"Leave it to Irvin to hit it out of the park with *Marbled, Swirled, and Layered.*
Every recipe is an inspiration! I want to make, and eat, every. single. one."

—ELISE BAUER, founder of *Simply Recipes*

"Irvin is not only an accomplished and creative baker, he is a generous
teacher. Home cooks will find all of the tips and techniques necessary to feel
supported and comfortable—as well as inspired—in the kitchen. No one
should miss the recipe variations! I love the modern versions of traditional
recipes, great new flavor combinations, and—of course—the invitation to
use flavorful flours other than wheat!"

**—ALICE MEDRICH, author of *Flavor Flours* and *Chewy Gooey
Crispy Crunchy Melt-in-Your-Mouth Cookies***

"Irvin Lin is a master at creative baking. I've admired his *Eat the Love* blog
for the delicious goodies and lovely storytelling. I'm excited to see desserts
with such interesting flavor combinations in his first cookbook. They are
truly works of art!"

**—LORI LANGE, author of *The Recipe Girl Cookbook* and founder
of *RecipeGirl.com***

"If th..d I
believ..ook
even..s
cove............8m 3x..r.

MARBLED, SWIRLED, AND LAYERED

MARBLED, SWIRLED, AND LAYERED

150 recipes and variations
for artful bars, cookies, pies, cakes, and more

Irvin Lin

photography by Linda Xiao

HOUGHTON MIFFLIN HARCOURT
Boston New York 2016

for A.J.

This book is as much yours as it is mine.
I love you and I'm so happy we're
making a life together.

For information about permission to reproduce selections
from this book, write to trade.permissions@hmhco.com or to
Permissions, Houghton Mifflin Harcourt Publishing Company,
3 Park Avenue, 19th Floor, New York, New York 10016.

www.hmhco.com

Library of Congress Cataloging-in-Publication Data
Names: Lin, Irvin F., author. | Xiao, Linda, photographer.
Title: Marbled, swirled & layered / Irvin Lin ;
photography by Linda Xiao.
Other titles: Marbled, swirled and layered
Description: Boston : Houghton Mifflin Harcourt, [2016]
Identifiers: LCCN 2015038040| ISBN 9780544453739
(paper over board) | ISBN 9780544454132 (ebook)
Subjects: LCSH: Baking. | LCGFT: Cookbooks.
Classification: LCC TX763 .L558 2016 | DDC 641.81/5—dc23
LC record available at http://lccn.loc.gov/2015038040

Designed by Kara Plikaitis

Printed in China
TOP 10 9 8 7 6 5 4 3 2 1

CONTENTS

INTRODUCTION

My friend Peter called me up to tell me all about the big weekend ski trip to Lake Tahoe that I had just missed—sadly, at the last minute, I got sick and had to cancel. There were eight couples there and their myriad children, and meals were all planned out potluck style. People brought casseroles and other items that could feed large groups, plus salads and bags of chips and plenty of beverages. But one thing Peter noticed in particular: Without me there, there wasn't a single dessert. Not a single person had brought one because they had all expected me to do it. I'm the baker who always has something in the oven. And my friends apparently count on it!

Baking has always been part of my life. It has been a constant, from the third grade, when I took a cooking class during the summertime and discovered the magic of making snickerdoodles, to college, where I coined the phrase "procrasti-baking" based on my tendency to bake instead of study or write papers, all the way to now. Whenever my roommates came home and found me baking, they knew I had a major test coming up. And even though I've gone through many different careers and lives, working at art galleries, selling books, designing packaging for chain restaurants, and copywriting for big-name clients, food and baking was always in the background. It was there for me when I needed to escape from the real world and relax. It's no wonder I ended up where I am now, developing recipes, photographing foods and drinks, baking for my blog and for clients, and writing this cookbook.

Despite the title, this book isn't just about making desserts that are marbled, swirled, or layered. This book is about making desserts for yourself and your loved ones. More important, it's about customizing desserts that you love and want to make. Most people are scared to deviate from recipes and adapt them for their own tastes, especially when it comes to baking. There's good reason, because baking is a complex science and once you start fiddling with the ingredients, you start messing up the chemistry. But I want people to explore and try new things. So you'll find that each recipe in this book has a core recipe and also an alternative recipe or two. Some are fairly easy alternatives, such as a simple swap of fruit. But others are a little more extensive. Read the main recipe completely before you read the alternatives; it will have more detailed instructions. But it's quite possible that the alternatives will be more appealing to you than the main recipe. That's why I included them!

This cookbook is also here for inspiration and as a reference for you. Even if you don't make a single recipe from it, I hope you'll take away some inspiration from the recipes and photographs. Perhaps a flavor combination will spark your interest and you'll use it in your own creation. Maybe a new-to-you baking technique will help you out the next time you make a cake. Or maybe you'll unlock a new passion for baking by reading about my own passion for it.

Finally, this book is here simply to share delicious baked goods and desserts. You can ignore all the stuff above about inspiring you or helping you find your passion and love of baking. Just flip the pages and pick a recipe at random. Bake it. Taste it. Share it with your friends and loved ones. For me, that's the best part of baking. Well, that and eating it myself! Enjoy.

BAKING EQUIPMENT

I'll be straight-up frank with you. My personal kitchen is exceedingly well-stocked with equipment. It has to be, because that's what I do for a living. However, I realize that most kitchens don't have—or need—the ridiculous number of specialty tools that I have. The majority of people won't run out and buy uni-taskers and fancy equipment to make a single dessert or baked good. And you shouldn't.

All that said, there are some standard pieces of kitchen and baking equipment that I think most people should have. Sure, a giant bowl (or in a pinch, a giant pot), a wooden spoon, and some elbow grease can still produce great things. But in today's world, we have electricity and modern appliances. There's no need to develop lopsided one-arm bulging muscles like Wimbledon champion tennis players from hand-whipping egg whites and whipped cream.

Most of the recipes in this cookbook rely on common equipment. The following list recommends items that you should have or might want to have, or that will just make your life easier when it comes to baking.

BAKING PANS

You should have a variety of standard-size baking pans. Buy heavy-duty commercial-grade ones if you can. They don't have to be expensive—I often find them at discount stores or at restaurant supply stores. The commercial-grade versions last longer, don't warp, and conduct heat better, which means you won't have part of your cake uncooked while another part is burnt. Try to avoid dark-colored pans, as they often heat up faster, causing a cake or other baked good to burn on the outside before the inside is done baking.

The sizes I recommend include:

ROUND CAKE PANS. I recommend at least two, if not three, 9-inch pans that are at least 2 to 3 inches deep. Any shallower and the cake batter might spill over as it rises in the oven.

SPRINGFORM PAN WITH REMOVABLE BOTTOM. I prefer a set that includes 8-inch, 9-inch, and 10-inch pans, but if you can only buy one, the 9-inch is the most commonly used. These pans are used for cheesecakes and other delicate cakes that can't be removed from the pan by turning it over. Don't ever trust the manufacturing promise that the pans "don't leak." Always place a piece of aluminum foil underneath the pan and wrap it around the bottom to prevent leakage of the batter. I usually place the pan on a rimmed baking sheet as well for added protection and to make it easier to remove the pan from the oven.

BUNDT PAN. I don't care for silicone Bundt pans even though they are convenient for unmolding a cake. They tend to be flimsy and not hold their shape properly. They also don't promote even browning, unlike metal. Buy a standard 10-cup-capacity metal Bundt pan. They come in a variety of shapes, but I opt for the classic. If you use a different shape, just make sure you grease the pan well (as the nontraditional shapes often have corners and edges that can cause the cake to stick) and unmold the cake when it is still warm. If you let the cake cool completely in the pan, it will stick and break and you'll curse up a storm.

TUBE PAN WITH REMOVABLE BOTTOM. If you want to make a chiffon or angel food cake, you need a tube pan with a removable bottom. The straight sides and bottom allow the cake to cling to the sides of the pan as it rises and also make it easy to remove the cake from the pan. I recommend getting one with "feet" or a longer center tube so you can invert it on a table or countertop for the cake to cool. But that's not a requirement. You could also invert the pan over the neck of a wine bottle and let it cool that way. If your tube pan doesn't have a removable bottom, line the bottom with a piece of parchment paper.

MUFFIN TIN/PAN. The standard 12-cup muffin tin is usually all you need. Each cup holds ½ cup of batter. Nonstick is great for easy cleanup, but don't feel obligated to get it. You can always generously grease the pan or use paper liners. The muffin tin is also what I use for my kouign amann recipe.

SQUARE BAKING PAN. I suggest a 9-inch square baking pan for most of these recipes. If you only have an 8-inch one, you can use it, but keep in mind that the resulting baked goods will be a little thicker and might take longer to bake. I prefer to use metal over glass, but pick what you feel comfortable with.

9 X 13 RECTANGULAR BAKING PAN. This is the standard size for brownies and sheet cakes. I prefer a metal one for brownies and sheet cakes and glass for savory casseroles and such.

HALF-SHEET PANS. The 13 x 18-inch half-sheet pan or rimmed baking sheet is the workhorse of the baking world. Get at least two for your kitchen and make sure they are heavy-duty professional or commercial grade. I use these for baking cookies (which I do a lot of), sponge cakes, and galettes, as well as for setting underneath smaller baking pans in the oven to catch any overflowing batter. This also makes it much easier to move a smaller cake pan in and out of the oven.

PIE PANS. A standard 9-inch pie pan and a deep-dish 9-inch pie pan should be in your arsenal if you plan on making pies! Glass, ceramic, or metal all work fine, and I usually opt for one over another mostly because of aesthetics.

TART PAN WITH REMOVABLE BOTTOM. I prefer a 10-inch round pan for my recipes. Tart pans with fluted edges make for great presentations, as you just press the tart dough into the pan, and then when you remove the tart from the pan, the edges are attractively fluted.

LOAF PAN. A 5 x 9-inch loaf pan is ideal for baking breads, like my babka.

JELLY-ROLL PAN. A 10 x 15-inch jelly-roll pan is probably one of those oddball baking pans that most people don't own. But if you plan on baking rolled cakes in general, I recommend getting one. I occasionally use it for brownies and blondies as well.

BALLOON WHISK

There is actually a wide variety of whisks out there, from ones with balls at the end to flat whisks to bouncy, spiral "galaxy" types. Each of them has a purpose, but if you just have room for one, go for the classic 11-inch balloon whisk. It's not just for beating eggs or whisking in liquids. It's also the perfect tool for blending dry ingredients together and aerating them.

CANDY THERMOMETER

You can certainly use the old-fashioned candy thread method (see page 190) to test the temperature of sugar when you cook it, but a candy thermometer is so much easier and more accurate. You can also use it to check the temperature of oil for deep frying.

CAST-IRON SKILLET/POTS AND PANS

I use a 10-inch cast-iron skillet for my tarte tatin as well as for upside-down cakes. I love how the cast iron retains heat and is both stovetop- and oven-safe. If you don't have a cast-iron skillet, you can still make these items in any ovenproof 10-inch skillet, or use a 10-inch cake pan for the upside-down cake (though you might have to make the caramel in a saucepan and then pour it into the cake pan).

I do recommend using a silver-bottomed (not non-stick) pan for making caramel and browned butter if you have never made them before, so you can see how the sugar and butterfat brown and adjust the heat as needed. If you're more experienced, though, a nonstick pan works as well and in fact is much easier for cleanup.

CUTTING BOARDS

I like to have separate cutting boards for savory and sweet cooking and baking. Certain pungent items, like garlic and onions, don't blend well with sweet baked goods. Wood, bamboo, or dishwasher-safe plastic is best. Avoid glass cutting boards; they dull your knives.

FLAT PARCHMENT PAPER

This is a "nice to have" item, but trust me when I say it's *really* nice to have! You can buy parchment paper in a roll at the grocery store, but it always curls up when you're trying to use it. You can buy precut flat paper (13 x 18 inches, the perfect size for standard half-sheet pans) online or at baking or restaurant supply shops.

If your only option is to buy rolled parchment paper, my best tip is to cut off a sheet of the paper in the size that you need, then wad the paper up into a ball in your hand (not too tightly). Flatten the wrinkly sheet out on the counter as much as you can. The act of crinkling the paper and then flattening it will help it to stay relatively flat instead of curling up on the baking pan.

FOOD PROCESSOR/BLENDER

I use a food processor to crush and grind everything from nuts to freeze-dried fruit. I like the shallow bowl of the food processor better than the taller blender, but either will work. You don't need anything super fancy; just make sure it's powerful enough to grind nuts.

HANDHELD MIXER

If you have a stand mixer you might not need this, but it is convenient to have a handheld mixer as well as a stand mixer. It's smaller, and you can maneuver the mixer around the bowl to scrape up all the side bits and such. It's also nice to have the stand mixer doing one thing, like mixing batter, and the hand mixer available for whipping egg whites at the same time. But if you have to pick one, I'd go with the stand mixer, even though it's more expensive.

ICE CREAM MAKER

There are a number of ice cream recipes in this book, and the best way to make ice cream is with an ice cream maker. Pick the ice cream machine that fits your budget and is most convenient to use, with some forethought on how often you plan on making ice cream and how much room you have in your freezer. If you pick the type that requires you to freeze the container beforehand, freeze it for a good 24 hours to ensure it is fully cold before churning.

KITCHEN KNIVES

Ideally, you should have at least three good knives in your kitchen: a long, thin, serrated bread knife (preferably at least 12 to 14 inches), which you can use to split cake layers (as well as cut bread). A chef's knife that feels comfortable in your hand (the most popular sizes are 8, 10, and 12 inches) to chop vegetables and chocolate. And a sharp, smaller paring knife for cutting fruit.

My best advice is to go to a kitchen supply store and try some out before investing in good-quality knives. Don't buy those cheap "ever-sharp" knives, as they are basically "never-sharp" in my opinion, and the flimsy blade is more likely to slip and cut you. But don't feel like you need to buy the most expensive knife out there, either. I know professional chefs who use less-expensive Dexter-Russell or Victorinox knives. Both brands can be found online or at restaurant supply shops. Remember that the higher the quality, the longer the knives will last. Get them professionally sharpened whenever you feel like they are starting to get dull (usually between 6 months and 1 year).

KITCHEN SCALE

This is probably the one piece of equipment that most American cooks don't have but absolutely should. They don't cost much (an inexpensive one is about $20), and they improve your baking by ensuring that all your ingredients are consistently measured. Ingredients like flour can range anywhere from 120 grams to 160 grams per 1 cup depending on how you fill the cup, the size of your cup (manufacturers' measuring-cup sizes are surprisingly inconsistent), the age and brand of the flour, and the ambient environment of your kitchen! But 140 grams of flour is the same amount across the board. Bonus: You don't have to wash all those

measuring cups afterward! If you are purchasing a scale, buy an electric one that switches between ounces and grams (I prefer grams because it's easier and more precise) and that tares, which means it goes back to zero once you press the button. This allows you to add an ingredient to the scale, tare back to zero, and then add the next ingredient, rather than adding each item to the scale separately.

KITCHEN TOWELS

Buy a bunch of 100 percent cotton kitchen towels (you can find them cheap at discount stores or in the clearance section of a cooking supply store). They work as oven mitts when you can't find your real ones (just make sure they are bone dry, as a wet towel will transfer the heat to your hand and burn you). And if you place a damp towel (like the one you just dried your hands with) on the counter or table, you can put a cutting board or bowl on top of it to keep it from sliding around. This is helpful when chopping anything or when whisking hot liquid into egg yolks when making custards or pastry cream.

MEASURING CUPS AND SPOONS, DRY

I'm definitely "Team Kitchen Scale" when it comes to measuring ingredients, but I understand that some people prefer otherwise. If you must use dry measuring cups and spoons, I recommend metal ones, as plastic ones tend to warp, melt, or get grubby over time. If you bake a lot, it's really handy to have two sets of measuring cups and spoons; otherwise, you have to wash and dry them between measurements.

MEASURING CUPS FOR LIQUIDS, GLASS

Glass measuring cups are important for liquids like milk, buttermilk, water, and oil. Pyrex makes coated glass measuring cups that are relatively heatproof, which means you can pour hot liquid in them (but you don't want to test the extremes by pouring super-hot molten caramel into a freezer-cold Pyrex cup—it will likely shatter). The best way to measure liquid is to put the cup on a level countertop, pour in the liquid, and then lower your eyes to the level of the cup to see where it lines up. If you raise the cup up to your eye level, you could be tilting the glass, giving a false reading. A 1-cup and a 2-cup capacity measuring cup are both handy to have. Don't measure your liquid ingredients in dry measuring cups or vice versa. You will get inaccurate readings.

METAL AND FLEXIBLE BENCH SCRAPERS

A bench scraper is one of those items you see in professional kitchens but don't find as much in home kitchens. This is unfortunate, because it's a really handy tool to have. The metal kind is good for cutting dough in half and for lifting up dough you've rolled out if it's sticking to the work surface. It also makes cleanup easy because you can simply scrape down the work surface with the scraper. The flexible variety is good for scraping out sticky doughs and batters from the bowl. They're pretty inexpensive, so I'd recommend picking up a few the next time you see them on sale or need to add something to your online shopping cart in order to get free shipping.

MICROPLANE GRATER

Since the introduction of the Microplane grater to the kitchen in the late 1990s, these handheld graters have become a staple in professional kitchens and have also moved into the home kitchen. It makes zesting citrus a breeze, and grating chocolate, fresh ginger, and whole spices like cinnamon and nutmeg easy work. Get one with a handle, designed for zesting citrus and hard cheeses.

MIXING BOWLS

Most people already have big mixing bowls in the house, but if you don't, I suggest running out and getting a nesting set of glass bowls and a nesting set of metal bowls. They're easy to store and include a variety of sizes. If you want to play "cooking show," you can set up all your ingredients in

them beforehand, but the novelty of that wears off after you realize you need to wash them all afterward.

Glass bowls are great because they are microwave-safe and usually heavy enough that you don't have to worry about them shifting around too much on the counter as you mix. Metal bowls are useful for making double boilers and ice water baths. They are also ideal for whipping egg whites, as the metal helps the whites cling to the sides of the bowl, and for whipping heavy cream, since you can place the bowl in the refrigerator beforehand to chill and keep the cream cool while whipping.

Ceramic bowls are attractive but heavy and potentially cumbersome. I don't recommend plastic bowls, because they are hard to clean after use and tend to get greasy over time. Plus, if you plan on whipping egg whites or cream, they will just slide down the sides of the plastic rather than clinging.

OFFSET SPATULA

I use an offset spatula to spread batter evenly in a pan and to frost cakes. If you plan on doing a lot of baking, the minimal cost of a basic one (under $5) is well worth it. A 4½-inch spatula is probably the most versatile size, large enough to spread batter and frosting effectively but not so big that it's cumbersome to use.

OVEN MITTS

I use silicone mitts because they work whether my hands are wet or not and it's easy to clean them. But use what you are comfortable with. I even know some people who swear by heat-resistant gloves from the hardware store. But you can also just use a dry kitchen towel folded over a few times.

OVEN THERMOMETER

The internal thermometers of home-kitchen ovens go out of whack all the time. Even brand-new ovens can be off by as much as 50°F. An oven thermometer will tell you

if your oven temperature is off, and then you can adjust it accordingly if necessary.

PASTRY BAG

A pastry bag, otherwise known as a piping bag, is a conical-shaped bag used to pipe frosting or batter into specific shapes. You can buy different tips for making flowers, leaves, or other decorative shapes. There are different types of bags, some disposable and some that are reusable. I don't use them often, but they do come in handy for piping éclairs and other batters. If you don't have a pastry bag, you can just scoop the batter or frosting into a zip-top bag, seal it, and clip off the bottom corner of the bag, then pipe the batter or frosting through the hole. You won't get fancy edges or shapes, nor will you get as much control as when using a pastry bag, but for baked goods like éclairs it works fine.

PASTRY BRUSH

A bristle brush is extremely useful. I brush flour off my dough before laminating it or placing it in the baking pan. I brush egg washes on my pie crusts. I brush the crumbs off my cake before I start frosting or glazing it. Don't bother with silicone brushes; buy a couple of cheap natural-bristle brushes and replace them when the bristles start to fall out. I've found the best way to wash them is to drop a little bit of liquid dishwashing detergent in the palm of my hand, wet the brush, and then just scrub the bristles in a circular motion around in my palm. Once I've stirred the detergent into a thick froth, I thoroughly rinse the bristles and brush, then make sure to let it air-dry completely before putting it away. You can get them inexpensively at a hardware store, kitchen supply store, discount store, or online.

ROLLING PIN

My suggestion is to find the style of rolling pin that you feel comfortable with and just go with it. I'm partial to a French rolling pin (ooh la la!), which is a solid piece of wood that is tapered at the ends. It allows me to have complete control over rolling and lets me easily whack away at cold butter and dough to soften them for laminated dough projects like kouign amann. But the standard rolling pin with the handles on the ends works just as well.

RULER

I really love having a kitchen ruler around! It's probably not necessary, as you can eyeball measurements most of the time or use your baking pan as a guide, but having a ruler dedicated to the kitchen soothes my nerves. It helps with precision for items like the Battenberg cake or kouign amann dough.

SIEVE/MESH STRAINER

I use these to rinse fragile berries, sift dry ingredients like powdered sugar, and strain custards and sauces to make sure they are super smooth. A fine-mesh one that fits over medium and large bowls is probably the most versatile.

SILICONE BAKING MAT/SILPAT

Again, a "nice to have" item. I'm a fan of using Silpat mats on baking sheets when making cookies. It's like a reusable piece of parchment paper that helps insulate the bottom of the cookies and keeps baked goods from burning. The baked goods slide right off. It also helps keep my baking sheets clean, with less wear and tear.

SILICONE HEATPROOF SPATULAS

I usually recommend having two or three of these around because they are so convenient and cheap, and you don't want to constantly be washing the only spatula you have over and over again as you're working. Get a couple of different sizes. My favorite money-saving tip is to find them at a discount department store with a kitchen section (like Marshalls or T.J.Maxx) or to go to a kitchen supply store right after a holiday, and buy seasonal spatulas on clearance. Right after Easter is especially great because the spatulas are usually inoffensive pastel colors, but if you don't have an issue with using Christmas-themed or Valentine's Day–themed spatulas year-round, then go for it!

SPICE/COFFEE GRINDER

I have a dedicated blade coffee grinder for my spices. If you need to grind different spices and you want to clean the grinder, pour 2 or 3 tablespoons of dry uncooked rice into the grinder, process it into a powder, then pour it out. Repeat, brushing out any residual rice powder with a pastry brush. The rice is a neutral ingredient that absorbs the oils left from the previous ingredient. I do this periodically just to keep my spice grinder fresh.

STAND MIXER

This may be the biggest investment in terms of money and space. But if you are serious about baking, a stand mixer is probably something you need to have on your counter, as a handheld mixer just won't cut it for some things. Keep in mind that a quality stand mixer will last for many years. I use a KitchenAid 5-quart Artisan mixer, but Breville and Cuisinart also make excellent stand mixers.

TIMER

It sounds pretty basic but you'd be surprised at how many times I've put something in the oven and then forgotten to turn on a timer. You can use the one built into your microwave or oven, a standalone version, or even a timer on your smartphone (my favorite because I tend to walk away from the kitchen, but I almost always have my phone on me).

WIRE COOLING RACKS

These come in a variety of shapes and sizes. I recommend two or three round ones (big enough to fit a 10-inch round cake) as well as a few rectangular ones for cookies, brownies, and other baked goods. For the rectangular ones, I recommend 12 x 17-inch racks that fit in a half-sheet pan and have mesh crisscross wires, so cookies won't slump through the wires as they cool.

My friend Shauna taught me a nifty way to hand-wash rectangular cooling racks when they get grubby and a run through the dishwasher doesn't quite clean them. Put the rack into a rimmed baking sheet and fill it with hot soapy water. Let it soak for a few minutes, then scrub the top side of the rack, flip it over, and scrub the bottom. Dump out the soapy water and rinse in the pan. The baking pan helps keep the rack rigid and gives you a surface to scrub the rack against, allowing you to really clean the rack thoroughly.

HOW TO USE THIS BOOK AND BASIC TROUBLESHOOTING FOR BAKING

Let's talk a little bit about how to use this book. Some of the recipes will look daunting because they require making more than one batter. But don't worry, I'm here to help.

Read the recipe completely before starting it. You don't want to be in the middle of a recipe and then realize that you needed to reserve ½ cup of the sugar for later use instead of adding it all at once, or that you don't have the right size pan! If you read the recipe completely beforehand, it will save you grief and much cursing.

While you're reading the recipe, take note of what it says about timing. Everyone's kitchen equipment is different, so I've tried to include visual and sensory clues as well as times. It sounds kind of new-age zen, but as you read the recipe, visualize yourself doing what is described in the directions.

Assemble all the ingredients before you start. What if you're out of brown sugar or it's rock hard? What if you *think* you have six eggs in the fridge but you only have four? Pulling out all your ingredients first will potentially save you stress and an emergency trip to the store.

Make sure to measure properly. I'm a huge proponent of using a kitchen scale, because you get more accurate results. Plus, when you use a scale you just dump the ingredients in the bowl. No measuring cups means less stuff to wash! But if you refuse to buy a scale, we can still be friends. I've included volume measurements in all the recipes. I use the "dip and sweep" method, where I dip the cup into the bag, then sweep across the top of the cup with a knife to level it out. The only exception is with brown sugar, which I measure tightly packed. A tip: Measure all your dry ingredients over a piece of parchment paper or waxed paper. Then pick up the paper and "funnel" any excess ingredients that fell out of the measuring cup back into the package. No mess, no waste!

If you are using cups and spoons to measure, be sure to use dry measuring cups for the dry ingredients and liquid glass measuring cups for the liquids. You'll get inaccurate readings otherwise. If you are measuring really sticky items like honey or molasses, a nice trick is to coat the inside of the measuring cup with some cooking spray before you measure the sticky liquid. The liquid should slide right out!

If you do choose to use a scale, here are some measurements of common baking ingredients:

ALL-PURPOSE FLOUR | 1 cup | 140 grams

CAKE FLOUR | 1 cup | 120 grams

BREAD FLOUR | 1 cup | 160 grams

CORNMEAL | 1 cup | 150 grams

CORNSTARCH | 1 cup | 115 grams

ROLLED OATS | 1 cup | 100 grams

GRANULATED SUGAR | 1 cup | 200 grams

POWDERED SUGAR | 1 cup | 115 grams

DARK OR LIGHT BROWN SUGAR | 1 packed cup | 220 grams

NATURAL COCOA POWDER | 1 cup | 110 grams

DUTCH-PROCESS COCOA POWDER | 1 cup | 100 grams

UNSALTED BUTTER | 1 cup | 225 grams | 2 sticks

HONEY | ¼ cup | 85 grams

MOLASSES | ¼ cup | 85 grams

MAPLE SYRUP | ¼ cup | 65 grams

NONFAT DRY MILK POWDER | 1 cup | 120 grams

Preheat your oven at least 15 to 30 minutes ahead of time. If you've got a fancy oven that makes a sound when it reaches the right temperature, wait an extra 5 minutes for the oven heat to stabilize after the alert goes off. Keep in mind that every time you open the oven door, the temperature inside can drop by as much as 50°F, so try to keep that to a minimum.

Prep the pans before making the batter or dough. With cookies, this might just mean pulling out the pan and lining it with a Silpat (silicone baking mat) or parchment paper. If you are using parchment paper and the baked good requires some sort of piping (like éclairs) or if your dough is sticky, you may want to anchor the paper to the baking sheet. You can do this by placing a little bit of dough underneath the paper as a "glue" to affix the paper to the baking sheet. Or, I opt to lightly coat the baking sheet with cooking spray. The oil keeps the parchment paper stuck nicely to the pan.

To cover the bottom *and* sides of a square or rectangular baking pan, cut a long piece of parchment paper to cover the bottom and two sides of the baking pan, leaving an overhang of 1 to 2 inches to help you remove the bars or cake from the pan once it's done. Then cut two thin strips to line the other two sides of the baking pan. It sounds fussy, but the extra minute of measuring and cutting saves you the grief of having to dig the baked good out of the pan, ruining those side pieces and potentially damaging the pan as well with your sharp knife.

Remember to set your timer! I don't know how many times I've forgotten to do this. If it's the first time you're making a recipe from this (or any) book, check the oven 5 to 10 minutes before the recommended baking time. Ovens can really vary. Nowadays I use my cell phone for a timer when baking so that I'll always hear it.

Get to know your oven. It will have hot spots and cold spots, and it may run warmer or cooler than the temperature you set it at. Even brand-new ovens can be completely off in temperature or go out of whack within a few months. If you have a separate oven thermometer, that's awesome (see page 7). But if you really want to get to know your oven, bake a batch of plain sugar cookies. Take note of how long they take to bake compared to the recipe. If the cookies take longer, your oven is probably too cool. If the cookies brown quickly, your oven is running hot. Also look to see which cookies are darker than the others. If the ones in the back left corner are darker brown than all the rest, then you know you have a hot spot in that corner of your oven. If you have extreme hot spots in your oven, you might want to swap and rotate your baking pans anywhere from halfway to three-quarters into the baking time. You can swap and rotate most cookies, brownies, or pies halfway through baking, but I don't recommend doing so for cakes or breads too early in the baking process. Both need time to rise and set, and if you open the oven and disturb them before that happens, they can deflate or collapse. If your oven heats evenly, skip rotating the pans, because it's a pain to do and drops the temperature of the oven when you open the door.

Finally, learn to trust your eyes and nose. If a pie or cake looks done after 45 minutes instead of the 50 minutes indicated in the recipe, take it out. Everyone's equipment, ingredients, and styles of baking are different. Enjoy!

INGREDIENTS

Like with all food, higher-quality ingredients used in baking will result in better-tasting baked goods. This doesn't mean that you need to spend a fortune on expensive vanilla beans or only use single-source artisan chocolate from Europe. But understand that there are times when splurging for a quality ingredient will take a recipe from good to great or from great to truly memorable. Other times, middle-of-the-road grocery store ingredients are perfectly acceptable to use. Here's a little insight into the ingredients I recommend as well as a little information about their role in baking.

ALCOHOL

I rarely drink, but I love the flavors of alcohol in baked goods: smoky bourbon and whiskey, dark exotic rums, coffee-tinged Kahlúa, and the boost of orange from Cointreau or Grand Marnier. Often a flavored alcohol (for example, Cointreau) works better than the base ingredient (orange juice). Keep in mind that much of the alcohol does burn off when heated. I try to suggest nonalcoholic options in most cases, but some recipes do require the flavor of the alcohol.

CHOCOLATE

Hard-core chocolate fiends are constantly talking about how the darker the chocolate, the better it is. I think chocolate is a very personal thing, and you shouldn't feel peer pressure to love that 85 percent cacao single-origin chocolate. If you love semisweet or milk chocolate or white chocolate, embrace it! Personally, I love all chocolates and find different uses for each sort.

In its purest unsweetened form, chocolate is cocoa solids and cocoa butter, both created from roasted cacao beans. Dark chocolate introduces sugar to the mix, milk chocolate has sugar and milk added (in the form of plain milk, milk powder, or condensed milk), and white chocolate is cocoa butter with milk and sugar but no cocoa solids.

When picking a chocolate, consider the application. If you are going to taste the actual chocolate in chunks or it will be mixed with very few ingredients, as in a ganache, you might want to get a very high-quality chocolate, one that you really enjoying eating. But if you are combining the chocolate with a lot of other ingredients, you can get away with a more everyday chocolate.

White chocolate has a bad reputation. Often it's cloyingly sweet and milky, without much dimension. But high-quality white chocolate is very good. Make sure to buy a white chocolate that has cocoa butter in it; otherwise you're just buying flavored sugary vegetable oil. Turn the bar over and look at the ingredient list; cocoa butter should be one of the first ingredients. My favorite white chocolates are made by Valrhona, El Rey, and Callebaut (all of which also make my favorite dark chocolates). Green & Black's and Ghirardelli both make good-quality white chocolate and other chocolates, and they can be found at most grocery stores.

Milk chocolate is required by the U.S. government to have a minimum of 10 percent cocoa solids, while in the EU the requirement is a minimum of 25 percent. Because it has a higher percentage of milk and milk fat, milk chocolate will melt at a lower temperature. You'll taste milk chocolate faster in your mouth than you would dark chocolate because milk chocolate melts in your mouth more quickly. Keep in mind that even though the government dictates a minimum amount of cocoa solids, quality milk chocolate often has more. Make sure to check the candy aisle in the grocery store for good-quality chocolate bars, as there is often a wider selection there than in the baking section.

Bittersweet or semisweet chocolate must have a minimum of 35 percent cocoa solids in the United States, but again, that's a low threshold, and most quality dark chocolates far exceed that. There is no specific definition of the difference between bittersweet and semisweet chocolate, but usually manufacturers will label dark chocolate with a higher percentage of cacao as bittersweet and chocolate with a lower percentage of cacao as semisweet. Valrhona is one of the standards in the pastry world, but it is expensive. Callebaut is one of my favorites and is priced slightly lower than Valrhona. Scharffen Berger is widely available in most grocery stores and is a quality chocolate. And if you don't want to break the bank, Ghirardelli and Guittard are both reasonably priced and easy to find.

I'm not a huge fan of chocolate chips. They are designed to hold their shape when heated, which means they don't provide the gooey chocolate texture that I like in chocolate chip cookies. The extra step of baking with chopped chocolate chunks really makes a difference! But if you're going to use them, pick a chocolate chip that tastes good when you eat it straight from the bag, and don't be afraid to buy a couple different brands and types and mix them up in the same batch of cookies. A blend of super-dark, bittersweet, semisweet, and milk chocolate chips makes for a really great cookie!

Unsweetened cocoa powder is divided into two different types: natural and Dutch-process. If the cocoa powder isn't labeled as Dutch-process (flip over the package and look at the ingredients to make sure), it's the natural stuff. Don't substitute natural or Dutch-process in a recipe designed for one or the other, because the acidity of each type is different. You might end up with unexpected results. That said, if you are really stuck with one kind of cocoa in your pantry and you want to make a recipe that calls for the other type, here's a way to substitute:

If the recipe calls for natural cocoa, substitute an equal amount of Dutch-process cocoa powder and replace the baking soda in the recipe with double the amount of baking powder.

If the recipe calls for Dutch-process cocoa, substitute an equal amount of natural cocoa powder and replace the baking powder in the recipe with half the amount of baking soda.

However, if it's a chocolate custard or frosting that doesn't require baking, you can probably swap cocoa powders with impunity. The resulting custard or frosting will look and taste different, but it will still be good.

Natural cocoa is cocoa solids from the cacao bean, with the cocoa butter extracted. It has a robust chocolate flavor and is slightly acidic. I use it when I want a stronger chocolate flavor. Because it's naturally acidic, most recipes with natural cocoa powder use baking soda as a leavening ingredient. Hershey's natural cocoa powder is a pretty nice, robustly flavored cocoa and is easy to find at the grocery store, but feel free to experiment with other brands. Dagoba, Scharffen Berger, and Ghirardelli also make natural cocoa powder.

Dutch-process cocoa can be more difficult to find at grocery stores. It is processed with an alkalized base solution to mellow it out and make it less acidic. It's usually darker in color and tastes less chocolaty, with its own specific flavor. If you've had Oreo cookies before, you'll know what Dutch-process cocoa tastes like. Since it is more neutral or even alkaline in pH, it is usually paired with baking powder in recipes. I use Dutch-process when I want to make a really dark-looking chocolate baked good or even as natural coloring to create darker contrasting batters. The most commonly found Dutch-process cocoas at grocery stores are Droste and Hershey's Special Dark. Guittard, Rodelle, and Callebaut also all make Dutch-process cocoa. Black Onyx, an ultra-Dutch-process cocoa, is super black in color. Because it has a very specific flavor, it is not often used by itself, and is instead frequently used in conjunction with another cocoa to give a dark color. You can find it online, and it does give chocolate cookies that traditional Oreo look and flavor.

COCONUT

I use unsweetened flaked, shaved, or shredded coconut in all my recipes. The sweetened stuff tends to be too sticky sweet for my taste and has a particular chew that I don't care for. You can often find unsweetened coconut in the same section of the grocery store as the raisins and dried fruit if it isn't in the baking section. Upscale grocery stores usually carry it, or you can order it online. But if you can only find sweetened coconut, that will work in a pinch. Be aware that the end result will be slightly sweeter. And if you plan on toasting the sweetened coconut, use low heat on

the stove and watch it like a hawk. The sugar in the sweetened coconut can burn really fast.

COFFEE

I love using coffee for its own flavor or as a way to boost chocolate. Instant espresso powder, instant coffee powder, and freshly brewed strong coffee all are used in this cookbook. Unless it's a very simple recipe with minimal ingredients (like a coffee ice cream or custard), don't worry about using the absolute best coffee beans. Use what you have available.

DAIRY AND NONDAIRY ALTERNATIVES

Dairy Milks

The recipes in this book are designed with whole milk in mind, and I don't recommend substituting a lower-fat milk in its place.

Cream is always heavy whipping cream. If you can find a regular pasteurized (not ultra-pasteurized) heavy cream, all the better. Ultra-pasteurization brings the cream to a higher temperature for a short time. It keeps longer, but it also doesn't whip up as easily, nor does it taste as fresh. That said, if all you have is ultra-pasteurized cream, it will work.

Always buy plain (unflavored) yogurt for baking. I choose to use full-fat yogurt in my baked goods and recommend you do the same for the best flavor.

Buttermilk initially was the leftover milk after you churned butter from cream. This is now called traditional buttermilk. Cultured buttermilk, the more commonly found buttermilk and the one used in this book, is fermented milk, similar to but not as thick as yogurt. It lends tenderness and tang to baked goods. If you don't have buttermilk at home, you can make a suitable substitute, called clabbered milk, by adding 1 tablespoon lemon juice or vinegar to 1 cup milk. Let it sit on the counter for 10 minutes, and it will thicken up and can be used in place of buttermilk in most recipes. Be forewarned that the resulting dessert won't have exactly the same flavor as it would if made with actual buttermilk.

When I use sour cream in recipes, I always opt for full-fat sour cream. Unless the recipe doesn't require baking (for example, if it is used as part of the whipped cream or topping), don't substitute nonfat sour cream.

Crème fraîche is thickened cream that is less sour than American sour cream. You can usually substitute sour cream for crème fraîche directly, but the end results will be tangier. A better substitution might be half sour cream and half heavy cream.

Cream cheese is an American-style cheese spread. I use full-fat cream cheese in my cheesecake and frostings. Make sure your cream cheese is at room temperature before using it or it will be lumpy, and no amount of beating will get those tiny little lumps out. If you need to warm up your cream cheese quickly, try placing the entire sealed brick (still in the foil wrapping) in a bowl of warm water, replacing the water as it cools. If the cream cheese is already open, seal it in a zip-top plastic bag first.

Powdered milk is exactly what it sounds like: milk that has had all the water removed, reducing it to a powder. Most home bakers don't have it around, but professional bakers use it fairly often to boost creaminess and give richness without throwing off the chemistry of the baked good by adding more liquid. You can use powdered milk, powered goat's milk, powdered buttermilk, or malted milk powder to boost flavor and richness.

Nondairy Milks

For more information about using alternative milks, see Alternative Milks for Flavor on page 286. I've listed a few of my favorite brands, but tastes vary, so you may want to play around with different ones.

I occasionally use almond milk in place of milk if I have a friend who is dairy sensitive or if I want to add a subtle vanilla-almond flavor to the end product. My favorite brands are Blue Diamond Almond Breeze unsweetened and Califia Farms unsweetened vanilla almond.

Oat milk has an earthy, grainy flavor and is slightly thicker than other nondairy milks. I prefer Pacific organic original oat milk. Keep in mind that oat milk is usually not gluten-free, in case that is a concern.

Coconut milk is a great subtly aromatic nondairy milk substitute. I use the canned version, which is nice and thick. My favorite brand is Chaokoh, a Thai coconut milk. Aroy-D also makes a good thick coconut milk. If you are looking for a thinner milk substitute to drink, Silk unsweetened is probably the best option.

Soy milk tends to be a little heavy, beany, or strangely chalky to my palate, so I don't use it very often. When I do, I use Silk or Whole Foods 365 Everyday Value brands.

Rice milk is rather thin, similar to skim milk. When I work with it, I usually go with Rice Dream Classic Original, which has a fairly pronounced rice flavor.

EGGS

All eggs used in this cookbook are large unless otherwise noted. Eggs help build structure in baked goods by creating a web of protein that sets when it bakes, and also bind together the other ingredients.

Cold eggs are easier to separate than room temperature eggs. First, crack an egg on a flat surface and not the edge of the bowl, which could potentially send shards of eggshell into your egg and puncture the yolk. Then pour the egg into your hand and let the white slip through your fingers into a bowl underneath. Just be sure your hands are clean to prevent introducing *any* oil into the egg white. Oil or any fat will prevent egg whites from whipping. The traditional method of passing the egg back and forth between the shell halves and letting the egg white fall through always seemed fraught with peril to me, as the sharp shell might break the yolk. Always separate eggs into two different bowls before adding them to the bowl you are mixing ingredients in. That way, if an egg yolk *does* happen to break, it won't contaminate the rest of the egg whites.

Most recipes call for room temperature eggs because they incorporate better into batter. If you haven't remembered to take the eggs out of the fridge ahead of time, a quick tip for bringing them up to room temperature is to place them in a bowl of warm water. Replace the water as it cools. Depending on the warmth of the water, the eggs should come to room temperature in 5 to 10 minutes. If you have already separated the eggs and you want to bring them to room temperature, you can still speed up the process by placing the separate components in zip-top plastic bags and placing the bags in warm water. The egg yolks might break when you put them in the bags, but that's okay. I usually snip the corner of the bag and just squeeze the contents into the mixing bowl when I'm ready to add them.

Egg whites are 80 percent water, with the remaining 20 percent protein and no fat, and they are often whipped to make meringue or to lighten batters or fillings. You can freeze egg whites for future use if you are using just the yolks. Place the egg whites in an ice cube tray, then pop them out once they are frozen solid and store them in a zip-top plastic bag, labeled with the date. Egg whites will keep frozen for up to 1 year. To thaw, place them in a bowl overnight in the refrigerator, or put as many as you need in a zip-top plastic bag and submerge it in a bowl of lukewarm water. Make sure to bring them completely to room temperature or at least to liquid form before using. Frozen egg whites won't incorporate into a batter very well, nor will they whip up. Cool liquid egg whites whip up best.

Egg yolks, on the other hand, are a little more difficult to freeze because the proteins in the egg yolk clump together when frozen and won't unclump, even when thawed or baked. If you find yourself with a surplus of egg yolks, stir in a scant ¼ teaspoon salt or sugar per egg yolk to help prevent the clumping and freeze them in ice cube trays. Thaw and use as directed in the recipe, decreasing the amount of salt or sugar in the recipe accordingly.

If you do plan to freeze egg whites or egg yolks, I recommend designating specific ice cube trays for this purpose.

Accidentally using a frozen egg white in your iced tea is not something you want to discover halfway through drinking it. And, of course, always wash your hands thoroughly before and after handling eggs to minimize the risk of salmonella.

FAT

Fat contributes moisture to baked goods and also tenderizes them. The reason shortening is called shortening is because it coats the gluten in baked goods, shortening the gluten formation, making foods less chewy and tough and more tender. Fat also carries flavor. A lot of flavor molecules and components are fat soluble, so you won't taste the flavor as much if you don't use enough fat. It's why I often add flavored extracts like vanilla to the butter first. Finally, fat lends richness and luxurious mouthfeel to baked goods.

Solid Fats

I'm a huge fan of using butter over margarine or vegetable shortening, although I occasionally use shortening if I want to achieve a specific bounce and chew in a cake. I almost always use unsalted butter. American-style unsalted butter contains about 80 percent butterfat and 20 percent water. European-style butter, however, has anywhere from 82 to 86 percent butterfat and less water. I usually stick with American-style butter for cost and convenience, but if there is a recipe where the butter is meant to be the shining star, I'll use a European-style butter like Kerrygold or Plugrá.

Most of the time I call for room temperature butter. The easiest way to get room temperature butter is to leave it out on the counter half an hour before you make the recipe. You want the butter to give a bit when you bend it or press down on it. If you can easily press down all the way through with your finger, then it's too soft. If it breaks when you try to bend it, it's too hard.

Of course, I'm a realist and understand that most people—myself included—don't always plan that far ahead when it comes to baking. So I take the butter out of the fridge first, cut it into ½-inch pieces (or smaller), and then do the prep for the rest of my recipe, pulling out the ingredients, greasing the pan, and preheating the oven. By the time I'm ready to use the butter, it has warmed up to the right temperature. If I'm really in a rush, I'll cut the butter into ½-inch pieces, place each butter chunk between two pieces of parchment paper, and then use the palm of my hand to smash the butter down into a flat disk. The warmth of my hand and the thinness of the disk will bring the butter to room temperature much more quickly. I don't recommend warming the butter in the microwave, as it does an uneven job.

Coconut oil is a solid fat that used to have a bad reputation but has recently come back into vogue as a healthy alternative to other fats. It can be persnickety to use, as the melting point is 76°F, which is just above room temperature, and placing it in the refrigerator makes it brittle. It does have a lovely tropical coconut scent to it, and can be great for anyone avoiding dairy. I recommend buying virgin unrefined coconut oil.

Shortening is a solid fat made from hydrogenated vegetable oil. It used to contain trans fats, but they have been phased out. I rarely use shortening in my baked goods, but occasionally it comes into play if I want my cookies to really have that melting quality in my mouth (like with snickerdoodles) or I want to add a little bounce to my cakes that I can't achieve with butter or oil. I also occasionally use it in my pie crust, blending it with butter to get the delicate balance of richness and flakiness (from the butter) and tenderness (from the shortening).

Liquid Fats

I occasionally use vegetable oil such as canola or corn oil in my recipes, when I want a neutral-flavored oil that doesn't clash with other flavors. Oils that are liquid at room temperature impart more moisture than solid fats. Olive oil can be really nice for certain recipes. Olive oil generally has a very particular flavor, which can range from buttery to fruity to spicy or peppery.

VANILLA

Obtaining vanilla from the plant is a really labor-intensive endeavor, from the hand pollinating of each orchid to manual harvesting of the beans. Once harvested, the beans go through a process of curing, killing, sweating, drying, and conditioning, all done by hand. From start to finish, it can take up to eight months to make one vanilla bean. No wonder they are crazy expensive!

You can buy individual vanilla beans at the grocery store, but if you plan on using a lot of vanilla beans, it might be worth investing in a large amount from an online retailer. A single bean can be as expensive as $5 to $6. If you are willing to buy 10 or 25 of them or more in bulk, you can get them as cheaply as $1 a bean (depending on how many you buy). See page 336 for sources. There is a wide range of vanilla beans, though the most popular ones are Mexican, Madagascar (sometimes called Madagascar Bourbon), and Tahitian.

Because of their price, I save vanilla beans for when I really want the vanilla flavor to shine through. I use them in vanilla ice cream, pastry cream, and buttercream frosting. If I'm feeling particularly luxurious, I'll use them in a vanilla cake where I want the vanilla to really stand out. Otherwise, I stick with using quality vanilla extract and paste.

I never dispose of the vanilla pod once I've used the seeds, though! Once I've scraped out the vanilla seeds, I'll either add the pod to the cream if I'm making an ice cream or pastry cream, for even more vanilla flavor, or I'll place the vanilla pod in vodka to make my own vanilla extract. I've also been known to add vanilla pods to sugar in a mason jar to make vanilla sugar or even add them to salt to make vanilla salt (which is absolutely lovely sprinkled on my malted chocolate chip and reverse chip cookies on page 81).

Real vanilla extract is made from vanilla beans steeped in alcohol to extract their flavor. Make sure to buy high-quality pure vanilla extract. It's worth the price, and if you can buy a large bottle (it keeps for quite a while) online or at a specialty store, it will be more cost-effective than buying small bottles at the grocery store. My favorite brands include Nielsen-Massey, Beanilla, Rodelle, and Lafaza.

Vanilla paste is a mix of extract and vanilla bean seeds suspended in a thick paste. It's lovely stuff, and is great for when you don't want to splurge or bother with a vanilla bean but still want those vanilla seeds freckling the buttercream frosting or ice cream. You use it just as you would vanilla extract, or 1 tablespoon paste for 1 whole vanilla bean.

Ground vanilla beans are exactly what they sound like: a powder made from ground whole vanilla beans. The slightly moist ground beans work just like vanilla paste, lending flavor and a speckled appearance to baked goods and custards, frostings, and ice creams. Don't confuse it with vanilla powder, which is mostly used in beverages.

I don't recommend using imitation vanilla extract. It's made with a synthesized chemical of vanillin, one of the flavor components of vanilla. Actual vanilla has over 170 different flavor components, with vanillin being only one of them. If you use imitation vanilla, you're shortchanging yourself of all those complex flavors.

FOOD COLORING

I rarely use food coloring in my baked goods, preferring to use natural ingredients like cocoa powder, matcha green tea powder, or freeze-dried fruit to add color. But every now and then I need to add a little bit of food coloring to boost the color, especially for reds and blues.

FREEZE-DRIED FRUIT

When I'm working with a dish that doesn't allow for the moisture of fresh fruit, or I want to add flavor without using an extract, I often reach for freeze-dried fruit. It's actually quite wonderful, as the freeze-dried fruit has a lot of the nutrients and flavor of the original fruit. Because it has all the water stripped out, it can be ground to a powder in a food processor, blender, or spice grinder and added to a baked good without altering the ratio of liquid to dry ingredients. Be forewarned that freeze-dried fruit is hygroscopic (it absorbs water fast), so if the air is humid or you have a drop of water in the food processor, the fruit will start to get sticky. Work fairly quickly with freeze-dried fruit powders, grinding the fruit right before you use it, or it will turn into a sticky mess as it absorbs moisture from the air.

You can find freeze-dried fruit at upscale grocery stores like Whole Foods or at specialty stores like Trader Joe's, or online.

LEAVENERS

To make a baked good rise in the oven, you need to put air and gas bubbles into the baked good. This is called leavening, and it is achieved in any of three ways: mechanically, chemically, or biologically.

Mechanical leavening means physically incorporating air into the batter. You do this when you whip egg whites, creating a matrix of protein strands that trap air in the whites. Then you fold the egg whites into the batter. You also mechanically leaven batter by blending the sugar and butter together in the recipe. The sugar crystals punch holes into the butter, and then those holes are filled with air. Once the batter is placed into the oven, the air expands from the heat and causes the baked good to rise. Science!

Baking powder and baking soda are chemical leaveners that produce carbon dioxide when moisture or heat is introduced.

Baking powder is a chemical leavener that has a built-in acid. It can be fast acting or slow acting or both. Fast-acting baking powder reacts when liquid is introduced to the batter. Slow-acting baking powder reacts when heat is introduced in the oven. Double-acting baking powder does both. Most baking powder is double acting, which ensures that your baked goods rise properly. Keep in mind that if your batter is thinner (as with some cakes), the gas created by the baking powder will move through the batter quickly, meaning you shouldn't take breaks between making the batter and putting it in the oven. In other words, if your phone goes off, or you get a text, check it *after* your place the cake in the oven! I try to use double-acting baking powder that is aluminum-free because I occasionally can taste the metallic aluminum.

Baking soda requires an acid to work. It's four times as powerful as baking powder, so you only need 25 percent of the amount you'd use for baking powder. But you need some sort of acidic ingredient to start the reaction. This could be an ingredient like buttermilk, natural cocoa powder, sour cream, molasses or brown sugar, honey, or lemon juice. Or you can add it to the batter in the form of cream of tartar or vinegar.

If your chemical leaveners have been sitting in your pantry for a while, you might want to check them to see if they still work. Ambient moisture in the air will react with the chemicals over time and slowly deactivate them. To check baking powder, add ¼ teaspoon baking powder to hot water. If bubbles form, it's fine. To check baking soda, do the same thing, but add ¼ teaspoon white vinegar to the water first.

Biological leavening is produced by yeast. Yeast can be intimidating if you've never used it before, but commercial yeast is actually very consistent and easy to use. I use active dry yeast for the recipes in this book.

NUTS

I love the crunch of nuts in baked goods. My favorite recommendation for using nuts of any sort is to toast them first in a dry skillet, stirring constantly. Once the nuts start to brown a bit and smell toasty and fragrant, pull them off the heat. A lot of people like to toast their nuts in the oven, but I like to see how they are browning and smell them so that I know when to remove them from the heat before they over-toast. That said, if you do happen to over-toast the nuts, don't toss them. Instead, steep them in milk overnight and then strain the milk and discard the nuts. The nutty flavor will infuse the milk, mellowing the over-toasted flavor. Then use the milk to bake with or to make ice cream. It's a nifty trick that salvages an ingredient that

you otherwise would throw away. You can do this with over-toasted coconut, too.

PEANUT BUTTER

Chunky or smooth—it's up to you. Although my recipes often specify a type, you can usually swap with no issues. That said, avoid natural-style peanut butters in baking, as they separate and result in dry baked goods.

SALT

Salt is probably one of the most underappreciated ingredients in sweet baking. Most people think that baked goods don't need salt at all, but salt functions in baking much like it functions in savory cooking. It helps amplify and round out the flavor of the dish. My mom taught me that if something tastes flat, adding salt brings out the flavor and dimension. Salt also strengthens gluten and helps build structure in breads. It has a hand in keeping baked goods from tasting too greasy in the mouth and promotes browning in the oven.

Nearly all the salt used in this cookbook is kosher salt because it dissolves easily, is evenly distributed in the dish or batter, and is inexpensive. I use Diamond Crystal brand kosher salt, which is less dense than Morton's kosher salt. If you use Morton's, you will want to use half the amount of salt specified in the recipe. I avoid table salt, which is iodized and has an odd chemical aftertaste to me. If you do use table salt, though, use half the amount listed in the recipe.

I occasionally call for finishing salt; these are flaky salts that have delicate crunch and are especially great to offset super-sweet desserts. Flavored salts—like vanilla salt or smoked salt—whether you make or purchase them, add another dimension to the final baked good as well. Finishing salts can also be used as a decorative touch; for example, black diamond salt or red Hawaiian salt can look quite striking. Basic finishing salts include Maldon salt or Cyprus pyramid salt, which has delicate, thin, pyramid-shaped flakes. You can get them at upscale or well-stocked

grocery stores like Whole Foods, specialty stores like Trader Joe's, or online. I like The Meadow, which stocks over 120 types of salt; it has a website and stores in Portland, Oregon, and New York City. If you don't have flake salt, substitute another sea salt or kosher salt in its place.

SWEETENERS

Though pure cane granulated sugar is the most common sweetener in baked goods, there is actually a wide range of sweeteners that can be used in baking and desserts, not just to sweeten but to add their own flavors as well.

These are not just there to make the baked goods sweet. Sugar and other sweeteners help keep baked goods moist, as sugar is hygroscopic, meaning it draws water in. It also tenderizes the baked good. When you cream granulated sugar and butter together, you're physically incorporating air into the mixture, which lightens the baked goods as well. Finally, sugar helps to brown baked goods. That nice crusty brown edge? That's the sugar caramelizing, making tasty little flavorful compounds and such.

Granulated sugar made from pure sugarcane lends a clean sweetness without having much of its own flavor, allowing other flavors to shine through. Avoid beet sugar, which is sometimes used to make cheaper granulated sugar. Organic and vegan versions of granulated sugar have a slight blond color because they don't go through the clarification process that regular granulated sugar goes through. They have a tiny, almost imperceptible molasses flavor but otherwise are interchangeable with regular granulated sugar.

Superfine sugar can be found at well-stocked grocery stores, sometimes under the name baker's sugar. It comes in a box and is basically the same thing as granulated sugar but with smaller crystals. It dissolves faster in liquids such as egg whites and also creates a finer crumb in cakes.

Powdered sugar, or confectioners' sugar, is cane sugar that has been ground to a fine powder. It is often mixed with cornstarch (or occasionally tapioca or potato starch) to prevent the sugar from clumping. It is primarily used for making frosting, icing, or glaze, or for dusting over baked goods right before serving. Just place the powdered sugar in a fine-mesh strainer or in a sifter and dust it over the baked good. If you want to get fancy, you can cut out your own stencils, use a paper doily, or buy a cake stencil from a specialty store and a place it on top of the cake before dusting it with sugar. When using in in recipes, I always measure the powdered sugar first, then sift it into the other ingredients.

Sparkling sugar is a coarse crystal sugar used for decoration. You can buy it in many colors, but I usually just stick to the bright white one. Brush your pastry with an egg wash or some heavy cream, then sprinkle the sparkling sugar over it before you bake it and the end result will look bakery worthy, with a sweet crunch. Even a quick sprinkle over muffins before putting them in the oven makes them extra special.

Swedish pearl sugar is large, irregular, opaque white chunks of hard sugar. It looks great on cinnamon rolls or on top of sweet breads (try using it in place of my crumb topping for the chocolate-cinnamon babka). This is a specialty ingredient, but keep an eye out for it, especially if you visit an Ikea, where it is often sold in the grocery section of the store.

Light and dark brown sugars are usually granulated sugar coated with a light spray of molasses. I'm a fan of using dark brown sugar for the extra molasses flavor, but you can substitute light brown sugar. If your brown sugar has hardened, place it in a microwave-safe bowl and cover with a damp paper towel. Microwave for 20 to 30 seconds. Finally, if you are out of brown sugar, you can make your own by adding 1 to 2 tablespoons molasses to 1 cup granulated sugar and mixing them together with a fork or hand mixer until the sugar is evenly coated.

Muscovado is an unrefined cane sugar that is dark brown. It's basically dark brown sugar on steroids, and it has a rich molasses flavor.

Turbinado sugar and demerara sugar are unrefined blond sugars with large crystals. They have a light molasses flavor and lend a lovely crunch to baked goods. I often sprinkle them on top of pies and cobblers because the big crystals and light caramel flavor work well with fruit fillings.

Coconut sugar, sometimes called coconut palm sugar, is made from the sap of coconut tree blossoms. Because it has a lower glycemic index than cane sugar, with some trace minerals and vitamins in it, it's popular with diabetics as well as with people on the paleo diet. It's a gorgeous brown sugar with deep hints of molasses and caramel and a complex, almost savory note to it. You can use it as a substitution for dark brown sugar if you want. If you are using volume measurements, you can substitute 1 cup coconut sugar for 1 cup packed brown sugar. Take note, though, that coconut sugar isn't as dense as brown sugar, so if you are measuring by weight, you should use about 70 percent of the total weight of the brown sugar for the coconut sugar. So if the recipe calls for 100 grams of brown sugar, use 70 grams of coconut sugar. Avoid the coconut sugar that comes in hard cakes at Asian grocery stores, as it is difficult to work with. You can find granulated coconut sugar at natural food stores, upscale markets, and specialty stores like Trader Joe's.

There are many grades of maple syrup, ranging from Golden Color with Delicate Flavor all the way to Very Dark Color with Strong Flavor. I prefer the Very Dark Color with Strong Flavor grade (formerly Grade B maple syrup), but it can be hard to find. Your best bet is to go to an upscale grocery store, natural food store, or specialty store like Trader Joe's. Avoid "pancake syrup" and that sort of thing. Maple sugar is basically maple syrup boiled into a crystallized form. It's expensive because it takes a lot of work to reduce maple sap into maple syrup and then into maple sugar. However, it's easier to substitute maple sugar for cane sugar in baked goods than it is to substitute maple syrup because it's granulated. It is sweeter than cane sugar, so reduce the amount of maple sugar to 75 percent of the amount of cane sugar.

Honey is truly fabulous sticky-sweet liquid ambrosia. It has a surprisingly broad range of flavors, though most people are familiar with the mild neutral-flavored honey found in bear-shaped bottles at the grocery store. If you can, find a local source for your honey and try to buy it raw.

Molasses is a by-product of making granulated sugar. It's a thick, dark brown syrup with a deep, earthy, sweet, and bitter flavor. Like maple syrup, molasses comes in different grades, from light, original, or mild molasses, which has a sweet, slightly burnt sugar flavor; to dark, robust, or full-flavored molasses, which is darker, richer, and deeper in flavor; to blackstrap, which is strong and quite bitter, with only a tinge of sweetness.

Regular store-bought corn syrup is mostly glucose and shouldn't be confused with high-fructose corn syrup. That said, I don't use it much because it's a relatively bland sweetener. Chemistry-wise, it helps keep ice cream smooth and prevents crystallization in both ice cream and caramel.

SPICES AND HERBS

If your ancient bottles of ground nutmeg and allspice are turning dusty brown or you can't remember when you bought them, it's probably time to toss them. Most ground spices should be used within a year. Technically they will keep longer, but their flavor and color will fade. I hate tossing old and expired ingredients, so I try to buy spices in smaller amounts if I can. See Resources, page 336, for sources for specialty spices.

As for herbs, unless otherwise stated in the recipe, stick with fresh herbs when baking or, if you can find them, herbal extracts (see Resources, page 336).

STARCHES

Starch is a white powder that is used as a thickener or stabilizer. It is made from processing starchy foods like corn, potato, or roots like cassava root or arrowroot. It's usually flavorless, though certain starches do add a slight flavor. They are mostly interchangeable, but they do have their specific uses. If you add any starch to a hot liquid, it will immediately seize up and create lumps. To prevent this, stir the starch into an equal amount of cold or room temperature liquid before adding it to the hot liquid.

Cornstarch is probably the most common and familiar starch. Cornstarch thickens at about 200°F, so you need to make sure the temperature of the filling or custard you are making reaches that point. After thickening, though, the more you cook or stir the filling or custard, the thinner it will get. Cook the filling or custard for a full minute after it has thickened, but there's no need to cook longer. Cornstarch doesn't work as well in acidic environments, so you might need to use more of it if you are using acidic ingredients like lemon or vinegar. It also isn't the best choice if you plan on freezing the dessert after baking. The filling or custard ends up spongy and icy. Try using tapioca starch or arrowroot instead.

Tapioca starch (sometimes sold as tapioca flour) is extracted from the cassava root and ground into a fine powder. I'm fond of using tapioca starch over cornstarch for fruit pie fillings because it sets faster at a lower temperature and works better in acidic environments. It also has a cleaner taste than cornstarch, though it can sometimes create a "stringy" filling if you use too much. See Tapioca Starch or Flour on page 68 for more information.

Arrowroot starch is made from a number of tropical plants. It's more expensive than other starches, but it's a great thickener because it works in acidic environments and also freezes well. It creates a really nice glossy sheen in pie fillings. It's a little more powerful than cornstarch or tapioca starch, so use a light hand when substituting, usually 2 teaspoons arrowroot per 1 tablespoon cornstarch or tapioca starch. It also holds up well to longer cooking times and higher temperatures as well. All that said, you don't want to use arrowroot when dairy is involved. You'll end up with a slimy substance that might be fun for a science experiment but not so much for eating.

Potato starch is best known for being the thickener of choice for kosher-for-Passover time. Many grocery stores carry it. It's a great neutral-flavored starch for thickening and lends moisture and softness to baked goods. If they don't have it in the baking section, look for it in the kosher section of the grocery store, or look for it at an Asian grocery store. Don't confuse it with potato flour, which is ground dried potatoes and has a potato flavor.

WHEAT FLOURS

Flour is the base ingredient for nearly all baked goods and desserts, and creates structure in the baked goods. Regular all-purpose is relatively neutral in flavor, letting other flavors shine through. Other specialty flours have more flavor. You can't talk about flour without talking about gluten, the protein in wheat and other grains like barley and rye that makes dough elastic and gives bread its signature chewy texture. Common wheat flours are divided into categories based on their gluten protein content, though different brands may vary slightly. I opt for unbleached flour because, to my palate, the bleached version tends to have a chemical taste, but you can substitute bleached versions. The three main types of white flour I use are cake flour, all-purpose flour, and bread flour.

Cake flour is 7 to 8 percent gluten, the lowest protein content of the wheat flours. If you want a really tender cake, use cake flour. If you don't have any cake flour on hand, you can substitute by combining 2 tablespoons (18 g) cornstarch with ¾ cup plus 2 tablespoons (122 g) all-purpose flour for each 1 cup cake flour.

All-purpose flour is 10 to 12 percent gluten. It is the most common, and the predominant flour used in this book.

Bread flour is 12.5 to 15 percent gluten, the flour with the highest protein content. This is used mostly for bread making (though I also use it in my pâte à choux paste for éclairs), and it's what gives bread its chewy texture.

Cake, all-purpose, and bread flours are made strictly from the endosperm, the center of the wheat berry. Whole-wheat flour is made from the entire wheat berry, including the outer bran layer, the germ, and the endosperm. This makes a nuttier speckled flour that is more nutritious and has a toasty flavor. It also leads to a heavier and denser baked good. If a recipe calls for all-purpose flour, you can substitute up to 25 percent of the amount with whole wheat flour. White whole-wheat flour is still whole wheat, but it is made from a specific soft albino type of wheat. It has all the nutrition that regular whole-wheat flour has, but is milder in flavor and less bitter. Whole-wheat flours are more likely to spoil quickly. Buy smaller amounts unless you plan on using it quickly; it will keep for 1 to 3 months in a cool pantry or 2 to 6 months in the freezer.

WHOLE GRAINS, ANCIENT GRAINS, AND OTHER FLOURS

There is a whole slew of specialty flours worth exploring, made from other grains and nuts. Some of my favorite gluten-containing ones include barley, khorasan, rye, and spelt. You can usually replace up to half of the all-purpose flour with another gluten-containing flour. Just expect the final product to be softer or more tender, depending on the flour. For gluten-free flours like amaranth, buckwheat, millet, quinoa, polenta, and teff, as well as nut flours like almond, hazelnut, and pistachio, you can usually substitute up to 20 percent of the all-purpose flour without affecting the recipe too much. Each flour has its own flavor and texture, which can add interesting new dimensions to desserts. If you have access to a natural food store or an upscale grocery store that has a well-stocked bulk food section, look for some of these flours there. You can often buy the flours at a cheaper price and in smaller amounts, allowing you to experiment without committing to a larger, more expensive prepackaged bag or box.

GLUTEN-FREE CONVERSIONS

Gluten is a protein found in wheat flour, as well as rye, barley, and a few other ancient grains related to wheat like khorasan, spelt, and emmer. The gluten forms long bonds, creating that web of sticky stretchiness that you may have noticed if you've ever made bread dough. Gluten is important in baking because it creates structure. Without gluten, most baked goods are either crumbly and fall apart or are heavy and dense.

However, if you can't eat gluten or are baking for friends who are gluten-intolerant, you can make your own home-made custom gluten-free flour blend, or try one of these popular commercial gluten-free flour mixes: Cup4Cup, Bob's Red Mill Gluten-Free 1-to-1 Baking Flour, or King Arthur Flour Gluten-Free Multipurpose Flour. To bake gluten-free, it's important to add a binder, like xanthan gum, to mimic the gluten. The Cup4Cup and Bob's Red Mill mixes include binders, but the King Arthur Flour mix and my blends do not, so you must add your own if you use those. Try using ½ teaspoon xanthan gum per 1 cup flour for cakes, muffins, and quick breads. For cookies and brownies, try using ¼ teaspoon per 1 cup. For breads, try using ½ teaspoon psyllium husk per 1 cup as the binder.

Here are three of my gluten-free flour blends:

My Standard All-Purpose Gluten-Free Flour Blend

STARCHES
2 cups (340 g) tapioca starch
2½ cups (325 g) sweet/glutinous rice flour
Total 665 grams

GRAINS
1½ cups (210 g) white rice flour
1¼ cups (150 g) millet flour
½ cup (70 g) brown rice flour
Total 430 grams

This makes a total of 7¾ cups or 1,095 grams of flour, or about 2½ pounds. Combine all the ingredients in a large bowl and stir the heck out of it with a whisk. Pour into a zip-top plastic bag and label it with the date. Since whole-grain flours go bad faster, use within 3 months or store in the freezer for 6 to 9 months.

My Whole-Grain Gluten-Free Flour Blend

3 cups (455 g) brown rice flour

3½ cups (420 g) millet flour

2 cups (270 g) teff flour

1½ cups (205 g) sorghum flour

Total 1,350 grams

This makes about 10 cups or about 3 pounds of flour. Combine all the flours in a large bowl and stir the heck out of it with a whisk. Pour into a zip-top plastic bag and label it with the date. Use within 3 months, or store in the freezer for 6 to 9 months.

My Chocolate Gluten-Free Flour Blend

3¼ cups (420 g) sweet/glutinous rice flour

2 cups (270 g) teff flour

2 cups (240 g) buckwheat flour

1 cup (120 g) millet flour

¾ cup (105 g) mesquite flour, sifted

¼ cup (35 g) carob powder, sifted

Total 1,190 grams

This makes about 9¼ cups or about 2½ pounds of flour. Combine all the flours in a large bowl and stir the heck out of it with a whisk. Pour into a zip-top plastic bag and label it with the date. Use within 3 months, or store in the freezer for 6 to 9 months.

COOKIES

THE FIRST THING I EVER LEARNED TO BAKE from scratch was a snickerdoodle. It was a revelation for my third-grade self. Throwing all these ingredients into a bowl, mixing them up, shaping into balls (like Play-Doh!), rolling in cinnamon sugar, and putting them in the oven seemed like play, not work! Twelve minutes later they came out as cookies. It was like magic. Melt-in-your-mouth unicorn magic.

Most people's first experience with baking is a cookie. It might even be slicing cookie dough from a plastic tube bought at the grocery store, but that still counts. Nowadays, whether the dough is homemade or store-bought, for most of us, the minute we smell fresh-baked cookies, we immediately revert to being kids again.

I've taken some of the traditional cookie doughs from your childhood and marbled or layered them together, infusing them with new life. I hope that these treats will inspire the kid in you. After all, it's hard to turn down a fresh-baked cookie right from the oven.

JUMBO ARNOLD PALMER COOKIES

makes 18 cookies

My one and only foray into selling my baked goods (besides the occasional bake sale) was a pop-up bakery/treats shop organized by several of my friends. All the other folks were experienced sweets salespeople, having sold at various farmers' markets before. Their advice to me, the newbie, was to underproduce so I'd be sure to sell out as much as possible. But because I throw a lot of dinner parties and have an innate fear of running out of desserts, of course I *over*produced. However, the first items to sell out were these Arnold Palmer cookies! The Arnold Palmer (otherwise known as a Half & Half in the South) combines lemonade and iced tea together and is named after the American golfer who popularized it, and this is my cookie version. One taste and you'll understand why it was such a best seller.

LEMONADE COOKIE DOUGH

10 tablespoons (140 g or 1¼ sticks) unsalted butter, at room temperature

1¼ cups (250 g) granulated sugar

Zest of 2 lemons

1½ teaspoons lemon extract

¾ teaspoon baking powder

½ teaspoon baking soda

½ teaspoon kosher salt

1 large egg

1¾ cups (245 g) all-purpose flour

ICED TEA COOKIE DOUGH

5 teaspoons (10 g or 5 to 6 tea bags' worth) finely ground Lipton Yellow Label tea

1 large egg

10 tablespoons (140 g or 1¼ sticks) unsalted butter, at room temperature

MAKE THE LEMONADE COOKIE DOUGH

Preheat the oven to 350°F and line baking sheets with parchment paper or Silpats. Cut the butter into ½-inch chunks and place them in the bowl of a stand mixer fitted with the paddle attachment. Add the sugar, lemon zest, and lemon extract and beat together on medium speed until the mixture looks lighter in color than when you started, about 1 minute. Add the baking powder, baking soda, and salt, beating until the batter is pale yellow, about 30 seconds. Add the egg and beat until incorporated. Add the flour and beat until a dough forms. Scoop out the dough and transfer to a clean bowl.

MAKE THE ICED TEA COOKIE DOUGH

Empty the tea bags into a small bowl. Grind the tea if it isn't finely ground enough (you can do this in a spice grinder or by placing it in a zip-top plastic bag and using a rolling pin to crush the leaves). Add the egg to the bowl and beat to blend. Place the butter and both sugars in the bowl of the stand mixer (no need to wash it). Beat together on medium speed until the mixture looks lighter in color than when you started, about 1 minute. Add the baking powder, baking soda, and salt and beat for about 30 seconds to incorporate. Scrape the egg and tea into the bowl and beat for about 30 seconds more to incorporate. Add both flours and beat until a dough forms.

·······>

¾ cup (165 g) packed dark brown sugar

½ cup (100 g) granulated sugar

¾ teaspoon baking powder

½ teaspoon baking soda

½ teaspoon kosher salt

1 cup (140 g) all-purpose flour

½ cup (75 g) whole-wheat flour

OPTIONAL GLAZE

4 tea bags Lipton Yellow Label tea

½ cup boiling water

3 cups (345 g) powdered sugar, divided and sifted

3 to 4 tablespoons fresh lemon juice

✳ *As I stated, these make large cookies. You can reduce the size to make 24 cookies by making the balls of dough slightly smaller, the size of a large cherry (about 25 g each). They will still spread, so make sure to place them 2 inches apart. Reduce the baking time to 12 to 15 minutes.*

Pinch off a chunk of lemon dough the size of a walnut (about 35 g) and roll into a ball. Pinch off a same-size chunk of iced tea dough and roll into a ball. Squish the two doughs together and roll into a single ball. If you aren't glazing the cookies, roll the dough in some additional granulated sugar. Place on the lined baking sheet and flatten the ball with the palm of your hand, so you have a disk about 2 inches across. Repeat with the remaining dough, spacing the disks about 2 inches apart (they spread a lot during baking). Bake until the edges of the cookies are golden brown, 15 to 18 minutes. Let cool on the baking sheets for 5 minutes before moving to a wire rack to cool completely.

MAKE THE GLAZE, IF USING

Add the tea bags to the boiling water. Let steep for 3 to 4 minutes. Measure out 2 tablespoons of the extra-strong tea and add it to 1 cup (115 g) of the powdered sugar in a medium bowl. Stir to dissolve the sugar. Place the remaining 2 cups (230 g) powdered sugar in a separate bowl and add 3 tablespoons lemon juice. Stir to dissolve, adding the additional 1 tablespoon lemon juice if necessary to thin the glaze. Spread a tablespoon of the lemon glaze onto each cookie. Drizzle a teaspoon of the tea glaze on top of the lemon glaze. Using a toothpick, drag the glazes around to marble them together. Let dry before serving.

STRAWBERRY AND CREAM COOKIES

Make the white chocolate cream cookie dough following the recipe for the lemonade cookie dough, omitting the lemon zest and extract and adding 2 teaspoons vanilla extract. Melt ⅔ cup (4 ounces or 115 g) chopped white chocolate over a double boiler and then let cool slightly. Add the melted white chocolate to the dough after adding the egg. Add ¾ cup (90 g) powdered dry milk to the dough along with the flour.

Make the strawberry cookie dough following the recipe for the tea cookie dough, replacing the tea with 1 cup (34 g) freeze-dried strawberries crushed into a powder. Add 1 teaspoon balsamic vinegar and 3 drops of red food coloring (optional) to the dough along with the egg. Omit the dark brown sugar and increase the granulated sugar to 1¼ cups (250 g). Omit the whole-wheat flour and increase the all-purpose flour to 1¾ cups (245 g).

Assemble the cookies as directed, then roll the cookies in granulated sugar before baking as directed. Skip the glaze.

CORN AND LIME COOKIES

Make the lime cookie dough following the recipe for the lemonade cookie dough, replacing the lemon zest and extract with the zest of 3 limes, 1 tablespoon fresh lime juice, and 2 drops of green food coloring (optional). Increase the flour to 2 cups (280 g) all-purpose flour.

Make the corn cookie dough following the recipe for the tea cookie dough, replacing the tea with 1 cup (45 g) freeze-dried corn crushed to a powder. Omit the dark brown sugar and increase the granulated sugar to 1¼ cups (250 g). Omit the whole-wheat flour, increase the all-purpose flour to 1¼ cups (175 g), and add ⅓ cup (50 g) yellow cornmeal along with the flour.

Assemble the cookies as directed, then roll the cookies in granulated sugar before baking as directed. Or, make an optional glaze by mixing 2 cups (230 g) powdered sugar with 3 tablespoons fresh lime juice. Adjust the thickness with more juice or powdered sugar, then glaze the cookies as directed.

CINNAMON HONEY BUN COOKIES

makes 48 cookies

I took these cookies to a holiday cookie swap years ago. The host, a fellow food blogger, let me know that she had invited a number of other food bloggers, which, in turn, made me feel the pressure to bring my A game. Not that food bloggers are judgmental, but you always want to present your best when faced with folks who write and make food for an Internet audience. Luckily these cookies more than did the trick and were snapped up quickly by everyone.

COOKIE DOUGH

1½ cups (175 g) powdered sugar, sifted

1 cup (225 g or 2 sticks) unsalted butter, at room temperature

½ teaspoon kosher salt

½ teaspoon baking powder

2 teaspoons vanilla extract

1 large egg

2½ cups (315 g) all-purpose flour

CINNAMON FILLING

6 tablespoons (85 g or ¾ stick) unsalted butter, at room temperature

¼ cup (55 g) packed dark brown sugar

3 tablespoons all-purpose flour

1 tablespoon honey

1 tablespoon ground cinnamon

½ teaspoon ground nutmeg

MAKE THE COOKIE DOUGH

Combine the powdered sugar, butter, salt, and baking powder in the bowl of a stand mixer fitted with the paddle attachment. Start mixing on low speed and slowly increase the speed to medium until the butter looks creamy and starts to cling to the sides of the bowl, about 2 minutes. Add the vanilla and beat on medium speed until incorporated. Add the egg and beat until incorporated. Add the flour and mix on low speed, then slowly increase to medium speed until the flour is incorporated and a dough forms. The dough will be soft.

Scrape the dough out onto a clean, floured surface and shape into a ball. Flatten into a circle and then square off the edges. Roll out the dough into a 13 x 14-inch rectangle with a long side facing you, occasionally adding more flour to the bottom and top of the dough so it doesn't stick.

MAKE THE CINNAMON FILLING

Combine the butter, brown sugar, flour, honey, cinnamon, and nutmeg in the mixer bowl (no need to clean it). Beat together until the filling is uniform in color, fluffy, and light, about 2 minutes. Scrape the filling out onto the rolled-out dough and spread to cover the entire surface. You may need to use your fingers for this, as the filling will need to be spread thinly. Tightly roll up the dough starting from the bottom edge. Wrap with plastic wrap and freeze for 1 hour. Preheat the oven to 350°F and line baking sheets with parchment paper or Silpats.

Remove the dough from the freezer and unwrap. Carefully slice ¼-inch-thick cookie disks from the rolled log, slicing straight down (do not saw back and

·······>

GLAZE

2 tablespoons honey

1 tablespoon buttermilk or whole milk

1 teaspoon vanilla extract

½ to ¾ cup (60 to 90 g) powdered sugar, sifted

✱ *Make sure the butter for the cinnamon filling is truly at room temperature or even slightly warmer than that. It makes spreading the filling so much easier.*

✱ *You can make and freeze this cookie dough for future baking. Once it's been frozen for an hour, place the log in a labeled zip-top plastic bag. Slice and bake cookies at your convenience. The dough should keep for up to 2 months in the freezer.*

forth). Place on the baking sheets, spacing the cookies about 1½ inches apart. Bake until the edges of the cookies start to turn golden brown, 12 to 14 minutes. Let cool on the baking sheets for 5 minutes, then move to a wire rack to cool completely. Repeat with the remaining dough.

MAKE THE GLAZE

Combine the honey, buttermilk, vanilla, and ½ cup (60 g) powdered sugar in a bowl and stir together. If the glaze looks too thin, add more powdered sugar, 1 tablespoon at a time, until it has thickened to the right consistency. Brush the glaze onto the cooled cookies with a pastry brush.

CHAI CHOCOLATE AND ORANGE COOKIES

Add the zest of 1 navel orange to the cookie dough when beating the butter. Make the filling as directed, but reduce the cinnamon to ½ teaspoon and the nutmeg to ⅛ teaspoon. Add 1½ teaspoons ground cardamom, 1 teaspoon ground ginger, and ¼ teaspoon freshly ground black pepper. Omit the flour and add 3 tablespoons powdered dry milk, 2 tablespoons natural cocoa powder, and 1 teaspoon (the contents of 1 tea bag) English breakfast tea to the filling. Beat together as directed.

Assemble, bake, and glaze as directed.

MALT CHOCOLATE–VANILLA SUGAR COOKIES

Make the cookie dough as directed, but at the beginning, split a vanilla bean lengthwise and scrape the seeds into the bowl with the butter and sugar. Proceed as directed. Alternatively, increase the vanilla extract to 4 teaspoons.

Omit the honey, cinnamon, and nutmeg from the filling. Reduce the flour to 1 tablespoon and add 2 tablespoons natural cocoa powder and 1 tablespoon malt powder. Spread on the cookie dough as directed. After rolling the dough into a log, roll the entire log in ¾ cup (180 g) sparkling sugar. Wrap and freeze as directed. Slice and bake as directed. Skip the glaze.

Flavor inspirations: the grocery store ....

One of my favorite places to look for flavor inspirations is the grocery store. I don't buy a lot of premade cookies and treats at the supermarket. With my job, there's not really any reason to, unless I'm making a cookie crumb crust for a pie. But I do love to walk down all the aisles of the grocery store just to see what people are making. From chai-flavored cookies to masala curry potato chips to rainbow-colored cake and caramel-swirled brownie mixes, grocery stores are often bursting with inspiration. Though I don't imitate these things directly when I get home, I keep a mental catalog of flavor ideas (with the occasional quick mobile phone pic as well for reference). When the occasion arises, or when I feel like playing in the kitchen, I am never without inspiration.

SPARKLING DARK CHOCOLATE AND RASPBERRY–CREAM CHEESE CHEWY COOKIES

makes 96 cookies

These cookies epitomize the perfect chewy texture that cookie fanatics crave. The use of cream cheese gives a soft, toothsome bite to the cookies, while raspberry and chocolate extracts give both sides of the cookies extra flavor punch. Because this recipe requires you to make two different doughs to marble together, it also makes quite a lot of cookies, which is perfect for parties or gatherings. You can also freeze the doughs for up to 1 month if you don't want to make as many cookies right away. Just tightly wrap the doughs in plastic wrap and seal the dough in a zip-top freezer bag. Thaw the dough in the fridge overnight before marbling and baking as directed.

RASPBERRY COOKIE DOUGH

1¼ cups (6 ounces or 170 g) fresh or frozen raspberries

1½ cups plus 2 tablespoons (325 g) granulated sugar, divided

6 tablespoons (85 g or ¾ stick) unsalted butter, at room temperature

2 ounces (57 g or ¼ brick) cream cheese, at room temperature

1 teaspoon baking powder

½ teaspoon baking soda

½ teaspoon kosher salt

2 teaspoons raspberry extract

1 teaspoon balsamic vinegar

1 large egg

1 large egg yolk

2¾ cups (375 g) all-purpose flour

MAKE THE RASPBERRY COOKIE DOUGH

Preheat the oven to 350°F and line baking sheets with parchment paper or Silpats. Place the raspberries and 2 tablespoons of the sugar in a small saucepan and cook over medium heat, crushing the berries with a potato masher or the back of a wooden spoon and stirring constantly, until the berries have broken apart. Continue cooking until the mixture darkens a bit and thickens, about 5 minutes. Remove from the heat.

Combine the butter, cream cheese, baking powder, baking soda, salt, and the remaining 1½ cups (300 g) sugar in the bowl of a stand mixer fitted with the paddle attachment. Beat on medium speed until light and fluffy, about 3 minutes. Add the raspberry extract, vinegar, and egg and beat on medium speed until incorporated. Add the egg yolk, beating until incorporated, and then the cooled raspberry jam, scraping down the sides of the bowl between additions.

Add the flour and mix on low speed until the dough starts to absorb some of the flour. Raise the speed to medium and mix until the flour is completely incorporated. Transfer the dough to a separate bowl and move to the refrigerator to cool and firm up slightly while you make the chocolate cookie dough.

·······>

DARK CHOCOLATE COOKIE DOUGH

¾ cup (170 g or 1½ sticks) unsalted butter, at room temperature

4 ounces (115 g or ½ brick) cream cheese, at room temperature

1 cup (200 g) granulated sugar

1 cup (220 g) packed dark brown sugar

1 teaspoon baking soda

1 teaspoon kosher salt

2 teaspoons chocolate extract (see note, below)

1 teaspoon balsamic vinegar

1 large egg

1 large egg yolk

1 cup (110 g) natural cocoa powder (not Dutch-process)

2 cups (280 g) all-purpose flour

TO ASSEMBLE

1 cup (200 g) granulated sugar

MAKE THE DARK CHOCOLATE COOKIE DOUGH

Combine the butter, cream cheese, both sugars, baking soda, and salt in the mixer bowl (no need to clean it). Beat on medium speed until light and fluffy, 2 to 3 minutes. Add the chocolate extract, vinegar, and egg and beat on medium speed until incorporated. Scrape down the sides of the bowl and then add the egg yolk and beat until incorporated.

Add the cocoa powder and mix on low speed until the dough starts to absorb some of the cocoa. Raise the speed to medium and mix until the cocoa is completely incorporated. Add the flour and beat, starting on low speed and then increasing to medium until incorporated.

ASSEMBLE THE COOKIES

Pour the granulated sugar into a small bowl. Pinch off about 1 teaspoon of the chocolate dough and roll it into a ball. Repeat with another teaspoon of chocolate dough. Then do the same with the raspberry dough, so that you have 4 balls of dough. Line them up in a row, alternating chocolate, raspberry, chocolate, raspberry. Now squish them together and roll the whole thing into a ball. The ball should look like marbled dough. Roll the ball in the sugar and place on the baking sheet.

Repeat with the rest of the dough, spacing the cookies about 2 inches apart. Bake until the edges of the raspberry part of the cookies start to look golden, 13 to 15 minutes. Don't overbake. Let cool on the baking sheets for 4 to 5 minutes and then move the cookies to a wire rack to cool completely. Repeat with the remaining dough.

✳ *This dough is fairly soft. If you have problems scooping or forming the marbled dough, refrigerate it for 30 minutes to firm it up first. Then proceed as directed.*

✳ *You can find chocolate extract at specialty cooking stores, some upscale grocery stores, and online. But if you can't find chocolate extract, just substitute 2 teaspoons vanilla extract in its place.*

ORANGE AND GINGER CHEWY COOKIES

Make a double batch of cookie dough following the recipe for the dark chocolate dough, but leave out the balsamic vinegar, chocolate extract, and cocoa powder. Instead, increase the flour to 5½ cups (770 g). Divide the dough in half.

To one half of the dough, add 2 teaspoons orange extract, the zest of 1 navel or Valencia orange, 2 tablespoons chopped candied orange peel, 25 drops yellow food coloring, and 15 drops red food coloring. To the second half, add 1 tablespoon ground ginger, 1 teaspoon ground turmeric, and 2 tablespoons chopped crystallized ginger. Assemble the cookies and bake as directed.

PEPPERMINT AND MILK CHOCOLATE CHEWY COOKIES

Make the peppermint dough following the recipe for the dark chocolate dough, omitting the balsamic vinegar, chocolate extract, and cocoa powder. Add 2 teaspoons peppermint extract and increase the flour to 2¾ cups (375 g). Add 12 drops green food coloring, if desired.

Make the milk chocolate dough following the recipe for the dark chocolate dough, omitting the balsamic vinegar and only using ½ cup (50 g) natural cocoa powder. Add ¾ cup (90 g) dry nonfat milk powder with the cocoa powder. Assemble and bake as directed.

CHOCOLATE-VANILLA CHECKERBOARD COOKIES

makes about 48 cookies plus 18 to 20 round marble cookies

Before I first attempted to make these cookies, I was intimidated. They basically look like something you'd buy at a fancy bakery, not something you'd make at home. But, as my college friend Krista once told me, there's something quite zen about making them. Krista is a food stylist who works with celebrity chefs, so I took her advice with a grain of salt. But it turns out she was right. Layering the pieces of dough and precisely cutting them out is really soothing, and the end result is immensely satisfying. I've adapted this recipe from the traditional version, called *Schwarz-weiss Gebäck* in German, to give it a little more chocolate and vanilla punch. And although I've impressed many a friend with these cookies, the secret is that they aren't really that hard. They do take a little bit of time, though, so keep that in mind and consider this a fun weekend project.

VANILLA DOUGH

1 cup (225 g or 2 sticks) unsalted butter, at room temperature

1 cup (115 g) powdered sugar, sifted

½ cup (100 g) granulated sugar

1 teaspoon kosher salt

1 teaspoon baking powder

1½ teaspoons vanilla extract

1 vanilla bean (optional, or increase the vanilla extract to 1 tablespoon)

1 large egg

2½ cups (350g) all-purpose flour

CHOCOLATE DOUGH

1 cup (225 g or 2 sticks) unsalted butter, at room temperature

1 cup (115 g) powdered sugar, sifted

½ cup (100 g) granulated sugar

1½ teaspoons baking powder

MAKE THE VANILLA DOUGH

Combine the butter, both sugars, salt, and baking powder in the bowl of a stand mixer fitted with the paddle attachment. Beat on medium speed until light and fluffy, about 3 minutes. Add the vanilla extract, then split the vanilla bean lengthwise and scrape the seeds into the batter with the back of a knife. Reserve the vanilla pod for another use. Add the egg. Beat until incorporated, about 30 seconds.

Add the flour in three portions, beating on low speed to incorporate and scraping down the sides of the bowl between additions. Divide the dough in half and pat each half into a 6-inch square that is ½ inch thick. Wrap tightly with plastic wrap and refrigerate until firm, about 30 minutes or overnight.

MAKE THE CHOCOLATE DOUGH

Add the butter, both sugars, baking powder, and salt to the mixer bowl (no need to wash it). Beat on medium speed until light and fluffy, about 3 minutes. Add the chocolate and vanilla extracts and the egg and beat until incorporated, about 30 seconds.

Add the cocoa powder, beating on low speed to incorporate and scraping down the sides of the bowl with a large spatula. Add the flour in two portions, beating to

·······>

1 teaspoon kosher salt

1 teaspoon chocolate extract (optional, or increase the vanilla extract to 1½ teaspoons)

½ teaspoon vanilla extract

1 large egg

½ cup (50 g) Dutch-process cocoa powder

2 cups (280 g) all-purpose flour

incorporate and scraping down the sides of the bowl between additions. Divide the dough in half and pat each half of the dough into a 6-inch square that is ½ inch thick. Wrap tightly with plastic wrap and refrigerate until firm, about 30 minutes or overnight.

Preheat the oven to 350°F and line two baking sheets with parchment paper or Silpats. Take the dough out of the refrigerator. Brush the top of one of the vanilla dough squares with water. Place one of the chocolate dough squares on top of it, and press down firmly so the dough adheres. Brush the top of this chocolate dough with water and place the remaining vanilla dough square on top of that, pressing down firmly. Finally, brush the top of the vanilla square with water and place the remaining chocolate dough on top, pressing down firmly. You should have a 2-inch-thick stack of dough 6 inches square with alternating layers. Wrap with plastic wrap and return to the refrigerator until firm, about 30 minutes.

Trim the edges of the dough to make a completely square piece. Set the trimmings aside to make marbled round cookies as a bonus (instructions in next step). Cut a ½-inch slice from the square and lay it down flat. Brush the top of it with water. Cut another ½-inch slice and rotate it 180 degrees so the pattern alternates with the bottom slice. Set it on the first slice and press down firmly. Repeat with the remaining cookie dough, chilling the dough as needed if it warms up and becomes sticky. Slice each stack of dough into ½-inch-thick cookies.

To make marbled round cookies with the extra dough, brush the top of one trimming with water and place another trimming on top, with the dough strips alternating. Repeat until all the trimmings are placed on each other. Flatten and twist the trimmings together, turning clockwise with one hand and counterclockwise with the other. Form the dough into a 1½-inch-thick log that is about 12 inches long. Press down firmly to make sure the different doughs stick together. Wrap the log with plastic wrap and chill while you bake the checkerboard cookies.

Place the cookies on the prepared baking sheets about 1 inch apart (keep the extra cookies chilled until ready to bake). Bake until the edges of the cookies start to brown ever so slightly, 12 to 14 minutes. Let cool on the baking sheet for 10 minutes and then move the cookies to a wire cooling rack to cool completely. Repeat with the remaining dough. Once you have finished baking the checkerboard cookies, remove the marbled log from the refrigerator and slice into ½-inch-thick cookies. Bake for 12 to 14 minutes. Let cool on the baking sheets for 10 minutes before moving to a wire cooling rack to cool completely.

LEMON AND GINGERBREAD CHECKERBOARD COOKIES

Make the lemon dough following the recipe for the vanilla dough, omitting the vanilla bean and reducing the vanilla extract to ½ teaspoon. Add 2 teaspoons lemon extract and proceed as directed.

To make the gingerbread dough, beat together ¾ cup (170 g or 1½ sticks) unsalted butter, ½ cup (57 g) powdered sugar, ⅓ cup (75 g) packed dark brown sugar, ⅓ cup (115 g) dark molasses, 1 teaspoon kosher salt, ¼ teaspoon baking soda, 2½ teaspoons ground ginger, 1½ teaspoons ground cinnamon, ½ teaspoon ground nutmeg, and ¼ teaspoon ground cloves in a stand mixer fitted with the paddle attachment until fluffy, about 3 minutes on medium speed. Beat in 1 large egg, then add 2½ cups (350 g) all-purpose flour in three portions, beating to incorporate and scraping down the sides of the bowl between additions. Shape the doughs into squares, assemble, and bake as directed.

STRAWBERRY-PEPPER AND ORANGE CHECKERBOARD COOKIES

Make the strawberry dough following the recipe for the vanilla dough, omitting the vanilla bean and reducing the vanilla extract to ½ teaspoon. Add 2 teaspoons natural strawberry extract (found online or at specialty stores), ¼ teaspoon balsamic vinegar, 1 teaspoon freshly ground black pepper, and 1 teaspoon red food coloring, and proceed as directed.

Make the orange dough following the recipe for the vanilla dough, omitting the vanilla bean and reducing the vanilla extract to ½ teaspoon. Add 2 teaspoons orange extract, ½ teaspoon ground turmeric, and ½ teaspoon fiori di Sicilia flavoring (optional, found online or at specialty stores). Shape the dough into squares, assemble, and bake as directed.

The importance of color

One thing that clearly shows off two different doughs is their contrasting colors. Color is much more than just aesthetics, though. When you eat something that is brightly colored, it signifies to your brain that the food is actually more intensely flavored as well. Humans are biologically wired to search out produce that is bright and vibrant (as opposed to dull and gray, which could signify rot or spoilage). The food industry knows this, and it's why grocery store mint ice cream is usually a vibrant green and why cherry candy is neon red. Color is a psychological indicator of flavor. I'm not a huge fan of artificial coloring, though I do use it on occasion for this specific reason. Most of the time, I opt for natural colorings, from freeze-dried fruit, spices, or other ingredients, as long as the flavors are complementary or will blend into the background.

The hardest colors to achieve are blues, purples, and reds. Blues and purples from natural sources like red cabbage or berries tend to fade to a rather unappealing zombie purple-blue-gray. The reason they become muddy is that the colors mix with the golden tones that are the natural colors of most baked goods. If you remember the color wheel from grade school, yellow is the opposite of purple and orange is the opposite of blue. When combined, they add up to a fairly ugly color. Thankfully, I don't bake a lot of items that are blue or purple, but when I do, I usually opt for a drop or two of blue or purple food coloring, which is more saturated in color and doesn't fade the same way diluted natural coloring does. Red is troublesome because you often need a large amount of a red ingredient (like beets) or one that is very concentrated in flavor as well as color, which can throw off the flavor of the baked good. Thus red food coloring (liquid or gel) is probably the one I use the most when it comes to the artificial stuff.

But natural food coloring works fairly well for non-baked items (frostings and decorations). Keep in mind that natural food colorings are still heat- and temperature-sensitive and might fade over time, so once you've decorated the cake or cookies, eat them within a day or two! If you want try your hand at using natural food coloring, here are some ideas:

RED: Hibiscus tea, pomegranate juice or concentrate, blood orange juice, beet juice or powder (look for powder at health food stores).

ORANGE: Carrot juice (try simmering it a bit to reduce the water content and concentrate the color) or paprika.

YELLOW: Turmeric (ground in the jar or grated fresh) or saffron (a little goes a long way).

GREEN: Matcha green tea powder. Buy the culinary grade, as it's usually cheaper and perfect for baking. Liquid chlorophyll, found at health food stores, is another option.

BLUE AND PURPLE: Boil a chopped red cabbage and then reduce the liquid to get a deep purple. To make it blue, add baking soda a little at a time, and stop when it turns blue. Red cabbage liquid is actually a pH indicator liquid. When you add a base like baking soda, it turns blue. If you add an acid (like lemon juice or vinegar), it will turn pink.

BROWN: Natural cocoa powder or instant espresso powder.

BLACK: Dutch-process cocoa powder or Black Onyx Dutch-process cocoa. Squid ink is another option, though it can be hard to find. It is relatively neutral in flavor unless you use a lot of it (which you rarely need to), but a lot of folks are hesitant to use it in non-savory applications because it does have a slight sea-salt metallic undertone.

CHOCOLATE, PEANUT BUTTER, AND BUTTERSCOTCH LAYERED COOKIES

makes 48 cookies

I have few regrets in life: eating that third doughnut (two is almost always enough). The rock-star mullet I had in high school (along with the accompanying attempt at a mustache that I'd rather not speak of). The unfortunate fashion choices I made in the 1980s (oh, acid wash, how you played me). But one major regret is not discovering this flavor combination earlier! I can't believe my world was ever bereft of a chocolate, peanut butter, and butterscotch cookie. It may sound fussy to make two different cookie doughs, but the chocolate–peanut butter dough is crazy easy to make, and the combination of flavors is life-changing.

BUTTERSCOTCH DOUGH

3 cups (420 g) all-purpose flour

½ teaspoon kosher salt

½ teaspoon baking soda

½ teaspoon baking powder

¾ cup (170 g or 1½ sticks) cold unsalted butter, divided

2 cups (440 g) packed dark brown sugar

2 large eggs

1 tablespoon vanilla extract

CHOCOLATE–PEANUT BUTTER DOUGH

¾ cup (105 g) all-purpose flour

7 tablespoons (50 g) natural cocoa powder (not Dutch-process)

¾ teaspoon baking soda

½ teaspoon baking powder

MAKE THE BUTTERSCOTCH DOUGH

Preheat the oven to 350°F. Line baking sheets with parchment paper or Silpats. Combine the flour, salt, baking soda, and baking powder in a large mixing bowl. Stir vigorously together with a balloon whisk until all the ingredients are evenly distributed. Set aside.

Place 10 tablespoons (1¼ sticks) of the butter in a large pan and cook over medium-high heat until the butter has melted and starts to foam. Lower the heat to medium-low and continue to cook until the fat solids start to brown. Turn off the heat and continue to swirl the butter in the pan until the residual heat of the pan turns the fat solids golden brown and the butter starts to smell nutty. Pour the browned butter into the bowl of a stand mixer fitted with the paddle attachment, add the remaining 2 tablespoons cold butter, and beat until the melted butter has cooled and the solid butter has melted, about 2 minutes.

Add the brown sugar and beat for about 30 seconds to blend. Add one egg and beat until incorporated, about 30 seconds, then beat in the second egg and the vanilla until incorporated. Add half of the dry ingredients, beating to incorporate before adding the second half of the dry ingredients. The dough should be stiff. Transfer the butterscotch dough to a different mixing bowl.

·······>

½ teaspoon kosher salt

6 tablespoons (85 g or ¾ stick) unsalted butter, at room temperature

6 tablespoons (75 g) granulated sugar

6 tablespoons (85 g) packed dark brown sugar

¾ cup (205 g) smooth peanut butter, at room temperature

1 large egg yolk

TO ASSEMBLE

½ cup (100 g) turbinado sugar or granulated sugar

MAKE THE CHOCOLATE–PEANUT BUTTER DOUGH

Combine the flour, cocoa powder, baking soda, baking powder, and salt in a clean mixing bowl. Stir vigorously together with a balloon whisk until all the ingredients are evenly distributed. Place the butter and both sugars in the stand mixer bowl (no need to clean it). Beat on medium speed until light and fluffy, about 2 minutes. Add the peanut butter and beat until incorporated, about 30 seconds. Add the egg yolk and beat until incorporated, about 15 seconds. Add the dry ingredients all at once and beat until incorporated, about 1 minute.

ASSEMBLE THE COOKIES

Pinch off a rounded tablespoon of the butterscotch dough and roll it in the palm of your hand to form a ball. Press your palms together with the ball in the middle to form a butterscotch cookie disk about 1½ inches in diameter. Dip one side of the disk into the turbinado sugar, lightly pressing down so the sugar sticks to the bottom of the cookie. Place the disk on the lined baking sheet with the sugar side down. Repeat, filling the baking sheets with the butterscotch disks, spacing them 2 inches apart.

Pinch off a rounded teaspoon-size chunk of the chocolate–peanut butter dough and roll it in your palm to form a ball. Brush the top of the butterscotch dough with a little bit of water, place the chocolate ball in the center of a butterscotch disk, and press down on the ball to flatten it onto the butterscotch disk. Use a fork to lightly press a crisscross pattern on the peanut butter–chocolate dough only.

Repeat for all the cookies. Bake until the edges of the cookies just start to look slightly dry, 10 to 12 minutes. Do not overbake them, as you want the butterscotch cookies to be chewy. Let cool on the baking sheets for 5 minutes and then move to a wire rack to cool completely.

Stacking the dough

Combining two doughs into one cookie will astound your friends and loved ones. The secret is finding a sturdy dough for the bottom layer (often adding ¼ to ½ cup all-purpose flour will make your dough sturdier). Make a normal batch of sturdy cookie dough for the bottom layer and then a half batch of whatever cookie dough you want on top. Brush some water on the bottom half so that the doughs stick together. Just be sure to pick flavors that go well together. Check your pantry or the grocery store shelves for ideas. Chocolate and peanut butter, cinnamon and oatmeal, and dried cherry and almond are all flavors that you see on packages and that you can use for inspiration in making your own stacked layered cookies.

CHUNKY PEANUT BUTTER AND SNICKERDOODLE COOKIES

Make the snickerdoodle cookie dough by combining 2¾ cups (385 g) all-purpose flour, 2 teaspoons cream of tartar, 1 teaspoon baking soda, and ½ teaspoon kosher salt in a large bowl. Vigorously stir together with a balloon whisk. In a stand mixer fitted with the paddle attachment, beat together ½ cup (115 g or 1 stick) unsalted butter, ½ cup (90 g) vegetable shortening, and 1½ cups (300 g) granulated sugar. Add 2 eggs, one at a time, waiting until the first is incorporated before adding the next. Mix in 2 teaspoons vanilla extract. Add the dry ingredients in two batches, mixing to incorporate before the second addition. Combine 2 tablespoons granulated sugar and 1½ teaspoons ground cinnamon in a bowl and use it to coat the bottoms of the cookies as directed.

Make the peanut butter dough as directed, using ½ cup (150 g) chunky peanut butter instead of the smooth peanut butter and omitting the cocoa powder. Assemble and bake as directed.

CINNAMON–PEANUT BUTTER AND OATMEAL-RAISIN COOKIES

Make the oatmeal-raisin cookie dough by combining 2¼ cups (270 g) rolled oats, 1½ cups (210 g) all-purpose flour, 1½ teaspoons ground cinnamon, and ¾ teaspoon each ground nutmeg, ground ginger, baking powder, baking soda, and kosher salt in a large bowl. Vigorously stir together with a balloon whisk. In a stand mixer fitted with the paddle attachment, beat together ¾ cup (170 g or 1½ sticks) unsalted butter, ¾ cup (150 g) granulated sugar, and ¾ cup (165 g) packed dark brown sugar. Add 1 large egg, 1 large egg yolk, and 1 tablespoon vanilla extract and mix to incorporate. Add the dry ingredients in two batches, beating to incorporate before the second addition. Mix in 1½ cups (225 g) raisins.

Make the peanut butter dough as directed, but omit the cocoa powder and add 1 teaspoon ground cinnamon to the dry ingredients. Assemble and bake as directed.

CHOCOLATE SANDWICH COOKIES WITH MAPLE-BACON FILLING

makes 48 sandwich cookies

Chocolate sandwich cookies are pretty classic. There are numerous recipes for variations online and in cookbooks, and even Nabisco is known to tinker with their Oreos by adding fun flavor combinations, especially for the holiday seasons. This one is worlds above any store-bought version but still has the signature look and bitter chocolate flavor due to the use of Dutch-process cocoa. If you can get ahold of Black Onyx Dutch-process cocoa (available by mail order), by all means use it, as it will give your cookies a super-black color, but Hershey's Special Dark cocoa powder works nearly as well. The maple-bacon filling is a surprisingly savory-sweet twist. The result is a sandwich cookie that will tickle both your inner child and your grown-up palate.

COOKIE DOUGH

6 tablespoons (85 g or ¾ stick) unsalted butter, at room temperature

½ cup (100 g) granulated sugar

¼ cup (55 g) packed dark brown sugar

1 teaspoon kosher salt

¼ teaspoon baking powder

¼ teaspoon baking soda

2 teaspoons vanilla extract

1 large egg

¾ cup (105 g) all-purpose flour

¾ cup plus 2 tablespoons (85 g) Dutch-process cocoa powder (see note, opposite)

2 tablespoons cornstarch

MAKE THE COOKIE DOUGH

Preheat the oven to 350°F and line baking sheets with parchment paper or Silpats. Combine the butter, both sugars, salt, baking powder, and baking soda in the bowl of a stand mixer fitted with the paddle attachment. Beat on medium speed until the butter starts to cling to the sides of the bowl and the mixture starts to look creamy, 2 to 3 minutes. Add the vanilla and beat until incorporated. Add the egg and beat until incorporated.

Add the flour, cocoa powder, and cornstarch to the batter and beat on low speed until the dry ingredients start to incorporate. Raise the speed to medium and beat until incorporated completely. The dough will be stiff.

Dust a clean surface with some extra cocoa powder and scrape the dough out of the bowl onto the surface. Gather it into a ball and press down to make a large, thick disk. Using a rolling pin, roll out the dough to ⅛ inch thick. Using a 2-inch round cookie cutter, cut out circles from the dough and place on the baking sheets. Bake until the cookies are firm to the touch, 7 to 8 minutes. Do not over-bake. Let cool on the baking sheets for 5 minutes and then move to a wire rack to cool completely. Continue with the rest of the dough, gathering the scraps, kneading the dough together, and rerolling. Make sure to continue to dust the surface and the rolling pin so the dough doesn't stick.

3 thick-cut slices (85 g) bacon, finely chopped

¼ cup (85 g) maple syrup (Very Dark Color with Strong Flavor preferred)

4 tablespoons (57 g or ½ stick) unsalted butter

1¾ cups (200 g) powdered sugar, sifted

½ teaspoon freshly ground black pepper

⅛ teaspoon kosher salt

✱ Bacon is easier to chop into small bits if it is partially frozen. Freeze the bacon for 30 minutes before chopping it with a sharp serrated knife.

✱ Because you roll out the dough with cocoa powder instead of flour, making these cookies can get pretty messy! Wear an apron or old clothes in case you get some cocoa on you.

✱ Black Onyx cocoa is an ultra-Dutch-process cocoa, meaning it has been extra-processed with an alkalizing agent that lowers the acidity and alters the flavor. The extra processing also results in a nearly purple-black cocoa powder and the signature flavor of Oreos and other store-bought chocolate sandwich cookies. Black Onyx cocoa can be found online (see Resources, page 336) and I highly recommend trying it out, but if you don't feel like investing, you can use regular Dutch-process cocoa, or a blended cocoa like Hershey's Special Dark cocoa, in its place. The flavor of Hershey's Special Dark is pretty close to Black Onyx, though the cookies won't be as midnight black.

MAKE THE FILLING

Cook the bacon until extremely crisp (this shouldn't take too long because the pieces are small; be careful not to burn them). Drain the bacon bits in a bowl lined with a paper towel. Place the maple syrup and butter in a small pot and melt over high heat, stirring constantly. Once the butter is melted, reduce the heat to medium and cook for about 4 minutes, stirring constantly to make sure the mixture doesn't boil over. Remove from the heat and pour into the bowl of a stand mixer fitted with the paddle attachment. Beat on medium speed for about 1 minute, until the syrup has cooled a bit. Add the powdered sugar and beat until incorporated. Mix in the bacon, pepper, and salt. Let cool to room temperature to thicken into a filling.

Assemble the cookies by pinching off ½ teaspoon of the filling and rolling it into a ball (about the size of a hazelnut or chickpea). Place the ball in the center of the bottom of one of the cookies and press another cookie (bottom side down) on top of the filling firmly, so the filling spreads evenly to the edges of the cookie. Repeat with the remaining cookies.

·······>

Cocoa types

One of the most confusing things about cocoa powder is the distinction between natural versus Dutch-process cocoa. Untreated cocoa powder is called natural cocoa powder, and it is what you find most commonly at the grocery store. Natural cocoa powder is acidic, lighter in color, and has a natural bitterness and more robust cocoa flavor.

Dutch-process cocoa has been treated with an alkalizing agent, giving it a neutral or slightly alkaline pH. It is darker in color, ranging from a dark reddish brown to midnight black, and is more soluble in liquid. It also has a smoother chocolate flavor and is often the type of cocoa used in making hot cocoa. The most commonly found Dutch-processed cocoa is Hershey's

Special Dark, which is a blend of Dutch-process and natural. It works for most recipes that require Dutch-process cocoa. Black Onyx is extra-Dutch-processed, making it a midnight-black cocoa that is perfect for the black cookie sandwiches in this recipe. It's also used in blackout cake and other recipes where you want a deep, dark chocolate-black color.

I don't recommend swapping out natural cocoa for Dutch-process cocoa or vice versa unless you are willing to tinker more with the recipe. The difference in their acidity means they will react differently with the other ingredients in the dough or batter. However, if you do need to substitute, refer to page 16 for instructions on how to do it.

MALTED CHOCOLATE SANDWICH COOKIES WITH MALTED BUTTERSCOTCH FILLING

Make the cookies as directed, but omit the cornstarch and Dutch-process cocoa powder. Instead, increase the flour to 1¼ cups (175 g) and add ¾ cup (80 g) natural cocoa powder and ½ cup (80 g) malted milk powder. Proceed as directed.

To make the filling, melt 4 tablespoons (57 g or ½ stick) unsalted butter in a medium skillet and cook over medium-high heat until the butterfat starts to brown and smell nutty and fragrant, 2 to 3 minutes. Reduce the heat to medium, add ⅓ cup (75 g) packed dark brown sugar, and cook, stirring constantly, for about 5 minutes. Carefully stir in ¼ cup (65 g) plain Greek-style yogurt (it will steam and bubble up) and cook for an additional minute or two, until any solid chunks of sugar have dissolved. Scrape into a clean bowl of a stand mixer fitted with the paddle attachment. Add ½ teaspoon vanilla extract, 1½ cups (175 g) sifted powdered sugar, ¼ cup (40 g) malted milk powder, and ½ teaspoon kosher salt. Beat until the dry ingredients are incorporated and the filling has cooled. Assemble the cookies as directed.

MINT CHOCOLATE SANDWICH COOKIES WITH STRAWBERRY FILLING

Make the cookies as directed, adding ½ teaspoon mint extract along with the vanilla. Proceed as directed.

Make the filling by crushing ⅔ cup (15 g) freeze-dried strawberries into a powder. Add it to ½ cup (85 g) vegetable shortening, 1 cup (115 g) powdered sugar, and ⅛ teaspoon kosher salt in the bowl of stand mixer fitted with the paddle attachment. Beat until the filling comes together. If the filling is too soft, add an extra ¼ cup powdered sugar. If it is too firm, thin it with 1 teaspoon of milk. Assemble the cookies as directed.

HAZELNUT-COCOA LINZER COOKIES WITH BLACKBERRY-MINT JAM

makes 36 cookies

I've often thought about where I would want to live if I didn't live in San Francisco. Though I have no desire to move away, Portland is definitely on the short list. I visit Portland often and I love its local food scene. Oregon is known for many things, but two of its major produce exports are blackberries and hazelnuts. Those happen to be two of my favorite flavors as well, and they work great together in a linzer-style cookie. You can certainly cheat and use store-bought blackberry jam if you want, but making it from scratch isn't difficult, especially since you aren't canning it. It also allows you to control the ingredients (no corn syrup) as well as add an extra layer of flavor (fresh mint).

BLACKBERRY-MINT JAM

2 cups (12 ounces or 340 g) fresh or frozen blackberries

2 cups (400 g) granulated sugar

1 tablespoon chopped fresh mint

2 teaspoons fresh lemon juice

COOKIE DOUGH

⅔ cup (100 g) hazelnuts

½ cup (110 g) packed dark brown sugar, divided

1 cup (225 g or 2 sticks) European-style unsalted butter, at room temperature

½ teaspoon baking powder

½ teaspoon kosher salt

½ teaspoon ground cardamom

1 large egg

1 teaspoon vanilla extract

MAKE THE BLACKBERRY-MINT JAM

Place two or three metal spoons in the freezer. Combine the blackberries, sugar, mint, and lemon juice in a large pot (nonstick is better for easy cleanup). Cook over high heat, crushing the blackberries with a potato masher or the back of a wooden spoon until they liquefy and the juices start to boil. Reduce the heat to a rapid simmer and cook, stirring frequently, until the jam starts to thicken slightly, 10 to 15 minutes. Scoop up a tiny bit of the jam with a spoon, then drop it onto one of the frozen spoons. Place the spoon with the jam back in the freezer for 1 minute. Take it out and push at it with a finger. If it wrinkles, then the jam is set. If not, continue to cook for an additional 2 to 3 minutes and then test again. The jam will continue to thicken as it cools, so don't worry if it seems too thin. Once the jam is done, let it cool in the pan to room temperature and then pour into a jar or bowl and refrigerate until ready to use. You can make the jam up to 1 week in advance, if you'd like.

MAKE THE COOKIE DOUGH

Toast the hazelnuts in a medium dry skillet over medium-high heat until they start to turn fragrant and darken, 5 to 6 minutes. Pour them into a clean kitchen towel and rub off as much of the skins as you can. Don't worry if you can't get all of them off. Discard the skins and scoop the hazelnuts into the bowl of a food

·······>

2¼ cups (315 g) all-purpose flour, divided

5 tablespoons (30 g) Dutch-process cocoa powder

TO ASSEMBLE

2 tablespoons powdered sugar, sifted

processor or blender. Add ¼ cup (55 g) of the brown sugar and process until the nuts are ground into a powder, taking care not to overprocess (or you will end up with hazelnut butter).

Place the remaining ¼ cup (55 g) brown sugar, the butter, baking powder, salt, and cardamom in the bowl of a stand mixer fitted with the paddle attachment. Beat on medium speed until the mixture is uniform in color and sticks to the sides of the bowl, 3 to 4 minutes. Stop the mixer occasionally to scrape down the sides of the bowl. Add the ground hazelnuts and beat for about 1 minute. Add the egg and vanilla and beat until incorporated, about 30 seconds.

Add 2 cups (280 g) of the flour and mix until just incorporated. Divide the dough in half (about 380 g each) and move one half to a different bowl, leaving the other half in the mixer bowl. To the remaining dough in the mixer bowl, add the remaining ¼ cup (35 g) flour and mix until incorporated. Scoop out the dough onto a piece of parchment paper or waxed paper, press into a disk, and then cover with a second piece of parchment or waxed paper. Roll out the dough between the two pieces of paper until it is about ¼ inch thick. Refrigerate the rolled-out dough (still in the papers). Return the reserved dough to the mixer bowl. Add the cocoa powder and mix to incorporate. Roll out the chocolate dough between two pieces of parchment or waxed paper as you did for the first piece of dough, and then refrigerate for 1 hour.

After 45 minutes, preheat the oven to 350°F and line two baking sheets with parchment paper or Silpats. Take the chocolate dough out of the refrigerator and use a 2-inch round cookie cutter to cut out circles, placing them on one of the lined baking sheets ½ inch apart. If the dough gets too soft, return it to the fridge for 5 to 10 minutes to firm up. Gather the remaining chocolate dough, reroll it between the papers, and place it back in the fridge. Take the plain dough out of the refrigerator and cut out more 2-inch circles. Use a smaller cookie cutter or the wide end of a piping tip to cut out a "window" in the center of each plain cookie. Place the plain cookies on the second lined baking sheet. Reroll any leftover dough and return it to the fridge.

Bake until the edges of the plain cookies are golden brown, 10 to 12 minutes. Keep an eye on the cookies, as they brown really fast. Because the chocolate dough is already so dark, it's best to bake a sheet of each at the same time so you can use the plain cookies to judge when both are done. Let the cookies cool on the baking sheets for about 5 minutes and then move to a wire rack to cool completely. Cut and bake the remaining cookie dough.

·······>

Once the cookies have completely cooled, dust the plain cookies with the "window" with powdered sugar. Place 1 heaping teaspoon of the blackberry jam on each of the chocolate cookies and then place a plain cookie on top to sandwich the jam.

✱ *Skip making your own jam and just use your favorite store-bought one. There are some really great artisan jams and preserves out there. Try to avoid any that have high-fructose corn syrup in the ingredients, however, as those tend to use inferior fruit and are overly sweet and one-dimensional in flavor.*

✱ *You will have some leftover jam after making these cookies. Save it and use it on your toast or croissant the next morning. It's absolutely lovely.*

✱ *These cookies are good the day you make them but improve the next day!*

American vs. European butter

Most recipes in this book are designed to be made with standard American butter, but occasionally European butter is better. European butter has less water than American butter and is richer in both fat and flavor. American butter is usually about 80 percent butterfat, while European butter is 82 to 86 percent butterfat. This particular cookie has very few ingredients and benefits from the richness of the European-style butter. You can certainly replace it with American-style butter, but if you have a chance to make these with European-style butter (common brands include Kerrygold, Plugrá, and a few national brands like Challenge and Straus), you'll be able to taste the difference.

HAZLENUT-COCOA LINZER COOKIES WITH SEEDLESS ROSEMARY-BLACKBERRY JAM

Make the cookies as directed. Make seedless rosemary-blackberry jam for the filling by omitting the fresh mint and using 1 teaspoon chopped fresh rosemary leaves instead. Press the cooked jam through a fine-mesh strainer into a bowl or jar while hot. The strainer will catch the seeds and rosemary leaves. Let cool and then assemble as directed.

alternatives

BROWNED BUTTER SHORTBREAD WITH MANDARIN ORANGE MARMALADE

Place 2 spoons in the freezer. To make the orange marmalade, peel 3 mandarin oranges. Slice the peel thinly then chop it into small bits and place in a medium saucepan along with the zest of 1 lemon and 1 cup water. Bring to a boil. Lower the heat to a simmer, cover, and cook for about 20 minutes. Meanwhile, cut off the bitter white pith from the lemon and any pith left on the orange. Slice both citrus fruit into cross sections, discarding any seeds. Puree the fruit in a food processor. Once the peel and zest have cooked for 20 minutes, add the orange and lemon puree to the saucepan and return to a boil. Lower the heat, cover, and simmer for 20 minutes. Uncover and add 1¼ cups (250 g) granulated sugar. Raise the heat to a boil and cook for 10 minutes, stirring frequently. Remove from the heat and place a drop of the marmalade on one of the frozen spoons. Place it back in the freezer for 1 minute, then push on the marmalade with your finger. If it wrinkles, the marmalade is done. If it's still liquid, return to a boil and cook a little longer, testing again after a couple of minutes. Let cool before using.

Make the cookie dough, but first, brown the butter by melting it in a large skillet over high heat. Reduce the heat to medium and cook until the butter solids start to brown, 2 to 3 minutes. Turn the heat off and let the residual heat finish cooking the butter until the solids are golden brown and smell nutty and fragrant. Let cool in the skillet to room temperature and then proceed with the recipe as directed, using ½ teaspoon ground cinnamon in place of the cardamom. Skip dividing the dough in half and omit the cocoa powder, increasing the flour to 2½ cups (350 g). Bake and assemble as directed.

······>

Place two spoons in the freezer. To make the peach butter, thoroughly wash 1 pound (455 g) peaches, then pit and chop them into ½-inch chunks (with their skin) and place them in a large pot along with 1 cup plus 2 tablespoons (225 g) granulated sugar. Add 2 tablespoons fresh lemon juice, 1 vanilla bean, split lengthwise, and two 2-inch-long cinnamon sticks. Cook over medium-high heat, stirring frequently, for 20 to 30 minutes, until the fruit pulp is soft and tender. Remove the vanilla bean and cinnamon sticks and puree the fruit with either an immersion blender or a blender or food processor. Return the puree to the pot if necessary. Cook over medium heat for an additional 10 minutes. Remove from the heat and place a drop of the peach butter on one of the frozen spoons. Return to the freezer for 1 minute, then push on the peach butter with your finger. If it wrinkles, the peach butter is done. If it's still liquid, return to a boil and cook a little longer, testing again after a couple minutes. Let cool before using.

Make the cookie dough as directed, omitting the cardamom and adding 2 teaspoons chopped fresh rosemary. Skip dividing the dough in half and omit the cocoa powder, increasing the flour to 2½ cups (350 g). Bake and assemble as directed.

GINGER AND PLUM SWIRLED ICE CREAM SANDWICHES WITH SOFT AND CHEWY OAT COOKIES

makes 12 ice cream sandwiches

It turns out that soft oatmeal cookies are perfect for ice cream sandwiches, as they don't get really hard when frozen. The best part about making ice cream sandwiches is that you can have a bunch of these in the freezer for unexpected guests, or whenever you are just craving something sweet. Consider yourself warned that the ginger in this ice cream is very assertive and strong. So if you love the heat of ginger, this is the ice cream for you!

PLUM SWIRL

2 cups (¾ pound or 3 medium) chopped and pitted firm red plums (skin left on)

½ cup (100 g) granulated sugar

1 tablespoon fresh lemon juice

GINGER ICE CREAM

3 ounces (85 g or about 6 inches long) fresh ginger

5 teaspoons tapioca starch (see note, page 68)

2 cups whole milk, divided

1¼ cups heavy cream

⅔ cup (135 g) granulated sugar

2 tablespoons mild-flavored honey

⅛ teaspoon kosher salt

3 tablespoons cream cheese, at room temperature

MAKE THE PLUM SWIRL

Combine the plums, sugar, and lemon juice in a medium saucepan and cook over high heat until the plum juices start to release and the sugar dissolves. Once the liquid starts to boil, lower the heat to a simmer. Cook, stirring frequently, until the fruit has disintegrated and the jam has thickened, 7 to 10 minutes. Remove from the heat and let cool completely. Pour the jam into a small jar or container and refrigerate overnight.

MAKE THE GINGER ICE CREAM

Rinse off the ginger, then slice it thinly (about ⅛ inch thick) with the peel on. Place the ginger slices in a medium saucepan and cover with water by about 1 inch. Bring to a boil and cook the ginger for about 2 minutes. Drain the ginger and rinse it with water. Boiling the ginger removes an enzyme in the root that makes dairy curdle and also removes any bitterness. Rinse out the saucepan and put the ginger back in the pan.

Combine the tapioca starch and 2 tablespoons of the milk in a small bowl, cover with plastic wrap, and refrigerate until ready to use. Add the remaining milk, the cream, sugar, honey, and salt to the saucepan with the ginger. Bring to a near boil over high heat, stirring constantly. Once you see bubbles start to form on the sides of the pan, turn off the heat and cover the pan. Let sit for 1 hour for the ginger to steep. Now's a good time to take the cream cheese out of the refrigerator to come to room temperature if you haven't already.

·······>

OATMEAL COOKIES

1 cup (225 g or 2 sticks) unsalted butter, at room temperature

1 cup (220 g) packed dark brown sugar

½ cup (100 g) granulated sugar

2 tablespoons mild-flavored honey

1 teaspoon vanilla extract

½ teaspoon ground cinnamon

1 teaspoon baking soda

1 teaspoon kosher salt

2 large eggs

2 cups (225 g) thick-cut rolled oats

1½ cups (210 g) all-purpose flour

1 cup (160 g) dried cherries

Use a slotted spoon to remove the ginger slices from the cream mixture. Don't worry if there are tiny bits of ginger still floating; just out get as much as you can. Bring the mixture back to a boil, then lower the temperature to a simmer. Take the tapioca mixture out of the refrigerator and stir to make sure the tapioca hasn't all settled on the bottom. Once the cream mixture is simmering, pour the tapioca mixture into the pan, stirring with a whisk. Cook until thickened slightly, about 1 minute. Remove from the heat and add the cream cheese, whisking to incorporate.

Open a 1-gallon zip-top plastic bag and set it in a large bowl. Put a mesh strainer inside the bag and pour the ice cream base into the bag through the strainer. Discard any solids caught in the strainer and seal the bag. Fill the large bowl with ice from two ice cube trays and water. Submerge the bag in the ice water and let sit for 30 minutes, or longer, until the ice cream base is cold. At this point you can refrigerate the ice cream base overnight (recommended) or proceed right away.

Churn the ice cream according to your machine's instructions. Once the ice cream is done churning, layer the ice cream with the cold plum jam in an airtight container. Press a piece of parchment paper on the surface of the ice cream, seal the container, and place in the freezer to harden, about 4 hours.

MAKE THE OATMEAL COOKIES

Preheat the oven to 350°F and line baking sheets with parchment paper or Silpats. Place the butter, both sugars, honey, vanilla, cinnamon, baking soda, and salt in the bowl of a stand mixer fitted with the paddle attachment. Beat on medium speed until the butter is fluffy and sticks to the sides of the bowl, about 2 minutes. Add the eggs, one at a time, waiting for the first one to incorporate and scraping down the sides of the bowl before adding the next. Add the oats and flour and mix on low, then increase the mixer speed as the dry ingredients are incorporated. Add the dried cherries and mix on low speed until just blended in.

Scoop the cookie dough in about 2-tablespoon amounts onto the lined baking sheets, spacing the cookies 2 inches apart. Flatten the dough slightly with the palm of your hand (the cookies will continue to spread a lot as they bake) and bake until lightly brown at the edges, 11 to 13 minutes. Don't overbake these cookies, as you want them soft for the ice cream sandwiches. Let cool on the baking sheets for 10 minutes and then move to a wire rack to cool completely. Repeat with the remaining dough. Once cool, stack the cookies in a plastic container and freeze for at least 2 hours or overnight.

To make the ice cream sandwiches, place a medium scoop of ice cream (3 to 4 tablespoons) on the bottom of one of the cookies. Place another cookie on top and squish together. Return to the freezer to firm up for about an hour before serving.

alternatives

SOFT AND CHEWY OAT AND BLUEBERRY ICE CREAM SANDWICHES WITH VANILLA AND PEACH-BOURBON ICE CREAM

Churn and use the peach-bourbon ice cream from the Vanilla and Peach-Bourbon Ice Cream Pie (page 225). Make the cookies as directed, swapping in 1 cup (160 g) dried blueberries for the cherries. Assemble as directed.

SOFT AND CHEWY OAT AND RAISIN ICE CREAM SANDWICHES WITH STRAWBERRY AND PEANUT BUTTER ICE CREAM

Make the strawberry jam following the recipe for the plum swirl, replacing the plums with 2 cups chopped fresh or frozen strawberries. Increase the sugar to ¾ cup (150 g) and 1 tablespoon of lemon juice. Cook and let cool as directed.

Make the peanut butter ice cream following the recipe for the ginger ice cream, but omitting the ginger and skipping the steeping. Increase the tapioca starch to 2 tablespoons and whisk in ½ cup (130 g) room temperature smooth natural peanut butter along with the cream cheese. No need to strain; just pour directly into the zip-top bag. Chill and churn as directed. Layer in the container with the cooled strawberry jam.

Make the cookies as directed, swapping in 1 cup (160 g) raisins for the cherries. Assemble as directed.

Easy cheat: store-bought ice cream

As much as I love to make everything from scratch, I know that not everyone has the time or wants to go through all the effort. But if you are willing to bake cookies, you can make ice cream sandwiches with store-bought ice cream and everyone will still be impressed! Use 1 quart of high-quality ice cream in a flavor that complements the oat cookies. I like vanilla bean, strawberry, salted caramel, or butter pecan.

Of course, if you feel like doing a little more work but still don't feel like churning ice cream, you can always add a fruit swirl, like the plum jam or the strawberry jam, and just layer it in with softened store-bought ice cream. Vanilla or cinnamon are both complementary to fruit jams as well as to the oatmeal cookies.

Tapioca starch or flour

Tapioca starch (sometimes sold as tapioca flour) is a gluten-free starch extracted from the cassava root. Tapioca is probably most commonly used in the United States for tapioca pudding, though the Taiwanese bubble tea with tapioca pearls has become quite popular. Tapioca starch is the same ingredient used for both of those items, but ground into a fine powder.

In this recipe, tapioca starch acts as a thickener in place of egg yolks and helps keep the ice cream smooth and less icy. Ginger has an enzyme that curdles both dairy and egg yolks. Boiling it helps, but to minimize curdling, this recipe uses starch instead of egg yolks, a method that is also used in Sicilian gelato. This produces a clean flavor, allowing the sharp ginger heat to come through in the ice cream.

You can find tapioca starch at upscale grocery stores, natural food stores, and online. If you can't source it, you can replace the tapioca starch with the same amount of cornstarch, but the flavor won't be quite as sharp and the resulting ice cream may not be as creamy-thick.

DARK CHOCOLATE WHOOPIE PIES WITH RASPBERRY MARSHMALLOW FILLING

makes 10 whoopie pies

The resurgence of vintage recipes and desserts means people are discovering local and regional items like whoopie pies. Whoopie pies are an odd novelty treat that has always been quite popular in the New England area but is spreading across the country. The curiously named treat isn't really a pie but rather a cross between a cake and a cookie, sandwiched together with marshmallow filling or buttercream frosting. They're pretty easy to make and delightfully old-fashioned looking—as if they should be piled up on a cake stand in the window of a bakery shop in a small Maine town where people don't lock their doors and the kids ride around on their bikes without worry. These are made with a raspberry marshmallow filling, but the classic version is made with vanilla filling, an option I give following this recipe.

WHOOPIE PIE BATTER

1 large egg

1 teaspoon vanilla extract

2 teaspoons instant coffee powder

½ teaspoon kosher salt

½ cup (115 g or 1 stick) unsalted butter, at room temperature

1 cup (220 g) packed dark brown sugar

1 teaspoon baking soda

½ teaspoon baking powder

¾ cup plus 2 tablespoons (85 g) Dutch-process cocoa powder

1 cup (220 g) buttermilk, well shaken

1¾ cups (245 g) all-purpose flour

MAKE THE WHOOPIE PIE BATTER

Preheat the oven to 350°F and line baking sheets with parchment paper or Silpats. Combine the egg, vanilla, instant coffee, and salt in a small bowl. Beat with a fork until uniform in color and the coffee has dissolved. Place the butter, brown sugar, baking soda, and baking powder in the bowl of a stand mixer fitted with the paddle attachment. Mix on medium speed until creamy and the butter clings to the sides of the bowl, about 3 minutes.

Reduce the mixer speed to medium-low and drizzle the coffee-egg mixture into the bowl; mix until completely incorporated. Add the cocoa powder and beat to incorporate. Add half the buttermilk, 1 cup (140 g) of the flour, and then the remaining buttermilk and remaining ¾ cup (105 g) flour, beating to incorporate and scraping down the sides of the bowl before each addition.

If you have a medium ice cream scoop, use it; otherwise, scoop out 2 to 3 table-spoons of batter onto the baking sheets, placing the mounds about 2 inches apart. Bake until the tops have cracked and they spring back when you gently push down on them, 10 to 12 minutes. Let cool on the baking sheets for 10 minutes and then peel them off the parchment paper and move them to a wire rack to cool completely. Repeat with the remaining batter.

·······>

RASPBERRY MARSHMALLOW FILLING

2 large egg whites

¼ teaspoon cream of tartar

⅛ teaspoon kosher salt

¾ cup (150 g) granulated sugar

½ cup (55 g) corn syrup

½ cup (2½ ounces or 75 g) fresh or frozen raspberries

½ cup (16 g) freeze-dried raspberries, crushed to a powder

4 tablespoons (57 g or ½ stick) unsalted butter, at room temperature

MAKE THE RASPBERRY MARSHMALLOW FILLING

Place the egg whites, cream of tartar, and salt in the clean bowl of a stand mixer fitted with the whisk attachment. Turn the mixer to high speed and beat until soft peaks form. Stop the mixer. Place the sugar, corn syrup, and raspberries in a medium pot and cook over medium-high heat, crushing the raspberries with a potato masher or wooden spoon as the sugar cooks until the berries fall apart. Continue to cook the raspberry syrup, stirring frequently, until it reaches 240°F (soft-ball stage).

Once the raspberry syrup has reached 240°F, turn the mixer to medium-high speed and slowly drizzle the syrup into the egg whites, making sure not to hit the whisk itself or the sides of the bowl too much. Whisk until all the syrup is incorporated, then raise the speed to high and whip until the outside of the bowl is cool to the touch, about 10 minutes. Switch the whisk to the paddle attachment (be sure to scoop out any filling from the middle of the whisk with a rubber spatula) and add the raspberry powder. Fold in the powder on low speed. Raise the speed to medium and add the butter, 1 tablespoon at a time, waiting for the butter to incorporate before adding the next tablespoon.

Assemble the whoopie pies by spreading about a heaping tablespoon of filling onto the flat bottom of one cake and then pressing the flat bottom of another cake onto the filling, sandwiching them together. Repeat with the remaining cakes.

alternatives

CLASSIC WHOOPIE PIES WITH VANILLA BEAN MARSHMALLOW FILLING

Make a plain vanilla bean marshmallow filling by omitting the raspberries when you cook the syrup, instead adding 2 tablespoons water. Cook the syrup and drizzle it into the whipped egg whites as directed. When mixing the marshmallow filling, omit the freeze-dried raspberries. Instead, add 2 teaspoons vanilla extract and the seeds from 1 vanilla bean, splitting the bean lengthwise and scraping out the seeds into the marshmallow filling when you add the last of the butter.

SWEET POTATO WHOOPIE PIES WITH TRIPLE-GINGER MARSHMALLOW FILLING

Omit the instant coffee from the whoopie pies. Reduce the brown sugar to ¼ cup (55 g) and add ¾ cup (150 g) granulated sugar. Replace the cocoa powder with ¾ cup (195 g) canned sweet potato puree. Reduce the buttermilk to ½ cup (110 g). Increase the flour to 2½ cups (350 g) and add 1 teaspoon ground cinnamon, ½ teaspoon ground nutmeg, and ¼ teaspoon each ground ginger and cloves. Bake as directed.

Omit the fresh raspberries from the marshmallow filling and add 2 tablespoons water in its place. Proceed with the recipe as directed, omitting the freeze-dried raspberries and adding 1 tablespoon ginger juice (found online or at upscale grocery stores or specialty stores), 1 tablespoon ground ginger, ½ teaspoon ground turmeric , and 1 teaspoon vanilla extract to the marshmallow filling before adding the butter.

When assembling the whoopie pies, right after spreading the marshmallow filling onto the cake, sprinkle with 1 teaspoon finely chopped crystallized ginger before sandwiching with the other cake.

BUTTERSCOTCH WHOOPIE PIES WITH APPLE–CREAM CHEESE FILLING

Omit the instant coffee from the whoopie pies. Melt the butter in a pan over high heat, then reduce the heat to medium and cook until the butter solids start to brown, 2 to 3 minutes. Turn off the heat and continue to stir until the butter solids are golden brown and smell nutty and fragrant. Let cool in the pan to room temperature. Proceed with the recipe as directed, omitting the cocoa powder and increasing the flour to 2½ cups (350 g). Bake as directed.

Make the apple–cream cheese filling by beating together 8 ounces (225 g or 1 brick) room temperature cream cheese and ½ cup (115 g or 1 stick) room temperature butter in the bowl of a stand mixer fitted with the paddle attachment. Sift 3 cups (345 g) powdered sugar into the bowl and add 2 tablespoons boiled cider (found at specialty stores or online) and ½ teaspoon ground cinnamon. Beat together until the frosting is smooth. If the filling is too runny, refrigerate for 15 to 30 minutes to firm up. Assemble as directed.

The whoopie pie

Some years ago, the once regional treat of whoopie pies, found commonly in New England and Amish areas of Pennsylvania, suddenly found themselves in the spotlight. Articles hailed them as a new trend and they were everywhere, from Trader Joe's to upscale bakeries. What makes them so appealing isn't just their down-home flavor but also their convenience and adaptability. The whoopie pie is basically a portable cupcake, but with a better frosting-to-cake ratio. And what I love most about the whoopie pie is that it's a blank slate for flavor.

Much like the cupcake, whoopie pies are flexible enough to be made with nearly any flavor you wish. Add more instant coffee to the batter and you have mocha; omit the coffee and cocoa, add more flour, use granulated sugar, and increase the vanilla and you have vanilla bean. Add lemon extract for lemon whoopie pies. In my alternative recipe I use sweet potato, but you can easily use pumpkin, carrot, or even beet puree for a different take. Make a matching filling, whether it's marshmallow or buttercream frosting, and you can make whoopie pies in whatever flavor you dream of.

COCONUT JAM ALFAJORES

makes 36 sandwich cookies

I wasn't always a huge fan of coconut. Its sticky, stringy threads of chewiness did nothing for me, and I steered far away from it whenever I saw it in a candy bar or dessert. But then I discovered that not all coconut is the same. The presweetened coconut that comes in a bag and in candy bars still isn't my favorite. But the pure flavor of coconut, whether it's in coconut milk, cream, oil, or unsweetened shredded coconut, is much more subtle. With hints of vanilla and tropical paradise, coconut adds an elusive flavor that I've come to appreciate. I've made a simple coconut jam to use in a filling for the South American sandwich cookies called alfajores. Traditionally filled with dulce de leche, these are similar but with a darker bittersweet edge from the coconut jam. The silky soft cookie, made with a blend of cornstarch and all-purpose flour, starts with a forgiving dough. The scraps easily reroll as often as you want.

COCONUT JAM

27 to 28 ounces (two 14-ounce cans) coconut milk (see note, page 74)

1 cup (165 g) packed coconut palm sugar (see page 25), or ¾ cup (165 g) packed dark brown sugar

½ teaspoon kosher salt

ALFAJOR DOUGH

2 cups (260 g) cornstarch

1½ cups (210 g) all-purpose flour

2 teaspoons baking powder

1 teaspoon baking soda

½ teaspoon kosher salt

1 cup (225 g or 2 sticks) unsalted butter, at room temperature

⅔ cup (135 g) granulated sugar

MAKE THE COCONUT JAM

Combine the coconut milk and coconut palm sugar in a large pot. Whisk together to make sure any coconut cream from the milk that rose to the top is blended in. Bring to a boil over high heat, then immediately reduce the heat to a very low, bare simmer. You'll be tempted to speed things up by raising the heat, but don't. If you heat it too fast, the coconut jam will come out chunky and the fat will separate. Simmer for 2½ to 3 hours, stirring occasionally and then stirring more frequently starting 30 to 45 minutes before the end of the cooking time. The jam is done when it is dark like chocolate ganache and thick like jarred caramel sauce and has reduced to about 1½ cups. Remove from the heat, stir in the salt, and let cool to room temperature.

MAKE THE ALFAJOR DOUGH

Combine the cornstarch, flour, baking powder, baking soda, and salt in a large bowl. Stir vigorously with a whisk until all the ingredients are blended and uniform in color.

Place the butter and sugar in the bowl of a stand mixer fitted with the paddle attachment. Beat on medium speed until they are fluffy and stick to the sides

·······>

4 large egg yolks

1 teaspoon vanilla extract

2 tablespoons Grand Marnier, Cointreau, brandy, pisco, or orange juice

TO ASSEMBLE

1 to 2 tablespoons powdered sugar, sifted

CHEAT SHORTCUT

If you can get ahold of jarred coconut jam, found in Asian grocery stores, use that instead of making the coconut jam yourself! Look for one that is dark in color and has only two ingredients: coconut milk and sugar.

of the bowl, about 2 minutes. Add the egg yolks, one at a time, waiting for the first one to incorporate before adding the next and scraping down the sides of the bowl between additions. Add the vanilla and Grand Marnier and mix to incorporate.

Add the cornstarch and flour mixture in three batches. Beat on low speed, increasing the speed to medium as the dry ingredients are absorbed, before adding the next batch. Scrape down the sides of the bowl between additions to make sure there are no dry spots. Divide the dough in half and flatten each piece into a ½-inch-thick disk. Wrap tightly in plastic wrap and refrigerate for at least 1 hour, or overnight.

Preheat the oven to 350°F and line baking sheets with parchment paper or Silpats. On a clean surface dusted with flour, unwrap one of the chilled dough disks, cut in half (rewrapping the remaining dough and returning it to the refrigerator), and roll out the dough to about ¼ inch thick. The dough might crack if it is cold but just patch and press it together or cut out the cookies around the cracks. Use a 2-inch round cookie cutter to cut out the cookies, rerolling the scraps as many times as you want. Place the cookie rounds on the baking sheets and bake until the edges of a few cookies have just barely started to brown (the top shouldn't brown at all, as you want these cookies to stay soft), 9 to 12 minutes. Let cool on the baking sheets for 5 minutes and then move to a wire rack. Repeat with the remaining dough.

ASSEMBLE THE COOKIES

Dab about ½ teaspoon of the coconut jam onto the bottom of one cookie and press the bottom of another cookie onto the jam, sandwiching it. Repeat with the remaining cookies and jam and then sift powdered sugar over the tops.

Coconut milk ....

Not all coconut milk is the same, and results might vary if you use a different brand. I prefer to use a popular Thai brand called Chaokoh. It can be found in Asian grocery stores, natural food stores, and online. If you are having difficulty making your coconut jam, the coconut milk may be the culprit, so I'd suggest switching to a different brand.

TRADITIONAL ALFAJORES WITH DULCE DE LECHE FILLING

Make the cookies as directed. Make the dulce de leche by preheating the oven to 425°F. Open and pour a 14-ounce can of condensed milk (not evaporated) into a deep-dish glass pie plate. Cover tightly with aluminum foil. Place in a larger baking pan and fill the baking pan with boiling water to come halfway up the sides of the pie plate. Bake for 45 minutes, then check the water level and add more if needed. Continue to bake for an additional 45 minutes (1½ hours total), then check the condensed milk by picking it up and looking at the bottom of the glass pie plate. It should be caramel colored. If not, cook for an additional 15 to 30 minutes. Let cool completely in the pie plate, then use as a filling in place of the coconut jam. Or buy a 16-ounce jar of dulce de leche and use that as a filling!

ALFAJORES WITH BLUEBERRY FILLING

Make the cookies as directed, but use 2 tablespoons limoncello in place of the Grand Marnier and add the zest of 1 lemon. Make the blueberry filling by placing 2 cups (12 ounces, or 340 g) fresh or frozen blueberries, ½ cup (100 g) granulated sugar, 1½ tablespoons fresh lemon juice, and 1 tablespoon cornstarch in a medium saucepan. Cook over medium-high heat, mashing down on the blueberries with a wooden spoon, until the berries release their juices and the mixture starts to boil. Reduce the heat to a simmer and cook until the jam has thickened, about 10 minutes. Let cool completely, then use the blueberry filling in place of the coconut jam. Or buy a 14-ounce jar of blueberry jam and use that as filling.

PUMPKIN S'MORES WITH MAPLE–BROWN SUGAR MARSHMALLOWS AND DARK CHOCOLATE

makes about 15 s'mores

I'm not going to lie: These s'mores are not something you whip up over a campfire. Or even like my friend Jen does, by toasting store-bought marshmallows over the blue flame of the stove. These s'mores are a weekend project, but totally worth the effort. Nothing in this recipe is overly difficult, but there are numerous components plus rest time in between; for example, the marshmallow filling, which needs to cure and dry for several hours or overnight. Once everything is done, though, it's glorious, like a giant bonfire made of a pile of leaves in autumn. One bite will make you forget how long it took to rake all those leaves, so to speak. Trust me when I say that you will never go back to store-bought once you've tasted homemade s'mores.

MAPLE–BROWN SUGAR MARSHMALLOWS

1 cup (115 g) powdered sugar, sifted, divided

½ cup cold water

2 tablespoons (3 packages) powdered gelatin

1 cup (220 g) packed dark brown sugar

1 cup (340 g) maple syrup

¼ teaspoon kosher salt

PUMPKIN GRAHAM CRACKERS

1 cup (270 g) pumpkin puree

1 fresh bay leaf

1 teaspoon ground cinnamon

½ teaspoon ground nutmeg

¼ teaspoon ground cloves

6 tablespoons (85 g or ¾ stick) unsalted butter

MAKE THE MAPLE–BROWN SUGAR MARSHMALLOWS

Coat a 9-inch square baking pan with cooking spray, then dust it liberally with about half the powdered sugar. Pour the water into the bowl of a stand mixer fitted with the whisk attachment. Sprinkle the gelatin over the water and let the gelatin soften, about 5 minutes. In a medium saucepan, combine the brown sugar, maple syrup, and salt. Cook over low heat, stirring, until the sugar dissolves. Increase the heat to medium-high and cook, stirring constantly, until the syrup reaches 240°F (firm-ball stage). Turn the mixer on medium-high speed and slowly drizzle the syrup into the gelatin until it is completely incorporated. Slowly raise the mixer speed to high and beat until opaque and fluffy and the outside of the bowl is cool to the touch, about 10 minutes. Scrape the marshmallow batter into the prepared pan and smooth it out. Dust the top with the remaining powdered sugar and let "cure" in the pan, uncovered, for 6 hours or overnight in a cool, dry place.

MAKE THE PUMPKIN GRAHAM CRACKERS

Place the pumpkin puree and bay leaf in a large nonstick skillet and cook over high heat, stirring constantly with a wooden spoon and scraping up any hard pieces of pumpkin, until the mixture has darkened and reduced to about ½ cup,

·······>

2 tablespoons whole milk

¼ cup (85 g) honey

1¾ cups (270 g) graham flour

½ cup (75 g) white whole-wheat flour

¾ cup (165 g) packed dark brown sugar

1 tablespoon baking soda

1 teaspoon kosher salt

TO DUST GRAHAM CRACKERS

¼ cup (55 g) packed dark brown sugar

½ teaspoon ground cinnamon

½ teaspoon ground cardamom

¼ teaspoon ground ginger

¼ teaspoon ground nutmeg

¼ teaspoon ground allspice

⅛ teaspoon ground cloves

¼ cup whole milk

TO ASSEMBLE

3 cups (450 g) chopped dark chocolate

about 10 minutes. Discard the bay leaf and stir in the cinnamon, nutmeg, and cloves. Add the butter and continue to cook, stirring constantly, until the butter has melted. Remove from the heat and stir in the milk and honey.

Combine both flours, the brown sugar, baking soda, and salt in a large bowl. Stir vigorously with a balloon whisk until all the ingredients are evenly distributed and uniform in color. Scrape the pumpkin mixture into the bowl with the dry ingredients and stir with a wooden spoon until all the liquid is incorporated and a dough forms. Pat the dough into a large disk, wrap tightly with plastic wrap, and refrigerate for at least 1 hour, or overnight.

DUST THE GRAHAM CRACKERS

Preheat the oven to 350°F and line baking sheets with parchment paper or Silpats. Combine the brown sugar, cinnamon, cardamom, ginger, nutmeg, allspice, and cloves in a large bowl. Roll out the graham cracker dough on a clean, well-floured surface to about ¼ inch thick. Cut into 2½-inch squares and set the squares on the lined baking sheets. Brush the top of each cracker with milk and then sprinkle with the brown sugar dusting mixture. Prick the top of the squares with a fork. Bake until the edges start to darken, 15 to 17 minutes. Let cool for 10 minutes on the baking sheets and then move to a wire rack to cool completely.

Invert the marshmallows onto a cutting board, using a butter knife to loosen from the pan. Lightly grease a sharp knife or pizza cutter with cooking spray and cut the marshmallows into to 3 rows, then cut each piece crosswise into thirds, making nine 3-inch square marshmallows. Take each marshmallow, stand it on its thin side, and slice down, splitting it lengthwise as if you were splitting a sandwich bun. You should have 18 flat marshmallows.

ASSEMBLE THE S'MORES

Line a baking sheet with a fresh piece of parchment paper or Silpat. Microwave the chocolate in a heatproof glass bowl in 30-second increments, stirring between each until the chocolate is melted and smooth. Using a butter knife, smear some chocolate onto the bottom of a graham cracker, then place a marshmallow on top. Smear some melted chocolate on top of the marshmallow and then place another cracker (bottom side down) on top. Toast the sides of the marshmallow with a kitchen torch. Dip the entire sandwich halfway into the melted chocolate, then place onto the lined baking sheet. Continue with the rest of the crackers and marshmallows. Refrigerate until the chocolate has hardened, about 20 minutes. These are best served the day you make them.

CLASSIC S'MORES WITH APPLE-CINNAMON MARSHMALLOWS

Make the marshmallows as directed, but replace the dark brown sugar with granulated sugar and the maple syrup with liquid apple juice concentrate (from the frozen food aisle). Add 1 teaspoon ground cinnamon to the marshmallows in the very last minute of whipping.

Make classic graham crackers by omitting the pumpkin puree and bay leaf and increasing the milk to ⅓ cup. Bake and assemble the s'mores as directed.

........>

To make the marshmallows, grease and dust the baking pan with powdered sugar as directed. Sprinkle 4½ teaspoons (2 packages) powdered gelatin over ½ cup cold water in a small bowl to soften. Place 4 ounces (115 g or ½ brick) room temperature cream cheese in the bowl of stand mixer fitted with the whisk attachment. Add 2 tablespoons vanilla extract and beat until fluffy. Scrape the cream cheese into a medium bowl and thoroughly clean the mixer bowl and whisk. To the clean bowl, add 2 large egg whites and ⅛ teaspoon cream of tartar. Whip on high until soft peaks form, then stop the mixer.

Make the syrup as directed, but using 1 cup (200 g) granulated sugar, ½ cup (155 g) light corn syrup, ¼ teaspoon kosher salt, and ¼ cup water. Cook until the sugar reaches 240°F (firm-ball stage). Remove from the heat and quickly whisk in the softened gelatin until dissolved. Turn the stand mixer back on at medium-high speed and slowly drizzle a little hot syrup into the eggs to warm them up. Continue to slowly drizzle in the syrup until completely incorporated, then beat for 5 minutes. Raise the mixer speed to high and beat for an additional 5 minutes, or until the marshmallow fluff has tripled in volume. Scoop out one-quarter of the fluff and add it to the cream cheese. Fold together with a large spatula, then scrape it all back into the mixer bowl and fold together on low speed for about 10 seconds, until just incorporated. Don't overmix or the marshmallow fluff will deflate. Pour into the prepared pan, dust the top with powdered sugar, and let cure for 6 hours, or overnight.

Make the red velvet graham crackers by omitting the pumpkin puree and bay leaf. Instead, add 2 tablespoons Dutch-process cocoa powder and increase the milk to ⅓ cup. Add 1 tablespoon plus 2 teaspoons red food coloring with the milk and honey and proceed as directed. Mix ¼ cup (55 g) dark brown sugar with 1 teaspoon ground cinnamon and ½ teaspoon Dutch-process cocoa powder and dust the graham crackers. Assemble the s'mores as directed.

Graham flour

A coarse, speckled flour that gives graham crackers their signature rough, crumbly texture, graham flour can be found in natural food stores, upscale or well-stocked grocery stores, and online. I always recommend using it if you want to make real graham crackers, but you can substitute regular whole-wheat flour in its place. The resulting crackers won't have exactly the same texture as the graham crackers you are used to eating, but they'll be pretty darn tasty nevertheless!

MALTED CHOCOLATE CHIP AND REVERSE CHIP COOKIES

makes 18 large cookies

I wasn't planning to include a recipe for chocolate chip cookies in this book until a friend of mine asked me about tips and tricks for customizing chocolate chip cookies. I came up with a list of 24 different tips and tricks! Apparently I have a lot to say. Better men and women than I have written about the best chocolate chip cookie recipe. I give them all the suspicious side-eye because everyone has different tastes—what is better for me might not be better for you. These cookies use a few specialty flours. You can substitute all-purpose if you don't have them; the cookies will still look impressive, with their magical reverse quarters of light batter and dark chocolate batter. Yet they are almost as easy to make as any regular chocolate chip cookie! Trust me on this one. Once you serve them up to people, they'll be asking you for your list of tips and tricks too.

COOKIE DOUGH BASE

2 cups (280 g) all-purpose flour

½ cup (90 g) teff flour
(see note, page 84)

¼ cup (35 g) mesquite flour/powder
(see note, page 84)

1½ teaspoons baking powder

1¼ teaspoons baking soda

1¼ cups (285 g or 2½ sticks) unsalted butter, at room temperature

1¼ cups (275 g) packed dark brown sugar

1 cup plus 2 tablespoons (225 g) granulated sugar

1 tablespoon vanilla extract

¼ teaspoon kosher salt

2 large eggs

1 large egg yolk

MAKE THE COOKIE DOUGH BASE

Combine the all-purpose flour, teff flour, mesquite flour, baking powder, and baking soda in a large bowl. Stir vigorously with a whisk until well blended and uniform in color.

Place the butter, both sugars, vanilla, and salt in the bowl of a stand mixer fitted with the paddle attachment. Beat together until a paste forms that is uniform in color with no streaks of butter or any other ingredients. Scrape down the sides of the bowl once or twice with a large spatula to make sure. Add the eggs, one at time, waiting for the first egg to incorporate before adding the second one. Add the egg yolk and mix to incorporate.

Scrape down the sides of the bowl again and add half the dry ingredients. Reduce the mixer speed to low and mix to incorporate, increasing the speed as the ingredients are absorbed. Add the rest of the dry ingredients and repeat. The dough will still be a little sticky.

MAKE THE MALTED COOKIE DOUGH

Transfer half of the dough to another bowl, leaving the remaining half in the mixer bowl (about 650 g of dough per half). To the dough in the mixer bowl,

.......>

MALTED COOKIE DOUGH

½ cup (85 g) malted milk powder

½ cup (70 g) all-purpose flour

1½ cups (8 ounces or 225 g) chopped dark chocolate

REVERSE CHIP DOUGH

½ cup (50 g) Dutch-process cocoa powder

1½ cups (8 ounces or 225 g) chopped white chocolate

TO ASSEMBLE

1 to 2 tablespoons flaky sea salt, like Maldon

add the malted milk powder and flour and mix on low speed to incorporate, increasing the speed as the ingredients are absorbed. Add the chocolate and mix on low speed until the chocolate is evenly distributed. Scoop the dough onto a large piece of plastic wrap and pat the dough into a 1-inch-thick disk. Wrap the dough tightly with the plastic wrap and refrigerate for at least 36 hours and up to 72 hours.

MAKE THE REVERSE CHIP DOUGH

Place the reserved half of the dough back in the mixer bowl (no need to clean it). Add the cocoa powder and mix on low speed to incorporate, increasing the speed as the cocoa is absorbed. Add the white chocolate and mix on low speed until the white chocolate is evenly distributed. Scoop the dough onto a large piece of plastic wrap and pat the dough into a 1-inch-thick disk. Wrap the dough tightly with the plastic wrap and transfer to the refrigerator. Refrigerate the dough for at least 36 hours and up to 72 hours.

ASSEMBLE THE COOKIES

Preheat the oven to 350°F. Line a baking sheet with a piece of parchment paper or Silpat. Break off a 1½-inch chunk of the malted dough (about 1¾ ounces or 50 g) and roll it into a ball. Break off a chunk of reverse chip dough the same size and roll it into a ball.

Squish the two balls of dough together and roll them in the palm of your hand to form one big ball. Place the ball on a cutting board. Press down to form a ¾-inch-thick disk that is 2½ to 3 inches wide. Cut the dough in half, perpendicular to the dough dividing line. Flip one half over and then firmly press the halves back together. You should have a disk with 4 quarters, alternating malted cookie dough and reverse chocolate cookie dough. Place on the baking sheet and sprinkle with a pinch of salt. Repeat with the remaining dough, spacing the cookie disks about 2 inches apart (they will spread during baking to about 5 inches in diameter).

Bake until the cookies are golden brown at the edges and are just set in the middle, 14 to 16 minutes. The cookies will puff up when baking, but will settle down once they cool. Let the cookies cool on the baking sheet for about 10 minutes and then move them to a wire rack to cool completely.

·······>

ORANGE CHOCOLATE CHIP AND REVERSE MOCHA CHIP COOKIES

Make the cookie dough base as directed, increasing the all-purpose flour to 2¾ cups (385 g) and omitting the teff and mesquite flours. Split the dough in half and to one half, add ¾ cup (105 g) all-purpose flour, the zest of 1 navel orange, and 1½ cups (8 ounces or 225 g) chopped dark chocolate chunks. To the other half, add ¾ cup plus 2 tablespoons (85 g) Dutch-process cocoa powder, 2 tablespoons instant coffee powder, and 1½ cups (8 ounces or 225 g) chopped white chocolate chunks. Assemble and bake as directed.

DOUBLE CHOCOLATE CHIP AND MATCHA GREEN TEA WITH WHITE CHIP COOKIES

Make the cookie dough base as directed, increasing the all-purpose flour to 2¾ cups (385 g) and omitting the teff and mesquite flours. Split the dough in half and to one half, add ¾ cup (105 g) all-purpose flour, 1 cup (5.3 ounces or 150 g) chopped dark chocolate chunks, and ½ cup (2.7 ounces or 75 g) chopped milk chocolate chunks. To the other half, add ½ cup (70 g) all-purpose flour, 3 tablespoons matcha green tea powder, and 1½ cups (8 ounces or 225 g) chopped white chocolate chunks. Assemble and bake as directed.

Teff flour and mesquite flour

I've opted to use teff flour, a popular gluten-free grain that has a ton of nutrients, in this recipe because it plays really well with chocolate. It's not used very often here in the United States but is popular in Ethiopia. If you ever dine at an Ethiopian restaurant, the spongy sour bread called injera is made with teff. But don't be fooled by the sourness of that flatbread, as teff is mildly nutty and slightly malty in flavor. You can get teff flour at upscale grocery stores, health food stores, and online.

Mesquite flour, sometimes called mesquite powder, is made from grinding the dried pods of the mesquite tree.

It has a slightly sweet, mildly nutty, woodsy flavor that also works amazingly well with chocolate. The subtle earthy, almost smoky, flavor of mesquite flour brings out the sweet toffee and butterscotch notes of the chocolate cookies and makes it worth tracking down, despite the expense and the difficulty of finding it. It's available online and in select upscale natural food stores.

If you can't find or don't have either flour, don't worry! You can use a total of 2¾ cups (385 g) all-purpose flour instead. The cookie will still be pretty spectacular!

Tips and tricks to improve your chocolate chip cookies

There are plenty of ways to improve your chocolate chip cookies, customizing in a way that is perfect for you. Here are a few ideas.

1 Don't overmix your butter and sugar. If you incorporate too much air, the cookies will be light and cakey instead of dense and cookie-like, but most people want chocolate chip cookies to be dense and chewy. Mix the sugar and butter together until just blended.

2 Let the dough rest in the refrigerator for 36 hours. This allows the flour to fully absorb the liquid ingredients properly. The dough becomes firmer and the cookies will be chewier, with deeper notes of caramel and butterscotch.

3 Try swapping some of the all-purpose flour for another flour. The most common swap is whole-wheat flour or white whole-wheat flour. I usually recommend substituting up to 25 percent of regular all-purpose flour with whole wheat or white whole wheat. But there's a whole range of flours that you can use as well.

For gluten-free flours, I recommend teff, mesquite, buckwheat flour, and grapeseed flour. Substitute only up to 20 percent of the all-purpose flour with gluten-free flour (though you'll want to be much more conservative with grapeseed flour, using it more like a spice and substituting only a couple of tablespoons). Any more than that and the cookies might start to get crumbly.

Flours that have gluten in them include khorasan flour (sold under the brand name Kamut) and spelt flour, rye flour, and barley flour. When using flours that have gluten in them, you can substitute up to 25 percent of the flour, but try experimenting with less first, to see what flavors you like.

4 Try using different sugars in the cookie dough. Try swapping the brown sugar with maple sugar or coconut sugar. Maple sugar, coconut sugar, and muscovado sugar all add different dimensions to the cookies. Turbinado sugar (sometimes sold by the brand name Sugar In The Raw) adds sweet crunch and texture. For all the sugars except turbinado, you can substitute the full amount for the brown sugar. For turbinado, substitute up to ¼ cup of the brown sugar.

5 Add salt to the top of the cookies to give them a little contrast. I like to use flaky sea salt like Maldon, but coarse sea salt is great as well. It tempers the sweetness of the cookies and brings out the deeper flavors of the brown sugar and chocolate. If you want to experiment, try flavored salts like smoked salt, red wine salt, black salt, and vanilla salt.

6 Mix up your chocolate! I prefer chopped chocolate over chocolate chips because chips are designed not to melt at high heat. A mix of different types of chocolates like super-dark (80 to 85 percent cacao), bittersweet (70 to 75 percent cacao), and semisweet (50 to 60 percent cacao) gives the cookies a little complexity. To make it all more convenient, I chop a bunch of chocolates ahead of time and store them in labeled zip-top plastic bags. That way it's ready when I need it!

7 Nuts are always an option. Toast the nuts first in a dry skillet until they darken slightly and smell fragrant and nutty. This will intensify the flavor. Let them cool and chop the nuts before adding them to the dough with the chocolate chunks. Try adding roasted cacao nibs as well. You can find them in upscale grocery stores, natural food stores, and online.

8 Finally, try varying the flavor by adding extracts or spices. Extracts range from common flavors like almond, raspberry, rum, maple, and lemon to wackier flavors like marshmallow, eggnog, and cheesecake.

Of course, common dried spices like cinnamon, ginger, nutmeg, and even black pepper all work well with dark chocolate, and you probably have all those in the pantry. A good starting point is to add ½ teaspoon of any of those spices or extracts to a batch of dough and then adjust the quantity as desired in subsequent batches.

BROWNIES AND BARS

IN THE BATTLE OF COOKIES VERSUS BROWNIES, it would be pretty hard to come up with the definitive winner. But the one thing that might give brownies and bars the advantage is that they are so much less time-consuming to make! Cookies require you to individually portion out the dough, and once you've baked a batch you have to do it all over again with the next batch. But brownies and bars! You can just pour the batter or dough into the pan and bake away. They may take longer to bake, but it's all walk-away time. A complete no-brainer task that can feed a bunch of people. Yep, brownies definitely win the convenience medal in this competition.

Of course, people who love brownies are divided into those who love dense and fudgy brownies or those who like fluffy and cakey brownies. Personally, I'll take either! And if that brownie happens to have a swirl of caramel or cream cheese (or both) in it? Get in my stomach now!

The brownies and bars you will find in this cookbook are a notch above the average. With a swirl of fruit or cream cheese, a layer of caramel or popcorn, or a smear of ganache icing, these are the perfect casual date for a coffee but also dressy enough to bring along to a dinner party. Who knows—maybe you'll end up in a long-term love affair with one of them. Stranger things have happened.

SALTED CARAMEL CHEESECAKE SWIRLED BROWNIES

makes 16 brownies

Caramel is one of those scary things that a lot of my friends, even those who are experienced in the kitchen, get freaked out about. They hear horror stories of the heated sugar burning hands like napalm. Worse, they fear that they'll overheat the sugar, leading to a charred black mess that is impossible to clean, ruining their expensive, fancy pots and pans. Thankfully, anyone with a microwave can make crazy-easy caramel, with practically no danger of burning or ruining a pan. With this trick, all of a sudden these brownies are a snap to make, which is totally dangerous in my household because we can devour a pan of them in no time.

CARAMEL

½ cup (100 g) granulated sugar

1 tablespoon light corn syrup

1 tablespoon water

4 tablespoons (57 g or ½ stick) unsalted butter, melted

3 tablespoons heavy cream

½ teaspoon salt

BROWNIE BATTER

½ cup (70 g) all-purpose flour

¼ cup (25 g) Dutch-process cocoa powder

½ teaspoon baking powder

¼ teaspoon kosher salt

4 ounces bittersweet chocolate, chopped into ¼-inch chunks

2 ounces unsweetened chocolate, chopped into ¼-inch chunks

½ cup (115 g or 1 stick) unsalted butter

1 cup (200 g) granulated sugar

3 large eggs

2 teaspoons vanilla extract

MAKE THE CARAMEL

Place the sugar, corn syrup, and water in a large microwave-safe glass bowl or glass measuring cup. Stir together, then place in the microwave, set the time for 6 minutes, and start to cook. Start watching through the microwave door at 1½ to 2 minutes (you might need anywhere from 2 to 6 minutes; see note, opposite). Once the sugar starts to color and turn a light amber brown, turn the microwave off and transfer the bowl to a light-colored surface (place a piece of paper on the surface if your surface is dark colored) to check the color. Watch the sugar continue to darken until it reaches the color of an old penny, and then carefully drizzle half the melted butter into the hot sugar. It will steam and bubble up a lot. Stir with a fork until the butter is incorporated, then add the remaining butter. Add the cream, 1 tablespoon at a time, and then the salt, stirring between each addition. Once the caramel is smooth and uniform, let the bowl sit on the table for 15 minutes, then transfer to the refrigerator to cool more quickly.

MAKE THE BROWNIE BATTER

Preheat the oven to 325°F. Lightly coat a 9-inch square metal baking pan with cooking spray and then fit a piece of parchment paper into the pan, with 2 inches of paper overhanging the edge of the pan on two sides. Combine the flour, cocoa powder, baking powder, and salt in a medium bowl. Using a balloon whisk, vigorously stir the dry ingredients together until they are uniform in color and well blended. Place the chocolates and butter in a large microwave-safe bowl and microwave for 45 seconds. Stir and microwave in 30-second intervals until all the chocolate and butter is melted.

CREAM CHEESE SWIRL

8 ounces (225 g or 1 brick) cream cheese, at room temperature

½ cup (100 g) granulated sugar

1 large egg yolk

1 teaspoon vanilla extract

1 teaspoon finishing salt (like Maldon, fleur de sel, or coarse sea salt)

Add the sugar to the melted chocolate and beat with a whisk by hand for about 30 seconds. Add the eggs one at a time, beating to incorporate after each one. Add the vanilla and beat to incorporate. Add the dry ingredients and, using a large spatula, fold until just incorporated and there are no more dry pockets.

MAKE THE CREAM CHEESE SWIRL

Place the cream cheese and sugar in the bowl of a stand mixer fitted with a paddle attachment. Mix on medium speed until the cream cheese mixture is fluffy, then add the egg yolk and vanilla and beat until incorporated. Remove the caramel sauce from the refrigerator (it might still be warm, which is fine) and scrape it into the bowl. Mix on medium speed until combined and the cream cheese mixture has lightened to the color and texture of peanut butter.

Spoon half of the brownie batter into the lined baking pan, then add three-quarters of the cream cheese. Swirl around with a knife. Repeat with the remaining brownie and cream cheese batters. Sprinkle the finishing salt over the batter and then bake until a toothpick inserted in the center comes out with a few crumbs adhering to it, 50 to 60 minutes. Let cool completely in the pan on a wire rack, and then cover and refrigerate overnight to set. To serve, remove the entire brownie from the pan by grabbing the overhanging parchment paper and lifting straight up. Move to a large cutting board and use a sharp knife to cut into bars.

✳ *Depending on the power and age of your microwave, you might need to cook the sugar all the way to 5½ to 6 minutes. Or it could start turning brown after around 2 minutes. Just keep an eye on the bowl through the window, and take note of how long it takes for the next time you make this recipe!*

✳ *One of the hardest parts of making a recipe with cream cheese is that the cream cheese often needs to be at room temperature, and rarely do I remember to take it out of the refrigerator early enough. So instead, I fill a large bowl with warm water from the tap. Then I remove the cream cheese from the paper box, leaving it in the foil wrap, and submerge it in the warm water, occasionally changing the water as it cools, for 3 to 5 minutes. This warms the cream cheese up much faster than just letting it sit on the counter. In fact, for a recipe like this, if the first thing you do is pull the cream cheese out and dunk it in the warm water, it'll be warmed up by the time you need it!*

✳ *If you don't have a microwave, you can make caramel the old-fashioned way: on the stovetop! Place the sugar in a large saucepan, preferably one with a light-colored bottom (so you see how dark the sugar turns). Skip the corn syrup and water. Follow the instructions for making caramel on page 104. Once the sugar has reached the color of an old penny, remove from the heat and add 1 tablespoon of the cream. It will steam and boil up furiously. Stir until smooth, then add another tablespoon of cream and stir until smooth. Finally, stir in the third tablespoon of cream. Add the melted butter and the salt. Continue with the recipe as directed.*

STRAWBERRY CHEESECAKE SWIRL BROWNIES

Skip making the caramel and puree 1 cup (7 ounces or 200 g) hulled strawberries with 2 tablespoons granulated sugar and 1 teaspoon balsamic vinegar in a food processor. Fold this into the cream cheese swirl in place of the caramel. Assemble, skipping the finishing salt, and bake as instructed.

ORANGE CHEESECAKE SWIRL BROWNIES

Skip making the caramel and add the zest of 1 orange and 1 tablespoon Cointreau to the cream cheese swirl in place of the caramel. Assemble, skipping the finishing salt, and bake as instructed.

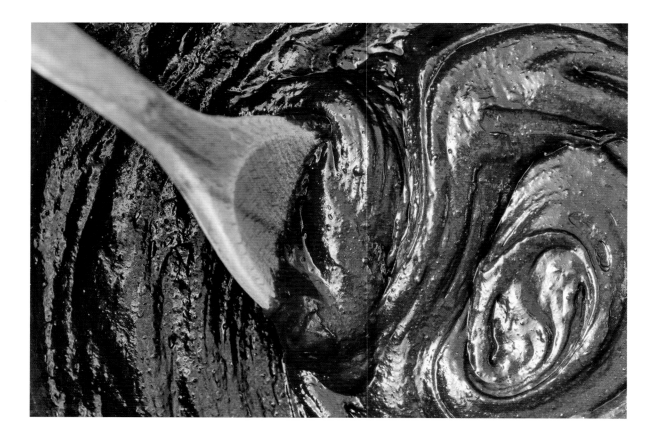

BANANA CRUNCH BEER BROWNIES

The minute a friend of mine mentioned that she was eating beer brownies, I became obsessed with the idea. I've made cakes using deep-roasted barley beer, like Guinness, but it had never occurred to me to make brownies with beer. It's a natural combination that makes sense, especially since the beer lends a toothsome quality that makes the brownies addictive. Here I've added a banana crunch crumble to give it some textural punch as well as a little banana in the brownie batter. If you're a fan of chocolate banana bread, this is basically the brownie version of that, on steroids.

BANANA CRUNCH MIX-IN

½ cup (60 g) nonfat dry milk powder

⅔ cup cornflakes, lightly crushed

⅓ cup (45 g) all-purpose flour

2 tablespoons cornstarch

2 tablespoons granulated sugar

¾ teaspoon kosher salt

4 tablespoons (57 g or ½ stick) unsalted butter, melted

1½ cups (70 g) freeze-dried bananas (see note, page 93)

3 ounces (85 g) white chocolate (see note, page 93)

BROWNIE BATTER

8 ounces (225 g) semisweet chocolate, chopped into ¼-inch chunks, divided

½ cup (115 g or 1 stick) unsalted butter

¼ cup (30 g) natural cocoa powder

½ teaspoon kosher salt

½ cup Guinness beer or other dry stout

3 large eggs

MAKE THE BANANA CRUNCH MIX-IN

Preheat the oven to 250°F and line a rimmed baking sheet with parchment paper or a Silpat. Combine the powdered milk, cornflakes, flour, cornstarch, sugar, and salt in a medium bowl and stir vigorously with a whisk until all the ingredients are evenly distributed. Drizzle the melted butter over the dry ingredients and toss until clumps start to form.

Pour onto the lined baking sheet and spread into an even layer. Bake for 10 minutes. Stir the crunch with a spatula, making sure the darker outer clumps get mixed with the inner clumps, and then bake for about 10 minutes more. Break up any big chunks and let cool completely on the baking sheet.

While the crunch is baking, put the freeze-dried bananas in a food processor and pulse until they are reduced to powder. Chop the white chocolate into small chunks and place them in a microwave-safe bowl. Microwave for 30 seconds, then stop and stir. Cook for another 30 seconds, and then stir until melted and smooth, letting the residual heat from the bowl finish melting the white chocolate. If there are any stubborn big pieces, microwave in 10-second intervals and stir until completely melted and smooth. Be careful of overheating, though, as white chocolate has a tendency to scorch easily.

Once the crunch has cooled, pour it into a bowl and add the banana powder. Drizzle the white chocolate over the bowl and toss until the crunch absorbs the white chocolate and banana powder. Refrigerate while you make the brownie batter.

·······>

1 medium banana, mashed

1 cup (200 g) granulated sugar

1 cup (220 g) packed dark brown sugar

½ teaspoon baking powder

2 teaspoons vanilla extract

1 cup (140 g) all-purpose flour

CHOCOLATE-BEER GANACHE

6 ounces (170 g) semisweet chocolate

2 tablespoons unsalted butter

¼ cup heavy cream

¼ cup Guinness beer or other dry stout

1 teaspoon flaky sea salt

✳ *Freeze-dried bananas are banana slices that have all the water extracted from them. You can find them at upscale grocery stores like Whole Foods and specialty stores like Trader Joe's. Don't substitute banana chips, which are fried banana slices. They don't have a lot of banana flavor.*

✳ *When using white chocolate, avoid white chocolate chips. They are often made with vegetable oil instead of actual cocoa butter and are designed not to melt at high temperatures. Instead, pick a white chocolate bar that lists cocoa butter in the ingredients.*

MAKE THE BROWNIE BATTER

Increase the oven temperature to 350°F. Coat a 9 x 13-inch baking pan with cooking spray and then line the bottom and sides with parchment paper, with 2 inches of paper overhanging the edge of the pan on two sides. Place 4 ounces (115 g) of the chopped chocolate in a large heatproof mixing bowl. Place the butter in a medium skillet and turn the heat to medium-high. Cook the butter, stirring constantly, until it has completely melted and the solid butterfat starts to brown. Turn the heat off and continue to stir until the heat browns all the butterfat and it smells fragrant and nutty. It should be bordering on reddish brown. Immediately pour the hot butter into the bowl with the chopped chocolate, making sure to scrape out all the brown bits in the pan. Stir the chocolate until it melts. Add the cocoa and salt and stir until the cocoa has been absorbed. Add the beer and stir to incorporate.

Combine the eggs, banana, both sugars, baking powder, and vanilla in the bowl of a stand mixer fitted with a paddle attachment. Beat the ingredients together on medium speed until they are combined and thick, about 30 seconds. Add the chocolate-beer mixture and mix on medium-low speed until incorporated. Add the flour and beat on medium speed until absorbed into the batter, about 15 seconds. Remove the bowl from the mixer, add the remaining 4 ounces (115 g) chocolate and half the banana crunch mix-in, and fold them in using a large spatula.

Pour the batter into the lined baking pan and spread evenly. Cover with aluminum foil and bake until a toothpick inserted in the center comes out clean, 35 to 40 minutes. Let cool completely on a wire rack.

MAKE THE CHOCOLATE-BEER GANACHE

Chop the chocolate into ¼-inch chunks. Place the chocolate and butter in a microwave-safe bowl and microwave for 30 seconds. Stir and then cook for another 1 minute, stopping after 30 seconds to stir again. Stir until completely smooth. If there are any stubborn big pieces, microwave in 15-second intervals and stir until completely melted and smooth. Add the cream and beer to the warm chocolate and stir until incorporated. Spread the ganache over the cooled brownies and sprinkle the reserved banana crunch mix-in and the sea salt over the ganache. Let cool completely before cutting and serving.

PUMPKIN SPICE CRUNCH PUMPKIN BROWNIES

Make the pumpkin spice crunch mix-in by increasing the flour to ½ cup (70 g) and adding 3 tablespoons carrot juice. Omit the freeze-dried bananas and instead add 1 tablespoon pumpkin spice blend (or a combined 1½ teaspoons ground cinnamon, ½ teaspoon ground ginger, ½ teaspoon ground nutmeg, ½ teaspoon ground allspice, and ¼ teaspoon ground cloves).

Make the brownie, omitting the banana and using 4 large eggs instead of 3. Instead of Guinness stout in both the brownie batter and the ganache, use ½ cup pumpkin ale in the brownie batter and ¼ cup pumpkin ale plus 1 teaspoon pumpkin spice blend in the ganache.

Bake and assemble as directed.

PISTACHIO BUTTER SWIRLED FUDGE BROWNIES

makes 24 small brownies

I know people who swear they could eat an entire jar of peanut butter. But as much as they love peanut butter, when I introduce these folks to pistachio butter, they often go crazy for it! This brownie, which incorporates swirls of homemade pistachio butter, is for all those people who haven't yet had the pleasure of pistachio butter in their lives. With a deep, fudgy chocolate brownie and a dense, salty pistachio batter married together, this is the showstopper brownie that will have you wondering where pistachio butter has been all your life.

PISTACHIO BUTTER BATTER

2½ cups (360 g) shelled pistachios

1 teaspoon kosher salt

6 tablespoons (80 g) extra-virgin olive oil or pistachio oil

1 cup (115 g) powdered sugar

1 teaspoon matcha green tea powder (optional)

BROWNIE BATTER

6 ounces (170 g) unsweetened chocolate, chopped into ¼-inch pieces

14 tablespoons (200 g or 1¾ sticks) unsalted butter

1¼ cups (250 g) granulated sugar

1 cup (220 g) packed dark brown sugar

4 large eggs

2 teaspoons vanilla extract

½ teaspoon kosher salt

¼ teaspoon baking soda

¾ cup (105 g) all-purpose flour

⅔ cup (75 g) natural cocoa powder (not Dutch-process)

MAKE THE PISTACHIO BUTTER BATTER

Place the pistachios, salt, and oil in a food processor or blender and process until a smooth paste forms. Add the powdered sugar and process until incorporated.

MAKE THE BROWNIE BATTER

Preheat the oven to 350°F. Coat a 9 x 13-inch baking pan with cooking spray and then line the bottom and sides with parchment paper, with 2 inches of paper overhanging the edge of the pan on two sides. Place the chocolate and butter in a microwave-safe bowl and microwave for 30 seconds. Stir and then microwave for another 30 seconds. Continue to cook in 15-second intervals, stirring in between, until the mixture is melted and smooth.

Add both sugars to the chocolate mixture and stir with a whisk or fork until incorporated. Add the eggs, one at a time, beating vigorously to incorporate after each. Stir in the vanilla and then the salt and baking soda. Switch to a large spatula and add the flour and cocoa, folding until just absorbed.

Scrape half of the brownie batter into the prepared baking pan and spread it out evenly to the edges (it's okay if it doesn't cover it completely). Spoon three-quarters of the pistachio butter batter over the brownie batter, then spread the remaining brownie batter on top. Stir the matcha green tea powder, if using, into the remaining pistachio butter batter. Spoon the pistachio batter on top of the brownie batter in dollops and use a butter knife or chopstick to swirl it into the brownie batter.

·······>

Bake until a toothpick inserted into the center comes out clean, 35 to 45 minutes. Let cool in the pan for 30 minutes on a wire rack, then remove the brownies by grabbing the parchment paper by the overhang and lifting straight up and out. Transfer the still-warm brownies to a wire rack to cool to room temperature.

alternative

PEANUT BUTTER SWIRLED FUDGE BROWNIES

Make the brownie batter as directed. For the peanut butter batter, stir together ¾ cup (225 g) smooth peanut butter (not natural), 6 tablespoons (85 g) melted unsalted butter, ½ cup (60 g) powdered sugar, 1 teaspoon vanilla extract, and ¼ teaspoon kosher salt. Assemble and bake as directed.

ROASTED WHITE CHOCOLATE BROWNIES WITH STRAWBERRY-BALSAMIC SWIRL

makes 24 small brownies

Every year, my partner, A.J., and I go to a black-tie benefit for our local Meals on Wheels nonprofit organization. It's a stellar fund-raising affair with food and wine from top chefs and vintners in the San Francisco Bay Area, and the thing I look forward to most is the desserts. Not only are the best local pastry chefs showcasing their top sweet treats, but the flavor combinations and inspirations are ridiculous! After tasting a dessert that used roasted white chocolate in it, I knew that I had to create something similar at home. Making a brownie out of the caramelized white chocolate results in bars with a deep, sweet flavor that are a cross between a brownie and a blondie. Just make sure to use actual white chocolate (check the ingredients; cocoa butter should be listed) and not white chocolate chips or cheap white chocolate (which uses vegetable oil in place of the cocoa butter). Those don't melt or caramelize well.

BROWNIE BATTER

1⅔ cups (10 ounces or 285 g) chopped white chocolate (in about ¼-inch chunks)

¾ cup (170 g or 1½ sticks) unsalted butter, at room temperature

¾ cup (150 g) granulated sugar

¾ cup (165 g) packed dark brown sugar

2 teaspoons vanilla extract

¾ teaspoon kosher salt

3 large eggs

½ cup extra-virgin olive oil

2¼ cups (315 g) all-purpose flour

ROAST THE WHITE CHOCOLATE

Preheat the oven to 300°F. Spread the white chocolate on a rimmed baking sheet and bake for about 10 minutes. Remove from the oven and stir with a clean spatula until the browned chocolate at the edges is evenly mixed with the uncooked white chocolate in the center. Once completely stirred, the white chocolate should be the color of dark peanut butter. If it isn't, continue to bake in 5-minute increments to darken it. Watch the white chocolate closely once it starts to brown, as it can burn pretty fast. Let cool on the baking sheet while you make the brownie batter.

MAKE THE BROWNIE BATTER

Lightly coat a 9 x 13-inch metal baking pan with cooking spray and then line it with parchment paper, with 2 inches of the paper overhanging the edges of the pan. Increase the oven temperature to 350°F.

Place the butter and both sugars in the bowl of a stand mixer fitted with the paddle attachment. Beat together on medium speed until light and creamy, about 2 minutes. Add the vanilla and salt and beat to incorporate. Add the eggs

......>

STRAWBERRY-BALSAMIC SWIRL

1 cup (5½ ounces or 160 g) chopped strawberries (in about ½-inch chunks)

1 tablespoon granulated sugar

1 teaspoon cornstarch

1 tablespoon cold water

2 teaspoons balsamic vinegar

one at a time, beating after each egg to incorporate completely and scraping down the sides and bottom of the bowl before adding the next one. Add the oil and beat to incorporate. Scrape the roasted white chocolate into the bowl (it may have hardened and gotten a little grainy, but don't worry about that) and mix it in. Add the flour and mix on low speed until absorbed. Scrape the batter into the prepared pan.

MAKE THE STRAWBERRY-BALSAMIC SWIRL

Place the strawberries and sugar in a small saucepan over medium heat. Cook, stirring frequently with a wooden spoon and smashing the berries, until the strawberries release their juice and fall apart, 10 to 12 minutes. Stir the cornstarch into the water and then drizzle it into the strawberries, continuing to stir and cook for a minute or two until the mixture has thickened into a jam. Continue cooking for about 2 more minutes, stirring constantly, then remove from the heat. Stir in the balsamic vinegar. Drop generous tablespoons of the strawberry swirl over the brownie batter and then use a butter knife or chopstick to swirl them together. Don't overmix; just gently pull the strawberry swirl here and there and pull some brownie batter over the strawberry swirl as well.

Bake until the brownie is golden brown and a toothpick inserted in the center comes out clean, 25 to 30 minutes. Let cool completely on a wire rack, then remove the brownies by grabbing the sides of the parchment paper and pulling directly up. Transfer the entire slab of brownies to a cutting board. Cut and serve.

The magic of roasted white and milk chocolate

Too many chocolate snobs dismiss white and milk chocolates as one-dimensional and too sweet, choosing dark chocolate with high cacao percentages. They clearly have not tasted roasted white and milk chocolates. Roasting these sweeter chocolates in the oven caramelizes the cocoa butter fats, creating complex flavors reminiscent of buttery caramel, toffee, butterscotch, and dulce de leche (the caramelized milk sauce popular in South America). Roasting white chocolate for baking is easy (just toss it into a 300°F oven for 10 to 15 minutes, or at lower temperature like 250°F for 20 to 30 minutes if you want a smoother end result). Milk chocolate requires longer in the oven (20 to 30 minutes at 300°F, or longer at lower temperatures). Either can be used in place of dark chocolate in recipes to create something closer to a caramel or blondie bar with chocolate undertones. Roasted or caramelized white chocolate has become so popular that some upscale professional chocolate companies like Valrhona are even selling commercial versions of it now.

ROASTED WHITE CHOCOLATE BROWNIES WITH CHOCOLATE-HAZELNUT SWIRL

Make the brownie batter. Omit the strawberry-balsamic swirl. Make the chocolate-hazelnut swirl by placing 1 cup (130 g) hazelnuts, 1 tablespoon granulated sugar, ¼ cup (30 g) natural cocoa powder (not Dutch-process), and ½ teaspoon kosher salt in a food processor. Turn the processor on and slowly drizzle in 3 tablespoons olive oil while the processor is running. Blend until a paste forms. Add up to 3 teaspoons more olive oil, 1 teaspoon at a time, if the paste is too thick (you want a peanut butter–like consistency). Swirl into the brownie batter in a decorative pattern. Assemble and bake as directed.

Or cheat and use ¾ cup Nutella to swirl into the brownie!

SALTED CARAMEL POPCORN DOUBLE-CHOCOLATE BROWNIES

makes 24 small brownies

I once had a boss who refused to allow our office kitchen to have a microwave because he hated the smell of microwave popcorn. Of course, he could have just banned microwave popcorn, but instead we all had to live without any microwave at all, which at least gave us a reason to get away from the office for lunch. I'm not a huge fan of microwave popcorn myself, but I love making it on the stovetop. The popcorn tastes immensely better, in my opinion. But even better than old-fashioned stovetop popcorn? Homemade caramel popcorn . . . on top of home-made brownies. Salted Caramel Popcorn Double-Chocolate Brownies. It's a thing.

BROWNIE BATTER

¾ cup (105 g) all-purpose flour

¼ cup (25 g) Dutch-process cocoa powder

¾ teaspoon baking powder

½ teaspoon kosher salt

6 ounces (170 g) unsweetened chocolate (do not use bittersweet), chopped

¾ cup (170 g or 1½ sticks) unsalted butter

1½ cups (300 g) granulated sugar

¾ cup (165 g) packed dark brown sugar

4 large eggs

1 teaspoon vanilla extract

1 cup (6 ounces or 170 g) chopped bittersweet chocolate

POPCORN

1 tablespoon olive oil

1 teaspoon kosher salt

⅓ cup (70 g) popcorn kernels

MAKE THE BROWNIE BATTER

Preheat the oven to 325°F. Lightly coat a 9 x 13-inch metal baking pan with cooking spray and then line it with parchment paper, with 2 inches of the paper overhanging the edges of the pan.

Combine the flour, cocoa powder, baking powder, and salt in a medium bowl. Using a balloon whisk, vigorously stir the dry ingredients together until they are uniform in color and well blended. Place the unsweetened chocolate and butter in a large microwave-safe bowl and microwave for 45 seconds. Stir and microwave in 30-second intervals until the chocolate mixture is completely melted.

Add the sugars to the chocolate mixture and beat with a balloon whisk by hand for about 30 seconds. Add the eggs one at time, beating to incorporate between each one. Add the vanilla and beat to incorporate. Add the dry ingredients and, using a large spatula, fold them in until just incorporated and there are no more dry pockets. Fold the bittersweet chocolate into the batter.

Scrape the batter into the prepared pan and spread evenly. Bake until a toothpick inserted in the center comes out with some crumbs attached, 30 to 35 minutes. Let cool completely on a wire rack before adding the caramel popcorn.

MAKE THE POPCORN

Place the oil and salt in a large Dutch oven or pot. Add 3 popcorn kernels to the pot, cover with the lid slightly ajar to let steam release, and turn the heat to high.

.......>

1 cup (200 g) granulated sugar

2 tablespoons light corn syrup

½ cup heavy cream

4 tablespoons (57 g or ½ stick) unsalted butter

½ teaspoon kosher salt

1 teaspoon finishing salt (like Maldon, fleur de sel, or coarse sea salt)

Cook, shaking the pot occasionally, until the kernels pop. Remove the pot from the heat and add the rest of the popcorn kernels. Shake the pot to coat with the oil and salt and wait 30 seconds. Return the pot to the stovetop and reduce the heat to medium-high. Cook, with the lid slightly ajar and shaking the pot occasionally, until there is a 2-second interval between popping. Remove from the heat and pour the popcorn into a large heatproof bowl.

MAKE THE SALTED CARAMEL

Combine the granulated sugar and corn syrup in a large pot, preferably one with a silver or light-colored bottom (so you can see the color of the sugar). Turn the heat to medium-high. As the sugar starts to melt and turn brown on the bottom and at the edges, stir with a wooden spoon or paddle to encourage the unmelted sugar to melt and caramelize. Continue to cook until all the sugar has reached the color of an old penny. Remove from the heat and add the cream and butter. The caramel will steam and bubble up, so do this carefully. Place back over medium-high heat and cook, stirring to dissolve any hardened bits, until the caramel reaches 245°F (firm-ball stage). Stir in the kosher salt.

Using an offset spatula or butter knife, quickly spread a thin layer of caramel over the brownie, making sure the caramel reaches the edges. Pour the rest of the caramel over the popcorn, tossing the popcorn to coat with caramel. Pour the still-warm caramel popcorn onto the brownie, and pat the popcorn down with a heatproof spatula or with a piece of parchment or waxed paper to create a layer of popcorn over the brownie. Sprinkle with the finishing salt and let cool to harden.

Once the popcorn has cooled and hardened, remove the entire brownie from the pan by grabbing the overhanging parchment paper and lifting straight up. Transfer to a large cutting board and, using a sharp serrated knife, cut and serve.

✱ *Though you probably are tempted to throw in a cup of chocolate chips instead of going to the trouble of chopping up a bar of chocolate, I implore you to reconsider. First off, you have more control over the type of chocolate that you use in the recipe if you use chopped chocolate, as most commercially available chocolate chips are made from inferior chocolate. But more important, chocolate chips are designed to hold their shape when heated up. Using chopped chocolate means the chocolate actually gets melty and gooey when baked, something that makes the brownies taste even better. Certainly you can use the shortcut of chocolate chips in place of the chopped chocolate, but these brownies will be better if you take the extra step and chop up some chocolate chunks.*

✱ *Even though I'm not a huge fan of microwave popcorn, I understand the appeal. It's so easy! Feel free to substitute a bag of low-salt, low-butter microwave popcorn if you prefer that to making it on the stove. Or make your own microwave popcorn: Place ½ cup popcorn kernels in a small bowl and toss with 1 tablespoon olive oil and 1 teaspoon salt to coat. Pour the popcorn into a brown paper bag (the sort you used to take school lunches in) and fold the top over twice. Microwave for 2½ to 3 minutes or until you hear 2-second pauses between the popping of the kernels. It's homemade microwave popcorn at a fraction of the price!*

SPICY CARAMEL POPCORN MEXICAN CHOCOLATE BROWNIES

For the Mexican chocolate brownie, add 1 teaspoon ground cinnamon, ½ teaspoon ground nutmeg, and ½ teaspoon cayenne pepper to the melted chocolate in the brownie batter, and proceed as directed.

For the spicy caramel, stir in ½ teaspoon cayenne pepper right before you remove the caramel from the heat.

Bake and assemble as directed.

CANDIED PEPPERMINT POPCORN MOCHA BROWNIES

For the mocha brownie, add 2 tablespoons instant coffee powder or 1½ tablespoons instant espresso powder to the melted chocolate.

For the candied peppermint popcorn, divide the popped popcorn into two bowls. Omit the cream, butter, and salt from the caramel. Instead, bring the sugar and corn syrup to 310°F (hard-crack stage) and immediately stir in 1 teaspoon peppermint extract (carefully, as the molten sugar will boil and steam). Immediately drizzle some liquid sugar over the brownie and pour half the remaining liquid sugar over the popcorn in one of the bowls, toss to coat, and then layer the popcorn onto the brownie. Add 3 or 4 drops red food coloring to the remaining liquid sugar (again being careful when you stir it in) and drizzle over the second bowl of popcorn, tossing to coat. Pour the red popcorn over the white popcorn on the brownie and press down to adhere. Let cool to harden, and then serve.

Caramel popcorn

The beauty of caramel popcorn is that pretty much everyone loves it. It's a little bit salty, a little bit sweet, a little bit crunchy, a little bit chewy. It's basically the perfect snack for those who have a sweet tooth but don't want to commit to a chocolate bar. Caramel popcorn has always been that secret magical treat that I never knew you could make at home. It seemed like something you just purchased at the store, preferably in large tins divided into three pie wedges filled with caramel, butter, and radioactive orange. The caramel always went first in my tin.

You can definitely follow the preceding recipe to make caramel popcorn just to enjoy it by itself. But if you like your popcorn to be extra crunchy, once the popcorn has been coated with the caramel, pour it onto a baking sheet lined with parchment paper or a Silpat. Quickly pat it into a single layer with a spatula and stick it in a preheated 300°F oven. Bake for 15 minutes, or until it has darkened a bit to a nice shiny reddish brown. Let cool on the baking sheet.

CITRUS SOUR SALTED CARAMEL BARS WITH DARK CHOCOLATE GANACHE

makes 24 bars

If my partner, A.J., had his way, pretty much everything I create in the kitchen would involve either caramel or chocolate—or preferably a combination of both, which might explain why these particular bars disappear almost immediately after I make them. At first glance, most people would think these bars are pretty sweet, but using a dark bittersweet chocolate (I usually pick something around 70 percent cacao), as well as bringing the caramel to a dark smoky edge when making them, helps temper the sweetness. The touch of citrus salt on top also pulls the bars in a different direction, just enough to make them interesting but not enough to make them oddball. Citric acid, an ingredient that is often used when making preserves, can be found online and at stores that sell canning supplies. If you don't have it, you can easily omit it, but it does add a nice subtly sour bite to the salt. One thing you should note: This recipe does require some rest time between steps, as well as an overnight rest in the refrigerator. So plan accordingly.

CRUST

2¼ cups (315 g) all-purpose flour

¾ cup plus 2 tablespoons (100 g) powdered sugar, sifted

1 cup plus 2 tablespoons (255 g or 2¼ sticks) unsalted butter, at room temperature

1½ teaspoons kosher salt

CARAMEL

2¼ cups heavy cream

2 teaspoons vanilla extract

2¼ cups (450 g) granulated sugar

¾ cup plus 2 tablespoons (200 g or 1¾ sticks) unsalted butter

MAKE THE CRUST

Preheat the oven to 350°F and lightly coat a 9 x 13-inch baking pan with cooking spray. Fit a piece of parchment paper inside the pan, overhanging the edges of the pan by 2 inches.

Combine the flour, powdered sugar, butter, and salt in the bowl of a stand mixer fitted with the paddle attachment. Mix together on low speed, raising the speed to medium as a dough forms. This might take a while depending on the butter temperature, and it may seem like the ingredients aren't coming together, but trust me, they do eventually and you will get a smooth dough. Pinch off a chunk of the dough and pat it down evenly into a ¼-inch-thick layer in the lined baking pan, starting at a corner of the pan. Continue to pinch off chunks of the dough and press them into the pan, patching together a flat layer of dough over the bottom of the pan. Prick the dough all over with a fork and then place a piece of parchment paper over the dough. Pour pie weights, uncooked rice, or dried beans over the paper and bake until the edges of the dough turn golden brown and the top of the crust looks dry and fully baked, 25 to 35 minutes. Carefully remove the paper with the weights. Let the crust cool to room temperature on a wire rack.

·······>

CITRUS SALT

2 tablespoons coarse sea salt

1 teaspoon lemon zest

⅛ teaspoon citric acid
(optional; see note on previous page)

CHOCOLATE GANACHE

3½ ounces (100 g) bittersweet chocolate
(70% or more cacao preferred)

6 tablespoons heavy cream

1 tablespoon balsamic vinegar

MAKE THE CARAMEL

Place the cream and vanilla in a small saucepan. Heat until bubbles start to form on the side of the pot. Turn off the heat and cover.

Place the granulated sugar in a large pot, preferably one with a silver or light-colored bottom (so you can see the color of the sugar). Turn the heat to medium-high. As the sugar starts to melt and turn brown on the bottom and at the edges, stir with a wooden spoon or paddle to encourage the unmelted sugar to melt and caramelize. Continue to cook until all the sugar has reached the color of an old penny.

Remove from the heat and carefully whisk in about ¼ cup of the cream. Be careful, as the caramel will sputter and steam up (some of the caramel might seize up and harden; that's okay). Continue to whisk in the cream in increments of ¼ cup until you have added all the cream. Add the butter in ½-inch chunks, stirring between additions. Once everything is added, cook the caramel over medium heat, stirring until any hardened pieces have dissolved. Once smooth, raise the heat to medium-high and cook, stirring frequently, until the caramel reaches 240 to 245°F (soft-ball stage), 8 to 12 minutes. Immediately pour the caramel onto the cooled crust. Let cool to room temperature.

MAKE THE CITRUS SALT

Turn the oven temperature to 250°F. Line a small baking sheet with parchment paper. Mix the salt, lemon zest, and citric acid together in a small bowl, then sprinkle over the parchment paper. Bake until the zest looks dry and brittle, 8 to 10 minutes. Let cool.

MAKE THE CHOCOLATE GANACHE

Chop the chocolate into ¼-inch chunks. Place the chocolate in a microwave-safe bowl and microwave for 30 seconds. Stir and then microwave for another 30 seconds. Stir and repeat if there are any large chunks remaining. If there are only small solid bits left, then don't worry about microwaving it again. Heat the cream in a small pan on the stove until tiny bubbles form on the sides of the pan. Add the heated cream to the chocolate, stirring until the chocolate is smooth and completely melted. Stir in the balsamic vinegar. Pour the ganache over the caramel, spreading it evenly. Sprinkle the citrus salt over the ganache, then refrigerate the entire pan overnight to let the caramel and chocolate firm up. Let sit at room temperature for 1 hour before cutting and serving.

SMOKED SALTED CARAMEL BARS ON CHOCOLATE SHORTBREAD

Make the crust as directed, but reduce the flour to 1¾ cups (245 g) and add ½ cup (50 g) Dutch-process cocoa powder. Bake as directed.

Make the caramel as directed. Skip the citrus salt. Make the chocolate ganache, but omit the balsamic vinegar and increase the heavy cream to ½ cup. Sprinkle 2 tablespoons smoked sea salt (found at specialty stores and online) over the ganache.

TOASTED SALTED COCONUT CARAMEL BARS WITH COCONUT-CHOCOLATE GANACHE

Make the crust as directed.

Make the caramel as directed. Skip the citrus salt. Make the chocolate ganache, but use ½ cup coconut cream in place of the heavy cream. Toast ¼ cup (25 g) unsweetened finely shredded coconut in a dry skillet over medium heat until brown. Let cool, then sprinkle over the chocolate ganache along with 2 tablespoons coarse sea salt.

Finishing salts

Salt is an important component of both savory and sweet foods. My mom taught me that if something tastes flat, adding salt brings out the flavor and dimension. Finishing salts, the type of salt you use at the very end of cooking or baking a dish, are different from the salt you use while making the dish. When cooking or baking, I use regular kosher salt in the main part of the dish, as it dissolves easily, is evenly distributed in the dish or batter, and is inexpensive. Kosher salt also has a cleaner taste than iodized table salt. Save the expensive salt until the end, as a finishing touch, where you can actually appreciate the flavor and texture of the salt. Flaky salts that have delicate crunch are great to help offset super-sweet desserts like these caramel bars. Flavored salts, whether you make or purchase them—like vanilla salt or smoked salt—add another dimension. Finishing salts can also be used as a decorative touch; for example, black diamond salt or red Hawaiian salt can look quite striking.

Nowadays it's fairly easy to buy finishing salts. Upscale grocery stores like Whole Foods and specialty shops like Trader Joe's carry finishing salts like Maldon or pyramid salt at a reasonable price. The Meadow, with a Web site and stores in Portland, Oregon, and New York City, stocks over 120 types of salt. You can also buy them online. Experiment with different types of finishing salts and you'll be surprised at how just a tiny investment in an ingredient can change the end result.

SEVILLE ORANGE BARS WITH SALTED SHORTBREAD AND GIN MERINGUE

makes 24 bars

I realize that I'm insanely lucky to live in San Francisco, ground zero for the seasonal and local food movement. And maybe I take it for granted that I can source hard-to-find produce like Seville oranges, the traditional bitter orange used in marmalade. But if you ever come across them at a farmers' market or upscale grocery, snatch up a bag of them as soon as you can! Sure, you can make marmalade or use them for an orange tart, but one of my favorite cocktails is a simple combination of gin and a splash of bitter orange juice. Flavored gins like orange or lemon used to be more popular but faded away in the mid-1980s. Even my yellowing 1988 copy of *Mr. Boston Official Bartender's Guide* has a cocktail using orange-flavored gin called the Leap Year Cocktail. So it was only natural that when I started tinkering with the classic lemon bar, I landed on a Seville orange curd bar with a touch of gin in the meringue topping. It's like a long-lost cocktail in dessert form.

SALTED SHORTBREAD CRUST

2¼ cups (315 g) all-purpose flour

¾ cup plus 2 tablespoons (100 g) powdered sugar, sifted

1½ teaspoons kosher salt

1 cup plus 2 tablespoons (255 g or 2¼ sticks) unsalted butter, at room temperature

SEVILLE ORANGE CURD

2 cups plus 1 teaspoon (404 g) granulated sugar, divided

½ cup (70 g) all-purpose flour

Zest of 4 Seville oranges

1 cup fresh Seville orange juice (from 6 or 7 medium oranges)

½ teaspoon vanilla extract

MAKE THE SALTED SHORTBREAD CRUST

Preheat the oven to 350°F and lightly coat a 9 x 13-inch baking pan with cooking spray. Fit a piece of parchment paper inside the pan, with enough paper to over-hang the edges of the pan by 2 inches.

Combine the flour, powdered sugar, salt, and butter in the bowl of a stand mixer fitted with the paddle attachment. Mix the ingredients together on low speed, raising the speed to medium as a dough forms. This might take a while depending on the butter temperature, and it may seem like the ingredients aren't coming together, but trust me, they do eventually and you will get a smooth dough. Pinch off a chunk of the dough and pat it down evenly into a ¼-inch-thick layer in the lined baking pan, starting at a corner of the pan. Continue to pinch off chunks of the dough and press them into the pan, patching together a flat layer of dough over the bottom of the pan. Prick the dough all over with a fork and then place a piece of parchment paper over the dough. Pour pie weights, uncooked rice, or dried beans over the paper and bake until the edges of the dough turn golden brown and the top of the crust looks dry and fully baked, 25 to 35 minutes.

........>

¼ teaspoon almond extract

6 large eggs

1 large egg yolk (save the white for the meringue)

¼ teaspoon kosher salt

1 tablespoon gin

MERINGUE

3 large egg whites

¼ teaspoon cream of tartar

1¼ cups plus 2 tablespoons (275 g) granulated sugar, divided

¼ cup water

2 tablespoons gin

✷ *If you can't find Seville oranges, don't substitute regular navel or Valencia oranges; they are both too sweet and your bars will end up tasting like orange sherbet. Instead, try using less sweet varieties like blood oranges, Cara Cara oranges, or even bergamot oranges if you can find any of those. If none of those are available, use a 50-50 combination of lemon and navel orange zest and juice to balance out the sweetness.*

MAKE THE SEVILLE ORANGE CURD

Meanwhile, add 2 cups (400 g) of the sugar, the flour, and zest to the bowl of the stand mixer fitted with the paddle attachment (wipe out any stray crumbs, but there is no need to clean it). Mix together on low speed. Pour in the juice, vanilla, and almond extract and continue to mix on low speed to incorporate. Stop the mixer and scrape down the side of the bowl. In a medium bowl, beat the eggs, egg yolk, and salt with a fork until uniform in color. Pour the eggs into the orange juice mixture and mix until incorporated, scraping down the sides of the bowl to make sure everything is well blended.

Carefully remove the parchment paper with the weights from the crust. Pour the orange curd onto the hot crust and carefully transfer the pan back to the oven (the curd filling will be very liquidy). Reduce the oven temperature to 300°F and bake until the center of the curd doesn't jiggle when you shake it, 30 to 40 minutes. Let cool on a wire rack to room temperature, about 1 hour. Stir the gin together with the remaining 1 teaspoon sugar in a small bowl (the sugar won't completely dissolve, but that's okay). Carefully brush the gin over the top of the bar with a pastry brush. Cover and refrigerate for at least 4 hours or up to overnight.

Once the bars have chilled, remove from the pan by grabbing the sides of the parchment paper and lifting straight up and out. Transfer to a cutting board. Cut into 24 bars and set them on a serving platter.

MAKE THE MERINGUE

Place the egg whites and cream of tartar in a clean metal bowl of the stand mixer fitted with a wire whisk. Whip on high speed until soft peaks form. Reduce the mixer speed to medium-high and sprinkle 2 tablespoons of the sugar into the whites, beating until dissolved. Turn the mixer off. Combine the remaining 1¼ cups (250 g) sugar and the water in a small saucepan and stir to wet all the sugar. Turn the heat to medium-high and cook until the sugar reaches 240°F (firm-ball stage). Turn on the stand mixer to high speed. Slowly drizzle the sugar syrup onto the egg whites, trying not hit the whisk itself or the sides of the bowl. Once all the syrup is incorporated, continue to whip the meringue until the bowl is cool to the touch, about 10 minutes. Add the gin and mix until just incorporated (10 seconds or so).

Spoon the meringue into a large pastry bag fitted with a round tip. Pipe the meringue on top of the bars. Use a kitchen torch to brown the meringue. Serve immediately.

LEMON-GINGER BARS WITH TEQUILA MERINGUE TOPPING

When making the shortbread, add ¼ cup (50 g) chopped candied ginger after the dough comes together and mix until evenly distributed. Bake as directed. When making the curd, replace the orange zest with lemon zest and the Seville orange juice with fresh lemon juice. Add 2 tablespoons grated fresh ginger to the curd with the juice. Omit the almond extract. Bake as directed. After the bars have cooled, mix 1 tablespoon tequila with 1 teaspoon granulated sugar and brush over the bars. Refrigerate as directed.

When making the meringue, replace the gin with tequila. Pipe and brown with a kitchen torch as directed.

Meringue

At its core, meringue is whipped egg whites with sugar added, nothing more. Since it is so sweet, meringue is often paired with something acidic or tart as a balance. This explains why you often see meringue on lemon or lime pies.

Making meringue involves whipping egg whites until a foam is created. When you agitate the egg whites (by whipping them), you are denaturing, or unraveling, the individual proteins that were originally wrapped in tight little pieces, allowing those loose protein ribbons to bind to adjacent unraveled protein ribbons. This forms a network of proteins that results in a larger three-dimensional foam. The more you agitate the egg whites, the more the proteins bind to each other and the bigger they get.

The reason that all recipes tell you to use a clean metal bowl and discard any egg whites that have a little bit of yolk in them is that glass and plastic bowls tend to have undetectable oil clinging to their sides and yolk has fat in it. If you introduce any fat, even a tiny bit, to the whipped egg whites, it will interfere with the protein-binding process. Imagine trying to open a door with greasy hands—you can't get a grip on the doorknob to open or turn it. The same thing happens to the egg white proteins: If you have a tiny bit of oil in them, they can't grab hold of each other and won't become as fluffy or as stiff as you'd need them to be.

The introduction of a bit of acid, like cream of tartar, lemon juice, or vinegar, helps speed the process of unraveling the egg white proteins and keeps them more stable. If you plan on whipping egg whites more than a few minutes before you use them, I'd definitely recommend adding about ⅛ teaspoon cream of tartar, lemon juice, or vinegar per egg white. Copper bowls function the same way as the acid, helping to stabilize the egg whites, which is why you sometimes hear old-school chefs touting the virtues of beating egg whites in copper bowls.

HONEY-LAVENDER CHEESECAKE BARS

makes 16 bars

It's a blessing and a curse living one block away from one of the most popular and best ice cream shops in San Francisco. My partner, A.J., and I were lucky to move into the neighborhood before it became the popular "gourmet ghetto" destination touted by Realtors and the food elite. A few years after we settled into our place, Bi-Rite Creamery opened up, with lines out the door. We were friendly with the owners and even once dressed up as their ice cream cartons for Halloween. A.J. was his favorite flavor (and their most popular flavor in general), salted caramel, while I went as my favorite flavor, honey lavender. The combination of the floral and the sweet works equally well in cheesecake form and inspired these bars. If you want to get really fancy, you can use homemade flavored graham crackers like the ones on page 77, but don't feel like you need to go overboard. Store-bought graham crackers are just fine, as the cheesecake layer is the real star.

LAVENDER SYRUP

1 cup (4¼ ounces or 120 g) fresh or frozen blueberries

2 tablespoons granulated sugar

2 tablespoons culinary-quality dried lavender

CRUST

9 ounces (255 g) graham crackers (store-bought or homemade, page 77)

2 tablespoons packed dark brown sugar

¼ teaspoon kosher salt

6 tablespoons (85 g or ¾ stick) unsalted butter, melted

MAKE THE LAVENDER SYRUP

Combine the blueberries, sugar, and lavender in a small saucepan. Turn the heat to high and cook until the blueberries have exuded their liquid, the sugar has dissolved, and the syrup starts to boil. Lower the heat to a simmer, then cook, covered, for about 5 minutes. Remove from the heat and let cool, still covered, for about 10 minutes. Once the syrup has cooled a bit and the lavender has had time to steep, pour the syrup through a fine-mesh sieve into a heatproof bowl. Press as much liquid as you can through the sieve with a rubber spatula. You should have about ½ cup. Discard the solids and let the liquid cool.

MAKE THE CRUST

Preheat the oven to 325°F and lightly coat a 9 x 13-inch baking pan with cooking spray. Fit a piece of parchment paper inside the pan, overhanging the edges of the pan by 2 inches. Place the graham crackers, brown sugar, and salt in a food processor and process until crumbs form. Drizzle the butter over the crumbs, pulsing until the crust starts to clump up. Dump the crumbs into the lined baking pan and press it down firmly with your fingers or the bottom of a flat drinking glass to form an even crust on the bottom of the pan. Bake until the crust is fragrant, about 5 minutes. Let cool on a wire rack while you make the filling.

·······>

CHEESECAKE LAYER

28 ounces (795 g or 3½ bricks) cream cheese, at room temperature

3 tablespoons all-purpose flour

1 vanilla bean or 2 teaspoons vanilla extract

½ cup plus 2 tablespoons (210 g) honey

3 large eggs

✳ *The blueberries used in this recipe add a subtle fruity berry dimension to the lavender syrup, but more important, also add the rich dark purple color that you can't get from lavender by itself. Frozen blueberries are the easiest to use, so you can make these cheesecake bars year-round, but feel free to use fresh blueberries if you have them.*

MAKE THE CHEESECAKE LAYER

Place the cream cheese and flour in the bowl of a stand mixer fitted with the paddle attachment. If using the vanilla bean, split it lengthwise and scrape the seeds into the mixer bowl with a knife. Save the pod for another use (see page 20 for ideas). If using vanilla extract, add it instead. Beat the cream cheese and flour together until incorporated, about 30 seconds. Add the honey and beat until incorporated. Add the eggs one at a time, beating to incorporate and scraping down the sides between each addition. Do not overbeat.

Pour about one-quarter of the cheesecake filling (about 300 g) into a separate bowl and add the lavender syrup to it. Stir with a large spatula until the batter is uniformly lavender in color. Gently spoon about half of the plain cheesecake batter over the graham cracker crust, trying not to disturb the crust too much. Layer the batters by adding most of the lavender batter, reserving 2 to 3 table-spoons of it, and then the remaining plain cheesecake batter to the pan. Use a spoon to drizzle the reserved lavender batter over the plain batter and then swirl it decoratively with a butter knife.

Bake until the center of the cheesecake slightly wobbles, 35 to 45 minutes. The cheesecake will puff up a lot while baking but will sink as it cools. Let cool to room temperature, then refrigerate, covered, overnight to firm up. Let sit at room temperature for 10 minutes before removing from the pan by grabbing the sides of the parchment paper and lifting straight up and out. Transfer to a cutting board to cut and serve.

SLOW-ROASTED BALSAMIC STRAWBERRY CHEESECAKE BARS

Instead of making the lavender syrup, preheat the oven to 275°F. Hull and quarter 1 pound (455 g) strawberries and place them in a large mixing bowl. Sprinkle them with 1 teaspoon vanilla extract, 2 tablespoons dark brown sugar, 1 tablespoon balsamic vinegar, and 1 tablespoon red wine. Toss gently to mix, then pour onto a rimmed baking sheet, scraping any juices out into the pan. Spread the strawberries in a single layer and roast until the berries have softened and darkened in color and the juices have thickened, about 2 hours, stirring every 30 minutes to make sure they don't stick to the pan. Let cool on the baking sheet, then use a food processor to puree.

Proceed with the recipe as directed, substituting the strawberry puree for the lavender syrup.

DOUBLE-CHOCOLATE CHUNK BLONDIE BARS WITH BOURBON GANACHE

makes 36 bars

Years ago, I brought a batch of these blondie bars (without the bourbon ganache) to the hospital as a gift for a friend who had just given birth to her first daughter. Upon receiving them, she proclaimed, "Now today is the best day!" as if birthing her first child wasn't enough! I love making these blondie bars, especially since I started using brown butter along with the almond meal and almond extract to give them a deeper nutty flavor. Of course, the bourbon ganache is literally icing on the dessert, but the butterscotchy, smoky bourbon really plays well with the blondie bar's brown sugar notes and is worth the bit of extra effort to make it.

BLONDIE BATTER

¾ cup (170 g or 1½ sticks) unsalted butter

2 cups (440 g) packed dark brown sugar

2 teaspoons vanilla extract

3 large eggs

2 cups (280 g) all-purpose flour

1 cup (140 g) almond meal or almond flour

2½ teaspoons baking powder

½ teaspoon kosher salt

1 cup (140 g) chopped semisweet chocolate (about 54% cacao)

1 cup (140 g) chopped bittersweet chocolate (about 70% cacao)

BOURBON GANACHE

2 cups (240 g) chopped bittersweet chocolate (about 70% cacao)

2 tablespoons unsalted butter

3 tablespoons bourbon

MAKE THE BLONDIE BATTER

Preheat the oven to 325°F. Line the bottom and sides of a 10 x 15-inch jelly-roll pan with a piece of aluminum foil, making sure about 1 inch of the foil hangs over the edges of the pan. Lightly coat the foil with cooking spray.

Place the butter in a large skillet (preferably one with a silver bottom, not non-stick) and turn the heat to high. Once the butter has melted completely, lower the heat to medium and stir constantly until the butter solids have started to brown at the bottom of the pan. Remove from the heat and let the butter continue to cook from the residual heat until it has turned a deep brown and smells fragrant and nutty. Pour the butter, scraping all the brown bits with a large spatula, into the bowl of a stand mixer fitted with the paddle attachment.

Add the brown sugar and vanilla to the butter and mix on medium speed until the outside of the bowl is barely warm to the touch, about 2 minutes. Add the eggs, one at a time, beating until each egg is incorporated before adding the next. Add the flour, almond meal, baking powder, and salt and mix until a batter forms. It will be wet. Add both chocolates and mix on low speed to evenly distribute.

Scrape the batter into the lined baking pan. Wet your hands with water and press the batter into the pan until it is evenly distributed to the edges. Bake until the sides of the blondie bar have started to turn golden brown and have darkened

1 teaspoon flaky finishing salt
(like Maldon) or coarse sea salt

✱ *If you don't have a 10 x 15-inch jelly-roll pan, you can bake the blondies in a 9 x 13-inch baking pan. Just increase the baking time by 5 to 10 minutes. Don't forget to line the baking pan with parchment paper or aluminum foil to help remove the bars from the deeper baking pan.*

slightly, 25 to 30 minutes. Let cool in the pan on a wire rack while you make the ganache.

MAKE THE BOURBON GANACHE

Place the chocolate and butter in a medium heatproof bowl. Microwave for 30 seconds. Stir the chocolate pieces (they won't have melted much) and microwave for 1 minute more, stopping to stir after 30 seconds. Stir until all the chocolate has melted; the warmth of the bowl and the melted chocolate will continue to melt the chocolate. If there are any stubborn pieces of chocolate chunks, microwave for another 15 seconds and stir again until smooth, but don't overcook. Stir in the bourbon. Pour the ganache over the warm blondie bars and spread to the edges with a large spatula.

FINISH THE BARS

Sprinkle the finishing salt over the warm ganache. Let cool completely in the pan. Remove the bar by grabbing the sides of the foil and lifting it straight up, transferring it to a cutting board. Cut and serve.

The magic of browned butter

Making browned butter, or *beurre noisette* in French (literally translated as "hazelnut butter"), isn't difficult, but the biggest mistake people make is burning the butterfat by either leaving the butter on the stove for too long or using too high heat.

Until you get the hang of making browned butter, I usually suggest making it in pan that isn't nonstick. Silver-bottomed pans allow you to watch the butterfat as it separates and browns, helping you remove the pan from the heat before the butter darkens too much. When starting out, I always suggest you remove the pan once the butterfat starts to brown and just let the residual heat from the pan continue to cook the butterfat. You can always nudge the fat to a darker color by placing it back on the heat, but it's impossible to go backward if you've browned it too much.

Once you start browning butter, it'll be hard to stop, as it adds an extra nutty dimension to baked goods like cookies, brownies, and cakes. The resulting baked good will have a deeper toffee butterscotch flavor and just taste richer. I often use it as a secret ingredient in chocolate chip cookies, and the results are outstanding. Sometimes that extra little step is all you need to take a baked good from good to great.

APPLE-TOFFEE BLONDIE BARS WITH CARAMEL GANACHE

Make the caramel ganache before you make the blondie. Place the chocolate in a large heatproof bowl. Combine ½ cup (100 g) granulated sugar, 1 tablespoon water, and 1 tablespoon fresh lemon juice in a large saucepan, stirring with a fork to moisten the sugar. Heat over medium-high heat until the sugar melts and turns a dark amber brown. Remove from the heat and carefully add ⅓ cup heavy cream. It will steam and bubble up. Add another ⅔ cup cream in two additions, stirring to incorporate in between (for a total of 1 cup cream). Add 2 tablespoons salted butter and then return the pan to the stove and cook over medium heat, stirring constantly, until the caramel is smooth and any hardened pieces of sugar have melted. Pour the caramel over the chocolate and let sit for 5 minutes to melt. Then stir slowly with a whisk until the chocolate is melted and the ganache is smooth and glossy. Let cool to a spreadable consistency, about 2 hours.

While the ganache is cooling, make the apple-toffee blondie. Omit the 1 cup semisweet chocolate and just use the bittersweet chocolate. Add 1 cup (40 g) chopped dried apple chips and ¾ cup (115 g) toffee bits to the batter along with the bittersweet chocolate. Bake as directed. Once the blondie bars have cooled, spread the caramel ganache over the bars and let cool completely before cutting and serving.

BERRY PIE BAR WITH CRUMB TOPPING

makes 12 bars

As much as I adore pie, my biggest complaint is that it's a dessert that needs to be plated and served. This is fine for a dinner party, but if I'm attending or hosting a more casual affair, I usually opt for a handy pie bar, which people can hold and eat while walking around without committing to a huge slice of dessert. The best part of these fruit pie bars is the ease of making them. The bottom crust does double duty as a crumb topping, meaning less work for you! If you use a fruit like berries, it's even faster because there's minimal chopping involved. This recipe can easily be doubled and made in a 9 x 13-inch pan; just increase the baking time by 5 to 10 minutes, or until the filling is bubbling and the top golden brown.

BASE DOUGH AND CRUMB TOPPING

1 cup (140 g) all-purpose flour

1 cup (150 g) whole-wheat flour

¾ cup (165 g) packed dark brown sugar

½ teaspoon kosher salt

6 tablespoons (85 g or ¾ stick) unsalted butter, cold, plus 3 tablespoons unsalted butter, melted

6 tablespoons whole milk

1 teaspoon ground cinnamon

½ teaspoon ground nutmeg

MAKE THE BASE DOUGH AND CRUMB TOPPING

Preheat the oven to 350°F. Lightly coat a 9-inch square baking pan with cooking spray. Line the bottom and sides with parchment paper, making sure about 2 inches of the paper hangs over the edges of the pan.

Combine the flours, brown sugar, and salt in a large mixing bowl and stir vigorously together with a balloon whisk until the ingredients are evenly distributed and uniform in color. Scoop out 1 cup (about 175 g) of the dry ingredient mixture and reserve in a small bowl to be used for the crumb topping. Cut up the cold butter into ½-inch chunks and sprinkle over the remaining dry ingredients in the large bowl. Using your fingers and hands, first toss the butter in the flour, then smash the butter into thin slivers, breaking them up as you go. Sprinkle the milk over the dough and continue to mix with your hands until clumps form.

Scrape the dough into the bottom of the lined baking pan and press down firmly with your fingers or the bottom of drinking glass into an even layer. Bake until the edges are starting to brown and the crust looks firm and dry, 15 to 20 minutes.

While the crust is baking, make the crumb topping by adding the cinnamon and nutmeg to the reserved dry ingredients and stirring with a fork to blend. Drizzle the 3 tablespoons melted butter over the ingredients and toss together with a fork until the mixture forms sandy crumbs. Refrigerate the crumb topping while you make the filling.

·······>

BERRY FILLING

2 tablespoons whole milk

1 teaspoon balsamic vinegar

3 tablespoons tapioca starch
(see note, below)

4 cups (18 ounces or 510 g) mixed fresh
berries (blueberries, blackberries,
strawberries)

½ cup (100 g) granulated sugar

¾ teaspoon ground cinnamon

½ teaspoon ground ginger

¼ teaspoon kosher salt

✱ *You can find tapioca starch at upscale
grocery stores, natural food stores,
and online. If you can't locate it, you can
replace the tapioca starch with the same
amount of cornstarch. You can learn
more about tapioca starch in the section
on starches (page 25).*

MAKE THE BERRY FILLING

Mix the milk, vinegar, and tapioca starch together in a small bowl. Place the berries, sugar, cinnamon, ginger, and salt in a medium bowl and drizzle with the tapioca starch mixture. Toss gently with a large spatula to coat. Once the crust has finished baking, spread the berry mixture over the hot crust in an even layer. Sprinkle the crumb topping over the berries and return to the oven to bake until the berries have burst and thickened and the top crumb is golden brown, 35 to 40 minutes more.

Let cool to room temperature before removing the pie bars from the pan by grabbing the overhanging parchment paper and lifting straight up and transferring the entire square to a cutting board. Cut and serve.

alternative

APPLE PIE BARS WITH OAT CRISP TOPPING

In the crust and crumb topping, replace the whole-wheat flour with 1 cup (100 g) thick-cut rolled oats. In the filling, omit the balsamic vinegar and replace the berries with 3½ cups (350 g) peeled and chopped (½-inch) apple chunks. Proceed with the recipe as directed.

SPICED PUMPKIN PIE BARS ON CHOCOLATE SHORTBREAD CRUST WITH MASCARPONE FROSTING

makes 24 bars

Every September, once the weather starts to cool off just a wee bit, my social media feed explodes with people getting all excited about pumpkin spice *everything*. I understand the frenzy because I do love pumpkin and spices, though maybe not to the same level as all of my fellow pumpkin spice aficionados. Nevertheless, I do want to take each and every one of them aside and say "Hey there. I know you love pumpkin spice. But you do realize that you can have it year-round if you want, right?" This pumpkin pie bar is the perfect example. Canned pumpkin is available year-round and plays well with both the chocolate shortbread crust and the sweet mascarpone frosting. Make a batch and serve them whenever you want!

CHOCOLATE SHORTBREAD CRUST

1¾ cups (245 g) all-purpose flour

¾ cup plus 2 tablespoons (100 g) powdered sugar, sifted

½ cup (55 g) natural cocoa powder (not Dutch-process)

½ teaspoon kosher salt

1 cup plus 2 tablespoons (255 g or 2¼ sticks) unsalted butter, at room temperature

PUMPKIN PIE FILLING

2 large eggs

1 (15-ounce) can pumpkin puree

1 cup heavy cream

¾ cup (165 g) packed dark brown sugar

1 teaspoon vanilla extract

1 teaspoon ground cinnamon

½ teaspoon ground nutmeg

½ teaspoon ground ginger

MAKE THE CHOCOLATE SHORTBREAD CRUST

Preheat the oven to 350°F. Lightly coat a 9 x 13-inch baking pan with cooking spray. Line the bottom and sides with parchment paper, with about 2 inches of the paper overhanging the sides of the pan.

Combine the flour, powdered sugar, cocoa powder, salt, and butter in the bowl of a stand mixer fitted with the paddle attachment. Mix together on low speed, raising the speed to medium as a dough forms. This might take a while depending on the butter temperature, and it may seem like the ingredients aren't coming together, but trust me, they do eventually and you will get a smooth dough. Pinch off a chunk of the dough and pat it down evenly into a ¼-inch-thick layer in the lined baking pan, starting at a corner. Continue to pinch off chunks of the dough and press them into the pan, patching together a flat layer of dough over the bottom of the pan. Prick the dough all over with a fork. Place a piece of parchment paper over the dough and add pie weights, uncooked rice, or dried beans. Bake until the surface of the crust looks dry, 25 to 35 minutes.

MAKE THE PUMPKIN PIE FILLING

Meanwhile, combine the eggs, pumpkin puree, cream, brown sugar, vanilla, cinnamon, nutmeg, ginger, cloves, and salt in a large bowl and stir vigorously with a balloon whisk until all the ingredients are evenly distributed and uniform in

·······>

½ teaspoon ground cloves

¼ teaspoon kosher salt

MASCARPONE FROSTING

⅔ cup heavy cream, cold

½ cup (60 g) powdered sugar, sifted

8 ounces (225 g) mascarpone cheese, at room temperature

½ teaspoon vanilla extract

color. Once the crust is done baking, carefully remove the parchment paper with the pie weights. Pour the pumpkin custard over the hot crust and return it to the oven to bake until the center of the filling no longer wiggles, about 30 minutes. Let cool to room temperature on a wire rack, then cover with aluminum foil and refrigerate overnight to set.

Once the pumpkin custard has set, remove the pumpkin pie bars from the pan by grabbing the parchment paper and lifting straight up. Transfer to a large cutting board and cut into 24 pieces.

MAKE THE MASCARPONE FROSTING

Pour the cream into the bowl of a stand mixer fitted with the whisk attachment. Sift the powdered sugar over the cream and then beat on high speed until soft peaks form. Scoop the whipped cream out of the bowl into another bowl. Add the mascarpone and vanilla to the mixer bowl (no need to clean it), and swap the whisk for the paddle attachment. Beat on medium-low speed until smooth. Remove the bowl from the mixer and add half the whipped cream, folding in the cream by hand with a large spatula. Fold in the remaining whipped cream.

Spread the frosting over the cut pumpkin pie bars and serve as is, or pull the bars apart and serve on individual plates.

PURPLE SWEET POTATO BARS WITH PECAN SHORTBREAD CRUST

Make the sweet potato puree before you make the crust, as the dense sweet potatoes take a while to cook. Peel 1 pound (455 g) purple sweet potatoes and cut into ½-inch-thick slices. Boil the sweet potatoes in a large pot of water until they are soft and easily pierced with a knife, 30 to 45 minutes. Drain and let cool. Mash the sweet potatoes with a potato masher or a large fork and use in place of the pumpkin puree. Replace the brown sugar with an equal amount of maple sugar and add 2 tablespoons bourbon to the custard. Bake as directed.

For the shortbread crust, toast ½ cup (55 g) chopped pecans in a dry skillet over medium heat until the pecans start to smell fragrant. Remove from the heat and let cool. Make the shortbread crust, omitting the cocoa powder, and increase the flour to 2 cups (280 g). Add the pecans at the very end, when the dough has just about come together. Bake as directed.

Replace the mascarpone in the frosting with room temperature cream cheese, and add 1 tablespoon of bourbon to the frosting along with the vanilla extract.

CAKES

BECAUSE OF THE CULTURAL IMPORTANCE OF cakes—from childhood cupcakes to homemade birthday cakes to extravagant multitiered wedding cakes—it's no wonder that there are cookbooks and TV shows dedicated to making and decorating show-stopping cakes. A cake all by itself is a symbol of celebration. But here's a little bit of a secret. You don't need professional culinary training to make fantastic cakes. You just need to have a little patience to create a few different components to build that fabulous cake.

The cake recipes you'll find in this book aren't fancy or lavish. A few might be considered a weekend project because of the time involved, but none of them require any special skills. But they all impress in different ways, whether it's a fun flavor combination or a cool and easy decorating tip. Who knows—maybe one of them might become your go-to celebratory cake in the future.

CLASSIC VANILLA AND CHOCOLATE MARBLED BUNDT CAKE

makes 1 bundt cake; 10 to 12 servings

Growing up in the Midwest, no potluck was complete without a marbled Bundt cake. My mom made them all the time, one of only two desserts that she was known for, so when I hosted a dessert potluck at a local nonprofit community center with the theme "Like Mom used to make!" I knew I had to replicate her Bundt cake. The secret to this recipe is the homemade chocolate syrup, which you make on the stove before adding it to the batter. Made with coffee and cocoa powder (and a touch of honey), it lends a rich, deep chocolate flavor because the cocoa blooms in the hot coffee. You don't necessarily taste the coffee or honey, but they both boost the chocolate goodness!

TO GREASE PAN

1 tablespoon unsalted butter, at room temperature

2 tablespoons all-purpose flour

CHOCOLATE SYRUP

½ cup (100 g) granulated sugar

½ cup (55 g) natural cocoa powder (not Dutch-process)

½ cup freshly brewed strong hot coffee

¼ cup (85 g) mild-tasting honey

½ teaspoon vanilla extract

CAKE BATTER

2 cups (400 g) granulated sugar

1 cup (225 g or 2 sticks) unsalted butter, at room temperature

2 teaspoons vanilla extract

4 large eggs, at room temperature

1 teaspoon baking powder

1 teaspoon baking soda

GREASE THE PAN

Preheat the oven to 350°F. Place the butter in a 12-cup Bundt pan and grease the pan with your fingers, making sure to grease all the nooks and crannies. Sprinkle the flour all over the pan and knock out the excess.

MAKE THE CHOCOLATE SYRUP

Combine the sugar, cocoa powder, coffee, and honey and in a small saucepan and cook over medium heat until the sugar has dissolved and the syrup starts to boil. Bring to a simmer, whisking to make sure there are no lumps. Remove from the heat and stir in the vanilla.

MAKE THE CAKE BATTER

Place the sugar and butter in the bowl of a stand mixer fitted with the paddle attachment. Beat on medium speed until the butter looks light in color and fluffy, about 2 minutes. Add the vanilla and mix until incorporated. Add the eggs one at a time, beating until completely incorporated and scraping down the sides and bottom of the bowl between each addition. Add the baking powder, baking soda, and salt and beat until the dry ingredients are absorbed.

Add the flour in three additions and the buttermilk in two, alternating between the flour and buttermilk and ending with the flour. Beat until incorporated and scrape down the sides and bottom of the bowl between each addition. Gently fold in the chocolate chips.

·······>

½ teaspoon kosher salt

2¾ cups (385 g) all-purpose flour

1 cup buttermilk

1 cup (210 g) semisweet chocolate chips

VANILLA BEAN GLAZE

1 vanilla bean or 1 tablespoon vanilla extract

¼ cup whole milk

2 to 2½ cups (230 g to 290 g) powdered sugar

FOR DECORATION

Chocolate pearls, chocolate shavings, or chocolate sprinkles (optional)

✳ *Skip making the glaze and just dust the cooled cake with powdered sugar before serving.*

Spoon one-third of the batter into a medium bowl and add the chocolate syrup. Stir to incorporate completely and set aside. Spoon half of the remaining vanilla batter into the prepared Bundt pan. Scrape the chocolate batter on top. Spread the remaining vanilla batter on top of the chocolate batter. Insert a butter knife or chopstick into the batter and make "figure eight" motions throughout the entire cake to marble the batter. You may want to sometimes dig deep to the bottom and sometimes lift up to make sure the batter really moves around. Just don't over-mix the batters, or else they will blend together instead of marbling.

Place the pan on a rimmed baking sheet. Bake until a toothpick or skewer inserted in the center comes out clean and the cake springs back when pressed down lightly, 50 to 60 minutes. Let cool in the pan on a wire rack for 20 to 30 minutes and then invert onto a serving plate while still warm. If the cake doesn't unmold, gently slip a very thin knife between the cake and the pan all the way around to loosen it and then try again.

MAKE THE VANILLA BEAN GLAZE

Slice the vanilla bean lengthwise, if using, and scrape the seeds into the milk in a large bowl. Chop the bean in half and toss the pod in with the milk as well. Let steep in the refrigerator as the cake cools. Once the cake has cooled completely (after about 2 hours), remove the vanilla bean from the milk and sift 2 cups powdered sugar into the milk. (If using the vanilla extract, add it to the milk right before sifting the powdered sugar; no need to steep it.) The glaze should be thin enough to pour, but thick enough to hold its shape on the cake, similar to honey in consistency. If the glaze is too thin, add more powdered sugar, 1 tablespoon at a time, until it reaches the desired thickness.

Drizzle the glaze on top of the cake, making sure the glaze drips down the sides of the cake. If decorating with chocolate pearls, shavings, or sprinkles, sprinkle them randomly on the cake before the glaze dries.

GINGERBREAD AND LEMON–POPPY SEED MARBLE BUNDT CAKE

Preheat the oven and prep the pan as directed. Skip the chocolate syrup. Combine ¼ cup fresh lemon juice with ¾ cup whole milk. Set aside to thicken. Make the cake batter as directed, adding the zest of 2 lemons along with the butter and sugar. Reduce the vanilla to 1 teaspoon and add 1 teaspoon lemon extract. Substitute the lemon milk in place of the buttermilk and omit the chocolate chips. Divide the batter as directed. To the one-third batter in the smaller bowl, fold in ¼ cup molasses, 2 teaspoons ground ginger, 1 teaspoon ground cinnamon, and ¼ cup (50 g) chopped crystallized ginger. To the larger bowl of batter, fold in 1 tablespoon poppy seeds. Assemble, marble, and bake as directed.

Once cooled, make a glaze as directed, omitting the vanilla and flavoring the glaze with 1½ teaspoons lemon extract instead.

STRAWBERRY AND BASIL-CORNMEAL SHORTCAKES WITH VANILLA WHIPPED CREAM

makes 4 strawberry shortcakes

Though we rarely had desserts in my home growing up, usually opting for fresh fruit at the end of the meal, occasionally my mom would make strawberry shortcake. This "shortcake" was composed of those prepackaged yellow sponge cakes found in the produce section along with out-of-season strawberries and imitation whipped cream topping from a plastic tub, which my mom stored in the freezer and never thawed. It wasn't until I grew up and moved out on my own that I discovered that actual strawberry shortcake meant a sweet biscuit with fresh (ideally in-season) fruit and real whipped cream. In this version, I've added a touch of fresh basil for an herbal dimension and some cornmeal to the shortcake for texture. Both additions keep the dessert from getting too sweet and pull the classic dish in an unexpected, modern direction.

STRAWBERRY FILLING

4 cups (1 pound or 455 g) strawberries, green tops cut off

2 tablespoons granulated sugar

1 tablespoon chopped fresh basil

1 teaspoon balsamic vinegar

WHIPPED CREAM

½ vanilla bean or 2 teaspoons vanilla extract

1 cup cold heavy cream

1 tablespoon granulated sugar

BASIL-CORNMEAL SHORTCAKES

1¼ cups (175 g) all-purpose flour

⅓ cup (50 g) yellow cornmeal

4 tablespoons (50 g) granulated sugar, divided

MAKE THE STRAWBERRY FILLING

Place about one-third of the strawberries in a medium nonreactive (glass or ceramic) bowl and crush them with a fork or potato masher. Add the remaining strawberries to the bowl and tear them up with your fingers into bite-size pieces, making sure any juice falls into the bowl. Sprinkle the sugar, basil, and vinegar over the strawberries and toss to coat. Let sit for at least 30 minutes or up to 3 hours before using.

MAKE THE WHIPPED CREAM

Split the vanilla bean lengthwise, if using, and scrape the seeds into the heavy cream in the measuring cup. (Or add the vanilla extract.) Add the sugar and stir to dissolve. Add the empty vanilla bean, cover with plastic wrap, and let steep in the refrigerator while you make the shortcakes.

MAKE THE BASIL-CORNMEAL SHORTCAKES

Preheat the oven to 425°F and line a baking sheet with parchment paper or a Silpat. Combine the flour, cornmeal, 3 tablespoons of the sugar, the baking powder, baking soda, salt, and basil in a large bowl. Cut the butter into ½-inch chunks, sprinkle over the flour, and toss to coat. Using your fingers, flatten the

·······>

1½ teaspoons baking powder

1 teaspoon baking soda

¼ teaspoon kosher salt

2 tablespoons chopped fresh basil

4 tablespoons (57 g or ½ stick) unsalted butter

1 large egg, separated

½ cup (115 g) plain Greek-style yogurt

1 tablespoon water

TO ASSEMBLE

1 tablespoon chopped fresh basil

cubes of butter and then rub and squeeze the butter and flour together until the butter is broken into small pieces, about the size of peas.

Set aside the egg white in a small bowl. Combine the egg yolk and the yogurt in a small bowl and beat together until the yolk is incorporated into the yogurt. Scrape the yogurt into the dry ingredients and toss first with a fork, then your hands, until a dough forms. It might seem dry at first, but keep tossing together and a dough will form. Divide the dough into 4 balls and place on the lined baking sheet, pressing down slightly to form disks. Add the water to the egg white and beat until frothy. Brush the top of each shortcake with a light coating of the egg white wash and sprinkle with the remaining 1 tablespoon sugar. Bake until the biscuits are golden brown on top and a toothpick inserted in the center comes out clean, 14 to 18 minutes. Let cool on the baking sheet for 5 minutes and then carefully move to a wire rack.

While the shortcakes are cooling, finish the whipped cream. Remove the vanilla pod from the cream and transfer the cream to the bowl of a stand mixer fitted with the whisk attachment. Whip on high speed until soft peaks form.

ASSEMBLE THE SHORTCAKES

Use a serrated knife to split the shortcakes in half. Spoon the whipped cream onto the bottom of each shortcake, add some strawberries, sprinkle with a little basil, add another dollop of whipped cream, and replace the top of each shortcake. Serve immediately.

Tearing strawberries ....

It sounds odd, but tearing the strawberries by hand in this recipe actually serves a purpose. If you slice the strawberries, the fruit tends to slip and slide off the whipped cream. However, if you tear the fruit with your fingers, the jagged edges of the fruit have nooks and crannies that help capture the whipped cream. It also helps bruise the fruit so that a little more juice is released for the shortcake. So get your hands dirty and start tearing away!

PEACH AND THYME SHORTCAKES WITH BROWN SUGAR WHIPPED CREAM

Replace the strawberries with about 4 medium juicy peeled fresh peaches (see Vanilla and Peach-Bourbon Ice Cream Pie on page 225 for instructions on peeling peaches). Mash one-third of the peaches into a sauce and slice the rest. In the shortcakes, increase the all-purpose flour to 1½ cups (210 g) and omit the cornmeal. Substitute 1 tablespoon fresh thyme leaves for the basil. In the whipped cream, use 1 tablespoon brown sugar instead of the granulated, and assemble the shortcakes with 1 tablespoon fresh thyme leaves instead of the chopped basil.

BLUEBERRY AND CORIANDER SHORTCAKES WITH LEMON-SCENTED WHIPPED CREAM

Make the blueberry filling by combining 4 cups (680 g) fresh blueberries (don't use frozen), ½ cup (100 g) granulated sugar, the zest of 1 lemon, and 1 tablespoon fresh lemon juice in a medium saucepan. Cook over medium heat, stirring constantly, until the juices start to boil and a few of the berries start to pop, 3 to 5 minutes. Remove from the heat and set aside to cool to room temperature or refrigerate overnight.

For the shortcakes, first toast 4 teaspoons coriander seeds in a dry skillet over medium heat until fragrant. Remove and let cool, then crush with a mortar and pestle or a spice grinder. Increase the all-purpose flour to 1½ cups (210 g) and omit the cornmeal, and substitute 2 teaspoons of the crushed toasted coriander for the basil. Sprinkle ¼ teaspoon crushed coriander over each shortcake with the sugar before baking. Make the whipped cream as directed, then fold in 1 tablespoon lemon zest or 2 teaspoons lemon extract. Sprinkle the remaining coriander over the blueberries when assembling in place of the basil.

MANGO, LIME, AND STRAWBERRY ANGEL FOOD CAKE WITH LEMON GLAZE

makes one 10-inch cake; 8 servings

Angel food cake has always been the dessert I resort to when I have accumulated too many egg whites. This is fairly often, because I use a lot of egg yolks making custards and ice cream. The problem with angel food cake, though, is that it's relatively benign, nothing too special in my eyes. I think of it as a base for other desserts, using slices to make ice cream sandwiches, or adding strawberries on top to make an ersatz strawberry shortcake. But I always knew I could do better. This triple-layer cake isn't much more difficult than the plain version, but it's bursting with spring fruit flavor, which means it can be served all on its own. I normally eschew food coloring in my baked goods, but sometimes you gotta do what you gotta do. The freeze-dried fruit by itself in the layers doesn't give quite enough color distinction. But if you are really averse to food coloring, just skip it and slather the cake slices with fresh strawberry sauce.

CAKE BATTER

1 cup plus 2 tablespoons (135 g) cake flour

1¾ cups (350 g) superfine sugar, divided (see note, page 325)

¼ teaspoon kosher salt

12 egg whites

1 teaspoon cream of tartar

2 cups (35 g) freeze-dried mangoes, crushed to a powder in a food processor (see note, page 138)

Yellow, red, and green liquid food coloring (optional but recommended)

1½ cups (34 g) freeze-dried strawberries, crushed to a powder in a food processor (see note, page 138)

1 teaspoon lime extract (see note, opposite)

MAKE THE CAKE BATTER

Preheat the oven to 325°F. Combine the cake flour, 1 cup (200 g) of the sugar, and the salt in a large bowl and stir vigorously with a whisk to remove any clumps and aerate the flour. Set aside.

Place the egg whites and cream of tartar in the clean bowl of a stand mixer fitted with whisk attachment. Whip on high speed until soft peaks form. Reduce the mixer speed to medium and slowly sprinkle the remaining ¾ cup (150 g) sugar into the bowl with the mixer running. Once all the sugar is incorporated, raise the speed to high and whip until firm peaks form and the egg whites are glossy and white.

Remove the bowl from the stand mixer and sift one-third of the dry ingredients over the egg whites. Fold in the dry ingredients with a large spatula, making sure there are no dry patches or streaks of flour. Repeat two more times with the remaining dry ingredients, making sure everything is incorporated before the next addition.

LEMON GLAZE

2½ cups (290 g) powdered sugar, sifted

5 to 6 tablespoons fresh lemon juice

Divide the batter into three bowls (about 285 g each). To one third, add the freeze-dried mango, 6 drops yellow food coloring, and 2 drops red food coloring (if using) and fold gently until the color is uniform. (Rinse the spatula in between folding each color.) To the second third, add the freeze-dried strawberries and 6 drops red food coloring (if using) and fold gently until the color is uniform. To the last third, add the lime extract, 3 drops green food coloring, and 3 drops yellow food coloring (if using) and fold gently until the color is uniform.

Scrape the mango batter into a 10-inch tube pan with a removable bottom (do not grease the pan) and place on a rimmed baking sheet. Layer the strawberry batter on top of the mango batter and then spread the lime batter on top. Tap the pan on the counter or table once to settle the batter. Bake until a toothpick inserted into the center comes out clean, 40 to 45 minutes.

Once you remove the pan from the oven, invert it with the center tube placed on top of a clean empty wine bottle and let the cake cool upside down completely. Run a thin knife around the sides of the pan and remove the sides. Then run the knife under the bottom of the cake to remove it from the bottom. Place the cake on a cake stand or serving platter and brush away any crumbs with a pastry brush.

MAKE THE LEMON GLAZE

Combine the powdered sugar and 5 tablespoons lemon juice in a large bowl. Stir to dissolve the sugar. If the glaze is too thick, thin it with more lemon juice, 1 teaspoon at a time, until it reaches the right consistency, like honey. The glaze should be a little bit on the thick side in order to get the nice drips on the side of the cake. Drizzle the glaze over the top of the cake, pushing some of the glaze over the edge of the cake with a spoon so that it drips down the sides and the middle. Let the glaze set for an hour or so before serving.

Lime extract

Lime extract is harder to find in stores than lemon extract. The best place to purchase it is online (see Resources, page 336). If you have a little bit of extra time, you can make your own lime extract. If you can get your hands on small, fragrant Key limes (the best place to find them is an ethnic grocery store that sells Mexican produce), they create a lovely lime extract. Zest 12 Key limes into a bowl, add 6 tablespoons vodka, and let sit for 2 hours. The resulting liquid should turn brilliant green. Strain the liquid into a small jar or bottle and store in a dark, cool place (the refrigerator is ideal). If you don't have access to Key limes, regular Persian limes will work as well. Zest 6 regular limes and let the zest steep in 6 tablespoons vodka for 1 week. Strain and store in the same manner.

If you can't get lime extract and you don't want to make your own, just swap in 1 teaspoon lemon extract and use 4 drops yellow food coloring to make a mango, lemon, and strawberry angel food cake.

PEPPERMINT AND RASPBERRY ANGEL FOOD CAKE WITH CHOCOLATE GLAZE

Make the recipe as directed, then divide the batter into two bowls (about 425 g each). Into one bowl, fold 1½ cups (35 g) freeze-dried raspberries, crushed to a powder, and 6 drops red food coloring. Fold ½ teaspoon peppermint extract into the other bowl. Add half of the peppermint batter to the pan, then half of the raspberry batter, then repeat with the remaining peppermint and raspberry batter to create four layers. Bake as directed.

Make the chocolate glaze by chopping 6 ounces (170 g) bittersweet chocolate into ¼-inch chunks and placing them in a large microwave-safe bowl. Add ½ cup (115 g or 1 stick) unsalted butter and microwave for 30 seconds. Stir and microwave again for two more 30-second intervals, stirring after each. Stir until all the chocolate is melted and smooth. If there are stubborn chocolate pieces, microwave in 15-second intervals, stirring until completely melted. Sift in 1½ cups (170 g) powdered sugar and then add ½ cup heavy cream. Stir until all the ingredients are combined. Spoon the glaze over the cooled cake, letting it drizzle down the sides. If the glaze is too thin, let it cool a little more. If it is too thick, microwave it for 15 seconds to warm it up.

VANILLA, ORANGE, AND CHOCOLATE ANGEL FOOD CAKE WITH WHITE RUM GLAZE

Make the recipe as directed, dividing the batter into three bowls. Into one bowl, fold 2 teaspoons vanilla paste or extract. Into the second bowl, fold the zest of 1 navel orange and 2 tablespoons Grand Marnier or Cointreau along with 6 drops yellow food coloring and 2 drops red food coloring. Into the third bowl, fold 3 tablespoons natural cocoa powder (not Dutch-process). Layer the cake batter in the pan, starting with the vanilla batter, then the orange, then the chocolate. Bake as directed.

Make the glaze as directed, replacing the lemon juice with white rum. Glaze the cake as directed.

Freeze-dried fruit

You can buy freeze-dried fruit at well-stocked grocery stores, upscale grocery stores, or specialty stores like Trader Joe's, and also find it online. Measure the fruit before crushing it into a powder in a food processor. Be warned that freeze-dried fruits are hygroscopic (they absorb water quickly), so if the air is humid or you have a drop of water in the food processor, the fruit will start to get sticky. Work fairly fast, or they will turn into a sticky mess as they absorb water from the air.

CARROT AND PARSNIP LAYER CAKE WITH HONEY–CREAM CHEESE FROSTING

I'm a creature of habit, so when my friend Annelies invited me to dinner in a neighborhood here in San Francisco that I rarely frequent, I jumped at the chance. Not only did I get to dine at a new restaurant, but I got to hang out with a friend too. After our meal, we agreed to split a dessert and were particularly smitten with the idea of the parsnip cake on the menu. Like carrot, parsnip has a subtle earthy and nutty sweetness when cooked. I've taken it even further, though, layering parsnip cake with carrot cake to really up the game. The deeper, almost creamy parsnip makes the common carrot brighter and more vibrant. With honey-sweetened cream cheese frosting and a sprinkling of toasted coconut, this dense winter vegetable cake is now one of my favorites.

CAKE BATTER

3¾ cups (525 g) all-purpose flour

¾ cup (90 g) almond flour or meal

1 tablespoon plus 2 teaspoons baking powder

1½ teaspoons baking soda

1 teaspoon kosher salt

3 cups (600 g) granulated sugar

1 cup plus 2 tablespoons olive oil

1 tablespoon vanilla extract

3 large eggs

1 large egg white

1 cup (6 ounces or 170 g) finely chopped fresh pineapple (or drained canned crushed pineapple)

1 pound (455 g) carrots, finely grated

1½ teaspoons ground cinnamon

1 teaspoon ground turmeric

½ teaspoon ground cardamom

MAKE THE CAKE BATTER

Preheat the oven to 350°F. Coat three 9-inch round cake pans with cooking spray and line the bottom of each with a round of parchment paper.

Place the flour, almond meal, baking powder, baking soda, and salt in a large bowl and stir vigorously with a balloon whisk until the ingredients are evenly distributed and uniform in color. Place the sugar, oil, and vanilla in the bowl of a stand mixer fitted with the paddle attachment. Beat together for about 30 seconds on medium speed to incorporate. Add the eggs, one at time, beating until each is incorporated before adding the next, then add the egg white. Scrape down the bowl with a rubber spatula and then add the dry ingredients and mix on low speed until incorporated. Add the pineapple and mix until incorporated.

Scoop about one-third of the batter into a separate bowl. To the remaining larger amount of batter in the mixer bowl, add the carrots, cinnamon, turmeric, and cardamom, and fold to combine. To the second bowl of batter, add the parsnips, ginger, and nutmeg, and fold to combine. Pour the parsnip cake batter into one cake pan and divide the carrot batter between the other two cake pans.

Bake until a toothpick inserted in the middle of the cake comes out clean, 35 to 40 minutes. Let cool in the pan for 15 minutes, then run a thin butter knife around the pan and invert the cakes onto wire racks to cool completely.

·······>

½ pound (225 g) parsnips, finely grated

1 teaspoon ground ginger

¼ teaspoon ground nutmeg

HONEY–CREAM CHEESE FROSTING

16 ounces (455 g or 2 bricks) cream cheese, at room temperature

1 cup (225 g or 2 sticks) unsalted butter, at room temperature

6 tablespoons (130 g) honey

1 cup (115 g) powdered sugar

2 teaspoons vanilla extract

TO ASSEMBLE

2 cups (170 g) unsweetened coconut flakes

✳ *Unsweetened coconut flakes can be difficult to find. Some upscale grocery stores carry it, and often you can find it in the bulk section, where you can buy just enough for your recipe. At regular grocery stores, if it isn't stocked in the baking section next to the sweetened shredded coconut, look for it near the dried fruit like raisins, dried ginger, and dried papaya. If you can't find it, though, the sweetened or unsweetened shredded coconut in the baking section will work. Just toast it over medium-low heat and pay extra attention if you use the sweetened shredded coconut. The sugar in the sweetened coconut will caramelize and burn faster than unsweetened shredded coconut.*

MAKE THE HONEY–CREAM CHEESE FROSTING

Combine the cream cheese, butter, honey, powdered sugar, and vanilla in the bowl of a stand mixer fitted with the paddle attachment. Beat until the frosting is pale and fluffy, 3 to 5 minutes. Refrigerate the frosting for at least 30 minutes to firm up.

ASSEMBLE THE CAKE

Toast the coconut in a large dry skillet over medium-high heat, stirring gently, until golden brown (some of the coconut will brown faster than the rest; that's fine). Immediately pour the coconut into a bowl to cool. Take the frosting out of the fridge and beat on medium speed for about 15 seconds to loosen it up. Place one carrot cake layer on a cake platter or stand, flat side up, and spread some frosting over the top of that layer. Place the parsnip layer over the frosting and repeat. Place the final carrot cake layer over the parsnip layer and frost the top and sides of the cake. Using your hands, pat the toasted coconut all over the sides of the cake. Brush any stray coconut off the platter before serving.

RAINBOW CARROT CAKE WITH MAPLE–CREAM CHEESE FROSTING

Make the cake batter as directed through the second step. Divide the cake batter equally into three separate bowls. Into one bowl, fold ½ pound (225 g) shredded orange carrots, ¾ teaspoon ground cinnamon, and ½ teaspoon ground cardamom. Into the second bowl, fold ½ pound (225 g) shredded yellow or white carrots, ¾ teaspoon ground ginger, and ¾ teaspoon ground turmeric. Into the last bowl, fold ½ pound (225 g) shredded purple or black carrots, 1 teaspoon freshly ground black pepper, and ½ teaspoon ground allspice. Bake as directed.

Make the cream cheese frosting as directed, substituting ¼ cup maple syrup and ¼ cup (30 g) maple sugar in place of the honey. Layer the cakes with the purple carrot layer at the bottom, the orange layer in the middle, and the yellow layer on top.

CHOCOLATE AND BROWN SUGAR BUTTERCREAM ROLLED CAKE WITH CRUSHED PISTACHIOS

makes 1 rolled cake; 10 to 12 servings

My partner was turning forty years old, and I was at a loss as to what sort of cake to make for him. It had to be something special, but nothing outlandish, as we weren't throwing a party but celebrating at home—a nice home-cooked meal for just the two of us. Luckily, the cookbook *Vintage Cakes* by Julie Richardson came to the rescue, inspiring this rolled cake. This recipe is different from Julie's recipe, except that it uses the same technique, rolling the cake and then standing it on its end so you can see the layers spiral out on top of the cake. It's like a large jelly-roll cake turned on its end! Somehow, it also seemed fitting that the book *Vintage Cakes* inspired a fortieth birthday cake.

CAKE BATTER

1 cup (16 ounces or 170 g) chopped bittersweet chocolate

3 tablespoons vegetable shortening

¼ cup hot fresh brewed coffee

2 teaspoons vanilla extract

¼ teaspoon almond extract (optional)

½ cup (70 g) all-purpose flour

1 teaspoon baking powder

¼ teaspoon kosher salt

6 large eggs, separated

½ teaspoon cream of tartar

½ cup (100 g) granulated sugar

BROWN SUGAR BUTTERCREAM

6 large egg whites

1½ cup (330 g) packed dark brown sugar

1 teaspoon kosher salt

2¼ cups (510 g or 4½ sticks) unsalted butter, cool but not cold

MAKE THE CAKE BATTER

Preheat the oven to 350°F and coat a 12 x 17-inch rimmed baking sheet with cooking spray. Line the bottom with a piece of parchment paper and spray the parchment with cooking spray too.

Place the chopped chocolate in a large microwave-safe bowl and microwave for 30 seconds. Stir and microwave again for 30 seconds. Stir until the chocolate is melted, heating the chocolate in additional 15-second intervals in the microwave if necessary.

Add the shortening, coffee, vanilla, and almond extract (if using) to the warm chocolate. Stir until the shortening has melted and incorporated. Add the flour, baking powder, and salt and mix until the dry ingredients are absorbed. Let the batter cool until it is barely warm and then add the egg yolks. Mix with a whisk until blended and smooth.

Place the egg whites and cream of tartar in the bowl of a stand mixer fitted with the whisk attachment. Whisk on high speed until soft peaks form. With the mixer still on, slowly sprinkle in the sugar and continue to whip until the whites become glossy.

Add about a quarter of the egg whites to the cake batter and fold gently to lighten the batter. Add the rest of the egg whites in three batches, folding to incorporate

·······>

1½ cups (210 g) chopped unsalted pistachios, divided (if you can only find salted nuts, omit the salt in the buttercream)

completely before adding the next batch. Scrape the batter onto the prepared baking sheet and spread evenly. Bake until a toothpick inserted in the center comes out clean and the cake feels firm to the touch, 14 to 16 minutes. Let cool in the baking sheet for 30 minutes.

MAKE THE BROWN SUGAR BUTTERCREAM

Place the egg whites, brown sugar, and salt in the bowl of the stand mixer. Set the bowl over a pot of simmering water and whisk by hand until the sugar and salt have dissolved and the temperature reaches 140°F (warm to the touch). Attach the bowl to the mixer fitted with the whisk attachment. Beat on high speed until stiff peaks form. Reduce the speed to medium and beat for an additional 5 to 6 minutes, until the egg whites have cooled and are fluffy. Switch out the whisk attachment for the paddle attachment and turn the speed to medium-low. Add the butter 2 tablespoons at a time, waiting for it to incorporate before each addition. Once the butter has all been added, reduce the speed to low and beat for an additional 2 to 3 minutes to smooth the buttercream and get rid of any air bubbles. If the buttercream looks like it is broken (curdled or separated), raise the speed to medium-high and beat for a minute or two to bring it back together.

ASSEMBLE THE CAKE

Unroll the cake and place it with the long side facing you. Trim ½ inch off the edges on the left and right to make a proper rectangle. Cut the cake vertically in the center with a serrated knife, making two 8 x 12-inch rectangles. Cut each rectangle vertically in half again, to make four 4 x 12-inch rectangles. Spread about half the buttercream over the cake, making sure to evenly spread it across the cake to the edges. Sprinkle ½ cup of the pistachios over the frosting.

Roll the first strip of cake by tucking the cake into the roll and continuing to roll tightly. Don't be concerned if the cake cracks a bit in the beginning. Place the rolled cake upright in the middle of the serving platter so that the flat edge is facing up and you can see the spiral on top. Then take the second strip of cake and wrap it around the first rolled piece of cake. Continue with the third and fourth piece, wrapping the cake around in a spiral pattern. Once you've rolled all the cake, frost the outside of the cake with the remaining frosting, making sure to leave the top of the cake exposed for everyone to see. Sprinkle some of the remaining pistachios on top of the cake, to help cover up any big holes or gaps in the cake roll, and then gently press the remaining pistachios around the outisde of the cake, over the frosting. Serve immediately, or refrigerate for up to 4 days, bringing to room temperature before serving.

PEANUT BUTTER AND JAM ROLLED CAKE WITH CHOPPED ROASTED PEANUTS

Make the cake as directed. Substitute ¾ cup (195 g) room temperature smooth peanut butter for the chocolate , and use ¼ cup hot water in place of the coffee.

Make the buttercream, using light brown sugar in place of the dark brown sugar. Fold in ¼ cup (65 g) room temperature smooth peanut butter at the very end.

When you assemble the cake, after spreading the buttercream onto the cake layer (before rolling), spread ¾ cup (245 g) good-quality store-bought strawberry jam (or grape jelly or whatever preserve you prefer) onto the buttercream. Sprinkle ½ cup (80 g) chopped unsalted peanuts over the jam and then roll and assemble the cake as directed, using another 1 cup (160 g) chopped unsalted peanuts in place of the pistachios.

MEYER LEMON ITALIAN CREAM CAKE WITH LEMON CUSTARD AND STRAWBERRY BUTTERCREAM

makes one 9-inch layer cake; 16 servings

Despite making over twenty desserts for my annual holiday dessert party, a version of this cake is almost always present, otherwise my guests would complain. It is so beloved that I've had friends request it as their wedding cake! This cake is one of those special-occasion labor-of-love cakes. It's not too difficult to make but there are a lot of components; trust me when I say it's worth it in the end! Make sure to read through all the instructions before starting so that you know what you're getting into, and prep all the ingredients beforehand. I usually make this cake over two days. Day one has me making the lemon custard and leaving it overnight in the fridge. Then I make the cake layers and frosting and assemble the whole thing the next day. But you can do it all in one day if you want. Keep in mind if you do split it into two days, you will need five 9-inch cake pans, as the two custard layers will be in the fridge while you make the three cake layers.

CAKE BATTER

2 small Meyer lemons (each about the size of a large egg)

1¼ cups heavy cream

8 large eggs, separated

¼ teaspoon cream of tartar

3 cups (600 g) granulated sugar, divided

¾ cup (170 g or 1½ sticks) unsalted butter, at room temperature

¾ cup (130 g) vegetable shortening

1½ teaspoons vanilla extract

1½ teaspoons baking soda

1½ teaspoons kosher salt

3 cups (360 g) cake flour

MAKE THE CAKE BATTER

Preheat the oven to 325°F. Coat three 9-inch round cake pans with cooking spray and then line the bottom of each pan with a round of parchment paper.

Zest the Meyer lemons into a bowl and set aside. Juice the Meyer lemons and add the liquid to the cream in the measuring cup or in a bowl. Stir and set aside to thicken. Place the egg whites and cream of tartar in the bowl of a stand mixer fitted with the whisk attachment. Whisk on high speed until soft peaks form. With the mixer still on, slowly sprinkle in ¾ cup (150 g) of the sugar and continue to whip until the whites become glossy. Turn the mixer off, scoop the whites out into a large bowl, and set aside.

Place the butter, shortening, the remaining 2¼ cups (450 g) sugar, the vanilla, baking soda, salt, and the reserved zest in the mixer bowl (no need to clean it) and switch to the paddle attachment. Beat until light and fluffy. Add the egg yolks, one at a time, waiting for each yolk to incorporate before adding the next. Occasionally stop the mixer and scrape down the sides of the bowl. The batter should look thick and rich.

LEMON CUSTARD

2¼ cups heavy cream

Zest of 4 lemons

6 large eggs

3 large egg yolks (reserve the whites for the buttercream)

1 cup plus 2 tablespoons (225 g) granulated sugar

1 cup plus 2 tablespoons fresh lemon juice

5 tablespoons cornstarch

STRAWBERRY ITALIAN MERINGUE BUTTERCREAM

6 large egg whites

¼ teaspoon cream of tartar

⅛ teaspoon kosher salt

2 cups (400 g) granulated sugar, divided

4 cups (1 pound or 455 g) fresh strawberries

1 teaspoon balsamic vinegar

2½ cups (570 g or 5 sticks) unsalted butter, at room temperature

TO ASSEMBLE

4 cups (1 pound or 455 g) fresh strawberries

Add one-third of the flour and mix on medium-low speed until incorporated. Add half the thickened cream and beat to incorporate. Repeat, alternating between the flour and the cream, ending with the flour. Remove the bowl from the mixer and scoop about 1 cup of the whipped egg whites into the cake batter. Gently fold it in by hand with a large spatula to lighten the batter. Once the initial egg whites are incorporated, scoop out more egg whites and repeat until all the egg whites are folded in.

Divide the batter among the prepared pans (about 665 g each) and bake until a toothpick inserted in the middle of a cake comes out clean, 30 to 35 minutes. Check the cakes after 20 minutes and rotate them if they are baking unevenly. Let cool in the pans until just warm to the touch, 15 to 20 minutes, and then unmold onto wire racks to cool completely. The cake layers will rise impressively while baking and then deflate a bit as they cool.

MAKE THE LEMON CUSTARD

Lower the oven temperature to 300°F. Coat two 9-inch round cake pans with cooking spray and then line the bottom of each pan with a round of parchment paper. Bring the cream to a boil in a medium pot. While the cream is heating, place the lemon zest, eggs, egg yolks, sugar, lemon juice, and cornstarch in a large bowl set on a damp towel (to keep it from shifting). Stir together. Once the cream is boiling, pour it over the mixture in the bowl while constantly stirring the custard with a whisk. Divide the custard between the prepared pans (about 700 g each). Bake until the center just barely moves and the edges of the custard have started to brown, 35 to 40 minutes. Immediately run a thin knife around the custard edge to help release it from the pan. Let the custard cool to room temperature in the pans, then cover and refrigerate for at least 2 hours or up to 24 hours.

MAKE THE STRAWBERRY ITALIAN MERINGUE BUTTERCREAM

Place the egg whites, cream of tartar, and salt in a clean bowl of the stand mixer fitted with the whisk attachment. Beat on high speed until soft peaks form. Slowly sprinkle in ½ cup (100 g) of the sugar and continue to whip until the egg whites look glossy. Turn off the mixer.

Cut the green tops off the strawberries, discarding the tops, and coarsely chop the strawberries into ½-inch chunks. Place the chopped strawberries (and any accumulated juice) in a medium pot along with the remaining 1½ cups (300 g) sugar. Bring to a boil, stirring constantly. Cook over high heat until the strawberries have released their juice, the sugar has dissolved, and the liquid is bubbling furiously and bright red, about 5 minutes. Remove from the heat and pour the

·······>

People always ask me if they can replace the shortening in this cake with butter. Yes, you can, but the cake won't have the same texture or crumb. Shortening gives the cake a spongy bounce that you can't get with butter, and I highly recommend it. But if you really are averse to shortening, you can certainly use all butter. Use 1¼ cups plus 2 tablespoons (170 g) butter in total and omit the shortening. The texture of the final cake will be a little heavier.

If you can't find Meyer lemons, you can substitute regular lemons.

strawberry sugar syrup through a fine-mesh strainer into another medium pot, catching all the solids. Place the strawberry solids in a food processor or blender and process into a smooth puree.

Heat the strawberry syrup over medium-high heat until it reaches 225°F (the early thread stage). Once it reaches that point, remove from the heat and turn the stand mixer with the whipped egg whites in it back on to high speed. Drizzle the strawberry sugar syrup carefully into the bowl, making sure it doesn't hit the whisk attachment or it will send the scalding hot syrup all over the place. Continue to drizzle the syrup until it is fully incorporated, then add the vinegar. Continue to beat for 8 minutes, or until the outside of the bowl is cool to the touch. Switch to the paddle attachment and reduce the mixer speed to medium-high. With the mixer running, add the butter 2 or 3 tablespoons at a time, beating until incorporated before each addition. If the frosting looks really loose and thin, the egg whites are probably still too warm. Try placing the bowl in the freezer for 10 minutes to cool it down, then continue. Once all the butter is incorporated, reduce the speed to low and add the strawberry puree. Mix until just incorporated.

ASSEMBLE THE CAKE

Place one cake layer on a cake stand or serving platter and peel off the parchment paper if you haven't already. Unmold the custard onto the cake; you may need to coax it out with a butter knife. Peel off the parchment paper. Repeat this process with the second cake layer, the second custard layer, and then the final cake layer on top. Frost the cake with the strawberry buttercream. Place whole strawberries on top of the cake around the edge for decoration. Cut the green tops off the remaining strawberries and thinly slice them. Press the strawberry slices all the way around the bottom of the cake. Serve immediately.

MANGO ITALIAN CREAM CAKE WITH PASSION FRUIT CUSTARD AND KIWI BUTTERCREAM

Omit the Meyer lemon zest and juice and instead use ½ cup (100 g) pureed mango (puree mango in a food processor or blender). Reduce the cream to 1 cup. For the custard, omit the lemon zest and replace the lemon juice with 1 cup plus 2 tablespoons (225 g) passion fruit puree (often found frozen in Latin or specialty grocery stores or online; make sure to thaw first). For the buttercream, use 4 fresh ripe kiwis (about ¾ pound or 340 g) in place of the strawberries and replace the balsamic vinegar with fresh lime juice. Assemble and decorate with half-moon slices of kiwi at the bottom of the cake.

Buttercream frosting 101

There are numerous styles of buttercream frostings. Here's a brief overview of the most popular.

American buttercream is one of the easiest and possibly the most common among home bakers. It's the frosting that I learned to make when I was a kid. It's made with just butter, powdered sugar, sometimes a little cream or milk to thin the consistency, and flavoring. You can whip it up pretty fast, but it's very sweet and doesn't have a lot of dimensional flavor. If you are going to make it, I highly recommend using good-quality European-style butter; there are so few ingredients in the recipe that the flavor of the European butter really shines. Other butters are fine but won't taste as rich.

Italian meringue buttercream is the frosting that I use for this recipe, and it's one of my favorites. It is made by drizzling a hot sugar syrup into whipped egg whites, then mixing in butter. It's a little fussier but allows you to add fruit flavors like strawberry by cooking the fruit in the syrup first. Adding hot syrup helps raise the temperature of the egg whites so they are safe for consumption. If you are really concerned about egg whites and safety, stick with Swiss meringue buttercream, which cooks the egg whites directly over a heat source.

Swiss meringue buttercream is easier to make than Italian. You place the egg whites and sugar in a double boiler and use the steam from the hot water to raise the temperature of the egg whites to 140°F (thereby killing any dangerous bacteria), then whip the meringue and add butter. I use this style of buttercream for the Chocolate and Brown Sugar Buttercream Rolled Cake with Crushed Pistachios on page 144.

French and German buttercreams are made with egg yolks instead of egg whites. Because there's usually a surplus of egg whites in pastry shops and bakeries, you rarely see these rich yellow frostings, and I don't use them in this book.

Ermine or boiled-flour buttercream is an old-fashioned frosting that is seeing a revival. It's made with a simple pudding of milk, flour, and sugar combined with whipped butter. I use it in my Smoky Butterscotch and Vanilla Cake on page 175.

MALTED MILK CHOCOLATE CAKE WITH SALTED CARAMEL FROSTING

makes one 9-inch layer cake; 12 servings

Though I always had a nostalgic soft spot for malted milk chocolate flavor, it took me a while to see its potential as an adult. To me, *malted* meant sickeningly sweet, probably because I associated it with spooning heaping mounds of Ovaltine into my milk until it was nearly syrup when I was a child. But my partner absolutely loves all things malted, so when his birthday came around a couple of years ago, I came up with this cake. It combines pretty much everything he loves about store-bought candy without being overly sweet. The coffee in the cake boosts the chocolate, and the salt in the burnt sugar–caramel frosting tempers the sweetness even further. The chopped malted milk balls add a nice touch and some childhood whimsy that says "birthday cake" no matter how old you are.

CAKE BATTER

3 ounces (85 g) milk chocolate, chopped into ½-inch chunks

1½ cups freshly brewed extra-strong coffee

1½ cups (300 g) granulated sugar

1½ cups (330 g) packed dark brown sugar

2 cups (280 g) all-purpose flour

1 cup (110 g) natural cocoa powder (not Dutch-process)

1 cup (150 g) malted milk powder

1¼ teaspoons kosher salt

1 teaspoon baking soda

¾ teaspoon baking powder

3 large eggs

1½ cups heavy cream

¾ cup vegetable oil

2 teaspoons vanilla extract

MAKE THE CAKE BATTER

Preheat the oven to 300°F. Coat three 9-inch round cake pans with cooking spray, then line the bottom of each pan with a parchment paper round. Place the chocolate in the hot coffee and stir to melt. Set aside to cool.

Combine the flour, both sugars, cocoa powder, malted milk powder, salt, baking soda, and baking powder in a large bowl. Stir vigorously with a whisk until the dry ingredients are blended and uniform in color.

Place the eggs in the bowl of a stand mixer fitted with the paddle attachment. Beat on medium-high speed until the eggs are well blended and have lightened to a pale lemon yellow color, about 2 minutes. Add the chocolate-coffee mixture, cream, oil, and vanilla and beat on medium speed for about 30 seconds, or until incorporated. Add the dry ingredients, roughly 1 cup at a time, beating to incorporate after each addition before adding the next cupful, until all the dry ingredients are incorporated.

Divide the batter among the prepared pans and bake until a toothpick inserted in the center comes out clean, 35 to 45 minutes. Rotate the pans if you need to after 25 to 30 minutes. Once you remove the cakes from the oven, immediately run a thin knife around the outside edge of the cake to help release it from the pan.

SALTED CARAMEL FROSTING

¾ cup (150 g) granulated sugar

¾ cup heavy cream

1 tablespoon vanilla extract

2¼ cups (510 g or 4½ sticks) unsalted butter, at room temperature

1½ teaspoons kosher salt

3 cups (345 g) powdered sugar

TO ASSEMBLE

2 cups (215 g) malted milk chocolate balls, such as Whoppers

1 teaspoon flaky salt, such as Maldon

Let cool in the pans for about 10 minutes, and then unmold the layers and let them cool completely on wire racks.

MAKE THE SALTED CARAMEL FROSTING

Place the granulated sugar in a large heavy-bottomed saucepan with a silver bottom (to help you judge the caramel color; avoid nonstick). Cook over high heat, stirring occasionally with a heatproof silicone spatula or wooden spoon. As the sugar melts, continue to stir and shake the pan so all the sugar melts evenly. Once the sugar starts to brown, turn the heat off and let the residual heat of the pan continue to caramelize the sugar. You want the caramel to turn a dark golden brown, closer to chestnut but not mahogany black. If the caramel has stopped browning or isn't dark enough, turn the heat back on to low to give it a nudge. It's better to go slow and let the residual heat caramelize the sugar, as you can always make the caramel darker, but you can't go backward and if you burn the sugar, you have to start all over. Once the sugar has reached the appropriate color, carefully pour a little of the cream into the pot. It will steam and bubble up. Continue to drizzle the cream into the pot a little at a time, stirring with a wooden spoon. Stir in the vanilla. If there are any hard chunks of caramel, place the pan back on the stove and cook over medium-low heat, stirring constantly, until the caramel smoothes out and the hard chunks dissolve. Remove from the heat and let cool until the pan is cool to the touch, about 30 minutes.

Place the butter in the bowl of the stand mixer fitted with the paddle attachment and add the salt. Beat on medium-high speed until fluffy, about 2 minutes. Sift in about half of the powdered sugar and beat to incorporate. Sift and beat in the remaining powdered sugar. Scrape down the sides of the bowl, then add the caramel and beat to incorporate, about 2 minutes. Cover and refrigerate for 45 minutes, or until the frosting is stiff. Beat it briefly to loosen it up before frosting the cake.

ASSEMBLE THE CAKE

Frost and stack the cake layers, and then frost the top and sides of the cake. Chop the malt balls and press them onto the sides of the cake. Sprinkle the finishing salt on top of the cake in a ring around the edge.

alternative

DEEP DARK CHOCOLATE CAKE WITH ERMINE VANILLA BEAN FROSTING AND ROASTED CACAO NIBS

Make the cake as directed, but substitute the milk chocolate with dark chocolate. Omit the malted milk powder. Increase the all-purpose flour to 2½ cups (350 g) and the cocoa powder to 1½ cups (135 g). Replace the cream with buttermilk. Assemble and bake the cake layers as directed.

Use the Vanilla Ermine Frosting recipe from the Smoky Butterscotch and Vanilla Cake on page 175.

Assemble and frost the cake as directed. Sprinkle ¼ cup (35 g) chopped cacao nibs on top of the cake in a ring around the edge as decoration.

8-LAYER ORANGE-SCENTED SMITH ISLAND CAKE

makes 1 layer cake; 12 servings

Smith Island cake in an intriguing dessert, with thin layers of sumptuous chocolate sandwiched between eight thin layers of yellow cake. It's a cake for chocolate lovers. The cake is named after an island in the Chesapeake Bay and is the official dessert of the state of Maryland. It's not hard to make from a technical standpoint, though it can be repetitive, especially if you only have two 9-inch pans, in which case you will need to bake the cake layers in four batches. The key to making the cake is a little bit of time and an offset spatula if you have one (though you certainly can make it with just a spoon or butter knife). But if you're a fan of fudgy chocolate frosting, this cake, with its high frosting-to-cake ratio, is the one for you.

CAKE BATTER

3⅓ cups (465 g) all-purpose flour

2⅓ cups (465 g) granulated sugar, divided

2 teaspoons baking powder

1 teaspoon kosher salt

½ teaspoon baking soda

½ cup plus 5 tablespoons (190 g) unsalted butter, melted

¼ cup extra-virgin olive oil

1 cup whole milk

Zest of 1 large orange

⅓ cup fresh-squeezed orange juice

1 tablespoon vanilla extract

4 large eggs, separated, plus 4 large egg yolks

¼ teaspoon cream of tartar

MAKE THE CAKE BATTER

Preheat the oven to 350°F. Coat two to four 9-inch round cake pans (depending on how many you have) with cooking spray, then line the bottom of each pan with a round of parchment paper and lightly spray the paper.

Combine the flour, 2 cups (400 g) of the sugar, the baking powder, salt and baking soda in a medium bowl. Vigorously stir with a balloon whisk until the ingredients are well distributed.

In a separate bowl, combine the butter, oil, milk, orange zest, juice, vanilla, and the 8 egg yolks. Using a whisk, vigorously stir the wet ingredients together until they are uniform in color.

Place the 4 egg whites and the cream of tartar in the bowl of a stand mixer fitted with the whisk attachment. Beat on high speed until soft peaks start to form and the egg whites are opaque. With the mixer still on, sprinkle the remaining ⅓ cup (67 g) sugar into the egg whites, continuing to beat until the sugar is incorporated and the egg whites are glossy white. Scoop the egg whites out into a separate bowl.

Add the dry ingredients to the stand mixer bowl (no need to wash it). With the whisk attachment still on the mixer, start to mix the dry ingredients on low speed. Drizzle the wet ingredients into the bowl, increasing the speed slightly

·······>

CHOCOLATE FUDGE FROSTING

12 ounces (350 g) bittersweet chocolate (about 70% cacao)

1¼ cups heavy cream

1¼ cups (250 g) granulated sugar

1½ teaspoons vanilla extract

¼ teaspoon kosher salt

10 tablespoons (140 g or 1¼ sticks) unsalted butter, at room temperature

to medium-low as more liquid is poured in. Once all the liquid is added, stop the mixer, scrape down the sides of the bowl and the whisk with a spatula to make sure there aren't any dry spots, then mix for another 15 seconds, or until the batter is well mixed.

Remove the bowl from the mixer and scoop about one-third of the egg whites into the batter. Fold in the egg whites with a large flexible spatula. Once incorporated, add the rest of the egg whites in two more batches, folding to incorporate after each addition.

Measure out 1 cup of the batter (about 200 g) and spread the batter in a thin layer in the bottom of one of the prepared pans, using an offset spatula if you have one, or the back of a spoon or butter knife if you don't. Repeat with the second cake pan (and the additional pans, if using). Bake until the edges of the cake are golden brown and the center springs back when you touch it, 9 to 10 minutes. Let cool in the pan for 5 minutes, then run a thin butter knife around the edge of the pan and invert the cake onto a wire rack. Carefully peel off the parchment paper and discard. No need to invert the cake layers; just let them cool upside down.

Wipe the edges of the pan with a damp paper towel, scraping off any brown bits from the cake. Spray each cake pan again with cooking spray, line it with parchment paper, and lightly spray the parchment as before. Fill the pans with another 1 cup of batter and bake for 9 to 10 minutes. Repeat as needed for a total of 8 cake layers. Let all the layers cool completely before assembling (the cake layers are so thin that this shouldn't take long).

MAKE THE CHOCOLATE FUDGE FROSTING

Chop the chocolate into ¼-inch chunks. Place in a large microwave-safe bowl and microwave for 30 seconds. Stir and then microwave for another 30 seconds. The chocolate will still be mostly solid but warmed up and the chocolate touching the sides of the bowl should be melty. Place the cream, sugar, vanilla, and salt in a medium saucepan and heat until the sugar has dissolved and the cream is on the verge of boiling. Pour the hot cream over the chocolate and stir with a whisk until all the chocolate has melted and it is smooth.

Add the butter, about 2 tablespoons at a time, stirring with the whisk to melt the butter after each addition. Once all the butter has been added and melted in and the chocolate frosting is shiny and smooth, cover the bowl and refrigerate for 1 hour. If the frosting becomes too stiff to spread, let it sit at room temperature for 5 to 10 minutes, then stir with a whisk before using.

Once the cake layers are cool, assemble the cake by placing one layer on a cake platter or stand. Add about ¼ cup frosting and spread it to the edges of the cake. Place another cake layer on top of the frosting and repeat until you have all 8 layers stacked with frosting in between. Frost the top and sides with the remaining frosting. Let sit at room temperature for 1 hour to set, then serve.

alternative

8-LAYER TRADITIONAL SMITH ISLAND CAKE

Replace the milk and orange juice in the cake with 1⅓ cups buttermilk and omit the orange zest. Use vegetable oil in place of the olive oil. Make, bake, and assemble as instructed.

Folding in egg whites or whipped cream

The act of folding egg whites or whipped cream into batter or frosting is a common one but tends to intimidate beginning bakers. The idea is to incorporate the whipped ingredient into the batter or frosting without deflating it. If you just vigorously stir the whipped egg whites or cream, all the air trapped in them will be lost, thus defeating the purpose of whipping them in the first place.

To fold whipped ingredients into a batter, start by first adding a scoop of the whipped whites or cream, about one-third, to the batter or frosting. This allows you to lighten the otherwise heavier batter, making it easier to then fold in the rest of the whipped whites or cream. Using a large flexible spatula, scoop down the sides of the bowl and lift up some of the batter from the bottom of the bowl, folding it over the whipped ingredient. Give the bowl a quarter turn and repeat, gently folding the batter or frosting over the whipped whites or cream. Continue doing this until the whipped ingredients are melded into the batter or frosting. Repeat with the remaining egg whites, folding in the same manner to incorporate.

THE MODERN LANE CAKE

makes one 9-inch layer cake; 12 servings

The Lane cake is a classic southern layer cake created in Alabama by Emma Rylander Lane: Four layers of white cake sandwiching three layers of bourbon-soaked dried fruit, coconut, and nuts in a custard, all wrapped up in a boiled-sugar frosting. Back in 1898, when Emma Lane submitted her cake to the county fair (and won first prize), it was rather difficult to make. There were no electric mixers (meaning you needed serious arm muscle to hand-whip all those egg whites!), and wood-burning stoves were the norm. Nowadays, the mixer does the hard work with those egg whites and there's no need to drag wood in from the backyard for the oven. My own twist on the cake separates the components of the classic filling into three distinct layers of flavor, subtly scents the cake with a touch of orange zest, and adds a hint of honey to the frosting to modernize and bring the entire cake together. But I've kept the bourbon in the custard, because some things you just don't mess with.

CAKE BATTER

8 large egg whites (reserve the yolks for the filling)

½ teaspoon cream of tartar

2 cups (400 g) granulated sugar, divided

1 cup (225 g or 2 sticks) unsalted butter, at room temperature

4 teaspoons baking powder

2 teaspoons vanilla extract

1 teaspoon orange zest

½ teaspoon kosher salt

¼ teaspoon ground nutmeg

3½ cups (420 g) cake flour

1 cup whole milk

MAKE THE CAKE BATTER

Preheat the oven to 350°F and lightly coat two 9-inch round cake pans with cooking spray. Line the bottom of each pan with a round of parchment paper.

Combine the egg whites and cream of tartar in the bowl of a stand mixer fitted with the whisk attachment. Turn the mixer on and gradually increase the speed to high. Beat on high speed until soft peaks form. Lower the speed to medium-high and slowly sprinkle in ½ cup (100 g) of the sugar, until all the sugar is incorporated and the egg whites are glossy. Scoop the egg whites into another large bowl and set aside.

To the stand mixer bowl (no need to clean it), add the butter, the remaining 1½ cups (300 g) sugar, baking powder, vanilla, orange zest, salt, and nutmeg. Switch to the paddle attachment and beat on medium speed until the ingredients are fluffy and uniform in color (with no butter streaks) and cling to the sides of the bowl, about 2 minutes. Add the flour and milk in four batches, alternating between the flour and milk and waiting for the ingredients to be absorbed into the batter before each addition. Scrape down the sides of the bowl between additions as well.

······>

FILLING

1 cup (140 g) mixed dried fruit (raisins, dried cherries, apricots, cranberries, blueberries, or whatever you want)

1 cup (100 g) pecans

1 cup (85 g) unsweetened shredded coconut

1 cup (200 g) granulated sugar

8 large egg yolks

½ cup (115 g or 1 stick) unsalted butter

1 teaspoon vanilla extract

½ teaspoon kosher salt

½ cup bourbon (or brandy)

1 tablespoon cornstarch

FROSTING

1½ cups (300 g) granulated sugar

2 tablespoons honey

1 teaspoon vanilla extract

¼ teaspoon kosher salt

4 large egg whites

Remove the bowl from the mixer stand and scoop about one-quarter of the egg whites into the batter. Using a large spatula, fold the egg whites into the batter to lighten it. Repeat with the remaining egg whites in three more batches, folding between each addition, until all the egg whites are folded in.

Divide the batter between the prepared pans (about 750 g each). Bake until a toothpick inserted in the center comes out clean and the cake bounces back when you press it, 30 to 35 minutes. Let cool for 10 minutes in the pan, then unmold the cake layers onto wire cooling racks and carefully peel off the parchment paper. Let cool completely before assembling.

MAKE THE FILLING

Chop the dried fruit and place it in a heatproof bowl. Toast the pecans in a dry skillet over medium heat, stirring constantly, until they have darkened slightly and smell fragrant. Pour onto a cutting board and coarsely chop, then transfer them to a different heatproof bowl. Toast the coconut in the same dry skillet (no need to clean it) over medium heat, stirring constantly, until the coconut flakes have turned golden brown. Pour them into a third heatproof bowl.

Make the custard by placing the sugar, egg yolks, butter, vanilla, and salt in a medium saucepan. Measure out the bourbon in a glass measuring cup and then add the cornstarch to the bourbon, stirring to dissolve the starch. Pour the bourbon into the saucepan, scraping out any starch that might have sunk to the bottom of the cup into the saucepan as well. Cook over medium-low heat, stirring constantly with a whisk, until the custard has thickened, 5 to 7 minutes. Pour the custard through a fine-mesh sieve, discarding any solids. Divide the custard among the three bowls (about 170 g per bowl) with the fruit, pecans, and coconut, stirring each until well mixed. Set aside until ready to assemble.

MAKE THE FROSTING

Place the sugar, honey, salt, vanilla, and egg whites in a clean bowl of the stand mixer. Set the bowl over a pot of simmering water and stir with a whisk until the sugar is dissolved and the temperature reaches 140°F. Attach the bowl to the mixer, fitted with the whisk attachment, and beat on high speed until firm peaks form.

To assemble the cake, first split each cake in half horizontally to make four layers. Place one layer on a cake stand or serving platter. Spread the dried fruit filling over the top of the cake, making sure the filling is evenly distributed all the way to the edges. Place the second layer on top of the filling and spread the coconut filling over the top. Place the third layer over the coconut filling. Spread the pecan layer over the top. Set the final layer over the pecan filling. Spread and swirl the frosting over the top and sides of the cake. Serve immediately, or refrigerate overnight for the custard and bourbon to infuse the cake layers.

alternative

MODERN LADY BALTIMORE CAKE

First, coarsely chop ½ cup (75 g) black raisins, ½ cup (75 g) golden raisins, and 8 (65 g) dried figs and place in a medium bowl. Add ½ cup brandy or bourbon, cover, and let sit overnight for the brandy to be absorbed.

Make the cake batter as directed, but divide it among three 9-inch round pans (greased and lined in the same manner). Bake until a toothpick inserted in the center comes out clean, 20 to 25 minutes. Let cool for 10 minutes, then invert onto a wire rack and carefully peel off the parchment paper. Let cool completely.

Skip making the custard filling. When you are ready to assemble the cake, toast 1 cup pecans as directed and then chop them. Make the frosting, increasing the amounts to 2¼ cups (450 g) granulated sugar, 3 tablespoons honey, ½ teaspoon kosher salt, 6 egg whites, and 1½ teaspoons vanilla extract. Scoop out about 2½ cups of the frosting and set aside. Split the remaining frosting into two bowls. Stir the brandy-soaked dried fruit into one bowl of frosting, and the toasted pecans into the other.

Place one cake layer on a cake stand or serving platter. Spread the fruit frosting onto the cake layer and place another cake layer on top of it. Spread the pecan frosting onto the cake layer and place the last cake layer on top. Frost the top and the sides of the cake with the reserved frosting.

Splitting cake layers ....

To split cake layers, you'll need a long serrated knife, preferably one that is at least 10 to 12 inches.

Insert 8 toothpicks halfway up the side of the cake layer where you want to split the cake, all the way around. Using the toothpicks as guides, carefully slice the cake horizontally, holding down the top of the cake with your other hand while you saw gently through the cake.

Now carefully slide a thin, rigid piece of cardboard between the sliced cake and remove the top layer. Repeat with other layers.

As always, the more you split cake layers, the easier it will be and the more comfortable you will get.

RASPBERRY AND ALMOND BATTENBERG CHECKERBOARD CAKE

makes 1 cake; 8 servings

Apparently Battenberg cakes are common and popular over in Britain, most often served with afternoon tea. According to my friend Jane, who lives in London, most Brits don't bother making it and just buy it at the supermarket, where it's stocked next to the sponge cake. Being a rather ignorant American, I was oblivious to its existence until I came across a reference to it in the book *The Eyre Affair* by Jasper Fforde, a delightfully kooky novel that takes place in an alternate-universe Britain. Even though the plot revolves around alternative dimensions, time travel, and stolen literary manuscripts, the one thing that stuck out in my head was "What the heck is a Battenberg cake?" With a dash of raspberry extract, some punchy almond extract, and the addition of cream cheese to give the cake some tender tang and flavor in each bite, this cake would be perfect in an alternative-universe America, one where Battenberg cakes are as common as cupcakes in my grocery store.

CAKE BATTER

6 large eggs

3 large egg yolks

6 tablespoons heavy cream

1½ teaspoons kosher salt

4½ cups (900 g) granulated sugar

2½ cups (510 g or 4½ sticks) unsalted butter, at room temperature

8 ounces (225 g or 1 brick) cream cheese, at room temperature

1 teaspoon vanilla extract

4½ cups (630 g) all-purpose flour

1 cup (105 g) almond meal

2 teaspoons raspberry extract

¼ teaspoon red liquid food coloring

2 teaspoons almond extract

MAKE THE CAKE BATTER

Preheat the oven to 300°F. Coat two 5 x 9-inch loaf pans with cooking spray, then line the bottom and sides with parchment paper, leaving 1 inch of overhang on the long sides. Combine the eggs, egg yolks, cream, and salt in a bowl and stir vigorously with a whisk until evenly colored.

Place the sugar, butter, cream cheese, and vanilla in the bowl of a stand mixer fitted with the paddle attachment. Beat on medium speed until the mixture is fluffy and pale white, about 3 minutes. Scrape down the sides of the bowl and turn the mixer back on to medium-low speed. Slowly drizzle the egg mixture into the bowl, stopping occasionally to scrape down the sides and let the egg incorporate. Once all the egg is incorporated, scrape down the sides of the bowl again (the batter will look a little curdled; that's fine).

Whisk together the flour and almond meal in a large bowl until uniform in color and thoroughly blended. With the mixer on low speed, add the flour mixture to the batter in three additions, mixing to incorporate and scraping down the sides of the bowl between additions.

·······>

TO ASSEMBLE

1 (12-ounce) jar raspberry jam

¼ cup (30 g) powdered sugar

14 ounces (400 g) marzipan

Silver dragées (optional)

Scoop half the batter (about 1,375 g) into the bowl that had the flour in it. Add the raspberry extract and food coloring and stir with a large spatula until the batter is a uniform pink color. Scrape into one of the lined loaf pans.

To the batter in the stand mixer bowl, add the almond extract. Beat to incorporate fully, then scrape into the other lined loaf pan. Bake both pans until a toothpick inserted in the center of each cake comes out clean, 1 hour 40 minutes to 1 hour 50 minutes.

Let cool in the pans for 15 minutes, then use a butter knife to loosen the cakes from the sides of the pan and use the overhanging parchment paper to lift the cakes out of the pans. Move to a wire rack to cool completely.

ASSEMBLE THE CAKE

Trim all the sides of the cakes to square them off. Cut each loaf into thirds lengthwise so you have 3 long, flat pieces. Then cut each long, flat piece in half lengthwise to make 6 long, square logs. Use a ruler if you need to, but make sure each log is the same shape and size, about 1 x 1 x 7 inches.

Take one log of the raspberry cake and brush raspberry jam on top and on one long side. Lay an almond log next to it, pressed up against the jam side. Brush the top and exposed side of the almond cake log with raspberry jam. Press a raspberry log on the jam side of the almond cake and brush the top of the raspberry cake log with raspberry jam. Build a second layer on top of the first, alternating the cakes to create a checkerboard pattern and using the jam as glue to secure the pieces together, then repeat with a third layer, alternating again. You'll have extra cake, so just consider that a treat to nibble on as you assemble this cake.

Dust a clean surface with the powdered sugar and then roll out the marzipan to a rough 7 x 10-inch rectangle, about ¼ inch thick. Carefully drape it over the cake and smooth it out with your hands. Trim any overhanging marzipan. If desired, lightly press a butter knife on the top of the marzipan to make a crisscross pattern. Place a single silver dragée where the indentations meet and press down gently to adhere. The cake will keep for about 3 days under a cake dome at room temperature, or you can freeze leftovers for up to 1 month.

ORANGE AND PISTACHIO CHECKERBOARD CAKE

Omit the almond extract, raspberry extract, and red food coloring from the cake batter. Process 1 cup (150 g) shelled unsalted pistachios in a food processor or blender until crushed into a powder (or at least very small bits); set aside. Omit the almond meal and use 4 cups all-purpose flour. Divide the batter into two bowls. To one bowl of batter, add 1 cup (140 g) all-purpose flour, the zest of 1 navel or Valencia orange, 2 tablespoons Cointreau or Grand Marnier, ¼ teaspoon yellow liquid food coloring, and 1 drop red food coloring. Stir to incorporate. Into the other bowl of batter, stir the ground pistachios and 2 drops green food coloring. Bake as directed.

To assemble the cake, replace the raspberry jam with the Mandarin Orange Marmalade on page 63 (try to remove any large chunks of orange peel as you spread it over the cake), and then cover with marzipan as directed.

APRICOT AND BING CHERRY COCOA CRUMB COFFEE CAKE

makes 1 coffee cake; 12 servings

Every year I go back to Indiana in the summertime with my partner, A.J., to visit his family. They've become my second family, quirks and all. I tend to bake at least one or two things during our trip there. It's a funny thing, baking in someone else's home: trying to figure out what ingredients are in the pantry, what pans they have, and what I can get at the local store. One time, I whipped up a version of this coffee cake using the last of the summer fruit from the local grocery store. My adopted family was pretty thrilled with it, especially A.J., who practically inhaled the leftovers the next day.

APRICOT MIX-IN

5 medium (225 g) ripe apricots

½ cup (110 g) packed dark brown sugar

1 tablespoon cornstarch

2 teaspoons vanilla extract

CAKE BATTER

3 cups (420 g) all-purpose flour

½ cup (65 g) almond meal

4 teaspoons baking powder

1 teaspoon kosher salt

1½ cups (300 g) granulated sugar

½ cup (115 g or 1 stick) unsalted butter, at room temperature

2 teaspoons vanilla extract

½ teaspoon noyaux extract or almond extract (see note, opposite)

2 large eggs

1 cup buttermilk

4 cups (1 pound or 455 g) fresh or frozen cherries, pitted and halved

MAKE THE APRICOT MIX-IN

Peel and cut the apricots into 1-inch chunks. Place the apricots in a medium saucepan with the brown sugar and cornstarch. Cook over medium-high heat until the apricot juices start to thicken a bit and the fruit starts to break down, about 5 minutes. Remove from the heat, stir in the vanilla, and let cool.

MAKE THE CAKE BATTER

Preheat the oven to 350°F. Coat a 9 x 13-inch baking pan with cooking spray and line the bottom and sides with parchment paper, leaving 2 inches of overhang on either side of the pan.

Place the flour, almond meal, baking powder, and salt in a medium mixing bowl. Vigorously stir together with a balloon whisk until uniform in color and well blended. Place the sugar and butter in the bowl of a stand mixer fitted with the paddle attachment. Beat on medium speed until the butter is lighter in color, creamy, and clings to the side of the bowl, about 1 minute. Add the vanilla and noyaux extracts and beat for an additional 30 seconds to incorporate. Add the eggs, one a time, beating until the first egg is incorporated before adding the second one.

Add half the dry ingredients and beat on low speed, increasing the speed to medium as the dry ingredients incorporate. Add the buttermilk and repeat. Beat in the remaining dry ingredients. Gently fold in the cherries by hand with a large rubber spatula, then scrape the batter into the prepared baking dish and spread

1 cup (140 g) all-purpose flour

⅔ cup (145 g) packed dark brown sugar

½ cup (55 g) chopped almonds

2 tablespoons natural cocoa powder
(not Dutch-process)

1 teaspoon ground cinnamon

½ teaspoon kosher salt

½ cup (115 g or 1 stick) cold
unsalted butter

evenly. Spoon the apricot mix-in over the cake batter and use a butter knife to marble and swirl the cake batter and apricot mix-in together.

MAKE THE COFFEE CAKE TOPPING

Combine the flour, brown sugar, almonds, cocoa powder, cinnamon, and salt in a medium mixing bowl. Cut the butter into ½-inch chunks and sprinkle over the ingredients. Using your fingers, squeeze and break up the butter until the butter has been incorporated and the topping starts to hold together in pebble-size chunks. Sprinkle the topping over the cake batter. Bake until a toothpick inserted in the center comes out clean (you may have to pick a few spots, as you more than likely will hit a cherry the first time), 50 to 60 minutes.

✱ Noyaux extract is basically homemade almond extract, made from the pits of summer stone fruit like apricots, cherries, and plums. You can make it by cracking open the pits of any of those fruits, picking out the inner kernels, and then soaking those kernels in vodka. To crack open the pit, place it between paper towels, whack it with a hammer, pull the kernel out, and repeat with 30 to 40 more pits. The more kernels you get,

the more intense the flavor and the less time you will need to steep it. Then put the kernels in a mason jar and add about 2 cups vodka. Let it steep for a month or so, occasionally shaking the jar. Be aware that the extract does contain trace amounts of cyanide, which freaks some people out, but in such a tiny amount that it's harmless. You can also use store-bought almond extract.

alternative

PEACH AND BLUEBERRY COFFEE CAKE WITH PECAN CRUMB TOPPING

Make the peach mix-in, substituting 2 medium ripe peaches for the apricots. Make the cake batter as directed, using 4 cups (2 pints or 630 g) fresh blueberries instead of cherries.

Make the crumb topping, omitting the cocoa powder, increasing the cinnamon to 2 teaspoons, adding ½ teaspoon ground nutmeg, and using ½ cup (55 g) chopped pecans instead of almonds. Assemble and bake as directed.

LEMON-SCENTED TWEED CHIFFON CAKE WITH IRISH CREAM GLAZE

makes 1 cake; 12 servings

The first time I heard of a tweed cake, I immediately vowed to make it as soon as possible, as tweed happens to be one of my favorite fabrics in life. After all, it's the fabric of choice for Doctor Who, Giles from *Buffy the Vampire Slayer*, and basically every male character in *Downton Abbey*. Tweed cakes get their name because of the grated chocolate folded into the cake batter. When baked, the tiny flecks of chocolate create a tweed-like pattern that looks great when you slice into the cake.

CAKE BATTER

7 large eggs

½ teaspoon cream of tartar

1½ cups (300 g) granulated sugar, divided

2 cups (260 g) cake flour

2½ teaspoons baking powder

¾ teaspoon kosher salt

Zest and juice of 1 lemon
(3 tablespoons juice)

¾ cup whole milk

½ cup vegetable oil

2 teaspoons vanilla extract

½ teaspoon lemon extract (optional)

2 ounces (55 g) unsweetened chocolate, grated on the small holes of a box grater

IRISH CREAM GLAZE

¼ cup Irish cream liqueur

2 cups (230 g) powdered sugar, sifted

MAKE THE CAKE BATTER

Preheat the oven to 325°F. Separate the eggs, placing the whites in the clean bowl of a stand mixer fitted with the whisk attachment and the yolks in a large bowl. Sprinkle the cream of tartar over the egg whites and then whip on high speed until soft peaks form. With the mixer still on high speed, gently sprinkle in ½ cup (100 g) of the sugar, whipping until the egg whites are glossy white.

In another bowl, place the remaining 1 cup (200 g) sugar, the flour, baking powder, salt, and lemon zest. Stir vigorously together with a whisk until the ingredients are evenly distributed. To the bowl with the egg yolks, add the milk, oil, lemon juice, vanilla, and lemon extract if you really like the flavor of lemon (otherwise skip it). Beat with a whisk to combine.

Add the dry ingredients to the wet ingredients and beat together until well blended. Add about one-third of the whipped egg whites and fold into the batter with a large spatula to lighten. Fold in another third of the egg whites to incorporate. Add the remaining egg whites and fold to incorporate, making sure to scrape the bottom of the bowl. Scoop out one-third of the batter into a separate bowl and fold the chocolate into this smaller amount of batter.

Pour the half the plain batter into a 10-inch tube pan with a removable bottom (do not grease the pan), then layer the chocolate batter over it, and finish with the remaining plain batter. Insert a butter knife into the batter and make "figure eight" motions to marble the batter. Place the pan on a rimmed baking sheet. Bake for 40 minutes, then raise the oven temperature to 350°F and continue to bake until a toothpick inserted in the center comes out clean, 10 to 15 minutes more. Once you remove the pan from the oven, invert it with the center tube over a clean, empty wine bottle and let it cool upside down completely. Once the cake is cool, run a thin knife around the sides of the pan and remove the sides. Then run the knife under the bottom of the cake to remove it from the bottom. Place the cake on a serving platter or cake stand and brush off any loose crumbs.

MAKE THE IRISH CREAM GLAZE

Combine the Irish cream with the powdered sugar in a bowl. If the glaze seems too thick, add a little more Irish cream, ½ teaspoon at a time, until it's the right consistency. If the glaze is too thin, add powdered sugar by the tablespoon until thickened. Carefully spoon the glaze over the cake, making sure some of it drizzles down the sides of the cake and the center. Let the glaze dry for at least 30 minutes before serving.

alternative

STRAWBERRY AND LEMON CHIFFON CAKE WITH HONEY-LEMON GLAZE

Make the cake as directed, omitting the chocolate. Once the batter is made, scoop about one-third of the batter into a bowl. Crush 1½ cups (34 g) freeze-dried strawberries into a powder and add to the smaller amount of batter, along with 1 teaspoon strawberry extract. Fold to incorporate. Scrape half the remaining lemon batter into the prepared pan, then scrape the strawberry batter on top of it, then finish with the remaining lemon batter on top. Insert a butter knife into the batter and make "figure eight" motions to marble the batter. Bake as directed.

To make the honey-lemon glaze, combine 3 tablespoons fresh lemon juice and 1 tablespoon honey in a medium bowl. Using a fork, stir to dissolve the honey. Sift 2 cups (230 g) powdered sugar into the bowl and stir until combined. If the glaze isn't thick enough, add more powdered sugar, 1 tablespoon at a time, until the glaze reaches the right thickness. If the glaze is too thick, add more lemon juice, ½ teaspoon at a time. Glaze as directed.

PLUOT-CARDAMOM UPSIDE-DOWN CAKE WITH CARAMEL

makes 1 cake; 8 servings

Caramel and fruit are one of those combinations I don't think of right off the bat. Usually it's caramel and chocolate or caramel and salt. But the pairing of caramel and fruit, specifically summer stone fruit like pluots (a cross between plums and apricots), needs to get some attention as well. The razor-sharp sweetness of the caramel cuts through the juicy, soft sweetness of the pluots. This particular caramel is easy to make, and it mingles with the fruit juices to make a gorgeous glaze for the cake. It's perfect for a casual dinner party or just a warm weekday dessert at home.

CARAMEL TOPPING

4 tablespoons (60 g or ½ stick) unsalted butter

4 whole cardamom pods

1 cup (200 g) granulated sugar

4 medium firm pluots, pitted and sliced into ½-inch pieces

CAKE BATTER

6 tablespoons (85 g or ¾ stick) unsalted butter, at room temperature

¾ cup (165 g) packed dark brown sugar

½ teaspoon baking soda

¼ teaspoon kosher salt

2 teaspoons vanilla extract

½ teaspoon ground cardamom

2 large eggs

1 cup (140 g) all-purpose flour

¼ cup (35 g) almond flour

⅓ cup (75 g) plain Greek-style yogurt

MAKE THE CARAMEL TOPPING

Preheat the oven to 350°F. Place the butter and cardamom pods in a 10-inch oven-proof skillet. Heat over high heat until the butter is completely melted. Sprinkle the sugar over the melted butter and lower the heat to medium. Cook, stirring constantly, until the mixture starts to melt and then turns caramel brown. Once the sugar has melted and the caramel has formed (the butterfat will separate out; that's natural), turn the heat off and remove the cardamom pods. Carefully place the pluot slices in the caramel. The caramel might sizzle and sputter a little, so be careful! Arrange the pluot slices so they cover the bottom of the pan in an even single layer and remove from the heat.

MAKE THE CAKE BATTER

Place the butter, brown sugar, baking soda, and salt in the bowl of a stand mixer fitted with the paddle attachment. Beat on medium speed until light and fluffy, about 2 minutes. Scrape down the sides of the bowl and add the vanilla and cardamom, beating for about 15 seconds to incorporate.

Add the eggs, one at a time, mixing to make sure the first one is incorporated before adding the second. Add both flours and mix on low speed until incorporated. Scrape down the sides of the bowl and mix in the yogurt. Pour the cake batter over the pluot slices in the skillet, spreading into an even layer that covers all the fruit.

Place the skillet on a large rimmed baking sheet. Bake until a toothpick inserted in the center comes out clean, 40 to 45 minutes. Let cool for about 15 minutes. Place a flat serving platter or cake platter upside down on the skillet. Wearing oven mitts (remember, the skillet is still hot), invert the skillet and serving platter together, then remove the skillet, leaving the cake on the platter upside down. Wipe up any unsightly dribble and replace any fruit that has stuck to the pan back onto the cake. Serve warm or at room temperature.

alternative

CARAMEL AND GINGER RHUBARB UPSIDE-DOWN CAKE

Make the caramel as directed, omitting the cardamom pods. Slice 2 medium stalks of rhubarb (about ¾ pound or 350 g) and sprinkle the rhubarb over the caramel. Sprinkle ¼ cup (45 g) chopped crystallized ginger over the rhubarb. Make the cake as directed, replacing the cardamom with ground ginger. Assemble and bake as directed.

SEMOLINA AND BLOOD ORANGE CAKE WITH PISTACHIO-THYME FILLING

makes 1 bundt cake; 12 to 14 servings

I don't drink much coffee, but when I do, I always want a little bit of a snack to go along with it. Coffee for me is strictly a mid-afternoon respite from work, something I do when I have been staring at the computer for way too long and need to take a break. A classic dense coffee cake with a hint of orange and an intriguing swirl of flavor in the middle is the perfect little accompaniment to coffee (or tea). The use of semolina seems unusual, but it adds a bite and moisture to the cake that you can't get with regular flour. It's worth tracking down, but if you can't find it, try substituting cornmeal in its place. It will result in a lighter and more crumbly cake that's still quite good.

TO GREASE PAN

1 tablespoon unsalted butter, at room temperature

2 tablespoons all-purpose flour

CAKE BATTER

2 cups (280 g) all-purpose flour

¾ cup (135 g) semolina flour

2 teaspoons baking powder

1 teaspoon baking soda

3 large eggs

1 large egg yolk

½ teaspoon salt

¾ cup extra-virgin olive oil

1 teaspoon vanilla extract

Zest and juice of 2 blood oranges (6 tablespoons juice)

1½ cups (300 g) granulated sugar

¾ cup (195 g) sour cream

GREASE THE PAN

Preheat the oven to 350°F. Generously grease a standard 12-cup Bundt pan with the butter, making sure to cover all the grooves and dips of the pan. Sprinkle the buttered pan with flour, then knock out any excess. Place the pan on a rimmed baking sheet or pizza pan.

MAKE THE CAKE BATTER

Combine the flours, baking powder, and baking soda in a medium bowl. Stir vigorously with a whisk until the ingredients are evenly distributed. Place the eggs, egg yolk, and salt in a small bowl and beat with a fork until the eggs are blended and uniform in color.

Add the oil, vanilla, blood orange zest, and juice to the bowl of a stand mixer fitted with the paddle attachment. Add the sugar and beat on medium speed for about 15 seconds, or until blended. Reduce the mixer speed to low and drizzle in the eggs. Add the dry ingredients and the sour cream in four additions, alternating between the dry ingredients and the sour cream and beating until incorporated between additions.

MAKE THE FILLING

Combine the sugar, flour, thyme, pistachios, and salt in a bowl and toss together with a fork. Spoon one-third of the cake batter into the prepared pan, then spoon half the filling on top of the batter. Spread another one-third of the cake batter

FILLING

6 tablespoons (75 g) granulated sugar

1 tablespoon all-purpose flour

1½ teaspoons chopped fresh thyme

½ cup (75 g) finely chopped
unsalted pistachios

½ teaspoon kosher salt (skip if the
pistachios are salted)

GLAZE AND DECORATIONS

2 to 2½ cups (230 to 290 g) powdered
sugar, sifted

1 tablespoon Cointreau, Grand Marnier,
or orange juice

2 to 3 tablespoons whole milk

¼ cup (38 g) finely chopped unsalted
pistachios

over the filling, then spread the remaining filling over the cake batter. Spread the remaining cake batter over the filling. Bake until a skewer inserted in the center comes out clean, 40 to 50 minutes. Let cool in the pan for 30 to 45 minutes, then invert and unmold the cake onto a wire rack to cool completely.

MAKE THE GLAZE

Combine 2 cups powdered sugar, the Cointreau, and 2 tablespoons milk and whisk with a fork to combine. If the glaze seems too thin, add more powdered sugar, 1 tablespoon at a time. If the glaze seems too thick, add more milk, 1 teaspoon at a time. You want the glaze to be the consistency of Elmer's glue to achieve the drips. Spoon the glaze over the cooled cake and let it drip down the sides. Immediately sprinkle the pistachios over the top of the glaze so they stick. Let the glaze set for 1 hour before serving.

alternative

LEMON CORNMEAL CAKE WITH COCOA-ALMOND FILLING

Use 2 tablespoons butter to prep the pan. Sprinkle and press ⅓ cup (40 g) sliced almonds all over the inside of the pan, on the bottom and the sides, making sure they adhere all over to the butter. Place the pan in the refrigerator to solidify the butter and make sure the almonds stay in place.

Make the cake as directed, using ¾ cup plus 2 tablespoons (130 g) cornmeal in place of the semolina flour, ¾ cup (170 g or 1½ sticks) melted unsalted butter in place of the oil, and lemon zest and juice instead of the blood orange zest and juice.

Make the filling, mixing together ¼ cup (55 g) packed dark brown sugar, 2 tablespoons granulated sugar, 1 tablespoon natural cocoa powder (not Dutch-process), ½ teaspoon ground cardamom, and ¼ cup (30 g) sliced almonds. Assemble and bake the cake as directed. Skip the glaze and dust the cake after it cools with 1 tablespoon powdered sugar.

SMOKY BUTTERSCOTCH AND VANILLA CAKE

makes one 9-inch cake; 12 servings

Despite my sweet tooth, I've never been a fan of those yellow butterscotch candies. At the bottom of every one of my childhood Halloween candy bags lingered those cellophane-wrapped hard candies, along with a couple stray orange-and-black-wrapped peanut taffy pieces. They were always the last-resort candy, one you couldn't trade with any of your friends, that you ended up eating grudgingly after all the good pieces were consumed. But then, as an adult, I had a taste of *real* butterscotch. The combination of brown sugar and browned butter, a cousin of caramel, was revelatory to me. Here I've paired it with a touch of Lapsang Souchong tea, an Asian black tea that is dry-smoked over pine wood, giving the marble cake a slightly smoky flavor as well.

VANILLA CAKE BATTER

2 cups (400 g) granulated sugar

1¼ cups (285 g or 2½ sticks) unsalted butter, at room temperature

1 tablespoon vanilla extract

5 large eggs

2¼ cups (315 g) all-purpose flour

2 teaspoons baking powder

½ teaspoon kosher salt

½ cup (140 g) sour cream

SMOKY BUTTERSCOTCH CAKE BATTER

10 tablespoons (140 g or 1¼ sticks) unsalted butter

1 cup (220 g) packed dark brown sugar

2 teaspoons vanilla extract

2 large eggs

1 large egg yolk

MAKE THE VANILLA CAKE BATTER

Preheat the oven to 350°F. Coat three 9-inch round cake pans with cooking spray, then line the bottom of each pan with a round of parchment paper. Combine the sugar, butter, and vanilla in the bowl of a stand mixer fitted with the paddle attachment. Beat on medium speed until the butter is fluffy and sticks to the side of the bowl, about 2 minutes. Add the eggs, one at a time, beating to incorporate and scraping down the sides of the bowl after each egg before adding the next. Don't be concerned if the batter looks "broken," as it will come together with the flour. Add the flour, baking powder, and salt, mixing on medium speed until incorporated. Scrape down the sides of the bowl and add the sour cream, mixing to incorporate. Scrape the vanilla cake batter into a separate bowl.

MAKE THE SMOKY BUTTERSCOTCH CAKE BATTER

Cook the butter in a large skillet over high heat until melted. Lower the heat to medium and cook, stirring constantly, until the butterfat solids start to brown and smell fragrant. Remove from the heat and pour into the bowl of the stand mixer (no need to clean it), scraping out any brown bits as well. Add the brown sugar and vanilla and beat for 2 to 3 minutes, or until the outside of the bowl has cooled enough that it is barely warm (it doesn't have to be completely cold). Add the eggs, one at a time, then the egg yolk, beating to incorporate and scraping down the sides of the bowl after each addition. Add the flour, tea, baking powder,

·······>

1 cup plus 2 tablespoons (160 g) all-purpose flour

2 teaspoons loose Lapsang Souchong tea, ground to a powder (see note, below)

1 teaspoon baking powder

¼ teaspoon kosher salt

¼ cup (70 g) sour cream

VANILLA ERMINE FROSTING

3 cups (600 g) granulated sugar

1 cup (140 g) all-purpose flour

3 cups whole milk

1 vanilla bean or 1 tablespoon vanilla extract

3 cups (685 g or 6 sticks) unsalted butter, at room temperature

1 tablespoon vanilla extract

¾ teaspoon kosher salt

1½ teaspoons Dutch-process cocoa powder

✷ *Lapsang Souchong is an Asian smoked tea that can usually be found at upscale grocery stores, as well as at specialty tea shops and online. If you can't find it, you can always substitute a regular black tea, but you won't get the lick of smoke that you would from the Lapsang Souchong.*

✷ *Tea from a tea bag usually is ground fairly fine, but if you use loose tea, be sure to grind the tea to a powder before using. Place the tea in a clean spice or coffee grinder and process into a pow- der. You can also grind the tea manually by placing it in a mortar and pestle or in a zip-top plastic bag and crushing with a rolling pin.*

and salt and mix on medium speed until incorporated. Scrape down the sides and add the sour cream, mixing to incorporate.

Spoon the vanilla and butterscotch batters into the prepared baking pans, alternating spoonfuls of each batter. Once you've evenly distributed the batters, spread them with a knife so they fill the pans, then swirl the knife through the batter in "figure eight" movements just to marble the cake batter together. Bake until a toothpick inserted in the center comes out clean, 30 to 35 minutes. Rotate the pans after 20 minutes if needed for even baking.

MAKE THE VANILLA ERMINE FROSTING

Meanwhile, place the sugar and flour in a large pot and stir together with a whisk to combine. Add the milk and mix with the whisk to dissolve the flour and sugar. Split the vanilla bean lengthwise and scrape the seeds into the pot, then add the vanilla pod as well. Cook over medium heat, whisking constantly, until the mixture thickens into a pudding, 8 to 12 minutes. Remove from the heat and place a piece of parchment paper over the pudding, directly on the surface, to prevent a skin from forming. Let cool to room temperature.

Once the cakes are done, let cool in the pans for 15 minutes, then run a thin knife around the sides of the cake and unmold onto wire racks. Let cool completely, then peel the parchment paper off the bottom of the cakes.

To finish the frosting, place the butter, vanilla extract, and salt in a clean bowl of the stand mixer fitted with the paddle attachment. Beat on medium speed until the butter is fluffy and clings to the sides of the bowl, about 2 minutes. Remove and discard the vanilla pod from the pudding. With the mixer running on medium speed, add the cooled pudding, a tablespoon at a time, to the butter. Gradually beat in all the pudding until the frosting is smooth and creamy, about 3 minutes. If the frosting looks broken or isn't smooth, continue to beat; it will come together eventually. If the frosting is too thin, refrigerate for 10 or 15 minutes to help the butter solidify, and then beat again.

Scoop ½ cup of the frosting into a bowl and add the cocoa powder to it, mixing to form a darker frosting. Assemble the cake by placing one layer on a cake stand or serving platter. Frost the top of the cake layer with the vanilla frosting, and then place the next layer on top. Repeat, frosting each layer, then frost the top and sides of the cake. Spoon a couple dots of the cocoa frosting on top of the cake and swirl it around with a knife or spoon. Decoratively spread a little cocoa frosting around the edge of the cake as well.

STRAWBERRY AND HIBISCUS VANILLA CAKE

Preheat the oven and prep the cake pans as directed. Make one base cake batter by beating together 1¾ cups plus 2 tablespoons (425 g or 3¾ sticks) unsalted butter with 3 cups (600 g) granulated sugar and 5 teaspoons vanilla extract. Add 7 eggs and 1 egg yolk, beating until each egg is incorporated before adding the next one, scraping down the bowl between additions. Mix in 2¼ cups plus 2 tablespoons (475 g) all-purpose flour, 1 tablespoon baking powder, and ¾ teaspoon kosher salt, then add ¾ cup (210 g) sour cream and mix to incorporate.

Spoon one-third of the batter into a medium bowl. Stir in 1¼ cups (28 g) freeze-dried strawberries that have been crushed to a powder, 2 teaspoons hibiscus tea from a tea bag, ground to a powder, and 5 drops red food coloring (optional). Divide the batter among the pans as directed, alternating spoonfuls of the batters, and bake as directed.

Make the frosting as directed. Scoop out ½ cup of the frosting into a small bowl and mix in ¼ cup freeze-dried strawberries crushed to a powder. Assemble the cake as directed, using the strawberry frosting to swirl onto the top and around the edge of the cake.

Ermine frosting ....

Most buttercream frostings are made with either powdered sugar and butter (American buttercream) or with egg whites that have been whipped with sugar added (Italian meringue or Swiss meringue buttercream). Ermine frosting is a cooked-flour frosting, soft and mellow and not overly sweet or sugary. Flour, sugar, and milk are cooked on the stove to a pudding consistency and then added to the whipped butter.

Ermine frosting is a classic vintage recipe, one that used to be the standard frosting paired with red velvet cake before cream cheese became the popular frosting choice. Ermine is still not a popular frosting, though its profile is rising thanks to interest in vintage recipes and popular bakeries that use it, like Baked in Brooklyn. Though not a difficult frosting to make, the biggest drawback is waiting for the cooked pudding to cool to room temperature before adding it to the butter. For a quicker way to cool it, see my tip for Quicker Cream Pies on page 203.

THE NEAPOLITAN LAYER CAKE WITH FRESH STRAWBERRIES

makes 1 layer cake; 8 servings

Growing up, we didn't have a lot of desserts in the house, but we always seemed to have a half-eaten box of Neapolitan ice cream languishing in the back of the freezer. And when I say half eaten, I mean more like two-thirds eaten, with the chocolate and vanilla scooped out and the strawberry left behind with only a few half-hearted spoonfuls taken out. My mom refused to buy a new box of ice cream until the old one was finished, so it usually took a few weeks. I'm not sure what it is about strawberry ice cream that I'm so lukewarm about, as I love ice cream and I love fresh strawberries. And every attempt I made at a Neapolitan-flavored dessert left me feeling blah—until I realized that the solution was just to use fresh strawberries. Thus this Neapolitan layer cake was born. Think of it as the best strawberry shortcake ever.

CAKE BATTER

3 ounces (85 g) white chocolate, chopped into ¼-inch pieces

4 large eggs, separated

¼ teaspoon cream of tartar

1¾ cups (350 g) granulated sugar, divided

¾ cup (170 g or 1½ sticks) unsalted butter, at room temperature

3 teaspoons vanilla extract, divided

¼ teaspoon kosher salt

1 teaspoon baking powder

½ teaspoon baking soda

2 cups (240 g) cake flour, divided

1 cup buttermilk

¼ cup (30 g) natural cocoa powder (not Dutch-process)

MAKE THE CAKE BATTER

Preheat the oven to 350°F and lightly coat a 12 x 17-inch rimmed baking sheet with cooking spray. Place a piece of parchment paper on the bottom of the pan.

Place the white chocolate in a microwave-safe bowl and microwave for 30 seconds. Stir and then microwave for an additional 30 seconds. Stir until completely melted and smooth. Set aside to cool.

Place the egg whites and cream of tartar in the bowl of a stand mixer fitted with the whisk attachment. Whip on high speed until soft peaks start to form. Reduce the speed to medium-high and sprinkle in ¼ cup (50 g) of the sugar. Once incorporated, raise the speed to high and whip until the egg whites are shiny and hold firm peaks. Scoop the egg whites into another large bowl and switch to the paddle attachment.

Place the butter, the remaining 1½ cups (300 g) sugar, 1 teaspoon of the vanilla, and the salt in the mixer bowl (no need to clean it). Beat on medium speed until the butter is creamy and light and clings to the side of the bowl, 2 to 3 minutes, occasionally stopping the mixer to scrape down the sides of the bowl. Add the baking powder and baking soda and beat until absorbed into the batter, about 30 seconds.

·······>

1½ teaspoons powdered gelatin

3 tablespoons cold water

2 ounces (57 g) semisweet chocolate, chopped into ¼-inch chunks

3 cups cold heavy cream, divided

3 tablespoons granulated sugar

2 pints (1½ pounds or 680 g) strawberries, hulled and quartered

Chocolate shavings (optional; see note, below)

✱ *To make chocolate shavings, just run a vegetable peeler along a room-temperature chocolate bar. A "Y"-style vegetable peeler pulled flat against the surface of a large bar of chocolate will yield wider shavings, while a regular-style vegetable peeler can yield smaller shavings if you peel it across the edge of a chocolate bar or at an angle against the surface of the chocolate. Avoid super-dark chocolate (anything over 60% cacao), since darker chocolate will yield more brittle shavings.*

Add 2 of the egg yolks and beat to incorporate. Scrape down the sides of the bowl and then beat in the remaining egg yolks. Add 1 cup (120 g) of the flour and beat to incorporate, scraping down the sides of the bowl. Add the buttermilk and then another ¾ cup (90 g) flour, reserving the remaining ¼ cup (30 g) for later.

Remove the bowl from the stand mixer and add one-third of the whipped egg whites to the batter. Fold together with a large spatula to lighten. Fold in another one-third of the egg whites, then add the remaining egg whites and partially fold them in, just until the egg whites are no longer visible on top of the batter, but you still see white streaks (three or four folds of the batter).

Pour half the batter (about 525 g) into the bowl that held the egg whites (no need to clean it). Into one bowl, add the remaining ¼ cup (30 g) flour and the remaining 2 teaspoons vanilla. Fold until the flour is absorbed and there are no more streaks of egg whites. Fold the cocoa powder into the batter in the other bowl.

Place the baking sheet on the counter with a short side facing you (portrait orientation). Carefully scrape the vanilla batter onto the right half of the baking sheet. You don't need to be precise, but err on pouring the batter near the right of the rim, not near the center part. You'll spread it out later. Pour the chocolate batter onto the left half of the baking sheet.

Using an offset spatula, carefully spread the vanilla batter all the way across the right of the pan, filling the right half of the baking sheet. Wipe the spatula off with a paper towel and spread the chocolate batter over the left until it touches the vanilla batter. Make sure to fill the entire pan, with no empty spots.

Tap the bottom of the pan once or twice firmly on the counter to settle the batter, then bake until the cake springs back when you touch the center and a toothpick inserted in the center comes out clean, 20 to 25 minutes.

Let the cake cool completely in the pan. Lightly coat the back of another 13 x 18-inch baking sheet with cooking spray, then cover with a piece of parchment paper. Invert the cake onto the clean parchment paper and peel off the parchment from the bottom of the cake.

ASSEMBLE THE CAKE

Use the parchment paper to pull the cake onto a large cutting board. Trim the ends of the cake by ½ inch on all sides. Cut the cake crosswise into three even pieces roughly 5½ x 12 inches so that each piece is half chocolate and half vanilla.

·······>

Sprinkle the gelatin in a small bowl and add the water. Let sit for 5 minutes for the gelatin to soften. Microwave for 10 to 15 seconds, until liquid. Set aside to cool.

Place the chocolate in a microwave-safe bowl and microwave for 30 seconds. Repeat in 30-second intervals, stirring after each, until completely melted and smooth. Stir in 3 tablespoons of the cream and set aside to cool.

Place the remaining cream and the sugar in the bowl of the stand mixer fitted with the whisk attachment. Whip on high speed until soft peaks form. Reduce the speed to medium and, with the mixer on, drizzle the gelatin into the whipped cream. Raise the speed to medium-high and whip until firm peaks form. Stop the mixer and remove the bowl from the mixer stand. Drizzle the chocolate mixture all over the whipped cream and gently fold two or three times, swirling in the chocolate but not mixing it completely.

Place one cake layer on a serving plate and spread about 1½ cups of the whipped cream on the cake. Lay one-third of the strawberries on the whipped cream and smear a little more cream on top of the strawberries. Place another cake layer on top, rotating it 180 degrees so the chocolate and vanilla sides are reversed from the first layer. Spread with another 1½ cups whipped cream, and layer with another one-third of the strawberries and more cream. Place the last cake layer on top in the same orientation as the first layer and top with the remaining whipped cream, the rest of the strawberries, and the chocolate shavings, if using. Refrigerate until ready to serve.

alternatives

SUPER-AWESOME STRAWBERRY SHORTCAKE

Simplify this recipe by skipping the cocoa and using all-purpose flour instead of cake flour. Spread the batter in the pan as one large single-flavor cake and bake as directed. Skip the melted chocolate in the whipped cream and you'll have a super-awesome strawberry shortcake!

FRESH FRUIT NAKED LAYER CAKE

Use a different berry or fresh fruit as the filling, like blueberries, raspberries, pitted cherries, peach slices, or kiwi. You can mix the fruit layers up as well, adding one type of fruit (such as strawberries) on one layer and then another type of fruit (such as kiwi) on the second layer.

PUMPKIN ROLL WITH BERRY–CREAM CHEESE FILLING

makes 1 pumpkin roll; 8 servings

I've often thought of the standard pumpkin roll as just that—standard. It's not that I don't love a pumpkin-spiced sponge cake rolled with cream cheese. But growing up in the Midwest, the pumpkin roll was ubiquitous at every holiday potluck, next to the green bean casserole and the sweet potatoes with the marshmallows on top. It was the sort of food you ate during the holidays but didn't think too much of outside of that annual meal. So I wanted to add something special to this dessert, without losing too much of its classic taste. Turns out all I needed to do was add a little bit of berry to help brighten it up. Suddenly the pumpkin roll feels new again.

CAKE

3 large eggs, separated

¼ teaspoon cream of tartar

½ cup (100 g) granulated sugar

⅔ cup (170 g) pumpkin puree (not pumpkin pie filling)

½ cup (110 g) packed dark brown sugar

1 teaspoon vanilla extract

2 teaspoons ground cinnamon

1 teaspoon ground ginger

½ teaspoon ground allspice

¼ teaspoon ground nutmeg

1 teaspoon baking powder

¼ teaspoon kosher salt

¾ cup (105 g) all-purpose flour

MAKE THE CAKE

Preheat the oven to 350°F and coat a 10 x 15-inch jelly-roll pan with cooking spray. Line the bottom with a piece of parchment paper. Place the egg whites and cream of tartar in the bowl of a stand mixer fitted with the whisk attachment. Whisk on high speed until soft peaks form. With the mixer still on, slowly sprinkle in the granulated sugar and continue to whip until the whites become glossy. Scoop the whites into another bowl and switch to the paddle attachment.

Place the egg yolks in the mixer bowl (no need to clean it) and beat on medium speed until the yolks have thickened and turned a pale lemon color. Add the pumpkin puree, brown sugar, and vanilla and beat to incorporate. Add the cinnamon, ginger, allspice, nutmeg, baking powder, and salt and mix until the batter absorbs the dry ingredients and is uniform in color. Scrape down the sides of the bowl with a spatula and add the flour. Beat until the flour is incorporated.

Remove the bowl from the mixer stand and add half of the egg whites. Gently fold the egg whites into the batter to lighten. Fold in the rest of the egg whites. Spread the batter in the prepared pan with an offset spatula. Bake until a toothpick inserted in the center comes out clean and the cake springs back when you touch it in the center, 12 to 14 minutes. Let cool in the pan for 5 minutes.

·······>

BERRY SPREAD

¾ cup (3 ounces or 85 g) fresh
or frozen raspberries

¾ cup (3 ounces or 85 g) fresh
or frozen blueberries

¼ cup (50 g) granulated sugar

1 tablespoon honey

1 tablespoon cornstarch

1 teaspoon balsamic vinegar

TO ROLL THE CAKE

Powdered sugar

CREAM CHEESE FILLING

16 ounces (455 g or 2 bricks) cream
cheese, at room temperature

½ cup (115 g or 1 stick) unsalted butter,
at room temperature

1 cup (115 g) powdered sugar

1 tablespoon honey

½ teaspoon vanilla extract

MAKE THE BERRY SPREAD

Meanwhile, combine the berries, sugar, honey, and cornstarch in a medium saucepan. Cook over medium heat, stirring constantly with a silicone spatula, until most of the berries have popped and the juices have thickened, about 5 minutes. Stir in the vinegar and set aside to cool.

ROLL THE CAKE

While the cake is cooling for 5 minutes, generously dust a clean surface with powdered sugar. Place a clean kitchen towel on top of the sugar and dust the towel with powdered sugar as well. Once the cake has cooled for 5 minutes in the pan (it should still be warm), invert the cake onto the kitchen towel, remove the pan, and peel off the parchment paper. Roll the cake up in the towel from the short end, making a 10-inch-long log roll with the towel rolled into it. Move to a wire rack and let cool for about 1 hour, still in the towel.

MAKE THE CREAM CHEESE FILLING

Combine the cream cheese, butter, powdered sugar, honey, and vanilla in the clean bowl of a stand mixer fitted with the paddle attachment. Beat together until smooth. Set aside until the cake has cooled.

Once the cake has cooled, unroll it and spread the cream cheese filling on top of the cake to within 1 inch of the edges. Spread the berry spread over the cream cheese. Roll the cake (this time without the towel), from the short end, making sure it is tightly rolled at the start. Trim the ends of the roll and place it on a serving platter. Refrigerate for 1 hour before serving to let the cream cheese filling firm up. Dust with powdered sugar before serving.

Make the cake, prepping the pan as directed. Dissolve ½ cup (60 g) natural cocoa powder (not Dutch-process) in ½ cup freshly brewed strong coffee. Set aside to cool. Whip the egg whites as directed. Beat the egg yolks as directed, adding the brown sugar but omitting the pumpkin puree. Omit the cinnamon, ginger, allspice, and nutmeg, increase the salt to ½ teaspoon, and add the chocolate-coffee syrup. Add the flour and then fold in the egg whites as directed. Bake and roll up the cake to cool as directed.

Skip making the berry spread. When you are ready to assemble the cake, place 1 teaspoon powdered gelatin in a small bowl with 2 tablespoons cold water. Stir and let sit for 5 minutes for the gelatin to soften. Microwave for 10 to 15 seconds to dissolve the gelatin. In the bowl of a stand mixer fitted with the whisk attachment, whip 1 cup heavy cream with 2 tablespoons granulated sugar and 1 tablespoon instant coffee powder until soft peaks form. Reduce the speed to medium-high and drizzle in the gelatin and 1 tablespoon Grand Marnier or Cointreau. Raise the speed to high and whip until firm peaks form. Fold in 1 tablespoon orange zest.

Make the chocolate buttercream frosting by chopping 2 ounces (57 g) bittersweet chocolate into ¼-inch chunks and placing them in a microwave-safe bowl. Microwave for 30 seconds, and then stir. Microwave for an additional 1 minute, stopping and stirring after each 30 seconds, until melted and smooth. In the bowl of the stand mixer fitted with the paddle attachment, beat 1 cup (225 g or 2 sticks) room temperature unsalted butter. Add the melted chocolate and 2 teaspoons vanilla extract. Sift in 3 cups (345 g) powdered sugar and ¼ cup (35 g) natural cocoa powder (not Dutch-process). Beat until smooth. You want a stiff frosting, but if it is too stiff, add whole milk, 1 teaspoon at a time, until the frosting is thin enough to spread. If it is too loose, continue to sift in up to 1 cup (115 g) more powdered sugar to thicken, ¼ cup at a time.

Assemble the roll, spreading the stabilized whipped cream over the cake up to 1 inch from the edges. Roll the cake (without the towel) from the short end, making sure it is tightly rolled at the start. Trim the ends of the roll and place on a serving platter. Cut off a 2-inch slice from one end at an angle. Using 1 tablespoon of the frosting, attach the slice to the top of the log, and then frost the entire cake. Use a fork to create "bark" lines in the frosting. Sprinkle ¼ cup (37 g) chopped pistachios over the log to resemble moss. Refrigerate until ready to serve, and dust the top of the cake with a little powdered sugar "snow" right before presentation.

Rolled cakes

Rolled cakes always seem like a fancy-pants dessert, but they actually aren't that hard. Here are few tips and tricks to make sure they work out for you.

Get the right pan. You need a 10 x 15-inch jelly-roll pan that is 1 inch deep. Anything taller and it will be hard to spread the batter evenly and hard to get the cake out of the pan. I also use this pan to make the blondie bars on page 118.

Spray the sides and bottom of the jelly-roll pan and line the bottom of the pan with parchment paper. This will allow you to get the cake out of the pan much more easily. Waxed paper is a suitable substitute if you don't have parchment.

Test the cake and make sure it's properly baked. An underbaked cake will be mushy and fall apart, but an overbaked cake will crack when you roll it. It should bounce back when you touch the center of the cake and a toothpick should come out clean when inserted in the middle of the cake.

Pick a filling that complements the flavor of the cake and that has a little bit of contrast in terms of color or texture. Berries make the filling pop in terms of color and brightness of flavor (fresh strawberries are an easy choice if they are in season). Or make a flavored filling like mocha, chocolate, or green tea. You can even crush some freeze-dried fruit to color the filling and give it fruit flavor. You've gone through the trouble of making a rolled cake, so you should use a filling that highlights its swirled nature!

Have a clean kitchen towel ready and dust both sides with powdered sugar. The sugar keeps the cake from sticking to the towel, and since you do the initial roll of the cake with the towel inside the cake, you want both sides to be dusted. Dusting the work surface before setting out the towel will coat the underside of the towel.

You can also use the towel to help roll the cake after you spread the filling. Just lift up the towel and use it as a guide to help lift and roll the cake, making sure the cake is tightly rolled. By lifting up the towel instead of lifting up the cake, you are less likely to break the cake.

Chill the cake before serving. This helps firm up the filling and the cake so it is easier to slice. If you're using whipped cream, stabilize it with gelatin to make it firmer. Otherwise, serve it as soon as you can.

Finally, remember that frosting and powdered sugar are your friends! If you have some slight cracks or blemishes on the cake, you can always cover them up with frosting or a dusting of powdered sugar. In the end no one will notice anyway, once you serve stunning slices of spiral cake!

THE NOSTALGIC MARSHMALLOW-FILLED CHOCOLATE CAKE

makes 1 tube cake; 12 servings

Nostalgia is powerful emotion. I'll be walking down the aisle at the grocery store, minding my own business, looking to buy some kale and maybe a free-range chicken to roast, and then *wham!* a box of mass-produced cupcakes with the little squiggly white loops are staring me in the face and I get weak in the knees. They're too sweet for my adult taste buds and the chocolate cake will be slightly dry and oily at the same time. But I still hesitate and think about buying them because the nostalgia draws me in. The solution is to make a version from scratch. My homemade tube cake version perfectly satisfies that nostalgic itch. Once you get a bite of this cake, you'll know what I mean.

CAKE BATTER

2 cups (280 g) all-purpose flour

1 cup (100 g) Dutch-process cocoa powder

1½ cups (300 g) granulated sugar

½ cup (110 g) packed dark brown sugar

1¾ teaspoons baking powder

1 teaspoon baking soda

1 teaspoon kosher salt

3 large eggs

1 cup buttermilk

1 cup freshly brewed coffee, cooled to lukewarm

¼ cup vegetable oil

2 teaspoons vanilla extract

MARSHMALLOW FILLING

2 large egg whites

¼ teaspoon cream of tartar

¾ cup (150 g) granulated sugar

MAKE THE CAKE BATTER

Preheat the oven to 350°F. Coat the sides, bottom, and center of a tube pan with a removable bottom (the kind you would use for an angel food cake) with cooking spray. Line the bottom of the pan with a round piece of parchment paper with a hole cut out in the middle. Set the pan on a rimmed baking sheet.

Combine the flour, cocoa powder, both sugars, baking powder, baking soda, and salt in a large bowl. Using a balloon whisk, vigorously stir until the ingredients are uniform in color and fully blended. Place the eggs, buttermilk, coffee, oil, and vanilla in another bowl and beat together with a fork. Make a well in the middle of the dry ingredients and pour the liquid into the center. Mix with a large spatula until a batter forms. Pour into the prepared baking pan (it should only come about one-third up the sides of the pan). Bake until a toothpick inserted in the center comes out clean, 50 to 55 minutes. Let the cake cool in the pan for at least 3 hours, or up to overnight.

MAKE THE MARSHMALLOW FILLING

Place the egg whites and cream of tartar in the bowl of a stand mixer fitted with the whisk attachment. Beat until soft peaks form, then stop the mixer. Combine the sugar, corn syrup, water, and salt in a medium saucepan and cook over high heat until the syrup reaches 245°F on a candy thermometer (the firm-ball stage). Remove from the heat and turn the mixer back on to medium speed. Slowly

·······>

½ cup (155 g) light corn syrup

¼ cup water

½ teaspoon kosher salt

½ cup (115 g or 1 stick) unsalted butter, at room temperature

1 tablespoon vanilla extract or vanilla paste

CHOCOLATE FROSTING

2 cups (230 g) powdered sugar, sifted

¼ cup whole milk

2 teaspoons light corn syrup

1 teaspoon vanilla extract

3 ounces (85 g) dark bittersweet chocolate (about 60% cacao)

WHITE SQUIGGLE ICING

1 cup (115 g) powdered sugar, sifted

2 teaspoons whole milk

2 teaspoons light corn syrup

drizzle a little bit of the hot sugar syrup into the egg whites, avoiding the moving whisk (or else the hot syrup will fly everywhere!). Raise the speed to medium-high and continue to drizzle the syrup into the egg whites until it is all added. Don't rush it—just slowly drizzle. Once it's all added, continue to beat for an additional 7 to 10 minutes, until the marshmallow fluff is stiff and glossy white. Scoop the fluff into another bowl and let cool completely.

Once the cake is completely cool and ready to assemble, place the butter and vanilla in a clean bowl of the stand mixer fitted with the paddle attachment. Beat until the vanilla is incorporated and the butter becomes creamy and sticks to the side of the bowl. Add the marshmallow fluff and beat until well blended.

Remove the cake from the pan and set it with the rounded side up (the way it baked in the pan). Create a tunnel in the cake for the filling by first making a "moat": With a small paring knife, cut a curved rectangle, 2 inches long by 1 inch wide, into the top of the cake about halfway between the center hole and the outside edge of the cake, following the curve of the cake. Cut into the cake about two-thirds deep and use the knife to lift the rectangle out from the cake. If the hole isn't deep enough, just use the knife to cut and scrape out more cake (but don't cut all the way through to the bottom). Repeat, working around the cake, cutting out rectangular pieces to make a continuous moat. Place the cake pieces right next to where you cut, so you can put them back when the time comes. Once you've gone all the way around the cake, spoon the marshmallow filling into the moat, filling it about halfway. You may not use all the fluff, but that's okay. Save it for another use.

Cut off about half of each rectangular piece of cake from the rough side (the inside part). Replace the remaining cake pieces in the moat over the marshmallow filling to plug up the cake. Repeat all the way around the cake. Nibble on the scraps if you want (I do). Turn the cake over so that the "flat" side of the cake is on top and the "plugged" rounded side is on the bottom, and place on a cake stand or serving plate.

MAKE THE CHOCOLATE FROSTING

Combine the powdered sugar, milk, corn syrup, and vanilla in a medium pan. Cook over medium heat, stirring constantly, until the sugar dissolves and the mixture starts to bubble on the sides of the pan. Reduce the heat to low and add the chocolate, stirring until the frosting is smooth. Now quickly spoon the warm frosting over the cake. The frosting is a bit finicky and will start to crust immediately as it cools. If this becomes a problem, spoon as much as you can, getting it where you want it, then wet your fingers and use them to smooth out the frosting.

·······>

Simplify the filling by beating ½ cup (115 g or 1 stick) room temperature salted butter with 2 teaspoons vanilla extract or paste until creamy. Add a 7-ounce jar of store-bought marshmallow creme or fluff and beat until incorporated. Use that as the filling.

MAKE THE WHITE SQUIGGLE ICING

Mix together the powdered sugar, milk, and corn syrup to form a thick paste. Scrape it into a pastry bag with a small round tip or a zip-top bag with a small part of the corner snipped off. Make some test squiggles on a piece of paper to get the feel of it, then squeeze squiggle loops over the top of the iced cake.

Candy temperature

Using a candy/deep-frying thermometer is the easiest way to know when your sugar syrup is ready to use. Insert and clip the thermometer into the pan of sugar syrup deep enough that it gets a good reading of the syrup but does not touch the pan, which can give a false reading. If the syrup only covers a tiny part of the thermometer, you can occasionally tip the pan (carefully!) to one side so the syrup runs and covers more of the thermometer. You'll get a much more accurate reading when more of the syrup covers the end of the thermometer.

If you don't have a candy thermometer, you can use the old-fashioned candy stage method by placing a glass measuring cup of cold water next to your stove. Cook the sugar until you think it might be at the right stage. Drop some of the syrup into the water and see how it reacts. If the syrup disappears in the water, it's nowhere close to being done.

The Thread Stage
At 230 to 235°F, the syrup will form a thread that won't ball up, but you can still use this to make ice cream syrup and that sort of thing.

The Soft-Ball Stage
At 235 to 240°F, the syrup will form a ball that flattens out on your finger when you pull it out from the water.

The Firm-Ball Stage
At 245 to 250°F, the syrup will form a ball that is a little squishy if you press it between your fingers.

The Hard-Ball Stage
At 250 to 265°F, the syrup will form a hard thread or ball but will still be pliable when you try to squish it.

The Soft-Crack Stage
At 270 to 290°F, the syrup will immediately form hard threads that bend a little but will crack if bent too hard.

The Hard-Crack Stage
At 300 to 310°F, the syrup will immediately form brittle threads that crack if you try to bend them at all. At this point the sugar is really hot, so be careful about pulling it out of the water! Wait for 5 to 10 seconds first, before testing.

Caramel
Anything over 320°F is the caramel stage. If you're making caramel, it's pretty easy to judge the temperature by just looking at how dark the sugar turns. Stay under 350°F if you are measuring, though, because anything over that and the sugar starts to burn and get bitter.

THE NOSTALGIC YELLOW MARSHMALLOW-FILLED CAKE

Generously grease a standard 10-cup Bundt pan with 2 tablespoons softened unsalted butter, then dust it with flour and knock out any excess. In the bowl of a stand mixer fitted with the whisk attachment, whip 3 large egg whites and ¼ teaspoon cream of tartar on medium-high speed until soft peaks form. Reduce the speed to medium and slowly sprinkle in ¼ cup (50 g) granulated sugar, mixing until absorbed. Raise the speed back to medium-high and whip until the egg whites are glossy and form stiff peaks. Scoop the egg whites into another bowl and swap the whisk for the paddle attachment.

Combine 2¼ cups (315 g) all-purpose flour, 1¾ cups (350 g) granulated sugar, 1¼ teaspoons baking powder, ¼ teaspoon baking soda, and 1 teaspoon kosher salt in the stand mixer bowl (no need to clean it). Turn the mixer on to low speed and blend the ingredients. In a separate bowl, combine ½ cup (115 g or 1 stick) melted and cooled butter, 1 cup buttermilk, 6 tablespoons vegetable oil, 6 large egg yolks, and 1 tablespoon vanilla extract, and beat together with a whisk until uniform in color. Pour into the dry ingredients and mix on low speed until the batter comes together. Scrape down the sides with a spatula and mix for 10 to 15 more seconds to incorporate.

Remove the bowl from the mixer, scoop about one-third of the egg whites into the batter, and fold together. Repeat with the remaining egg whites in two additions, folding until all the egg whites are incorporated. Pour the batter into the pan and bake until a toothpick or skewer inserted in the center comes out clean, 40 to 50 minutes. Let the cake cool in the pan for 15 minutes, then invert and unmold the cake onto a wire cooling rack to cool completely (a minimum of 2 hours).

Make the filling as directed. Cut a "moat" in the bottom of the Bundt cake and fill with the marshmallow filling. Skip the frosting and the squiggle icing, but dust the top of the Bundt cake with powdered sugar before serving, if you like.

This version is inspired by a recipe in Shauna Sever's *Pure Vanilla*.

PIES, TARTS, COBBLERS, AND CRISPS

I GREW UP IN THE MIDWEST, WHERE FRUIT PIES and cobblers rule. Cakes were for formal affairs, but pies were down-home and friendly—the dessert you baked and brought over to welcome the new next-door neighbor. Cobblers were made to use up the overflowing fruit from the backyard tree. And crisps were to pretend you were eating something healthy for dessert. After all, if it has oats in it, it has to be good for you!

Summertime is pie heaven, with berries and stone fruit bursting at the market. Now that I live in San Francisco, where I have easy access to produce and local farmers' markets mere blocks away from me, it's hard for me to not stop and purchase a near bushelful of seasonal fruit at every opportunity. We can never eat it all before it goes bad. That's when I start baking up a storm.

Of course, wintertime brings apples, pears, and quinces, along with winter citrus and cream and custard pies. You really never go in and out of pie season. It's a year-round endeavor. From the soothing Zen of making dough to making the filling or weaving the crust on top, the process of pie baking is almost as good as eating it for me. *Almost* as good. Cakes may be the traditional showstoppers at most celebratory events, but pies are what warm the heart at home.

STRAWBERRY-RHUBARB PIE WITH PISTACHIO CRUMB TOPPING

makes one 9-inch deep-dish pie; 8 servings

The secret to this pie isn't the filling or the crust (though both are stellar). It's in the pistachio crumb topping. It looks like a lot of ingredients but it's not difficult and it's totally worth it in the end. My friend Hadley still raves about this pie as one of his all-time favorites. So much so that every time he orders strawberry-rhubarb pie at a restaurant, he texts me to say, "This is good . . . but not as good as yours!"

CRUST

1¾ cups (245 g) all-purpose flour

1 tablespoon granulated sugar

1 teaspoon kosher salt

10 tablespoons (140 g or 1¼ sticks) cold unsalted butter

¼ cup cold vodka

3 to 4 tablespoons cold water

PISTACHIO CRUMB TOPPING

1 cup (135 g) chopped unsalted pistachios

¾ cup (105 g) all-purpose flour

2 tablespoons packed dark brown sugar

2 tablespoons granulated sugar

2 tablespoons turbinado sugar

½ teaspoon kosher salt

¼ teaspoon ground nutmeg

½ cup (115 g or 1 stick) unsalted butter, melted

MAKE THE CRUST

Combine the flour, sugar, and salt in a large bowl. Stir vigorously with a balloon whisk until the ingredients are evenly distributed. Cut the butter into ½-inch cubes and sprinkle over the dry ingredients. Using your fingers and hands, first toss the butter in the flour, then smash the butter into thin slivers, breaking them up as you go. Once they have been broken and flattened into small bits the size of peas, sprinkle the vodka and 3 tablespoons of the water over the butter and flour. Toss with a fork until the dough starts to come together. If the dough still isn't forming, add the remaining 1 tablespoon water. Massage the mass with your hands until it forms a cohesive dough. Flatten into a disk about 1 inch thick, wrap with plastic wrap, and refrigerate for at least 1 hour. Preheat the oven to 375°F.

Roll out the dough into a 12-inch circle on a surface liberally sprinkled with flour. Fit it into a deep-dish 9-inch pie pan, pressing the dough so it drapes over the top edge of the pie pan, anchoring it to the top of the pan. Prick the bottom of the dough with a fork. Line with a piece of parchment paper and fill with dried beans, uncooked rice, or pie weights. Bake for 20 minutes. Remove the paper with the pie weights and bake for an additional 15 minutes. Let cool on a wire rack while you make the topping and pie filling. Reduce the oven temperature to 350°F.

MAKE THE PISTACHIO CRUMB TOPPING

Combine the pistachios, flour, sugars, salt, and nutmeg in a medium bowl. Drizzle the melted butter over the dry ingredients and toss with a fork until the mixture starts to clump and the ingredients are evenly distributed. Refrigerate the crumb topping until ready to use.

STRAWBERRY-RHUBARB FILLING

4 cups (1¼ pounds or 565 g) ½-inch-thick chopped pieces of rhubarb

2 cups (1 pound or 455 g) hulled and quartered fresh strawberries

1 cup (200 g) granulated sugar

3 tablespoons tapioca starch (see note, below)

2 tablespoons pistachio oil or extra-virgin olive oil

1 teaspoon vanilla extract

✳ *Tapioca starch is a thickener similar to cornstarch, but it sets at a lower temperature. You can substitute an equal amount of cornstarch in its place, though you might need to increase the baking time. If the crust starts to brown too much, cover it with aluminum foil.*

MAKE THE STRAWBERRY-RHUBARB FILLING

Combine the rhubarb, strawberries, sugar, tapioca starch, pistachio oil, and vanilla in a large bowl and toss with a large silicone spatula. Pour the fruit filling into the baked crust. Sprinkle the crumb topping over the top of the filling, breaking up any big chunks into smaller bits. Place the pie pan on a rimmed baking sheet in case of drips and bake until the juices from the filling are bubbling, 60 to 70 minutes. If the crust starts to burn, cover it with aluminum foil. Let cool to room temperature before serving.

alternative

CRANBERRY-APPLE PIE WITH WALNUT-CINNAMON CRUMBLE TOPPING

Prepare and pre-bake the crust as directed.

While the crust is baking, make the crumb topping as directed, replacing the pistachios with 1 cup (140 g) chopped walnuts and replacing the nutmeg with 1 teaspoon ground cinnamon.

Make the filling, substituting 7 cups (about 7 apples, 2½ pounds or 1,135 g) peeled, cored, and sliced Braeburn, Gala, or Jonagold apples and 1 cup (100 g) fresh cranberries in place of the rhubarb and strawberries. Add 1 teaspoon ground cinnamon and replace the pistachio oil with walnut oil or melted butter. Pour the filling over the baked crust, sprinkle the cold crumb topping over the filling (breaking up any large chunks), and bake as directed.

LEMON-BLACKBERRY CHESS PIE

makes one 9-inch pie; 6 servings

About five months after I started blogging about food, I decided to enter a local pie contest. Unlike other pie contests where you make two pies—one for display and one for the audience to look at—this pie contest required me to make enough pie for 200 people to sample. I didn't know what I was getting into. I bought props to decorate the booth (lemons and chess pieces) and even built a tiny little grid out of balsa wood so I could stencil a chessboard shape out of blackberry jam on top of the pie. I spent the entire day before making pie crust and pies for the event: twenty pies in all in my tiny little kitchen. My hard work paid off, as I won both Judge's 1st Place and People's Choice. The write-up in the local paper got picked up by *Bon Appétit* magazine's daily blog links, and all of a sudden my winning pie was all over the place. To this day, I still have people come up to me randomly on the street and talk about that pie. This is a streamlined version of it.

CRUST

1 cup (140 g) all-purpose flour

½ cup (75 g) whole-wheat flour

½ teaspoon kosher salt

½ cup (115 g or 1 stick) cold unsalted butter

3 tablespoons cold vodka

4 to 5 tablespoons ice-cold water

BLACKBERRY FILLING

1½ cups (6 ounces or 170 g) fresh or frozen blackberries

3 tablespoons granulated sugar

2 teaspoons cornstarch

1 teaspoon fresh lemon juice

MAKE THE CRUST

Combine the flours and salt in a large bowl. Stir vigorously together with a balloon whisk until the ingredients are evenly distributed. Cut the butter into ½-inch cubes and sprinkle over the dry ingredients. Using your fingers and hands, first toss the butter in the flour, then smash the butter into thin slivers, breaking them up as you go. Once they have been broken and flattened into small bits the size of peas, sprinkle the vodka and 4 tablespoons of the water over the butter and flour. Toss with a fork until the dough starts to come together. If the dough still isn't forming, add the remaining 1 tablespoon water. Massage the mass with your hands until it forms a cohesive dough. Flatten into a disk about 1 inch thick, wrap tightly with plastic wrap, and refrigerate for at least 1 hour.

Roll out the chilled dough into a 12-inch circle on a surface liberally sprinkled with flour. Fit into a standard 9-inch pie pan and trim the edges of the dough with a pair of kitchen scissors. Press the dough so it drapes over the top edge of the pie pan, anchoring it to the top of the pan. Refrigerate, uncovered, for about 15 minutes. Preheat the oven to 375°F.

Prick the bottom of the dough with a fork. Line with a piece of parchment paper and fill with dried beans, uncooked rice, or pie weights. Bake for 20 minutes.

·······>

CHESS PIE FILLING

2 cups (400 g) granulated sugar

½ cup (115 g or 1 stick) unsalted butter, melted

4 large eggs

2 large egg yolks

1 cup heavy cream

¼ cup (37 g) cornmeal

Zest of 2 lemons

6 tablespoons fresh lemon juice

2 tablespoons cornstarch

1 teaspoon vanilla extract

Remove the paper with pie weights and bake for an additional 15 minutes. Let the crust cool on a wire rack while you make the filling. Reduce the oven temperature to 350°F.

MAKE THE BLACKBERRY FILLING

Combine the blackberries, sugar, cornstarch, and lemon juice in a medium saucepan and cook over medium-high heat, stirring and breaking up the blackberries as much as possible with a wooden spoon or a potato masher, until the filling has thickened and the berries have fallen apart, 3 to 5 minutes. Remove from the heat and let cool.

MAKE THE CHESS PIE FILLING

Combine the sugar, cream, butter, eggs, egg yolks, cornmeal, lemon zest, juice, cornstarch, and vanilla in a large pot and stir together with a balloon whisk. Cook over medium heat, stirring constantly with the whisk, until the filling has thickened a bit and coats the back of the spoon, about 7 minutes. It should be the consistency of thin lemon pudding. Remove from the heat.

Assemble the pie by spooning most of the blackberry filling into the bottom of the baked crust and spreading it evenly onto the bottom of the crust. Reserve about 2 tablespoons of the blackberry filling for the top. Gently pour or spoon the lemon chess filling over the blackberry filling, trying to disturb the blackberry filling as little as possible. Once you've poured all the lemon filling, spoon and drizzle the remaining blackberry filling over the lemon filling, then decoratively swirl the blackberry filling with the lemon filling. Bake until the edges of the pie filling start to brown, 35 to 45 minutes. Let cool to room temperature before serving.

WHITE AND DARK CHOCOLATE CHESS PIE

Make and bake the pie crust as directed.

Skip the blackberry filling. For the chess pie filling, melt 12 tablespoons (170 g or 1½ sticks) unsalted butter with 2 ounces (60 g) chopped white chocolate in a small saucepan over low heat, stirring constantly until smooth. Combine 3 cups (600 g) granulated sugar, 6 large eggs, 4 large egg yolks, 1½ cups heavy cream, 6 tablespoons cornmeal, 2 teaspoons vanilla extract, and ¼ cup (30 g) cornstarch in a large bowl with the melted butter mixture and stir together. Omit the lemon zest and juice. Pour one-third of the filling into a smaller bowl and add ¼ cup (30 g) Dutch-process cocoa powder. Mix to incorporate. Reserve about 2 tablespoons of the chocolate filling and pour the rest into the baked pie crust, then carefully spoon or pour the white chocolate filling over it. Spoon the reserved 2 tablespoons dark chocolate filling over the white chocolate and decoratively swirl together. Bake until the edges of the pie turn golden brown, about 45 minutes.

What the heck is a chess pie?

Whenever I mention chess pie to folks, unless they grew up in the Deep South, they look at me like I'm crazy. What the heck is a chess pie? A chess pie is a sweet custard pie with a little cornmeal added for texture. The classic is made without any flavorings, though lemon and chocolate are fairly common variations. The vintage pie is similar to a sugar pie, a vinegar pie, or a buttermilk pecan pie. It's rather sweet, so small slices are all that are needed.

Various origin stories tell how the pie came to be called chess pie. In the South, before iceboxes came into normal use, pies were such a popular baked good that pie safes, or pie chests, were specific pieces of furniture used to store pies as well as other perishables like meat and bread. The story goes that southern cooks would make plain sugar pies and place them in the pie chest. Because these pies weren't specifically flavored with fruit or anything else to describe them, they became known as "chest pies," which eventually ended up being "chess pies."

Other stories say the pie filling itself looks so much like cheese that the pies were often called "cheese pies," which over time morphed into "chess pies." But my favorite story is the one that probably makes the most sense. Because southern housewives would make pies for their husbands and kids over and over again, the common question was always "What sort of pie is that?" Because chess pies don't have a specific flavor, the normal reply was "It's just pie!" which, said in a southern twang, came out as "It's jest pie!" which, of course, became "chess pie." This is the story I always tell when someone asks me where the name came from. Because even if it's not true, I just like the mental image of a hassled southern woman, exasperated at her husband and kids always asking the same question, finally yelling out loud, "It's jest pie, y'all!"

ROASTED BANANA–PEANUT BUTTER CREAM PIE

makes one 9-inch pie; 8 servings

It took me a few tries to really decide if I liked the combination of peanut butter and banana. For a lot of people this seems like crazy talk, as they absolutely love the combination. Of course, I just assumed they were all mad Elvis fanatics. But the turning point for me was this pie. The super-rich peanut butter topping and the extra banana-flavored cream filling just play so well together. I finally understand the appeal, and it's hard to hold back from taking slice after slice of this pie. I have to bring it somewhere to share with people. I can't have it around the house or I end up eating the entire thing.

PEANUT BUTTER CRUST

1½ cups (210 g) all-purpose flour

1 tablespoon packed dark brown sugar

½ teaspoon kosher salt

6 tablespoons (85 g or ¾ stick) cold unsalted butter

¼ cup (65 g) cold smooth peanut butter

4 to 6 tablespoons ice-cold water

BANANA CREAM FILLING

4 ripe bananas (unpeeled)

2 tablespoons packed dark brown sugar

2 tablespoons dark rum

1 cup heavy cream

½ cup whole milk

½ cup (100 g) granulated sugar

5 teaspoons cornstarch

⅛ teaspoon kosher salt

2 large eggs

1 tablespoon vanilla extract

2 tablespoons unsalted butter

½ teaspoon ground cinnamon

MAKE THE PEANUT BUTTER CRUST

Combine the flour, brown sugar, and salt in a large bowl. Cut the butter into ½-inch cubes and sprinkle over the dry ingredients. Using your fingers and hands, first toss the butter in the flour, then smash the cold butter into thin slivers, breaking them up as you go. Making sure your hands are covered with flour, add the peanut butter and cover with flour. Gently squeeze the peanut butter into the flour with your hands, making sure to keep it completely covered in flour. Continue until it is worked into the flour and is in small pieces. Once both the butter and peanut butter have been broken and flattened into small bits the size of peas, sprinkle in 4 tablespoons of the water. Toss with a fork until the dough starts to come together. If the dough seems really dry, add 1 to 2 more tablespoons water. Massage the mass with your hands until it forms a cohesive dough. Flatten into a disk about 1 inch thick, wrap tightly with plastic wrap, and refrigerate for at least 1 hour.

MAKE THE BANANA CREAM FILLING

Preheat the oven to 400°F. Place the 4 unpeeled bananas on a rimmed baking sheet. Roast until the banana peels are dark brown, verging on black, about 15 minutes. Let cool. Reduce the oven temperature to 375°F.

Roll out the dough into a 12-inch circle on a surface liberally sprinkled with flour. Fit into a 9-inch pie pan, pressing the dough so it drapes over the top edge of the pie pan, anchoring it to the top of the pan. Prick the bottom of the dough with a fork. Line with a piece of parchment paper and fill with dried beans, uncooked

PEANUT BUTTER FILLING

4 ounces (115 g or ½ brick) cream cheese, at room temperature

½ cup (57 g) powdered sugar

1 teaspoon vanilla extract

½ cup (130 g) smooth peanut butter

¾ cup heavy cream

TO ASSEMBLE

2 ripe but firm bananas

2 tablespoons dark rum

rice, or pie weights. Bake for 20 minutes. Remove the paper with the pie weights and bake for an additional 15 minutes. Let cool on a wire rack while you make the pie filling.

Peel the roasted bananas and place them in the bowl of a stand mixer fitted with the whisk attachment. Add the brown sugar and rum and mix on medium-high speed until the bananas are pureed. Place the cream, milk, granulated sugar, cornstarch, salt, eggs, and vanilla in a large pot. Stir briskly with a balloon whisk until the dry ingredients are dissolved and the eggs are incorporated. Cook over medium heat, stirring constantly, until the custard has thickened and boiled, about 5 minutes. Remove from the heat, add the butter, and stir until melted and incorporated. Fold in the banana mixture and the cinnamon, then spread the filling over the cooled pie crust. Refrigerate to firm up, about 1 hour. Place the cream cheese on the counter to come to room temperature while the banana filling is chilling.

MAKE THE PEANUT BUTTER FILLING

Combine the cream cheese, powdered sugar, and vanilla in a clean bowl of the stand mixer fitted with the whisk attachment. Whip until the cream cheese is fluffy and clings to the side of the bowl. Add the peanut butter and whip until the peanut butter is incorporated, scraping down the sides and bottom of the bowl once or twice. Add the cream and whip on high speed until incorporated and the peanut butter filling is lighter in color. The filling will still be thick.

ASSEMBLE THE PIE

Carefully spoon the peanut butter filling over the banana filling. Refrigerate to chill and firm up the peanut butter filling, about 2 hours or up to overnight. Before serving, slice the 2 bananas diagonally and toss with the rum. Arrange them on top of the pie and serve.

·······>

SLOW-ROASTED STRAWBERRY–BAY LEAF CREAM PIE

Make the crust as directed, but omit the peanut butter. Increase the flour to 1¾ cups (245 g) and the butter to 10 tablespoons (140 g). Bake and cool as directed. Make the slow-roasted strawberries by preheating the oven to 275°F. Hull and quarter 8 cups (2 pounds or 910 g) fresh strawberries and place in a large mixing bowl. Add ¼ cup (55 g) brown sugar, 2 teaspoons vanilla extract, 2 tablespoons balsamic vinegar, 2 tablespoons red wine, and ½ teaspoon freshly ground black pepper. Toss to coat, then pour onto a rimmed baking sheet, scraping the bowl to make sure all the juices get onto the baking sheet. Roast, stirring once every 30 minutes, until the strawberries have softened and darkened in color and the juices have thickened, 2 to 2½ hours. Let cool in the pan to room temperature, then move the strawberries to a glass bowl and refrigerate to cool for 1 hour or overnight.

Make the bay leaf filling by combining ¾ cup (150 g) sugar, 2 tablespoons cornstarch, ¼ teaspoon kosher salt, 1½ cups heavy cream, ¾ cup whole milk, 3 large eggs, and 1 teaspoon vanilla extract in a large pot. Stir briskly with a balloon whisk until the dry ingredients are dissolved and the eggs are incorporated. Add 3 fresh bay leaves (not dried) and cook over medium heat, stirring constantly, until the custard has thickened and boiled, 6 to 7 minutes. Remove from the heat, add 3 tablespoons unsalted butter, and stir until melted and incorporated. Remove the bay leaves and pour the filling into the baked pie crust. Place a piece of plastic wrap on the surface of the hot custard (to prevent a skin from forming) and refrigerate for at least 1 hour or up to overnight.

Spoon the strawberries over the filling before serving.

Quicker cream pies

"Cream pie" is a bit of a misleading name, as the pies themselves are often made of custard, a combination of cream and eggs or egg yolks. It's a fairly easy pie to make since the pie filling is made on the stovetop, not baked in the oven, and cream pies usually aren't dependent on seasonal fruit (you could even use a no-bake graham cracker or cookie crust if the day is warm and you don't want to turn on the oven). In fact, the hardest part of making a cream pie is the wait time, as the custard needs to cool in the fridge to make the pie easier to slice.

There is a shortcut for cooling the custard if you are impatient. Pastry chefs do it all the time. Line a rimmed baking sheet with plastic wrap and pour the hot custard onto the lined baking sheet. Using a large flexible spatula, push the custard back and forth on the baking sheet, spreading it out into a thin layer. The thinner layer of custard will cool quickly, within a matter of minutes. Then scrape up the custard with the spatula and pour it into the pie shell. Make sure to line the baking sheet with plastic wrap completely. If you try to cool the custard directly on the baking sheet, the custard will start to turn gray and pick up a metallic taste from the baking sheet.

Refrigerating the pie to firm it up will go much faster, allowing you to serve the pie in an hour or two instead of 6 hours or more. Quicker cream pies! That's a win-win situation all the way around.

RHUBARB–WHITE CHOCOLATE TART WITH CANDIED KUMQUATS

makes one 9-inch pie; 8 servings

I'm madly in love with rhubarb as an ingredient, and not just paired with strawberry (though I adore that combination as well). When rhubarb hits the market, I know that spring is just around the corner, and I'm ready to say goodbye to my winter citrus and hello to warmer weather and T-shirts. There's a small seasonal window when rhubarb and the last of the kumquats are both available, but you can make this pie with frozen rhubarb if you want. And if kumquats (those tiny grape-size citrus fruits with the thin sweet skin and tart sour interior) aren't available, try using sliced fresh strawberries or fresh blueberries over the tart. Kumquats can be difficult to find even when they are in season.

WHITE CHOCOLATE CRUST

3 ounces (85 g) white chocolate, chopped into ¼-inch chunks

¾ cup (170 g or 1½ sticks) unsalted butter, at room temperature

¼ cup plus 2 tablespoons (75 g) granulated sugar

¼ teaspoon kosher salt

Zest of 1 lemon

1 tablespoon fresh lemon juice

2¼ cups (315 g) all-purpose flour

RHUBARB "CURD"

1½ pounds (680 g or 3 or 4 medium stalks) fresh or frozen rhubarb

1 cup (200 g) granulated sugar

¼ cup (30 g) cornstarch

1½ cups silken tofu

¼ cup (57 g or ½ stick) unsalted butter

¼ teaspoon kosher salt

MAKE THE WHITE CHOCOLATE CRUST

Preheat the oven to 350°F. Place the white chocolate in a microwave-safe bowl and microwave for 30 seconds. Stir, then microwave for 30 seconds more. Stir until melted and completely smooth. If there are a few stubborn solid pieces, microwave for an additional 15 seconds, but be cautious, as white chocolate scorches much faster than dark or milk chocolate.

Place the butter, sugar, salt, lemon zest, and juice in the bowl of a stand mixer fitted with the paddle attachment. Mix on low speed to slowly cream the ingredients together. Once they start to mix, raise the mixer speed to medium. The ingredients will tend to slide around a bit in the beginning because of the lemon juice. Eventually the butter will absorb the majority of the liquid and sugar, but don't worry if it still slides around a bit. Add the white chocolate and beat to incorporate. Again, don't worry if it doesn't look like it is completely coming together; just mix until the white chocolate is as incorporated as you can get it.

Add the flour and mix until a dough forms. Press the dough into a 10-inch round tart pan with a removable bottom, making sure to cover the entire bottom and up the sides. You may have a little bit of dough left over, depending on how thick you make it. Just discard any leftovers or use it to reinforce the sides of the dough.

.......>

CANDIED KUMQUATS

2¾ cups (1 pound or 455 g) kumquats

1½ cups (300 g) granulated sugar

1 cup water

TO ASSEMBLE

2 ounces (57 g) white chocolate, chopped into ¼-inch chunks

1 tablespoon heavy cream

1 teaspoon kumquat sugar syrup (from the candied kumquats)

Place the tart pan on a rimmed baking sheet. Prick the bottom of the dough all over with a fork. Bake for about 20 minutes (no need for pie weights), or until the edges of the crust start to turn golden brown. Let cool on a wire rack.

MAKE THE RHUBARB "CURD"

Cut the rhubarb into ½-inch chunks and place in a large pot. Add the sugar and cornstarch and cook over medium-high heat, stirring constantly, until the rhubarb has fallen apart and the puree has thickened, about 10 minutes. Pour the hot rhubarb into a food processor. Add the tofu, butter, and salt and process until smooth. Pour the rhubarb curd into the baked tart shell and bake until the filling is set and the center just barely jiggles, 30 to 35 minutes. Let cool completely.

MAKE THE CANDIED KUMQUATS

Slice each kumquat in half lengthwise. Place in a medium saucepan and add the sugar and water. Bring to a boil, then reduce the heat to a simmer and cook until the kumquats are translucent, about 10 minutes. Let cool completely before using.

ASSEMBLE THE TART

Place the white chocolate in a microwave-safe bowl and microwave for 30 seconds. Stir and then microwave for an additional 30 seconds. Stir until completely melted and smooth. Add the cream and the kumquat sugar syrup and stir to incorporate. Drain the kumquats thoroughly (reserve the remaining syrup for another use). Arrange the candied kumquats, cut side down, on the curd in concentric circles from the center of the tart to the edge. Using a spoon, drizzle the white chocolate sauce over the tart. Refrigerate for about 1 hour to chill and set before serving.

✳ *Rhubarb "curd" is a bit of a misnomer for this recipe. Though I could have used egg yolks to thicken the curd, I opted to go a different route because the yellow egg yolks muddy the vibrant reddish pink of the pureed rhubarb and dull the fruit flavor. Silken tofu, often used in vegan cooking as a substitute for eggs, leaves the rhubarb bright and clean. Don't worry, though: You won't taste the tofu, as the tart rhubarb flavor and candied kumquats shine through.*

✳ *Make sure to use actual white chocolate, not just white chocolate chips. Read the ingredients on the label and make sure it lists cocoa butter. Cheaper stuff uses vegetable oil and other fillers that don't melt properly and taste waxy and unappetizing.*

alternative

KIWI, PASSION FRUIT, AND DARK CHOCOLATE TART

Make and pre-bake the crust as directed, substituting semisweet chocolate for the white chocolate.

Make the passion fruit curd by whisking together 8 large eggs, 1½ cups passion fruit puree (you can buy this frozen at Latin grocery stores, or you can use fresh passion fruit if you have access to it), 2 cups (400 g) granulated sugar, and ¼ cup (35 g) tapioca starch. Pour into the baked crust and bake for 25 to 30 minutes.

Peel and cut 4 kiwis into thin slices and arrange the slices on top of the tart. Skip the white chocolate glaze and drizzle 2 tablespoons honey over the top of the tart instead.

QUICK SHORTCUT

If kumquats aren't available, try slicing 4 cups (1 pound or 455 g) fresh strawberries and using them on top of the tart, drizzling the white chocolate over the strawberries as directed. Or use 2½ cups (¾ pound or 340 g) fresh blueberries or blackberries on top of the tart. Drizzle half the white chocolate directly on the rhubarb tart first, then sprinkle the berries over the white chocolate, using the melted chocolate to adhere the berries to the tart. Then drizzle the remaining chocolate on top of the berries.

ROSEMARY CARAMEL AND DARK CHOCOLATE–POTATO CHIP TART

makes one 10-inch tart; 10 to 12 servings

If you talk to any pastry chef, you'll notice that they have a slight obsession with salt. Perhaps they crave it because they are constantly surrounded by sweets and sugars. Perhaps it's because they know that the pull of salt in desserts gives a counterbalance and contrast in your mouth. Or maybe it's just because they know that salt is like a magnifying glass: it enhances pretty much everything it touches, even desserts. In this salty sweet dessert the addition of fresh rosemary not only plays well with the salty potato chips but gives the caramel a beautiful earthy depth. The chunks of potato chips in the crust and on top of the tart add a salty, satisfying crunch to each bite.

CRUST

½ cup (115 g or 1 stick) unsalted butter, at room temperature

¾ cup (90 g) powdered sugar

¾ cup (105 g) all-purpose flour

3 cups (150 g) lightly crushed salted thick-cut crinkle potato chips

1 large egg

CARAMEL FILLING

1 cup (200 g) granulated sugar

1 sprig fresh rosemary (5 to 6 inches)

1 cup heavy cream

6 tablespoons (100 g or ¾ stick) unsalted butter, at room temperature

1 teaspoon vanilla extract

½ teaspoon kosher salt

MAKE THE CRUST

Place the butter, powdered sugar, and flour in the bowl of a stand mixer fitted with the paddle attachment. Beat on medium speed until blended and light and fluffy, about 1 minute. Crumble the potato chips in your hand and add them to the bowl. Mix on low speed, raising the speed to medium as the potato chips break down and incorporate into the dough, 15 to 30 seconds. Add the egg and beat until incorporated, about 30 seconds. Scrape the sticky dough into a 10-inch round tart pan with a removable bottom. Wet your hands and press the dough evenly into the bottom and up the sides of the tart pan. Freeze for about 10 minutes to chill. Preheat the oven to 350°F.

When the dough has chilled and is firm to the touch, place it on a rimmed baking sheet. Line with a piece of parchment paper and fill with dried beans, uncooked rice, or pie weights. Bake for 25 minutes, or until the edges of the crust start to turn golden brown. Carefully remove the paper with the weights and bake for an additional 10 minutes, or until the bottom of the crust looks dry. Let cool on a wire rack to room temperature.

MAKE THE CARAMEL FILLING

Place the sugar and rosemary in a large pan with a single handle (see note, page 210). Cook over medium-high heat, occasionally shaking the pan, until the

.......>

CHOCOLATE FILLING

6 ounces (170 g) semisweet chocolate
(54% cacao), chopped into ¼-inch chunks

¾ cup heavy cream

TO FINISH

½ teaspoon coarse sea salt or flaky
finishing salt, such as Maldon

1 cup (50 g) lightly crushed salted
thick-cut crinkle potato chips

＊ *Having an extra hand to help you strain
the rosemary out of the caramel is
handy but not necessary. It's best to use
a saucepan with a single long handle and
a heatproof mesh metal strainer that
has a single long handle as well. If you
don't, you'll need someone around to
help you with the straining as you pour
the caramel into the tart pan.*

＊ *You might be tempted to substitute
dried rosemary in this recipe, but please
don't. Fresh rosemary gives an elusive
green herbal note that you can't get
from dried. It's subtle and adds an extra
dimension without being harsh or over-
powering. Most people will recognize
that there's something different in the
caramel but won't be able to place the
flavor. Save the dried herbs for soups,
stews, or other liquid-based recipes
that require long cooking times. The
fresh rosemary is key to flavoring the
caramel.*

sugar starts to melt. Stir the caramel with a wooden spoon or heatproof silicone spatula. Once the sugar starts to melt and brown on the edges of the pan, stir with a wooden spoon or paddle to make sure all the sugar melts. Continue to cook the caramel until it reaches a deep dark golden brown, the color of an old penny. You don't want to burn it.

Remove from the heat and carefully drizzle a little bit of the cream into the caramel while stirring with a whisk. The caramel will steam and bubble, so be careful! Continue to slowly drizzle in the cream, a little bit at a time, stirring with a whisk. Add the butter, 2 tablespoons at a time, stirring until it melts before adding more. Stir in the vanilla.

Return to the heat and cook over medium-high heat, stirring, until any solids have dissolved. Continue to cook until the caramel reaches 240°F (somewhere between the soft- and hard-ball stage). The caramel will start to thicken and look viscous. Stir in the salt and pour the caramel through a heatproof fine-mesh metal strainer directly into the tart crust (see note, at left). Press the caramel carefully through the mesh sieve so it all goes through and the strainer catches the rosemary twig and leaves. Tilt the tart sideways left and right to evenly distribute the caramel over the crust. Let the caramel cool completely before making the chocolate filling, about 1 hour.

MAKE THE CHOCOLATE FILLING AND FINISH THE TART

Place the chocolate in a medium bowl. Bring the cream to a boil in a small saucepan. Pour the hot cream over the chocolate and let it sit for 5 minutes, then stir until smooth. Pour over the cooled caramel, tilting the tart to evenly distribute the chocolate filling. Sprinkle the finishing salt over the top of the ganache, then crumble the potato chips over the salt. Refrigerate for about 1 hour to set up before serving.

PRETZEL, CARAMEL, AND MILK CHOCOLATE TART

Replace the potato chips in the crust with 3 cups (120 g) broken small pretzel twists and reduce the flour to ½ cup (70 g). Omit the rosemary from the caramel, which means you don't need to strain the caramel.

In the chocolate filling, replace the semisweet chocolate with milk chocolate. Use 1 cup (40 g) broken pretzel pieces for the topping instead of the chips.

PRETZEL, PEANUT, AND CHOCOLATE-BEER GANACHE TART (A TASTE OF BASEBALL SEASON)

Replace the potato chips in the crust with 1 cup (135 g) chopped salted peanuts and 2 cups (80 g) pretzel pieces. Omit the rosemary from the caramel, which means you don't need to strain the caramel.

In the chocolate filling, replace the semisweet chocolate with milk chocolate. Microwave the chocolate and 4 tablespoons (57 g or ½ stick) unsalted butter in a bowl for 30 seconds. Stir and cook again for 30 seconds. Stir until smooth, cooking in additional 15-second intervals if necessary. The chocolate should be fairly warm. Add ½ cup beer and stir to incorporate.

Pour over the tart and assemble, topping the tart with ½ cup (20 g) broken pretzel pieces and ¼ cup (34 g) chopped peanuts.

TRIPLE-BERRY PIE WITH TRIPLE-OAT CRUST

makes one 9-inch pie; 8 servings

One of the biggest issues with berry pies is getting them to set up properly. Nothing is more discouraging than spending the money and effort on a berry pie, only to end up with berry soup. I've made mixed berry pies numerous times before, and the only thing that was ever consistent is how inconsistently they set. Turns out, even though I was following the same recipe, berries themselves range in water content and don't always set up the same way. Which explains why you can make the same recipe twice and have one come out award-winning and one turn out drinkable. This recipe resolves the runny-filling issue in a number of ways. The thickener is tapioca starch, which sets up at a lower temperature than cornstarch or flour. It also produces a cleaner, less starchy flavor that allows the taste of the berries to come through. The filling is cooked slightly on the stove first to give it a head start in setting up before being baked. I've also added a grated apple to the filling, which not only thickens the pie (apples are naturally full of pectin, the protein that makes jams and preserves gel) but also subtly sweetens it, which means less sugar in the filling. Finally, there is the most unorthodox method of adding an extra crust, rolled out and placed in the middle of the filling. This helps give the slices extra structure. Surprisingly, the middle crust mostly disappears into the filling, leading to a slice of pie that looks as great as it tastes.

OAT CRUST

3 cups (420 g) all-purpose flour

1½ cups (150 g) rolled oats

1 teaspoon kosher salt

½ teaspoon ground ginger

1½ cup (340 g or 3 sticks) cold unsalted butter

¾ cup ice-cold water

MAKE THE OAT CRUST

Combine the flour, oats, salt, and ginger in the bowl of a food processor. Process until the oats have been reduced to smaller pieces but aren't completely ground to powder. Cut the butter into ½-inch cubes and sprinkle over the dry ingredients. Pulse the processor about 10 times, or until the butter is roughly the size of peas. Drizzle the water into the processor while you pulse it on and off until the dough starts to clump together. Stop the processor and dump the dough out onto a clean, well-floured surface. Gather the dough together and separate into three parts (about 350 g each). Flatten each dough ball into a disk about 1 inch thick, wrap tightly with plastic wrap, and refrigerate for at least 1 hour. Preheat the oven to 425°F.

·······>

4 cups (1 pound or 455 g)
strawberries, divided

2 cups (9 ounces or 255 g) blackberries

2 cups (9 ounces or 255 g) blueberries

1 apple (Jonagold or Gala)

½ cup (100 g) granulated sugar

¼ cup (35 g) tapioca starch
(see note, below)

1½ teaspoons balsamic vinegar

TO ASSEMBLE

1 large egg yolk

1 tablespoon water

2 tablespoons sparkling sugar
or granulated sugar

✳ *Tapioca starch is a thickener similar
to cornstarch, but it sets at a lower
temperature. I highly recommend it for
thickening pie fillings, as it also imparts
a lovely glossy look to the filling, has a
cleaner, more neutral taste than cornstarch, and works better with acidic
ingredients. You can find it at upscale
grocery stores or natural food stores,
but if you can't locate it or you don't
want to buy an extra ingredient, you
can substitute ⅓ cup (45 g) cornstarch
in its place in this recipe and omit the
balsamic vinegar. Once you start seeing
the cornstarch thicken on the stovetop,
cook the filling for an additional 2
minutes and then remove it from the
heat. Prolonged stirring of cornstarch
will thin it out again.*

MAKE THE FILLING

Hull and cut in half (or quarter if they are large) each strawberry, placing half of them in a large pot and reserving the other half in a bowl. Add the blackberries and blueberries to the pot. Peel and cut the apple into quarters. Cut out the seeds and stem, then grate the apple with the large holes of a box grater. Add the grated apple to the pot. Add the sugar and tapioca starch and fold together with a large spatula. Cook over medium-high heat, folding the berries constantly to make sure they don't fall apart, until the filling starts to thicken and the cloudy tapioca starch starts to turn clear, 4 to 5 minutes. The filling might initially look stringy, but keep going; it will loosen as more juice is released and the shredded apple cooks down. Remove from the heat, stir in the vinegar, and let cool.

ASSEMBLE THE PIE

Remove one disk of the dough from the fridge and roll it out into a 12-inch circle on a surface liberally sprinkled with flour. Fit into a deep-dish 9-inch pie pan. Pour half the filling (it may still be warm) into the dough, then sprinkle half the reserved fresh strawberries over the filling. Repeat with the second disk of dough and fit it over the filling. Trim any excess dough so the disk just barely fits in the middle of the pan. Pour the remaining berry filling and the rest of the reserved fresh strawberries over the dough.

Roll out the remaining dough disk into a 12-inch circle. Cut into strips. Working quickly, place the longest strip over the filling in the center and then rotate the pie 90 degrees. Place the second-longest strip perpendicular to the first. You should have an "X" on the pie. Rotate another 90 degrees and place the third and fourth strips on the right and left of the center strip. Rotate again and place two more strips of dough, lifting up the previous strips to "weave" the strips together. Continue until you have topped the entire pie. Fold the ends of the top crust into the edges.

Beat the egg yolk with the water and brush the top of the dough with the egg wash. Sprinkle sparkling sugar over the top of the pie. Bake for about 20 minutes. Reduce the oven temperature to 375°F and bake until the center of the pie is bubbling, about 40 minutes more. Let cool completely to room temperature for the filling to thicken before serving.

BLUEBERRY-RHUBARB PIE WITH CORNMEAL CRUST

Make the crust as directed, but omit the rolled oats. Instead, increase the flour to 2 cups (280 g) and add ¾ cup (113 g) cornmeal. Omit the ground ginger and make the pie dough as directed.

For the filling, use 4 cups (510 g) blueberries and replace the blackberries and strawberries with 4 cups (1 pound or 455 g) ½-inch pieces sliced rhubarb. Add ½ teaspoon ground cinnamon. Cook on the stovetop as directed, and then assemble and bake the pie as directed.

Different flours for texture

The problem with all-purpose flour is that it is finely ground and powdery with little actual flavor. This is fine for most purposes, as it's usually the filling or flavoring of a baked good that you want to shine through. The flour itself is just there for structure, meant to fade more into the background.

But the many different flours available can add flavor and texture in ways that all-purpose flour cannot. Various whole-grain and ancient-grain flours add way more flavor than all-purpose flour. But more coarsely ground flours like cornmeal, home-ground oat flour, or nut flours like almond flour add texture as well as flavor. The key is picking a flour that works with the filling or flavoring rather than clashing with it.

Cornmeal not only has a slightly sweet corn flavor to it but also has a coarse texture that works with berries like blueberries and strawberries as well as summer stone fruits like cherries and peaches. Rolled oats are basically uncooked oatmeal, so anything that works well with oatmeal will work well with oat flour. Cinnamon, brown sugar, berries, and apples are all perfect with rolled oats. And nut flours like almond or hazelnut work with chocolate, as well as berries or stone fruits that have an underlying almond flavor, like peaches or apricots.

Making your own oat or nut flour is as easy as placing the oats or nuts in a food processor and grinding into a powder. What's nice about making it at home is that you can also control how fine you grind the oats or flour. Keep it a little chunkier if you like more texture, or keep on grinding until it is much finer. With nut flours, just be forewarned that if you keep on grinding it for too long, it will turn into nut butter.

When you use any of these flours, keep in mind that cornmeal and nut and oat flours are inherently gluten-free. Gluten is the sticky protein that creates structure in baked goods. You can usually substitute up to 20 percent total of the all-purpose flour with a gluten-free flour without negatively affecting the structure.

MEAD AND FRANGIPANE POACHED PEAR GALETTE

makes one 11-inch galette; 8 to 10 servings

I've poached pears before in different liquids, including red wine, white wine, and dessert wine. But there's something fragrant and special about mead, a wine made from honey, that marries so well with pears. Mead has long been associated with Renaissance fairs, but there's a growing interest in artisan meaderies across the country that make mead with local honey. You can often find quality mead at upscale grocery stores and liquor stores. It comes in dry, semisweet, and sweet varieties. This recipe is meant for sweet, dessert-style mead, so be sure to increase the sugar and honey if you use a semisweet or dry version. Your initial poaching liquid should taste sweet, like apple juice, and any leftover liquid can be saved in the refrigerator to use as a glaze over cakes or for making cocktails. One thing to note about this recipe is that you need to let the pears soak in the liquid overnight, so plan accordingly. The crust dough can also be made a day ahead.

POACHED PEARS

2 pounds (about 5 medium) ripe but firm pears (Bosc or Anjou)

2 cups sweet mead

½ cup water

¼ cup (50 g) granulated sugar

2 tablespoons honey

1 cinnamon stick

CRUST

2½ cups (350 g) all-purpose flour

¼ cup (50 g) granulated sugar

¼ teaspoon kosher salt

1 cup (225 g or 2 sticks) cold unsalted butter

2 large egg yolks

½ cup cold water, plus 1 tablespoon if needed

MAKE THE POACHED PEARS

Peel each pear, slice it in half, and use a melon baller or spoon to scoop out the seeds. Place in a medium saucepan. Add the mead, water, sugar, honey, and cinnamon stick. Bring the liquid to a boil, then reduce the heat to a low simmer. Poach until you can easily pierce a pear with a knife, 10 to 15 minutes. Remove the pears from the poaching liquid and place them in a glass or ceramic bowl. Let the poaching liquid cool to room temperature, then discard the cinnamon stick, reserve 2 tablespoons of the liquid for the frangipane filling, and pour the remaining liquid over the pears. Cover and refrigerate overnight, or for up to 3 days (the longer you let the pears marinate in the poaching liquid, the more it will taste of the honey mead).

MAKE THE CRUST

Combine the flour, sugar, and salt in a large bowl. Stir vigorously together with a whisk until the ingredients are evenly distributed. Cut the butter into ½-inch cubes and sprinkle over the dry ingredients. Using your fingers and hands, first toss the butter in the flour, then smash the butter into thin slivers, breaking them up as you go. Once they have been broken and flattened into small bits the size of peas, add the egg yolks to the ½ cup water in a glass measuring cup and beat

·······>

FRANGIPANE FILLING

4 tablespoons (57 g or ½ stick) unsalted butter, at room temperature

¼ cup (50 g) granulated sugar

1 large egg

1 teaspoon vanilla extract

¼ teaspoon almond extract

¼ teaspoon kosher salt

1 cup (105 g) almond meal

2 tablespoons pear poaching liquid (from page 216)

TO FINISH

1 large egg yolk

1 tablespoon cold water

2 tablespoons granulated sugar or sparkling sugar

together with a fork. Drizzle the eggy water over the butter and flour. Toss with a fork until the dough starts to come together. If the dough still isn't forming, add the remaining 1 tablespoon water. Massage the mass with your hands until it forms a cohesive dough. Flatten into a disk about 1 inch thick, wrap tightly with plastic wrap, and refrigerate for at least 1 hour or up to 24 hours. When you are ready to proceed, preheat the oven to 375°F.

MAKE THE FRANGIPANE FILLING

Combine the butter and sugar in the bowl of a stand mixer fitted with the paddle attachment. Beat on medium speed until the butter is fluffy and sticks to the sides of the bowl, about 2 minutes. Add the egg and beat to incorporate. Scrape down the sides of the bowl and add the vanilla, almond extract, and salt. Mix and scrape down the sides, then add the almond meal and the 2 tablespoons pear poaching liquid. Mix to incorporate and scrape down the sides of the bowl.

On a clean surface dusted with flour, roll out the dough into a 15-inch circle. Slip a clean piece of parchment paper under the dough. Spread the frangipane filling out in the middle of the dough, leaving a border about 2 inches all the way around the edge of the dough. Cut each pear half lengthwise into 3 slices. Arrange the pear slices in concentric circles on top of the frangipane.

Once all the pears are arranged, start folding the edge of the dough over the pears in a circle, "pleating" the dough to make it fold around the pears. You should have a 2-inch border of dough and a 7-inch circle of exposed pears in the center; the whole galette should be about 11 inches in diameter and fit in the center of the parchment paper.

FINISH THE GALETTE

Carefully use the parchment paper to lift and slide the galette onto a 13 x 18-inch rimmed baking sheet. Beat together the egg yolk and the water in a small bowl. Brush the top crust (as well as under the pleats of dough to "seal" the dough to itself) with the egg wash, trying not to get any of the egg wash on the parchment paper. Sprinkle with the sugar and bake until the crust is a deep golden brown, 45 to 50 minutes. Let cool completely on the baking sheet before slipping the galette onto a serving platter.

GRILLED PINEAPPLE WITH VANILLA PASTRY CREAM ROSEMARY GALETTE

Make the crust as directed, adding 2 teaspoons finely minced fresh rosemary leaves (do not use dried rosemary) to the dry ingredients.

Instead of poaching pears, preheat a grill to high heat. Remove the crown of 1 whole fresh pineapple and cut off the prickly skin. Cut the pineapple in half lengthwise and reserve one half for another use. Slice the remaining half lengthwise again, making two long spears. Cut out the tough center core and then grill the pineapple spears. Cook until grill marks form, 2 to 3 minutes, then flip the pineapple spears and repeat. Then flip to the third "rounded" edge and repeat. Let the pineapple cool while you make the filling.

Replace the frangipane with vanilla pastry cream: Stir together 2 large egg yolks, 2 tablespoons cornstarch, 2 tablespoons granulated sugar, and ⅛ teaspoon kosher salt in a medium bowl until a paste forms. Combine 1 cup whole milk and 2 tablespoons granulated sugar in a medium saucepan. Split 1 vanilla bean lengthwise and scrape the seeds into the milk, then add the empty vanilla pod as well. Bring to a boil, then drizzle the hot milk into the egg yolk paste, whisking constantly. Once all the hot milk has been added, pour the entire mixture back into the saucepan and cook over medium-high heat, stirring constantly with a whisk, until thickened. Remove from the heat and whisk in 1 tablespoon unsalted butter and 1 teaspoon vanilla extract. Press a piece of parchment paper on the surface of the custard and allow the pastry cream to cool for 30 minutes before assembling the galette.

Assemble as directed, using the pastry cream (discarding the vanilla pod) instead of the frangipane. Slice the pineapple into ½-inch-thick wedges and arrange on the pastry cream. Fold and brush the crust with the egg yolk wash as directed. Sprinkle with 2 tablespoons turbinado sugar. Bake as directed, and let cool before serving.

Make the crust as directed, adding 1 tablespoon chopped fresh mint leaves to the dry ingredients.

Instead of poaching pears, use 4 ripe but firm fresh raw mangoes (no need to poach them), peeled and sliced into 1-inch strips.

Replace the frangipane with pastry cream: Stir together 2 large egg yolks, 2 tablespoons cornstarch, 2 tablespoons granulated sugar, and ⅛ teaspoon kosher salt in a medium bowl until a paste forms. Combine 1 cup whole milk and 2 tablespoons granulated sugar in a medium saucepan. Bring to a boil, then drizzle the hot milk into the egg yolk paste, whisking constantly. Once all the hot milk has been added, pour the entire mixture back into the saucepan and cook over medium-high heat, stirring constantly with a whisk, until thickened. Remove from the heat and whisk in 1 tablespoon unsalted butter and 1 teaspoon vanilla extract. Press a piece of parchment paper on the surface of the custard and allow the pastry cream to cool for 30 minutes; then stir in 1 teaspoon chopped fresh mint leaves before assembling the galette.

Assemble as directed, using the pastry cream instead of the frangipane and using the fresh mangoes instead of the poached pears. Fold and brush the crust with the egg yolk wash as directed. Sprinkle with granulated sugar. Bake as directed, and let cool before serving. Garnish plated slices with a fresh mint leaf.

What is a galette?

A galette is a free-form tart that doesn't use a mold or tart pan but instead just folds the crust over the fruit, allowing for a more rustic appearance and a greater crust-to-fruit ratio. You can fold the edge of the tart over by a tiny amount, showcasing the fruit inside, or you can fold the tart almost all the way over, making a free-form double crust tart with just the barest hint of fruits peeking through. I tend to let my dough chill overnight because it's easier to work with and creates a flakier crust when it's properly chilled. I roll the dough a little thicker as well so that the crust is sturdier to hold the fruit. Assembling the galette on parchment paper means it's easier to move it to a baking sheet and then to the serving platter.

Because the galette is customizable and doesn't conform to a pie or tart pan, you can easily make individual galettes, something that is always impressive for a dinner party. Just make sure to adjust the baking time, as smaller galettes may bake in less time. But one of the best parts of making galettes is the fact that they aren't supposed to look perfect and are really forgiving. Pleat the crust a little with tiny folds, or just do big folds. Make the galette square and do four corner folds however you want. You can even make triangle galettes if you like. How you make them and how you serve them (I often serve with a scoop of ice cream) is up to you!

LEMON AND FRESH MINT SHAKER TART WITH MASA HARINA CRUST

makes one 10-inch tart; 10 servings

I've experimented with a number of different citrus fruits when making Shaker pie, an ingenious recipe that requires very little work, just some time to allow the citrus to soak in sugar and let the pith soften. But my favorite version of the Shaker pie is the classic one with lemons. Meyer lemons make a wonderful change of pace, while blood oranges are brilliantly red in the middle and fun to serve. But the lemon Shaker pie is a classic for a reason. Here I've paired it with a touch of fresh mint to give an herbal brightness, and used a little masa harina flour in the crust, which is a corn flour mixed with lime water that is used to make corn tortillas. Just this tiny shift makes for a toothsome crust that really shines and goes so well with the lemon filling.

FILLING

3 medium lemons

2 cups (400 g) granulated sugar

4 large eggs

⅛ teaspoon kosher salt

3 tablespoons finely chopped fresh mint

CRUST

2¼ cups (315 g) all-purpose flour

¾ cup (120 g) masa harina
(see note, opposite)

3 tablespoons finely chopped fresh mint

1 teaspoon kosher salt

1 cup plus 5 tablespoons (300 g)
cold unsalted butter

⅔ cup ice-cold water

START TO MAKE THE FILLING

Cut the lemons in half lengthwise. Place each lemon on its flat side and slice it as thinly as you can with a sharp knife (or a mandoline). The slices should be paper-thin if possible! Place the lemon slices in a medium glass or ceramic bowl and add the sugar. Cover and let sit overnight, or for at least 8 hours and up to 24 hours, occasionally stirring the lemons to distribute the sugar. If you can't get your lemons paper-thin, I recommend letting them sit in the sugar for the full 24 hours.

MAKE THE CRUST

Combine the flour, masa harina, mint, and salt in a large bowl. Stir vigorously with a balloon whisk until the ingredients are incorporated and uniform in color. Cut the butter into ½-inch cubes and sprinkle over the dry ingredients. Using your fingers and hands, first toss the butter in the flour, then smash the butter into thin slivers, breaking them up as you go. Once they have been broken and flattened into small bits the size of peas, sprinkle the water over the dry mixture. Toss with a fork until the dough starts to come together. Massage the mass with your hands until it forms a cohesive dough. Divide the dough in half, flatten each half into a disk about 1 inch thick, and wrap tightly with plastic wrap. Refrigerate for about 1 hour or up to overnight.

1 large egg yolk

1 tablespoon cold water

2 tablespoons sparkling sugar
or granulated sugar

✳ *Masa harina can be found in upscale grocery stores, Mexican or Spanish grocery stores, and online. If you can't find it, you can use regular cornmeal or corn flour in its place. The resulting crust will be a little coarser.*

To finish making the filling, beat the eggs and salt in a medium bowl with a fork until well blended. Pour the eggs into the lemon mixture, add the mint, and stir to incorporate completely.

Generously flour a clean surface, then roll out one of the dough disks into a 12-inch circle. Fit the dough into a 10-inch tart pan with a removable bottom. Dust the surface with flour again and roll out the remaining dough into a 12-inch circle.

Pour the lemon filling into the bottom of the tart crust, making sure to distribute the lemon slices evenly. Brush some of the liquid filling up into the edges of the dough and fit the second crust over the top of the filling. Press the dough together firmly at the edges and trim them all the way around the tart pan. Decoratively crimp the edges together. Refrigerate the tart for about 30 minutes. Preheat the oven to 350°F.

MAKE THE TOPPING
Beat the egg yolk with the water and then brush it over the top of the crust. Cut decorative vent holes in the top and sprinkle the sugar over the top. Place the tart on a rimmed baking sheet and bake until the filling is bubbling through the vent holes, 40 to 50 minutes. Let cool on a wire rack to room temperature before serving.

What is Shaker pie?

Shaker pies are one of the creations of the ever-ingenious Shakers, a religious sect known for function-over-form architecture and furniture design as well as for frugal living. The idea behind a lemon Shaker pie is to make a hybrid marmalade-curd filling that doesn't waste any parts of the lemons. To do this, the lemons are sliced paper-thin and left to macerate in sugar for anywhere from 8 to 24 hours. The sugar softens and pulls out the bitterness in the lemon pith (the pith is the white part of the citrus fruit). Then eggs are added to thicken the filling. I use a tart pan because the filling, with its large amount of sugar, can be rather sweet; a thinner filling means you don't have an overload of sweet with each bite. I've found a number of citrus fruits can be used in the filling. Depending on the fruit, the maceration time can range. If you use Meyer lemons, which have thinner pith and are less bitter, you can get away with letting the slices soak in the sugar for only an hour. Fruits with a more bitter pith, like regular lemons or oranges, need longer. Limes aren't recommended, as the pith is so bitter that it makes the filling inedible. Since most of the work is done by just letting the citrus slices soak in the sugar, the hardest part of making a Shaker pie is planning ahead and starting the process a day ahead of time!

MEYER LEMON SHAKER TART WITH FRESH THYME CRUST

Replace the regular lemons with Meyer lemons. Slice the Meyer lemons paper-thin, toss with the same amount of sugar, and let sit for a minimum of 1 hour or up to 24 hours. (The rind of the Meyer lemon isn't as bitter, so they don't need to sit for as long.) For the filling, substitute 2 teaspoons fresh thyme leaves for the chopped mint. To make the crust, omit the masa harina and increase the flour to 3 cups (420 g). Substitute 1 tablespoon fresh thyme leaves for the fresh mint. Proceed as directed.

BLOOD ORANGE SHAKER TART WITH ROSEMARY-ALMOND CRUST

Replace the lemons with blood oranges, letting the oranges sit in the sugar for the same amount of time. For the filling, substitute 1 teaspoon chopped fresh rosemary leaves for the mint. To make the crust, substitute ¾ cup (120 g) almond flour for the masa harina and stir ½ teaspoon almond extract into the water before adding it to the dough. Substitute 2 teaspoons chopped fresh rosemary leaves for the fresh mint. Proceed as directed.

VANILLA AND PEACH-BOURBON ICE CREAM PIE WITH HONEY-CORNFLAKE CRUST

makes one 9-inch deep-dish pie; 6 to 8 servings

San Francisco is full of artisan ice cream shops, and none is more infamous than Humphry Slocombe, home of salt-and-pepper ice cream, foie gras ice cream (which got them featured in *The New York Times*), and their signature flavor, Secret Breakfast. A blend of bourbon and cornflakes, Secret Breakfast apparently sells four times as much as their next most popular flavor. It's one of my favorites, but I never really gave much thought to doing my own twist on it until I came across a vintage recipe for cornflake crust. Similar to graham cracker crust but made with cornflakes, it's a crisp, crunchy, and slightly sweet crust. Suddenly I knew exactly what I wanted to do the next time I pulled out my ice cream maker.

VANILLA ICE CREAM CUSTARD

2 cups heavy cream

1 cup whole milk

¾ cup (150 g) granulated sugar, divided

1 vanilla bean

6 large egg yolks

¼ teaspoon kosher salt

2 teaspoons vanilla extract

PEACH-BOURBON MIX-IN

¾ pound (340 g or 2 or 3 medium) ripe peaches

¾ cup (150 g) granulated sugar

2 tablespoons fresh lemon juice

1 tablespoon cornstarch

¼ teaspoon kosher salt

1 cinnamon stick

1 vanilla bean pod (from the custard, above)

¼ cup bourbon

MAKE THE VANILLA ICE CREAM CUSTARD

Combine the cream, milk, and ¼ cup (50 g) of the sugar in a medium saucepan. Bring the cream to a near simmer over medium-high heat. Stir constantly until you see small bubbles start to form on the sides of the pan. Turn off the heat. Split the vanilla bean lengthwise and scrape the seeds into the cream, then add the vanilla bean pod as well. Cover the pan and let steep for 30 minutes.

Combine the egg yolks, salt, and the remaining ½ cup (100 g) sugar in a heatproof bowl. Reheat the cream to a near simmer as before, then remove from the heat. Drizzle about ½ cup of the hot cream mixture into the bowl of egg yolks, stirring constantly with a whisk. Repeat with another ½ cup of hot cream. Return the egg yolk mixture to the pan with the hot cream mixture, whisking constantly.

Cook over medium-low heat, stirring constantly with a rubber spatula and making sure to scrape the sides and bottom of the pan so nothing cooks too fast or scorches, until the custard thickens and coats the back of a spoon and holds a line when you draw a finger across the custard, 3 to 5 minutes. Open a 1-gallon zip-top plastic bag and set it in a large bowl. Place a fine-mesh strainer inside the bag and pour the ice cream base through the strainer into the bag. Rinse off the vanilla bean pod and save it for making the peach mix-in. Fill the bowl with ice from 2 ice cube trays and water. Submerge the bag in the ice water and let sit for 30 minutes,

........>

CORNFLAKE CRUST

3 cups (105 g) cornflakes

1 tablespoon extra-virgin olive oil

2 tablespoons honey

2 tablespoons hot water
(from the tap is okay)

½ teaspoon kosher salt

6 tablespoons (85 g or ¾ stick)
unsalted butter

QUICK SHORTCUT

Skip making the ice cream and buy a quart of good-quality vanilla bean ice cream. Make the crust and peach-bourbon mix-in the day before. When you are ready to assemble the pie, take the ice cream out of the freezer and let it sit on the counter for 10 to 20 minutes, until it softens enough to spread and layer. Assemble the pie as directed.

or longer, until the ice cream base is cold. Move the bag to a smaller bowl and refrigerate overnight. (You will add the vanilla extract to the base later.)

MAKE THE PEACH-BOURBON MIX-IN

Peel the peaches. The best way to do this is to bring a large saucepan filled with water to a boil. Fill a bowl with ice cubes and water. Cut an "X" on the bottom of each peach with a sharp paring knife. Then submerge the peaches in the boiling water for 30 seconds. Once the time is up (don't wait for the water to boil again), remove the peaches with a slotted spoon and plunge them into the ice water. Let sit for 10 seconds, then peel the skins off with your fingers.

Cut the peaches in half and discard the pits. Puree the peaches in a food processor or blender. Measure out 1 cup of the puree and place it in a medium saucepan. Add the sugar, lemon juice, cornstarch, salt, cinnamon stick, and the reserved vanilla bean pod. Cook over medium-high heat until the puree starts to boil. Continue to cook, stirring constantly, for about 8 minutes. The puree will have reduced a bit and thickened to the consistency of applesauce. Let cool completely. Discard the cinnamon stick and vanilla pod, stir in the bourbon, and pour into an airtight container. Freeze overnight.

MAKE THE CORNFLAKE CRUST

Crush the cornflakes lightly. You want them to look roughly the size of thick-cut rolled oats and fill about 2 cups. Toast the cornflakes in a large nonstick skillet over medium heat until they start to darken, 2 to 3 minutes. Stir in the oil and cook for an additional 1 minute. Mix the honey, warm water, and salt together in a small bowl until the honey and salt dissolve. Drizzle the honey mixture over the cornflakes in the skillet and continue to cook until the honey has been absorbed and the cornflakes have darkened slightly, 3 to 4 minutes. There should be no liquid left in the skillet and the cornflakes will still feel a little moist (don't worry; they crisp as they cool). Pour the cornflakes onto a large rimmed baking sheet and spread evenly. As the cornflakes cool, break up any big chunks into smaller and smaller bits, until you have cool loose cornflake bits. Melt the butter in a large bowl, then add the cornflakes and toss them in the butter. Pour the cornflakes into a 9-inch deep-dish pie pan and press them into the bottom and up the sides of the pan. Place the crust in the freezer while you churn the ice cream.

Stir the vanilla into the ice cream custard base. Churn the custard in your ice cream machine according to the manufacturer's instructions. Smear some of the ice cream on the bottom of the pie crust. Add a layer of peach mix-in, then repeat the layers two more times, ending with the ice cream on top. Smooth the top of the ice cream, and freeze overnight to firm up before serving.

PUMPKIN AND GINGER SWIRL ICE CREAM PIE WITH PECAN-MAPLE CRUST

Make the ice cream, replacing the whole milk with 1 cup (255 g) canned pumpkin puree (not pumpkin pie filling). Replace the granulated sugar with packed dark brown sugar. Omit the vanilla bean and add 1 teaspoon pumpkin spice blend. Stir in 1 tablespoon bourbon with the vanilla at the end, right before churning.

Make the ginger swirl with 1 medium regular orange, cutting the top and bottom off to create a flat surface. Put the orange on a cutting board and cut off the zest and some (but not all) of the pith (the white part of the orange). Place the orange zest in a medium saucepan. Juice the orange and add the juice to the pan. Rinse off a 4-inch piece (about 60 g or 2 ounces) fresh ginger, then slice it thinly and add it to the pan. Peel, core, and slice a Granny Smith apple and grate it through the large holes of a box grater into the pan. Add 1 cup (200 g) granulated sugar. Cook over high heat until the juices start to release and the mixture comes to a boil. Reduce the heat to a simmer and cook until the juices start to thicken slightly, 12 to 15 minutes. Pour the mixture through a fine-mesh strainer into a bowl, discarding the solids. You should have about ½ cup. Mix 1 tablespoon tapioca starch with 1 tablespoon cold water and add the mixture to the orange mixture. Return the contents to the saucepan and bring back to a boil. Cook until the mixture thickens slightly, to the consistency of maple syrup, 3 to 4 minutes. Let cool to room temperature, and then freeze until ready to use.

For the crust, toast 3 cups (330 g) pecans in a dry skillet over medium-high heat, stirring frequently, until they darken and smell fragrantly nutty. Pour the pecans into a bowl to cool. Once cool, process into a powder in a food processor (don't overprocess). Add ¼ cup (30 g) maple sugar (found at upscale grocery stores and specialty stores like Trader Joe's), ½ teaspoon ground cinnamon, and 4 tablespoons (57 g or ½ stick) melted unsalted butter and pulse a few times, until all the ingredients are blended. Pour into the deep-dish pie pan and press the crumbs into the bottom and up the sides of the pan. Freeze until the pie is ready to be assembled.

Assemble the pie as directed, layering the ice cream with the ginger swirl.

·······>

Make the ice cream custard as directed, omitting the vanilla bean and using packed dark brown sugar in place of the granulated sugar.

Instead of making the peach-bourbon mix-in, make a salted caramel swirl by stirring together 1 cup (200 g) granulated sugar, 2 tablespoons light corn syrup, 2 tablespoons water, and ¼ teaspoon fresh lemon juice in a medium heatproof glass bowl. Set the microwave for 7 minutes and microwave the caramel. Start watching through the microwave door at around 3 minutes. Once the sugar starts to turn a light amber brown, remove the bowl (it may not take all 7 minutes). Place it on a light-colored table (or place a piece of paper on the table if your table is dark colored). Watch the sugar darken until it reaches the color of an old penny, and then carefully spoon in 1 tablespoon cream. It will steam and bubble up a lot. Stir with a fork until the cream is dissolved and incorporated into the caramel, then add another 1 tablespoon. Continue until you've added 16 tablespoons cream (1 cup). Once you've added about half the cream (8 tablespoons), you can start adding more cream at once. Once all the cream is incorporated and smooth, stir in ½ teaspoon vanilla extract and ½ teaspoon kosher salt. Set aside to cool to room temperature, then freeze overnight.

Make an oat cookie for the crust: Preheat the oven to 350°F and line a baking sheet with parchment paper or a Silpat. Combine 4 tablespoons (57 g or ½ stick) room temperature unsalted butter, ¼ cup (55 g) packed dark brown sugar, 2 tablespoons granulated sugar, 1½ teaspoons honey, ¼ teaspoon vanilla extract, ¼ teaspoon baking soda, ¼ teaspoon kosher salt, and ⅛ teaspoon ground cinnamon in the bowl of a stand mixer fitted with the paddle attachment. Beat together until a paste forms and is uniform in color with no streaks of butter. Add 1 large egg yolk and beat to incorporate. Add ½ cup (60 g) thick-cut rolled oats and 6 tablespoons (50 g) all-purpose flour and mix to blend. Spread the dough onto the baking sheet and bake until the edges are turning golden brown and the center looks set (try not to overbake it), 12 to 14 minutes. Let it cool on the baking sheet completely. Then crumble the cookie into a food processor. Melt 4 tablespoons (57 g or ½ stick) unsalted butter and process the cookie with the melted butter. Pour into the deep-dish pie pan and press the crust into the bottom and up the sides of the pan. Freeze until the pie is ready to be assembled.

Assemble the pie as directed, layering the ice cream with the caramel swirl.

TRIPLE-CHOCOLATE LAYER PIE

makes one 9-inch deep-dish pie; 10 servings

My partner, A.J., is absolutely obsessed with chocolate. At one point we had a chocolate bowl in the house, always filled with random candy bars and treats. Finally he drew the line at having that much easily accessible chocolate around, and we switched the bowl to a healthier fruit bowl. This means that anytime I make a chocolate dessert, it's that much more exciting. This no-bake triple-layer pie has dark, milk, and white chocolates along with a chocolate cookie crust and a chocolate swirled whipped cream top. Who needs a chocolate bowl?

CHOCOLATE COOKIE CRUST

9 ounces (255 g) store-bought chocolate cookie wafers

6 tablespoons (85 g or ¾ stick) unsalted butter, melted

CHOCOLATE LAYERS

3 ounces (85 g) bittersweet chocolate (70% cacao), chopped into ¼-inch chunks

3 tablespoons Dutch-process cocoa powder

4 ounces (115 g) milk chocolate, chopped into ¼-inch chunks

6 ounces (170 g) white chocolate, chopped into ¼-inch chunks

CUSTARD FILLING BASE

1½ cups (300 g) granulated sugar

½ cup (60 g) cornstarch

6 large egg yolks

1 tablespoon vanilla extract

3 cups whole milk, divided

1½ cups heavy cream

MAKE THE CHOCOLATE COOKIE CRUST

Place the chocolate wafers in a food processor and pulse until fine crumbs form. Drizzle the melted butter over the crumbs and pulse until the crumbs start to clump together and look moist. Dump the cookie crumbs into the middle of a 9-inch deep-dish pie pan. Press the crumbs evenly into the bottom and up the sides of the pan. Refrigerate while you make the filling.

MAKE THE CHOCOLATE LAYERS

Place the dark chocolate and cocoa powder in a medium bowl. Place the milk chocolate in another bowl and the white chocolate in a third bowl.

MAKE THE CUSTARD FILLING BASE

Combine the sugar, cornstarch, egg yolks, vanilla, and ¾ cup of the milk in a large bowl and whisk together. Combine the remaining 2¼ cups milk and the cream in a large pot. Cook over high heat, stirring occasionally, until bubbles start to form on the edges of the pot.

Turn off the heat and slowly drizzle a little bit of the hot milk mixture into the bowl with the egg yolks while stirring with a whisk. Continue to whisk and slowly pour the rest of the hot milk mixture into the bowl. Return the entire custard base to the pot (don't bother to clean it) and cook over medium-high heat, stirring constantly with the whisk, until thickened, 5 to 7 minutes.

Pour about one-third of the hot custard base through a sieve into the bowl with the white chocolate. Pour another one-third into the milk chocolate, and the rest

······>

CHOCOLATE SWIRLED WHIPPED CREAM

1 teaspoon powdered gelatin

2 tablespoons cold water

1 ounce (28 g) semisweet chocolate (about 54% cacao)

2 cups cold heavy cream, divided

2 tablespoons granulated sugar

into the dark chocolate (about 450 g custard per bowl). Stir with a spatula until all the chocolate is melted, first the white chocolate custard, then the milk chocolate, then ending with the dark chocolate. If you stir in that order, you don't have to worry about cleaning the spatula; just wipe it against the edge of the bowl.

Pour the dark chocolate custard into the bottom of the pie crust and spread it evenly over the crust to the edges with an offset spatula if you have one, or the back of a spoon or butter knife. Scoop out the milk chocolate custard and spread it over the dark chocolate custard layer. Repeat with the white chocolate custard. Place a piece of plastic wrap directly on the surface of the white chocolate custard and refrigerate the entire pie overnight.

MAKE THE CHOCOLATE SWIRLED WHIPPED CREAM

Sprinkle the gelatin over the water in a small microwave-safe bowl and let sit for 5 minutes to soften. Chop the chocolate into ¼-inch chunks and place in a medium bowl. Microwave for 30 seconds, stir, and microwave for an additional 30 seconds. Stir until completely melted and smooth. Add 2 tablespoons of the cream to the chocolate and mix until incorporated. Set aside.

Once the gelatin has softened, microwave for 10 to 15 seconds, until the gelatin has turned to liquid.

Combine the remaining cream and the sugar in the bowl of a stand mixer fitted with the whisk attachment. Whip on high speed until soft peaks form. Reduce the speed to medium and, with the mixer on, drizzle the gelatin into the whipped cream. Raise the speed to medium-high and whip until firm peaks form. Stop the mixer and remove the bowl. Drizzle the chocolate mixture all over the whipped cream and gently fold two or three times to swirl in the chocolate, but not mixing it completely.

Spread the chocolate swirled whipped cream over the top of the pie. Return to the refrigerator for the whipped cream to set up, about 30 minutes, before serving.

DOUBLE-LEMON PIE WITH EUREKA AND MEYER LEMONS

Make the crust, using store-bought gingersnaps instead of store-bought chocolate cookie wafers.

Skip the chocolate and instead make two different custards. Make the Meyer lemon custard by combining 1½ cups (300 g) granulated sugar, ½ cup (70 g) tapioca starch, and 6 large egg yolks in a large bowl. Add ½ cup whole milk and stir with a whisk into a paste. Heat 2 cups whole milk and 1½ cups heavy cream in a large pot until bubbles start to form on the edges of the pan. Drizzle the hot milk into the egg yolk paste, whisking constantly, until all the hot milk is incorporated. Pour the custard back into the pot and cook until the custard has thickened, 5 to 7 minutes. Stir in 4 tablespoons (57 g or ½ stick) unsalted butter. Remove from the heat, strain half of the custard through a sieve into a bowl, and stir in the zest of 3 Meyer lemons and ½ cup fresh Meyer lemon juice. Pour the remaining custard through the sieve into a different bowl and stir in the zest of 3 Eureka lemons (regular lemons) and ½ cup fresh Eureka lemon juice.

Pour the Meyer lemon custard into the pie crust, smoothing it out. Then layer the Eureka lemon custard on top. Place a piece of plastic wrap directly on the surface of the custard and refrigerate the entire pie overnight.

Once the pie has chilled, make the whipped cream, omitting the chocolate and increasing the sugar to 3 tablespoons. Add 1 teaspoon vanilla extract or paste along with the melted gelatin and whip until firm peaks form. Spread over the top of the pie and refrigerate for 30 minutes before serving.

Combining adjacent flavors

Much like a color wheel, flavors work in tandem and in complementary ways. You don't want flavors to clash with each other, as they tend to bounce around in your mouth fighting against each other. But oftentimes a bitter flavor (coffee) goes well with a sweeter flavor (chocolate). Or a tart flavor (cranberries) goes well with a sweet flavor (orange). Contrast is good with flavor combinations, but you need to have some sort of common tie. After all, coffee and chocolate are both earthy flavors, while cranberries and orange are both strong flavors that can stand up to each other.

However, there is something to be said about working with flavors that are similar to each other, but just different enough to add push and pull. The layering of three different chocolates helps bring out the flavor of each type. Citrus is another good example, as lemons work well with limes or with oranges. And butterscotch and the caramelized notes of roasted white chocolate are adjacent favors that are different enough to bring out the nuances of each.

Try exploring adjacent flavors by using fruits in the same family or season. Citrus in the wintertime, apples and pears in the fall, and summer stone fruits like apricots and pluots or berries like blueberries and raspberries all common adjacent flavors that work well together. Wintry spices like cinnamon, allspice, cardamom, and nutmeg are also great adjacent flavors, while fresh herbs like thyme, rosemary, and basil can work off each other as well, bringing the herbal notes out in each.

APPLE-BLACKBERRY TARTE TATIN

makes one 10-inch tart; 8 servings

Not to brag, but I'm a great dinner guest because I tend to bring dessert along with my winning personality and charming good looks. When there are leftovers, of course I always offer to leave them with the guests, as I don't need more desserts in my house. Usually the host will keep a slice or two but refuse more because "they are watching their weight," which seems ridiculous to me because all of my friends are significantly skinnier than I am. However, this tarte tatin is so fabulous that leftovers are never refused.

CRUST

1½ cups (210 g) all-purpose flour

½ teaspoon kosher salt

½ cup plus 3 tablespoons (155 g) cold unsalted butter

3 tablespoons spiced rum, bourbon, or vodka

3 to 4 tablespoons cold water

APPLE FILLING

8 medium apples (Gala, Jonagold, or Honeycrisp)

Juice of 1 lemon

1½ cups (300 g) granulated sugar, divided

6 tablespoons (85 g or ¾ stick) unsalted butter

2 fresh bay leaves

1 cup (6 ounces or 170 g) fresh blackberries

MAKE THE CRUST

Combine the flour and salt in a large bowl. Stir vigorously together with a balloon whisk until the salt is incorporated. Cut the butter into ½-inch cubes and sprinkle over the dry ingredients. Using your fingers and hands, first toss the butter in the flour, then smash the butter into thin slivers, breaking them up as you go. Once they have been broken and flattened into small bits the size of peas, sprinkle the rum and 3 tablespoons of the water over the butter and flour. Toss with a fork until the dough starts to come together. If the dough still isn't forming, add the remaining 1 tablespoon water. Massage the mass with your hands until it forms a cohesive dough. Flatten into a disk about 1 inch thick, wrap tightly with plastic wrap, and refrigerate while you prep and cook the apple filling.

MAKE THE APPLE FILLING

Peel, core, and cut each apple into 8 slices and place them in a large bowl. Sprinkle the lemon juice over the apples, followed by ½ cup (100 g) of the sugar. Toss to coat the apples, then set aside.

Place the butter and bay leaves in a 10-inch ovenproof skillet and melt over high heat. Sprinkle the remaining 1 cup (200 g) sugar over the melted butter and lower the heat to medium. Cook until the mixture starts to melt and then turn caramel brown, stirring constantly, 5 to 7 minutes. Once the caramel has formed and the sugar has melted into a liquid brown (the butter will separate out, which is natural), remove the bay leaves and turn the heat to medium-low. Carefully spoon the apples out of the bowl with a slotted spoon and place them in the caramel. The caramel might sizzle and sputter a little, so be careful! Leave any remaining liquid from the apples behind in the bowl. Distribute the apples evenly throughout the skillet (they will be piled rather high, but they will cook down). Preheat the oven to 425° F.

Continue to cook the apples on medium-low heat until the bottom ones start to soften, 3 to 4 minutes. Dip a pastry brush into the liquid on the side of the skillet and brush and baste the apples as they cook. Cover the skillet once the apples start to soften, and cook, frequently checking and basting the apples, for 10 to 15 minutes more, until the liquid starts to thicken and the apples look softened and golden. Remove from the heat and place the skillet on a rimmed baking sheet. Sprinkle the blackberries over the apples.

Roll out the dough into a 12-inch circle on a surface liberally sprinkled with flour. The dough will be soft and difficult to pick up, so fold it into quarters for ease of placement and set it on top of the apples. Unfold the dough and carefully tuck the sides of the dough into the skillet. (Beware: The skillet will still be hot!) Cut a few steam holes into the top of the dough. Place the skillet on a rimmed baking sheet to catch any drips. Bake until the crust looks golden brown, 25 to 30 minutes. Let cool slightly, for about 15 minutes. Place a flat serving platter or cake platter upside down on the skillet. Wearing oven mitts (remember, the skillet is still hot), invert the skillet and serving platter together, then remove the skillet, leaving the tarte tatin on the platter upside down. Wipe up any unsightly dribble and place any fruit that has stuck to the pan back onto the tart. Serve warm or at room temperature.

alternative

MANGO, BLUEBERRY, AND STAR ANISE TARTE TATIN

Substitute 1 whole star anise for the bay leaves in the caramel. Substitute 4 peeled, pitted, and sliced ripe but firm mangoes (about 4 pounds, or 1.9 kg) for the apples. Cook the mangoes for 3 to 4 minutes, but then do not cover and continue to cook. Replace the blackberries with blueberries. Bake for the same amount of time.

APPLE ROSES AND SPICED BROWN BUTTER TART

makes one 10-inch tart; 10 servings

When I know I have to bust out an impressive dessert, I opt for something like this show-stopping tart, which only requires a little bit of dexterity. Despite the way it looks, this recipe isn't too difficult, but it's always a gorgeous presentation dessert for dinner parties. The best part is that it looks like you spent a lot of money at the fancy-pants local bakery. Act all indignant when your guests ask you where you bought it, but secretly know that it actually didn't take too much effort.

CRUST

1¼ cups (175 g) all-purpose flour

½ cup (75 g) whole-wheat flour

¼ cup (50 g) granulated sugar

¼ teaspoon sea salt or kosher salt

¾ cup (170 g or 1½ sticks) cold unsalted butter

2 large egg yolks

¼ cup dark rum

BROWNED BUTTER FILLING

½ cup (115 g or 1 stick) unsalted butter

6 whole cloves

2 cinnamon sticks

3 cardamom pods

1 star anise

1 large vanilla bean or 2 teaspoons vanilla extract

½ teaspoon ground nutmeg

Zest of 1 orange

2 large eggs

½ cup (100 g) granulated sugar

¼ cup (35 g) all-purpose flour

¼ teaspoon kosher salt

MAKE THE CRUST

Combine both flours, the sugar, and salt in a large mixing bowl. Cut the butter into ½-inch cubes and sprinkle over the dry ingredients. Toss the butter cubes with your hands to coat, then squeeze until they flatten out, squeezing and tossing until the dough starts to resemble crumbly cornmeal with bits of butter still in flattened chunks. In a small bowl, beat the egg yolks with the rum, then drizzle the liquid over the flour-butter mixture and fold together. As the dry ingredients become moister, work the ingredients together with your hands until they come together and form a dough. If the dough seems too sticky, sprinkle a little more flour into it. If the dough seems too dry, add a little more rum or cold water. The dough should be soft. Flatten the dough into a disk about 1 inch thick, wrap with plastic wrap, and refrigerate for about 30 minutes.

Roll out the dough into a 14-inch circle, but don't worry if isn't perfect. This dough is really forgiving. Fit the dough into a 10-inch round tart pan with a removable bottom. This recipe makes a little more dough than necessary, so if you need to, use the extra dough to patch up any holes or tears. Prick the bottom of the dough with a fork all over, then line with a piece of parchment paper and fill with dried beans, uncooked rice, or pie weights. Freeze the lined pan for about 15 minutes. Preheat the oven to 400°F.

Set the tart pan on a rimmed baking sheet and bake until very lightly golden brown around the edges, about 10 minutes. Let the crust cool on a wire rack, and reduce the oven temperature to 350°F.

.......>

APPLE ROSES

2½ pounds (about 5 medium) red-skinned firm apples, such as Braeburn, Gala, or Jonagold

2 tablespoons fresh lemon juice

¼ cup (50 g) granulated sugar

2 tablespoons unsalted butter, melted

CRUMBLE TOPPING

¼ cup (55 g) packed dark brown sugar

⅓ cup (50 g) all-purpose flour

½ teaspoon ground cinnamon

¼ teaspoon kosher salt

3 tablespoons unsalted butter, melted

MAKE THE BROWNED BUTTER FILLING

Combine the butter, cloves, cinnamon sticks, cardamom pods, and star anise in a saucepan. Split the vanilla bean lengthwise and scrape the seeds into the pan, then add the vanilla pod as well. Add the nutmeg and orange zest. Cook over medium heat, stirring frequently, until the butter melts and starts to brown and turn fragrant. Once the butter starts to brown, turn the heat off and let the residual heat bring the butter to the right point. You don't want to burn the butterfat, you just want it golden brown. Discard the cloves, cinnamon, cardamom, star anise, and vanilla pod. Let cool to room temperature.

Whisk together the eggs, sugar, flour, and salt in a medium bowl. Whisk in the butter, scraping the brown bits at the bottom of the pan into the bowl. Pour the filling into the crust.

MAKE THE APPLE ROSES

Cut the apples by placing the apple on its bottom and slicing down near the core, but not close enough to get any seeds. Rotate the apple 90 degrees and slice down again. Repeat two more times until you have a rectangular core, which you can discard, and 4 apple chunks with skin on them. Place the apple chunks flat side down on the cutting board and cut thin lengthwise slices with a sharp knife (or use a mandoline). Each slice should have one flat edge and one rounded edge with a thin piece of red skin. Place the apple slices in a large microwave-safe bowl with the lemon juice. Toss to coat to prevent the apple slices from turning brown. Slice all the apples, continuing to toss the apple slices with the lemon juice as you go. Add the sugar and butter and toss to coat.

Microwave the apple mixture for 1 minute. You don't want to completely cook the apples, just soften them enough to make them pliable. If they are still too crisp and break when you bend them, cook in additional 15-second increments, testing until they are bendable. The amount of time will depend on how thick you cut the apples and how powerful your microwave is.

Starting with the thinnest, smallest piece you can find, curl the apple slice, with the skin side at the top, into a spiral, forming a rose-like shape. Wrap another, larger slice around the first slice. Build a rose with as many slices as you can. Use a spatula (or the side of a large chef's knife) to move the apple rose to the filled tart crust. The filling should help hold the apple roses together. Repeat with the rest of the apple slices, until you have tightly filled the entire surface of the tart. Any gaps in the tart where the roses don't quite fit can be filled with extra apple slices and smaller roses.

Combine the sugar, flour, cinnamon, and salt in a bowl and stir together with a fork. Drizzle the butter over the dry ingredients and toss until crumbs start to form and stick together. Sprinkle the crumble in a ring, about 1 inch wide, around the edge of the tart on top of the apples.

Bake until the apples are a rich golden brown and the filling has set and looks puffy and slightly golden, 50 to 60 minutes. Let cool on a wire rack for at least 30 minutes before releasing the tart from the sides of the pan.

alternatives

NECTARINE ROSES BLACKBERRY TART

Make, chill, and pre-bake the crust as directed.

Toss 2 cups (9 ounces or 270 g) blackberries with 2 teaspoons cornstarch and 1 tablespoon granulated sugar. Line the bottom of the tart with the blackberries.

Instead of the browned butter filling, melt 3 tablespoons unsalted butter in a large glass bowl in the microwave, then add 1 egg, 2 tablespoons fresh-squeezed orange juice, ½ teaspoon ground cardamom, and ¼ teaspoon sea salt. Whisk with a fork to combine, and then pour over the blackberries.

Cut 1 nectarine in half, discarding the pit. Place the nectarine halves flat side down the cutting board and cut into thin slices with a sharp knife or mandoline as you did with the apples. Slice 7 more nectarines. Shape the roses as directed and transfer them to the filled tart. Continue until you have tightly filled the entire surface of the tart. Fill in any gaps with extra slices of nectarines and smaller roses.

Make and sprinkle the crumble topping as directed. Bake until the edges of the tart are golden brown and the center of the filling starts to look puffy, 40 to 45 minutes. Let cool to room temperature before serving.

Make, chill, and pre-bake the crust as directed.

Make the browned butter filling as directed, omitting the cloves, cinnamon, cardamom, star anise, nutmeg, and orange zest and adding 3 fresh bay leaves, torn in half. Add the vanilla bean seeds and pod and cook as directed. Discard the bay leaves and vanilla pod. Proceed with the filling as directed, and then pour into the crust.

Cut 1 black or red firm but ripe plum in half, discarding the pit. Place the plum halves flat side down on the cutting board and cut thin slices with a sharp knife or mandoline as you did for the apples. Slice 5 more plums and 8 apricots. Shape the roses as directed, starting with a plum slice, then alternating apricot and plum slices. Transfer the fruit roses to the filled tart. Continue until you have tightly filled the entire surface of the tart. Fill in any gaps with extra slices of apricots or plums and smaller roses.

Make and sprinkle the crumble topping as directed. Bake until the edges of the tart are golden brown and the center of the filling starts to look puffy, 40 to 45 minutes. Let cool to room temperature before serving.

RASPBERRY-GRAPE CRÈME FRAÎCHE TART WITH PEANUT BUTTER CRUST

makes one 10-inch tart; 10 to 12 servings

The idea of clafoutis always sounds more interesting to me than it turns out to be in reality. No disrespect to the classic dessert (a custard studded with seasonal fruit, traditionally cherries), but I always want something a little more dynamic. So when I ran across a tart recipe by Deborah Madison that uses a batter underneath the custard, I knew it was exactly what was missing. Adding a crust, made from a thick batter that doesn't require rolling out, gives an extra dimension of flavor and texture that anchors the dessert. This custard also has less egg in it than a traditional clafoutis, so expect more of a cake-like tart that's not as custardy-creamy. I've used raspberries and grapes, as well as peanut butter in the crust, a subtle nod to the classic PB & J sandwich.

PEANUT BUTTER CRUST

½ cup (100 g) granulated sugar

⅓ cup (95 g) smooth peanut butter (do not use natural)

¼ cup (57 g or ½ stick) unsalted butter, at room temperature

¼ teaspoon kosher salt

3 large eggs

1 teaspoon vanilla extract

½ cup (70 g) all-purpose flour

½ cup (75 g) whole-wheat flour

CRÈME FRAÎCHE BATTER

¾ cup (200 g) crème fraîche

¼ cup (50 g) granulated sugar

1 large egg

½ teaspoon vanilla extract

MAKE THE PEANUT BUTTER CRUST

Preheat the oven to 375°F. Place a 10-inch tart pan with a removable bottom on a rimmed baking sheet.

Combine the sugar, peanut butter, butter and salt in the bowl of a stand mixer fitted with the paddle attachment. Beat together on medium speed until creamy. Add the eggs all at once and the vanilla and beat to incorporate. Scrape down the sides of the bowl with a spatula and then add both flours. Mix until the dry ingredients are absorbed. Scrape the batter into the tart pan and spread it evenly over the bottom and up the sides using the back of a spoon.

MAKE THE CRÈME FRAÎCHE BATTER

Combine the crème fraîche, sugar, egg, and vanilla in the mixer bowl (no need to clean it). Mix on medium speed until well blended. Pour into the crust and spread to the edges. The custard will be thin.

ADD THE FRUIT TOPPING

Place a ring of grape halves all the way around the edge of the tart in the custard, and then place a ring of raspberries right inside the grapes. Repeat, making

·······>

1 cup (200 g) green grapes,
sliced lengthwise

1 cup (200 g) fresh raspberries

2 tablespoons granulated sugar

Powdered sugar, for dusting

concentric rings of fruit, until all the fruit is used up. Sprinkle the sugar over the tart and bake until the edges of the tart start to look golden brown and nicely baked, 40 to 45 minutes. Let cool in the pan, then dust lightly with powdered sugar right before serving.

alternatives

BLACKBERRY AND FIG MASCARPONE HONEY TART WITH TAHINI CRUST

Preheat the oven and prepare the tart pan as directed. Make the crust as directed, replacing the peanut butter with tahini.

Make the custard by mixing together 1 cup (8 ounces or 225 g) mascarpone cheese, 3 tablespoons honey, 1 large egg, 1 large egg yolk, and 1 teaspoon vanilla extract.

To assemble the tart, use 1 cup (170 g) fresh blackberries and 10 to 12 fresh figs, sliced in half. Lay the fig halves around the edge of the tart pan, with the figs sideways and the stem half overlapping the bottom of the neighboring fig half for a "shingled" look. Sprinkle the blackberries all over the inside of the tart. Sprinkle with the granulated sugar, and then bake as directed. Let cool in the tart pan, then drizzle 2 tablespoons honey over the figs and blackberries before serving.

APRICOT AND CHERRY GOAT CHEESE TART WITH NUTELLA CRUST

Preheat the oven and prepare the tart pan as directed. Make the crust as directed, replacing the peanut butter with Nutella and reducing the sugar to ¼ cup (50 g).

Make the custard by mixing together ¾ cup (6 ounces or 170 g) soft goat cheese, ¼ cup heavy cream, ¼ cup (50 g) granulated sugar, 1 large egg, 2 teaspoons vanilla extract, and ½ teaspoon almond extract.

To assemble the tart, use 1 cup (115 g) pitted and halved sweet cherries and 6 to 7 medium apricots, sliced and pitted. Place a ring of apricots around the edge of the tart, then a ring of cherry halves inside the apricots, then alternating rings of apricots and cherries. Sprinkle with the granulated sugar, and then bake as directed. Let cool in the pan, then dust with powdered sugar right before serving.

Flavoring your crust

When the subject of pies and tarts comes up, the focus is nearly always on the flavor of the filling. From fruit pies packed with apples or peaches to cream pies made with chocolate, banana, or coconut, pies are nearly always defined by their filling. But the crust is an integral structural component of the pie, and a bad, soggy, or dense crust can ruin it. There's no reason crusts can't also have their own flavor to give the pie an extra dimension.

In this recipe, I use peanut butter in the crust as well as tahini and Nutella in the alternatives. You can do this in a traditional pie crust recipe as well, just replacing some of the butter used. Because those spreads are moister than butter, you may find that you will need less water to bind the crust together.

You can also use different whole grains like teff, buckwheat, or sorghum flour to pull the crust in different directions. Adding a bit of sugar to the crust, whether muscavado, a deep, dark molasses-rich unrefined sugar; or autumnal maple sugar; or tropical coconut sugar, contributes a little extra flavor. You can get a little bolder by adding an herb like fresh rosemary, thyme, or sage or a winter spice like cinnamon, ginger, nutmeg, or allspice.

Even oils and extracts like lemon or vanilla can give a little subtle flavor that helps complement the filling of the pie.

Finally, you'll notice that I sometimes use vodka in my crust. I talk about the use of alcohol in pie crust and why I do it on page 255. Try using another alcohol like bourbon, whiskey, rum, or tequila to add a subtle touch of flavor as well. Don't bother with the top-shelf stuff, though. The cheap booze works just as well since it's being blended in with the flour and butter and baked in the oven!

BLACK PLUM AND RAINIER CHERRY COBBLER WITH CHOCOLATE AND VANILLA BISCUITS

makes 10 servings

The argument over chocolate desserts versus fruit desserts seems to rage amongst my friends. On one side are those that proclaim chocolate cake and chocolate chip cookies as king of the world. On the other are the fanatics of fruit pies, cobblers, and crisps. I don't envy those folks (like my friends Rita and Damon) who are married but feel so strongly about their differing dessert loves. For them, and other couples like them, I present this peace offering: a dessert with both chocolate and fruit.

FRUIT FILLING

3 pounds (12 cups or 1.4 kg) Rainier cherries, pitted and cut in half

3 pounds (1.4 kg) firm black plums, pitted and sliced

⅔ cup (135 g) granulated sugar

½ cup (70 g) all-purpose flour

2 teaspoons vanilla extract

1 teaspoon almond extract

1 teaspoon ground cinnamon

½ teaspoon freshly ground black pepper

BISCUIT DOUGH

1¾ cups (245 g) all-purpose flour, divided

½ cup (100 g) granulated sugar

1½ teaspoons baking powder

½ teaspoon baking soda

½ teaspoon kosher salt

¾ cup (170 g or 1½ sticks) cold unsalted butter

⅔ cup plain yogurt (regular, not Greek-style)

2 tablespoons half-and-half

MAKE THE FRUIT FILLING

Preheat the oven to 425°F. Toss together the cherries, plums, sugar, flour, vanilla, almond extract, cinnamon, and pepper in a large bowl until the fruit is evenly coated, then pour it into a 9 x 13-inch baking pan. Bake for about 20 minutes.

MAKE THE BISCUIT DOUGH

Combine 1½ cups (210 g) of the flour, the sugar, baking powder, baking soda, and salt in a clean large bowl. Stir vigorously with a whisk until the ingredients are evenly distributed. Cut the butter into ½-inch cubes and sprinkle over the dry ingredients. Using your fingers and hands, first toss the butter in the flour, then smash the butter into thin slivers, breaking them up as you go. Start rubbing and squeezing the butter with the dry ingredients until they start to clump.

Mix the yogurt, half-and-half, and vanilla together in a small bowl, then drizzle over the flour-butter mixture. Toss a few times with a fork until the ingredients are just starting to moisten but haven't incorporated completely. Move half of the dough to another bowl. To the dough in one bowl, add the remaining ¼ cup (35 g) flour and toss until absorbed and a dough forms. To the remaining dough, add the cocoa powder and toss until absorbed and a dough forms.

ASSEMBLE THE COBBLER

Once the fruit has cooked for 20 minutes, pull the pan out of the oven and drop the biscuit batter over the fruit in 2- to 3-inch rounds, alternating the doughs over the fruit to make a checkerboard pattern and covering the top of the fruit.

.......>

1 tablespoon vanilla extract

¼ cup (30 g) natural cocoa powder
(not Dutch-process)

TO ASSEMBLE

1 large egg yolk

1 tablespoon water

2 tablespoons granulated sugar

Beat the egg yolk with the water until frothy. Brush the top of the biscuit dough with the egg wash and sprinkle with the sugar. Bake until the biscuit tops are golden brown and the fruit filling has thickened and is bubbly, 18 to 20 minutes more. Let cool for at least 15 minutes for the filling to thicken before serving.

alternatives

STRAWBERRY AND PEACH CHAMPAGNE COBBLER WITH FRESH MINT BISCUITS

Preheat the oven to 375°F. Make the filling by peeling, pitting, and cutting 3 pounds (1.4 kg) firm peaches into chunks and placing them in a large bowl. Hull and quarter 1 pound (455 g) strawberries and add them to the bowl. Peel, core, and quarter 1 Gala, Jonagold, or Braeburn apple, and grate through the large holes of a box grater into the bowl. Add 1 cup (200 g) granulated sugar, ¼ cup (35 g) tapioca starch, ½ teaspoon ground cinnamon, ¼ teaspoon ground nutmeg, 1 tablespoon balsamic vinegar, 1½ cups Champagne, and ¼ cup (70 g) honey. Toss to coat, and then bake for about 20 minutes.

While the fruit is baking, make the biscuits. Combine 2 cups (280 g) all-purpose flour, ¼ cup (50 g) granulated sugar, 2 teaspoons baking powder, 3 tablespoons chopped fresh mint, and ½ teaspoon kosher salt in a bowl. Cut 6 tablespoons (85 g or ¾ stick) cold unsalted butter into ½-inch chunks. Sprinkle over the dry ingredients. Using your fingers and hands, first toss the butter in the flour, then smash the butter into thin slivers, breaking them up as you go. Rub and squeeze the butter with the dry ingredients until they start to clump. Drizzle ⅔ cup buttermilk over the mixture and toss until a dough forms. Refrigerate until the fruit is baked.

Once the 20 minutes are up, pull the pan out of the oven and drop the biscuit batter over the fruit in 2- to 3-inch rounds, covering all the fruit. Brush the top of the biscuits with the egg wash and sprinkle the top generously with the sugar as directed. Bake until the biscuit tops are golden brown and the fruit filling has thickened and is bubbly, 30 to 40 minutes more. Let cool for at least 20 minutes for the filling to thicken more before serving (the filling will still be a bit thin).

Preheat the oven to 375°F. Make the filling by peeling, slicing, and coring 2½ pounds (1.1 kg) apples (a mix of Jonagold, Gala, Braeburn, and Granny Smith) and 3 pounds (1.4 kg) pears (a mix of Bartlett, Comice, and Bosc). Cut the fruit into ½-inch chunks and combine in a large bowl. Add ¾ cup (165 g) packed dark brown sugar, ¼ cup (50 g) granulated sugar, ¼ cup (35 g) all-purpose flour, 1 teaspoon ground cinnamon, ½ teaspoon ground ginger, ½ teaspoon ground allspice, and ½ teaspoon kosher salt. Toss to coat the fruit, and bake for about 40 minutes.

While the fruit is baking, make the biscuits. Combine 2 cups (280 g) all-purpose flour, ¼ cup (55 g) dark brown sugar, 2 teaspoons baking powder, 2 tablespoons chopped fresh sage, 1 teaspoon ground cinnamon, and ½ teaspoon kosher salt in a bowl. Cut 6 tablespoons (85 g or ¾ stick) cold unsalted butter into ½-inch chunks. Sprinkle over the dry ingredients. Using your fingers and hands, first toss the butter in the flour, then smash the butter into thin slivers, breaking them up as you go. Rub and squeeze the butter with the dry ingredients until they start to clump. Divide the mixture into two bowls. To the first bowl, add ⅓ cup (85 g) pumpkin puree (not pie filling) and 1 tablespoon buttermilk. Toss until a dough forms. To the second bowl, add ⅓ cup plain yogurt (not Greek-style) and 1 tablespoon buttermilk. Repeat tossing until a dough forms. Refrigerate both doughs until the fruit is baked.

Once the 40 minutes are up, pull the pan out of the oven and drop the biscuit batter over the fruit in 2- to 3-inch rounds, alternating the doughs over the fruit to make a checkerboard pattern and covering all the fruit. Brush the top of the biscuits with the egg wash and sprinkle the top generously with the sugar as directed. Bake until the biscuit tops are golden brown and the fruit filling has thickened and is bubbly, 20 to 25 minutes more. Let cool for at least 15 minutes for the filling thicken more before serving.

BLUEBERRY, BLACKBERRY, AND CORN GRUNT

makes 6 servings

A few years ago, a friend's oven broke. An avid baker, she was annoyed that the replacement oven she ordered couldn't be delivered for a week, and meanwhile, she was tasked with bringing a dessert to an upcoming party. I suggested perhaps it was the perfect time for her to make a grunt, a cobbler-like dish made on the stovetop. It was a hit at the party. For this version of the old-time homey dessert, I combine blueberries and blackberries together with sweet summer corn. It sounds like an odd combination, but the pop of the berries and the pop of the corn kernels really work with each other.

DUMPLING DOUGH

⅓ cup whole milk

1 tablespoon fresh lemon juice

1 cup (140 g) all-purpose flour

2 tablespoons cornmeal

2 tablespoons granulated sugar

1½ teaspoons baking powder

¼ teaspoon salt

3 tablespoons unsalted butter

1 ear fresh corn, cooked and kernels cut off or ¾ cup (125 g) frozen or canned corn kernels

FILLING

4 cups (2 pints or 510 g) fresh or frozen blueberries

2 cups (1 pint or 300 g) fresh or frozen blackberries

⅓ cup (65 g) granulated sugar

¼ teaspoon ground cinnamon

Zest of 1 lemon

1 teaspoon fresh lemon juice

1 tablespoon tapioca starch (see note, opposite)

1 medium apple (Gala, Golden Delicious, or Jonagold)

MAKE THE DUMPLING DOUGH

Stir together the milk and lemon juice in a small bowl or glass measuring cup. Place the flour, cornmeal, sugar, baking powder, and salt in a medium bowl. Cut the butter into ¼-inch chunks and blend into the dry ingredients with your fingers until the mixture forms small pebble-size pieces, like sand. Add the corn and toss to distribute evenly. Drizzle the milk over the dry ingredients and toss with a fork just until a dough starts to form. Set aside.

MAKE THE FILLING

Place the berries, sugar, cinnamon, lemon zest, juice, and tapioca starch in a 10-inch sauté pan or skillet with a lid. Peel, core, and quarter the apple. Grate the apple through the large holes of a box grater into the pan. Stir the filling ingredients together and then cook over medium-high heat, stirring constantly, until the filling is boiling and starting to thicken, 3 to 4 minutes. Lower the heat to the point where the filling is at a bare simmer.

Spoon the dumpling dough over the filling and sprinkle a little extra granulated sugar over the top of the dumplings and filling. Cover the pan. Cook over low heat, maintaining a bare simmer, until the dumplings are fully cooked and a thin knife slipped into the center of a dumpling comes out clean, 30 to 35 minutes. Serve warm.

PLUM, FIVE-SPICE, AND GINGER GRUNT

Make the dumplings as directed, omitting the cornmeal and corn and adding ½ teaspoon five-spice blend and 2 tablespoons diced crystallized ginger.

Make the filling as directed, substituting 6 cups (2¼ pounds or 1 kg) chopped black plums for the berries.

Assemble and cook as directed.

✳ *You can find tapioca starch at upscale grocery stores, natural food stores, and online. If you can't source it, you can replace the tapioca starch with the same amount of cornstarch.*

✳ *To cook the ear of corn, microwave the entire unhusked ear for 4 minutes. Let cool for 5 minutes, then remove the husk and cut the kernels off. If you don't have a microwave, you can steam or boil the husked corn for 10 minutes; then let it cool and cut the kernels off.*

Grunts, slumps, cobblers, and more ....

Most people are familiar with cobblers and crisps. Fewer people know about grunts, slumps, and brown Bettys. Here's a breakdown of some of these old-school treats.

Cobbler: Fruit filling on the bottom with biscuits on top. When baked, the biscuits tend to expand and meet up with each other, creating a "cobbled" look.

Grunt & Slump: Basically a cobbler that is cooked on the stovetop, steaming the biscuits or dumplings instead of baking them.

Crumble: Fruit filling on the bottom and an oat or rolled-grain streusel on top.

Crisp: Fruit filling on the bottom and a streusel that doesn't have oats in it.

Brown Betty: Crumbs made from bread toasted golden brown and layered on the bottom and top, with fruit filling sandwiched in between.

Buckle: Basically a coffee cake with fruit piled on top. The cake rises and the batter "buckles" around the fruit.

Pandowdy: Fruit filling on the bottom with a flaky, biscuit-like dough on top. Similar to a cobbler, but midway through baking, you push the biscuit dough down into the fruit juices, then continue to bake, so that the dough soaks up the juices and also caramelizes on top.

APPLE-CINNAMON CORIANDER SWIRL COBBLER

makes 12 servings

Apples, of course, pair lovingly with cinnamon, but my current spice love affair is the combination of fruit and coriander. Coriander, a plant that produces the polarizing herb cilantro, is often used in Indian, Mediterranean, and Middle Eastern cuisine. The seed (actually the dried fruit of the plant) tastes nothing like the herb. Instead, ground coriander has a citrusy sage flavor with notes of spicy wood. It's one of those spices that plays well with savory food (pork and fish especially) as well as desserts featuring fruit like apples, pears, citrus, mango, and summer stone fruit like peaches and apricots. In this updated version of a cobbler, I've paired it with cinnamon, but the coriander adds an elusive dimensional depth that will keep your friends guessing as to what you added to the mix to make it taste so good.

APPLE FILLING

5 pounds (2.3 kg) apples (get a mix of at least 3 types)

1 cup (120 g) dried cranberries

½ cup (110 g) packed dark brown sugar

3 tablespoons tapioca starch or cornstarch

1 teaspoon ground cinnamon

½ teaspoon ground coriander

½ teaspoon kosher salt

COBBLER DOUGH

2½ cups (350 g) all-purpose flour

2 tablespoons granulated sugar

1¼ teaspoons baking powder

½ teaspoon baking soda

½ teaspoon kosher salt

¼ cup (57 g or ½ stick) unsalted butter, melted

1 cup buttermilk

MAKE THE APPLE FILLING

Preheat the oven to 375°F. Coat a 9 x 13-inch baking pan with cooking spray.

Set aside 2 apples of different types and peel, core, and slice all the other apples into 8 pieces each. Place the apple slices in a large bowl. Peel, core, and quarter the reserved 2 apples. Grate those apples through the large holes of a box grater into the bowl. Add the cranberries, brown sugar, tapioca starch, cinnamon, coriander, and salt, and toss with a large spatula until the apples are evenly coated. Pour the apples and any juices from the bowl into the prepared baking pan. Bake, uncovered, for about 30 minutes.

MAKE THE COBBLER DOUGH

Combine the flour, sugar, baking powder, baking soda, and salt in a large bowl. Stir vigorously with a balloon whisk until the ingredients are evenly distributed. Drizzle the butter over the dry ingredients and toss with a fork until small clumps form. Drizzle the buttermilk over the mix and toss with a fork until a soft, sticky dough forms. Dump the dough onto a clean surface generously dusted with flour. Press the dough into a 9 x 12-inch rectangle, dusting your hands as often as needed to keep the dough from sticking.

······>

¼ cup (65 g) packed dark brown sugar

2 tablespoons granulated sugar

1 teaspoon ground coriander

½ teaspoon ground cinnamon

¼ teaspoon freshly ground black pepper

⅛ teaspoon kosher salt

3 tablespoons unsalted butter, melted

TO ASSEMBLE

2 tablespoons unsalted butter, melted

1 tablespoon granulated sugar

MAKE THE SWIRL FILLING

Combine both sugars, the coriander, cinnamon, pepper, salt, and butter in a large bowl and stir until a paste forms. Spread the paste thinly over the cobbler dough. Roll up the dough from the long side, using a flat spatula or bench scraper to help scrape the sticky dough from the surface. You should have a 12-inch-long log. Cut the log into twelve 1-inch-thick disks.

ASSEMBLE THE COBBLER

Once the apples are done baking, pull the pan out of the oven and baste the apples with the juices from the bottom of the pan. Place the cobbler disks on top of the apples, swirl side up. Brush the tops with the melted butter and sprinkle the sugar on top. Bake until the filling is thick and bubbly and the cobbler top has turned golden brown, 30 to 35 minutes more.

alternatives

PEACH–BLACK PEPPER GINGER SWIRL COBBLER

Make the filling, replacing the apples with 4 pounds (1.9 kg) peaches, peeled and sliced. Replace the dried cranberries with dried blueberries. Peel, core, quarter, and grate 1 apple into the bowl with the peaches. Replace the cinnamon and coriander with 1 teaspoon ground ginger and ½ teaspoon freshly ground black pepper. Toss to coat, and then bake for about 20 minutes.

Make the cobbler dough as directed. Make the swirl filling, replacing the coriander and cinnamon with 1 teaspoon ground ginger and increasing the black pepper to ¾ teaspoon. Assemble the cobbler swirl biscuits and bake as directed.

SWEET CHERRY–APRICOT NUTELLA SWIRL COBBLER

Make the filling, replacing the apples and dried cranberries with 3 pounds (1.4 kg) fresh cherries, pitted and halved, and 2 pounds (1.1 kg) apricots, pitted and sliced. Replace the brown sugar with granulated sugar. Replace the coriander with ½ teaspoon freshly ground black pepper and add 1 teaspoon vanilla extract and ½ teaspoon almond extract to the filling. Toss to coat, and then bake for about 25 minutes.

Make the cobbler dough as directed. Skip the swirl filling, and instead mix together ⅔ cup Nutella, 2 teaspoons ground cinnamon, and 1 teaspoon freshly ground black pepper. Spread over the dough, and roll and cut as directed. Assemble and bake as directed.

There are so many apples on the market, from the common Red Delicious that always ended up at the bottom of the elementary school bag to heirloom varieties that you can only find at farmers' markets with poetically descriptive names like Arkansas Black, Wolf River, Blushing Golden, and Porter's Perfection. Not all apples are best for cooking, as some tend to fall apart when heated.

Keep in mind that apples, like all of Mother Nature's produce, aren't always consistent. The same variety may be crisp and tart one day and mealy and flavorless the next, due to growing conditions, storage, or the season. This is why I always recommend buying and using two or three varieties of apples when baking. Not only do you get a deeper apple flavor with a variety of textures, but also it ensures that if one apple variety at the store is a dud, the rest are there to take up the slack. That being said, these are your best bets when buying apples for baking.

Braeburn: A red and green apple that is sharp and crisp without being overly sweet or hard.

Gala: A fairly reliable crisp and sweet apple. Holds up well in baking but not particularly complex in flavor.

Golden Delicious: A classic standby, it's gotten a bad reputation as a boring supermarket apple mostly because the supermarket version is mass harvested early, when the skin is green, and then stored, leading to a rather bland apple. If you can find riper ones (at farmers' markets or directly from a U-pick farm) with actual golden-green skins, you'll be surprised to find a bright and rich apple packed with sweetness. Either way, though, these apples are fine for baking and hold their shape well.

Granny Smith: These tart green apples are popular in baking because they always hold their shape. Their tartness makes them difficult to use on their own in baked goods, but a couple of them in the mix is always a good thing for an apple dessert.

Gravenstein: Probably one of the more difficult-to-find apples in grocery stores because they don't store very well (which means you can only find them seasonally in late summertime and early fall). This older variety apple, originally from Denmark, is tart-sweet, juicy, and used a lot for baking, applesauce, and apple cider.

Honeycrisp: Like the name says, these round apples are crisp without being too dense and are sweetly refreshing. Nice for baking and eating raw but lacking a lot of dimension and complexity, so I recommend pairing with another apple when baking.

Jonagold: A cross between Jonathan and Golden Delicious, this apple is great for baking, with a nice acidity and crispness. If I find Jonagolds at the store, I usually add a few to my basket.

BUTTERSCOTCH-PUMPKIN ZEBRA PIE WITH CHOCOLATE CRUST

makes 12 servings

I always groan when I am confronted with the idea of making yet another pumpkin pie. I've been making them every year for Thanksgiving, with every possible twist. Caramel. Chocolate. Molasses. Orange. It all comes down to that darn ubiquitous cinnamon-heavy pumpkin spice. Everyone goes crazy over "pumpkin spice," but I've always given it the side eye. Then I decided to stop fighting the crazy and just embrace it and join the frenzy. My solution is to temper the pumpkin spice with warm old-fashioned butterscotch flavor. Finally, a pumpkin spice that I can fall in love with.

CHOCOLATE CRUST

1¼ cups (175 g) all-purpose flour

½ cup (55 g) natural cocoa powder (not Dutch-process)

2 tablespoons powdered sugar, sifted

½ teaspoon kosher salt

½ cup (115 g or 1 stick) cold unsalted butter

3 tablespoons cold vodka

4 to 5 tablespoons ice-cold water

MAKE THE CHOCOLATE CRUST

Combine the flour, cocoa powder, powdered sugar, and salt in a medium bowl. Stir vigorously with a whisk until the ingredients are evenly distributed. Cut the butter into ½-inch cubes and sprinkle over the dry ingredients. Using your fingers and hands, first toss the butter in the flour, then smash the butter into thin slivers, breaking them up as you go. Once they have been broken and flattened into small bits the size of peas, sprinkle the vodka and 4 tablespoons of the water over the butter and flour. Toss with a fork until the dough starts to come together. If the dough still isn't forming, add the remaining 1 tablespoon water. Massage the mass with your hands until it forms a cohesive dough. Flatten into a disk about 1 inch thick, wrap tightly with plastic wrap, and refrigerate for at least 1 hour, or up to overnight.

Preheat the oven to 350°F. Roll out the dough into a 12-inch circle on a surface liberally sprinkled with flour. Fit into a 9-inch pie pan and prick the bottom of the dough with a fork. Line with a piece of parchment paper and fill with dried beans, uncooked rice, or pie weights. Bake for 15 minutes. Remove the paper with the pie weights, and bake the crust for an additional 10 minutes. Let cool on a wire rack while you make the filling.

MAKE THE BUTTERSCOTCH FILLING

Combine the egg yolks, ¼ cup (55 g) of the brown sugar, the cornstarch, and salt in a medium bowl. Stir with a whisk to form a paste. Heat the cream in a small saucepan until small bubbles start to form on the sides of the pan. Remove from the

BUTTERSCOTCH FILLING

8 large egg yolks

¾ cup (165 g) packed dark brown sugar, divided

6 tablespoons (45 g) cornstarch

½ teaspoon kosher salt

2 cups heavy cream

¼ cup (57 g or ½ stick) unsalted butter

1 tablespoon vanilla extract

1 teaspoon natural cocoa powder (not Dutch-process)

1 cup (200 g) pumpkin puree

2 teaspoons pumpkin spice blend

heat and cover to keep warm. Place the butter in a large saucepan and cook over medium-high heat until the butter melts and the milk solids start to brown. Add the remaining ½ cup (110 g) brown sugar and stir until the sugar starts to dissolve. Add the hot cream and stir until all the sugar is dissolved and the mixture starts to boil, with bubbles forming on the sides of the pan, 2 to 3 minutes.

Turn off the heat. Drizzle about ½ cup of the hot cream mixture into the egg yolks while whisking. Repeat with another ½ cup of the hot cream, whisking constantly as you add the hot liquid. Add the hot egg yolk mixture back to the pan and turn the heat back on to medium-low. Stirring constantly with a heatproof spatula, cook the custard until it starts to thicken and coats the back of a spoon, holding a line when you draw a finger across the custard, 7 to 10 minutes. Stir in the vanilla.

Pour half the custard through a fine-mesh strainer into a bowl (about 330 g) and stir in the cocoa powder. Pour the remaining custard through the strainer into a different bowl and stir in the pumpkin puree and pumpkin spice blend.

Place the cooled pie crust on a rimmed baking sheet. Spoon about 2 tablespoons of the pumpkin custard into the middle of the crust. Spoon about 2 tablespoons of the butterscotch custard on top of the pumpkin custard. Repeat, alternating between the two custards, occasionally tapping the bottom of the pie crust on the counter gently to spread the custard out. Once all the custard is added, bake until the center of the pie just barely jiggles, 25 to 30 minutes. Let cool for at least 2 hours to set the custard. Serve right away, or refrigerate overnight. Bring to room temperature before serving.

·······>

Why booze in your pie crust?

Pie crust is made of flour, fat (usually butter, but shortening or lard can work too), and a liquid to bind it all together. You can make a perfectly decent pie crust using nearly any liquid, ice water being the classic or sometimes milk or eggs. But a few years ago, *Cook's Illustrated* magazine developed a recipe using a blend of ice water and vodka to bind the crust. The alcohol in the vodka prohibits the gluten from forming (gluten makes bread chewy and can make pie crust tough).

Vodka is great because you can add more of it to the crust dough, creating a dough that's wonderfully easy to roll out without fear of cracking or toughening. (If you were to add the same amount of water, it would make the dough tough in the end.) Vodka is also neutral in flavor.

But if you want to give your crust a little pizzazz, try experimenting with different liquors like gin, rum, or bourbon. Pretty much any alcohol that is transparent and not overly sweet will work. The alcohol evaporates to negligible amounts in the oven, so don't worry that your pie will taste boozy. You should only taste the subtle flavorings of the liquor.

SWEET POTATO–BUTTERMILK PIE WITH ROSEMARY CRUST

Make the pie crust as directed, omitting the cocoa and powdered sugar and increasing the flour to 1½ cups (210 g) and adding 1 teaspoon chopped fresh rosemary leaves (don't use dried rosemary) with the flour and salt. Chill and bake as directed.

Make the pie filling, stirring ¼ cup (50 g) granulated sugar (instead of the ¼ cup [55 g] brown sugar) into the egg yolks along with the cornstarch and salt. Melt the butter in a large pot, then add ½ cup (100 g) granulated sugar (instead of brown sugar) to the butter along with the cream. Cook until the sugar has dissolved and small bubbles start to form on the sides of the pan. Remove from the heat. Finish making the custard as directed.

Pour half the custard through a fine-mesh strainer into a bowl (about 330 g) and whisk in ¼ cup (35 g) buttermilk powder (it might take some stirring, as the buttermilk powder has a tendency to clump together). Pour the remaining custard through a fine-mesh strainer into another bowl. Mash and stir in 1 cup (275 g) canned sweet potatoes along with 1 teaspoon ground cinnamon and ½ teaspoon ground nutmeg. Place the pie crust on a rimmed baking sheet. Spoon the custards into the crust as described, starting with 2 tablespoons of the sweet potato custard and alternating with the buttermilk custard, occasionally tapping the bottom of the pie crust on the counter gently to spread the custard out. Bake and let cool as directed.

CARROT AND HONEY PIE WITH
CREAM CHEESE–CORIANDER CRUST

makes one 9-inch pie; 8 servings

Though I love earthy, sweet carrots roasted and drizzled with a little bit of floral honey, I've never really thought about honey as the main vehicle of flavor. This all changed when I went to a workshop that highlighted the variety of honey flavors. Depending on what sort of flowers the bees are sipping on for nectar, honey can range from light and floral to dark and molasses-like. For this pie, I've opted to play up the honey flavor, with a touch of the pureed carrot to cut the sweetness. Don't forget to generously sprinkle the pie with salt as well!

CRUST

1 cup (140 g) all-purpose flour

¾ teaspoon ground coriander

¼ teaspoon ground cinnamon

⅛ teaspoon kosher salt

⅛ teaspoon baking powder

6 tablespoons (85 g or ¾ stick) cold unsalted butter

2 ounces (65 g or ¼ brick) cold cream cheese

2 tablespoons vodka

FILLING

¾ pound (340 g or 3 or 4 medium) carrots

½ cup plus 2 tablespoons heavy cream, divided

½ cup plus 2 tablespoons (125 g) granulated sugar, divided

½ teaspoon ground coriander

¼ teaspoon ground cinnamon

½ cup (115 g or 1 stick) unsalted butter, melted

MAKE THE CRUST

Combine the flour, coriander, cinnamon, salt, and baking powder in a medium bowl. Stir vigorously with a balloon whisk until the ingredients are evenly distributed. Cut the butter into ½-inch cubes and sprinkle over the dry ingredients. Do the same to the cream cheese. Using your fingers and hands, first toss the butter and cream cheese cubes in the flour, then smash them into thin slivers, breaking them up as you go. Once they have been broken and flattened into small bits the size of peas, sprinkle the vodka over the dough. Toss with a fork until the dough starts to come together. Massage the mass with your hands until a cohesive dough forms. Flatten into a disk about 1 inch thick, wrap tightly with plastic wrap, and refrigerate for about 30 minutes.

MAKE THE FILLING

Peel and slice the carrots into ½-inch-thick coins. Steam the carrots in a steamer basket until the carrots fall apart when you poke them with a fork, 20 to 25 minutes. You want them soft. Put the hot carrots into the bowl of a food processor or blender. Add 2 tablespoons of the cream, 2 tablespoons of the sugar, the coriander, and cinnamon. Process or blend until smooth.

Roll out the dough into an 11-inch circle and fit it into a 9-inch pie pan, trimming any excess. Crimp the edges of the crust, then cover with plastic wrap and freeze for about 15 minutes. Preheat the oven to 375°F.

.......>

2 tablespoons cornmeal

½ teaspoon kosher salt

1 tablespoon vanilla extract

½ cup plus 2 tablespoons (210 g)
honey of your choice

3 large eggs

2 teaspoons balsamic vinegar

TO FINISH
2 large pinches of flaky sea salt

Combine the remaining ½ cup cream, ½ cup sugar, the butter, cornmeal, salt, vanilla, honey, eggs, and vinegar in a large bowl. Stir vigorously with a whisk until well blended. Pour half of the mixture (about 385 g) into another bowl and add the carrot puree.

Set the crust on a rimmed baking sheet. Pour the carrot puree into the crust. Then drizzle the plain honey custard over the carrot puree in a circular motion. The honey custard is thin, so it will just blend into the carrot puree, but you should have a few variegated shades of both custards on the top of the pie. Carefully transfer to the oven and bake until the top of the pie is dark brown and orange and the center of the pie jiggles a little bit but isn't completely liquid, 50 to 55 minutes.

FINISH THE PIE

Let cool on a wire rack to room temperature, about 2 hours. Sprinkle generously with sea salt just before serving.

HAZELNUT, CHOCOLATE, AND HONEY PIE

Make the crust as directed, omitting the coriander and cinnamon.

Skip making the carrot puree, and instead toast 1 cup (150 g) hazelnuts in a dry skillet over medium heat until they darken and smell toasty fragrant. Pour the hot hazelnuts into a clean kitchen towel and rub the nuts in the towel to remove the skins. Don't worry if you can't get all the skins off. Chop 4 ounces (115 g) of dark chocolate into ¼-inch chunks. Place in a microwave-safe bowl with 2 tablespoons unsalted butter. Microwave in 30-second intervals three times, stirring between each interval until smooth and melted. Place the nuts in a food processor along with the melted chocolate, 2 tablespoons heavy cream, and 2 tablespoons natural cocoa powder (not Dutch-process). Process until smooth. Let cool in the bowl.

Make the honey custard as directed. Divide the custard in half into two bowls and stir the hazelnut-chocolate paste into one half. Assemble and bake as directed.

LEMON, MASCARPONE, AND HONEY PIE WITH PISTACHIO CRUST

Grind ⅓ cup (40 g) unsalted pistachios to a powder in a food processor or blender, making sure not to over-process into nut butter. If there are still some larger chunks of pistachio, that's fine. Make the crust as directed, using ¾ cup (105 g) all-purpose flour and the pistachio powder. Chill and roll out as directed.

Skip the carrot puree. Make the honey custard as directed. Divide the batter in half into two bowls and stir 1 cup (8 ounces or 225 g) room temperature mascarpone cheese and 1 teaspoon lemon extract into one half. Assemble and bake as directed.

MUFFINS, BREADS, AND BREAKFAST GOODS

THEY ALWAYS SAY THAT BREAKFAST IS THE most important meal of the day, and I agree. Any meal that allows me to eat bacon, pour maple syrup over a pan-fried piece of batter, or eat a muffin is a darn important meal in my eyes. I'm a fan of baking muffins and breads because it's an excuse to make items that aren't as sweet as their dessert counterparts. Not that I have anything against the desserts. But baking less-sweet sweets means I can eat a little bit more of them and it's totally socially acceptable. Win-win.

Most muffins you buy are either heavy and greasy or gigantic and overly sweet. I pretty much have to take a nap after I eat them. But more than anything, they are one-dimensional in flavor and execution. I need more from a muffin than a few blueberries thrown in. Unless they are extraordinary blueberries, in an exceptionally well-made muffin, I just end up feeling dissatisfied. These recipes solve that issue. They are fairly sophisticated without being overly complicated and once you start making them, you'll truly understand why breakfast is the most important meal of the day.

BLUEBERRY AND CINNAMON SWIRL BRIOCHE ROLLS

makes 8 rolls

There's a stark, minimal, hipster tea shop here in my San Francisco neighborhood. I rarely go there, even though I love tea, because buying and making my own tea at home is much more cost-effective, not to mention more convenient. But that shop has a selection of pastries that I adore, and every now and then they carry blueberry brioche rolls, which I must get. The combination of rich brioche works so well with the silky pastry cream filling and the tart fresh blueberries. It's fantastic for breakfast: not too sweet nor too rich but with just enough balance to give me a slight kick in the morning, right when I need it most. I've added a cinnamon swirl to my version, giving the pastry a little more of a sugary bite. Think of this as a mash-up of a cinnamon roll with a blueberry Danish.

BRIOCHE DOUGH

2 tablespoons whole milk

2¼ teaspoons (1 package) active dry yeast

1¼ cups (200 g) bread flour

1 cup (140 g) all-purpose flour

2 tablespoons granulated sugar

1 teaspoon kosher salt

3 large eggs

1 egg yolk

¾ cup (170 g or 1½ sticks) unsalted butter, at room temperature

CINNAMON SPREAD

¼ cup (55 g) packed dark brown sugar

¼ cup (50 g) granulated sugar

3 tablespoons ground cinnamon

4 tablespoons (57 g or ½ stick) unsalted butter, melted

MAKE THE BRIOCHE DOUGH

Heat the milk in a small saucepan until warm to the touch (this should only take 5 to 10 seconds on medium-high heat, as there is very little milk). Pour the warm milk into the bowl of a stand mixer fitted with the dough hook attachment. Sprinkle the yeast over the milk and stir with a whisk to dissolve. Add both flours, the sugar, salt, eggs, and egg yolk to the milk and mix on low speed until all the ingredients are incorporated. You might need to occasionally scrape down the dough hook and hand-knead in some of the dry ingredients, but eventually all the ingredients will incorporate.

Raise the speed to medium and knead the dough until it starts to look elastic, like bread dough, and pull away from the sides of the bowl, 3 to 4 minutes, stopping the mixer occasionally to pull the dough off the hook if needed.

Reduce the mixer speed to low and add the butter in 1- to 2-tablespoon chunks. At first the dough won't take the butter, but keep pressing on, adding more butter once most of the butter disappears. This should take 2 to 3 minutes. Once all the butter is mixed in, raise the speed to medium and continue to knead. The dough will look really sticky, almost as if it's a batter and not a dough, but eventually, after about 5 minutes, it will form a really shiny dough.

·······>

PASTRY CREAM

2 large egg yolks

2 tablespoons cornstarch

4 tablespoons (50 g) granulated sugar, divided

⅛ teaspoon kosher salt

1 cup whole milk

2 teaspoons vanilla extract

1 tablespoon unsalted butter

TO ASSEMBLE

2 cups (9 ounces or 255 g) fresh blueberries

1 large egg yolk

1 tablespoon cold water

¼ cup (50 g) granulated sugar

MAKE THE CINNAMON SPREAD

Mix the both sugars and cinnamon together in a small bowl. Add the melted butter and stir with a fork until a paste forms.

Dust some flour on a clean surface, then dump the dough onto it. Sprinkle the top of the dough with more flour and roll the dough out to a 10 x 16-inch rectangle. Spread the cinnamon mixture over the dough, making sure to spread it all the way to the edges. Roll up the dough, starting from the short side, to make a 10-inch log. Slice the dough into 8 even portions using a sharp knife (the dough will be soft and it might squish a little, but don't worry about it).

Place 4 cut rolls, flat swirl side down like a cinnamon roll, onto a baking sheet lined with parchment paper or a Silpat. Press each roll down with the palm of your hand, to form a flat ¾-inch-thick disk about 4 inches in diameter. Repeat with the other 4 rolls on a second lined baking sheet. Cover the rolls with plastic wrap and let rise for 2½ hours.

MAKE THE PASTRY CREAM

While the rolls are rising, combine the egg yolks, cornstarch, 2 tablespoons of the sugar, and the salt in a medium bowl. Stir together into a paste with a whisk. In a medium saucepan, combine the milk, the remaining 2 tablespoons sugar, and the vanilla and bring to a boil. Immediately remove from the heat and slowly drizzle a little bit of the hot milk into the egg yolk paste, stirring with a whisk. Continue to slowly drizzle the hot milk into the bowl, stirring constantly, until all the milk is incorporated. Whisk to make sure everything is dissolved, then pour the entire mixture back into the saucepan.

Cook over medium-high heat, whisking constantly, until the pastry cream thickens, 2 to 3 minutes. Scrape the pastry cream into the bowl of a stand mixer fitted with the paddle attachment and add the butter. Mix on low speed until the butter has melted and mixed in. Then raise the speed to medium and mix to cool the pastry cream, about 4 minutes. Fit a piece of plastic wrap over the pastry cream, directly on the surface of the cream to prevent a skin from forming, and let cool completely in the refrigerator while the rolls finish rising.

ASSEMBLE THE ROLLS

About 20 minutes before the rolls are finished rising, preheat the oven to 350°F. Once the rolls have finished rising, press the middle of each roll to make a well. Spoon about 2 tablespoons of pastry cream into the middle of each roll, then top with ¼ cup blueberries. Beat together the egg yolk and water with a fork to make

✻ I don't recommend frozen blueberries for this recipe because they shed too much water. If blueberries aren't in season or are not available, try one of the alternatives given below instead.

✻ If you have Swedish pearl sugar, this could be a nice place to use it instead of the granulated sugar to sprinkle over the rolls before you bake them. This white, crusty sugar can be found at specialty food stores, online, or occasionally at Ikea, in its food section.

an egg wash, then brush the sides of each roll with the egg wash and sprinkle ½ tablespoon sugar over each roll. Bake until the sides of the rolls are deep golden brown, 16 to 20 minutes. Let cool on the baking sheet for 5 minutes and then move to a wire rack to cool completely.

alternatives

STRAWBERRY AND COCOA SWIRL BRIOCHE ROLLS

Make the brioche dough as directed.

Make the cinnamon spread as directed, reducing the ground cinnamon to 1 tablespoon and adding 3 tablespoons natural cocoa powder (not Dutch-process).

Make the pastry cream as directed.

Assemble and bake as directed, using 2 cups (455 g) sliced fresh strawberries in place of the blueberries.

HONEY, APPLE, RASPBERRY, AND CORIANDER SWIRL BRIOCHE ROLLS

Make the brioche dough as directed.

Make the coriander-cinnamon spread as directed, using a combination of 2 tablespoons ground cinnamon and 1 tablespoon ground coriander.

Make the pastry cream as directed, using 3 tablespoons honey in place of the sugar. Increase the cornstarch to 3 tablespoons.

Peel, core, and chop 1 medium apple (Braeburn, Gala, Golden Delicious, or Jonagold) into ½-inch chunks. Cook the apples in a nonstick skillet with 2 tablespoons unsalted butter over medium heat until the apples are soft, about 10 minutes. Toss with 1 tablespoon honey. Use the cooked apple chunks and 1 cup (125 g) fresh raspberries instead of the blueberries. Assemble and bake as directed.

BLACK FOREST CHOCOLATE MUFFINS WITH CREAM CHEESE SWIRL

makes 12 muffins

"Muffins are just an excuse to eat cake in the morning," says my friend Susie. I disagree, but I wouldn't want to go into the boring details with her about the differences in texture and sweetness between the two. These muffins, though, definitely walk the line between cake and muffin. You'll find a coarser texture and less sweetness, both hallmarks of muffins. But let's face it, it's chocolate and cherries and cream cheese. It's pretty close to a cake. Still, since it's a muffin, it's totally acceptable to eat it for breakfast!

CHERRY SWIRL

1 cup (115 g) fresh or frozen cherries, pitted and quartered

¼ cup (50 g) granulated sugar

1 tablespoon cornstarch

1 tablespoon cold water

CREAM CHEESE SWIRL

4 ounces (115 g or ½ brick) cream cheese, at room temperature

1 egg yolk

2 tablespoons granulated sugar

1 teaspoon vanilla extract

MUFFIN BATTER

1½ cups (210 g) all-purpose flour

½ cup (100 g) granulated sugar

¼ cup (55 g) packed dark brown sugar

¼ cup (30 g) natural cocoa powder (not Dutch-process)

2 teaspoons baking powder

½ teaspoon baking soda

Preheat the oven to 400°F and coat a standard 12-cup muffin tin with cooking spray or line it with paper cups.

MAKE THE CHERRY SWIRL
Combine the cherries and sugar in a small saucepan and cook over medium-high heat. Once the juices start to release, lower the heat to medium-low and cook for about 10 minutes, stirring frequently. Stir the cornstarch into the water and then pour the mixture into the pan. Cook until the cherry juices have thickened, about 2 minutes more. Set aside to cool.

MAKE THE CREAM CHEESE SWIRL
Combine the cream cheese, egg yolk, sugar, and vanilla in the bowl of a stand mixer fitted with the paddle attachment. Mix on medium speed until well blended.

MAKE THE MUFFIN BATTER
Place the flour, both sugars, cocoa powder, baking powder, baking soda, and salt in a large bowl. Stir vigorously together with a whisk until the dry ingredients are evenly distributed. In another bowl, combine the buttermilk, oil, egg, and vanilla and whisk together until smooth. Pour the liquid mixture into the dry ingredients and fold together until the batter is mostly (but not completely) formed and there are still some dry streaks. Add the chocolate and fold until the muffin batter is just combined. Don't overwork the batter, though. If there are still some dry spots here and there, that's okay.

½ teaspoon kosher salt

1 cup buttermilk

½ cup vegetable oil

1 large egg

2 teaspoons vanilla extract

½ cup (4 ounces or 115 g) chopped
semisweet chocolate (¼-inch chunks)

In each muffin cup, layer 2 tablespoons of the muffin batter, 1 tablespoon of the cherry swirl, ½ tablespoon of the cream cheese swirl, and then another ½ tablespoon of the muffin batter on top. Using a chopstick, swirl the batter around once. Bake for 5 minutes, then lower the oven temperature to 375°F and continue to bake until a toothpick inserted in the middle of a muffin comes out clean, 15 to 20 minutes more. (You might want to test a few spots in case you hit a cherry.) Let cool in the pan for 10 minutes before transferring the muffins to a wire rack.

alternative

PUMPKIN-VANILLA LATTE CREAM CHEESE MUFFINS

Preheat the oven and prep a muffin tin as directed. Skip the cherry swirl.

Make the cream cheese swirl by mixing 8 ounces (225 g or 1 brick) cream cheese, 1 large egg, ¼ cup (50 g) granulated sugar, and 1 teaspoon vanilla paste or extract. Divide the cream cheese mixture in half and stir 1 tablespoon instant coffee powder into half of the mixture.

To make the muffin batter, increase the flour to 1¾ cups (245 g) and omit the cocoa powder. Omit the baking soda, decrease the baking powder to 1½ teaspoons, and add 1 teaspoon ground cinnamon, ½ teaspoon ground ginger, ¼ teaspoon ground nutmeg, and ¼ teaspoon ground allspice to the dry ingredients. To the wet ingredients, add 1¼ cups (320 g) canned pumpkin puree (not pumpkin pie filling), omit the buttermilk, and decrease the oil to ⅓ cup. Mix as directed, omitting the chocolate chunks.

Into each muffin cup, spoon 2 tablespoons of the pumpkin batter, then ½ tablespoon of the coffee–cream cheese batter, ½ tablespoon of the plain cream cheese batter, and then another ½ tablespoon of the pumpkin batter on top. Using a chopstick, swirl the batter once around. Bake as directed.

BLUEBERRY-LEMON MUFFINS WITH CINNAMON-CARDAMOM SWIRL

makes 12 muffins

I throw around the word *obsessed* a lot. I'm obsessed with *Gilmore Girls* (even though that TV show ended years ago). I'm obsessed with cookbooks (which clearly led me down a path to writing my own). And I'm obsessed with blueberry muffins—even though they so often go wrong. Heavy, dense, super sweet, or somehow sticky *and* dry at the same time, bad blueberry muffins are a coffee-shop epidemic. Luckily, the solution is to bake your own, with a bulletproof recipe. The batter needs to be dense so that the blueberries don't sink to the bottom, but not so dense that the muffin's crumb is tough and chewy or hard and oily. This version solves all that by using the time-tested method of the wet and dry mix. I scoop out some of the batter and add a healthy punch of cinnamon and cardamom to give the muffins a little something extra. These are going to be your new go-to muffins.

2¼ cups (315 g) all-purpose flour

1 tablespoon baking powder

2 large eggs

6 tablespoons vegetable oil

Zest and juice of 1 lemon

1 cup (200 g) granulated sugar

1 cup (225 g) plain Greek-style yogurt

1 teaspoon vanilla extract

½ teaspoon kosher salt

1½ cups (190 g) fresh blueberries

2 teaspoons ground cinnamon

1 teaspoon ground cardamom

Sparkling sugar, for topping

Preheat the oven to 425°F and grease a standard 12-cup muffin tin by coating it with cooking spray. (I don't recommend paper cups, as they stick to this muffin.) Place the flour and baking powder in a large bowl and vigorously stir together using a balloon whisk until well blended.

Place the eggs in a large bowl. Add the oil, lemon zest and juice, sugar, yogurt, vanilla, and salt and beat to incorporate.

Make a depression in the middle of the dry ingredients and pour the wet ingredients into the middle. Using a large rubber spatula, start folding the wet and dry ingredients together two or three times. Add the blueberries and continue to fold a couple more times. The batter shouldn't be completely mixed at this point.

Scoop out about one-third of the batter, transfer it to the bowl that previously held the wet ingredients, and set aside. Go back and continue folding the remaining two-thirds of the batter until the dry ingredients are incorporated. Don't overmix; it's okay if there are some small dry patches.

Add the cinnamon and cardamom to the reserved one-third of the batter and stir until just incorporated. Again, it's okay to have some small dry patches.

Into each muffin cup, spoon some of the cinnamon batter and then some of the plain batter, alternating spoonfuls in the same muffin cup to get a marbled muffin. The muffin cups will be pretty full. Once all the batter is used, swirl the batters together a couple of times using a chopstick. Sprinkle the tops of the muffins with sparkling sugar.

Bake for 5 minutes. Reduce the oven temperature to 375°F and continue to bake until a toothpick inserted into the middle of the center muffin comes out clean, 18 to 20 minutes. Let cool in the muffin tin for about 20 minutes before carefully lifting the muffins out of the pan and placing them on a wire rack to cool completely.

alternative

PLUM-ORANGE MUFFINS WITH GINGER SWIRL

Replace the blueberries with 1½ cups (250 g) diced plums (2 or 3 medium red or black plums), and substitute orange zest and juice for the lemon zest and juice. Use 2 teaspoons ground ginger and 1 teaspoon ground turmeric in place of the cinnamon and cardamom.

The muffin method of mixing

Do you ever wonder why muffin recipes always tell you to be careful not to overmix the batter and how it's okay to leave dry pockets of flour in the mix? It's because you want your muffins to be light and fluffy, not miniature bricks.

The muffin method of mixing requires you to pour all the wet ingredients into the dry ingredients and then fold them together until a batter just forms, and not any longer. The reason you don't want to overstir your ingredients is because the more you agitate the dry ingredients and get them wet, the more you activate the gluten in the muffins. Gluten is the stringy protein that creates the chew of bread. For that reason (chew), you *want* to activate the gluten protein in bread; but you want muffins to stay tender, which means mixing as little as possible.

If you have solid mix-ins like berries or chocolate chunks, try to add them halfway through mixing or even at the beginning. If you wait until the batter is fully mixed to add them, you'll end up overmixing. Remember, mix until the batter just forms; even leaving a few dry patches is okay. Now go make some muffins!

GRAPEFRUIT AND EARL GREY BREAD

makes one 9-inch loaf

The first time I made this quick bread, my partner, A.J., was suspicious, because he isn't terribly fond of grapefruit *or* Earl Grey tea. But one slice was enough to win him over. The bergamot orange oil used in Earl Grey tea works well with the grapefruit flavor, and the cake has a great tender crumb. It's a perfect quick and easy bread to make anytime.

1½ cups (300 g) granulated sugar

½ cup (100 g) olive oil

1 teaspoon vanilla extract

Zest of 1 ruby red grapefruit, plus ⅔ cup ruby red grapefruit juice (from about 1 medium grapefruit)

4 large eggs

1 teaspoon baking powder

½ teaspoon kosher salt

½ teaspoon baking soda

2½ cups (350 g) all-purpose flour

⅔ cup (140 g) sour cream

1 tablespoon Earl Grey tea (from 2 or 3 tea bags)

1 teaspoon Dutch-process cocoa powder

4 drops red food coloring (optional)

Preheat the oven to 350°F. Generously coat a 5 x 9-inch loaf pan with cooking spray. Line the bottom and long sides with a piece of parchment paper, with 1 inch of the paper hanging over the sides of the pan.

Combine the sugar, oil, vanilla, and grapefruit zest in the bowl of a stand mixer fitted with the paddle attachment. Beat on medium speed until the ingredients are incorporated completely and uniform in color. Add the eggs, one at a time, beating to incorporate between additions. Add the baking powder, salt, and baking soda, then beat to incorporate completely. Add the grapefruit juice and beat to incorporate.

Add the flour and blend on low speed until the flour is incorporated. Add the sour cream and beat until incorporated. Scoop one-quarter of the batter into a medium bowl and stir in the tea leaves and cocoa powder until uniform in color. Add the red food coloring (if using) to the larger amount of batter and stir until uniform in color. Pour half the plain grapefruit batter into the pan, then half the Earl Grey batter, then the rest of the grapefruit batter and the rest of the Earl Grey batter. Using a butter knife, swirl the batter together a few times, making "figure eight" motions in the batter.

Bake until a skewer or toothpick inserted in the center of the loaf comes out clean, 60 to 70 minutes. Let cool in the pan for about 5 minutes before using the parchment paper overhang to lift the loaf out of the pan and transfer it to a wire rack to cool completely.

MATCHA-MINT AND LEMON-GINGER BREAD

Preheat the oven and prep the loaf pan as directed. Stir 2 tablespoons fresh lemon juice into 1¼ cups whole milk and set aside to thicken. When making the batter, replace the grapefruit zest with the zest of 1 lemon and omit the grapefruit juice and yogurt. After mixing in the salt and baking powder, add half of the lemon-milk mixture and mix on low speed until incorporated. Add the flour and mix until incorporated. Add the remaining milk and mix until incorporated.

Scoop out one-third of the batter and stir in 1 tablespoon matcha green tea powder and 1½ teaspoons mint tea (about the content of 1 tea bag) instead of the Earl Grey and cocoa powder. Into the remaining two-thirds of the batter, fold in 2 teaspoons ground ginger and ½ teaspoon ground turmeric. Pour half the lemon-ginger batter into the pan, then half the green tea batter over it, then the rest of the lemon-ginger batter and the rest of the green tea batter. Swirl, bake, and cool as directed.

Quick batter breads and muffins

Quick batter breads are basically similar to muffins except baked in a loaf pan (obviously). You can usually use the same batter to make breads or muffins, though sometimes a little tinkering might be needed, since muffins might bake up a little drier than breads. Because of their sizes, the biggest difference is the baking time.

If you are baking a loaf at 350°F, usually the baking time is anywhere from 50 to 70 minutes, depending on the batter. Muffins are usually baked at a slightly higher temperature, 375°F, since they are smaller and there is less risk of burning the outside before the inside bakes through. The muffins can be done anywhere between 15 and 30 minutes. The easiest way to check is with a toothpick or skewer inserted into the middle of the bread or muffin (test one close to the middle of the muffin tin), but the most accurate way is to check with an instant-read thermometer. The inside of a loaf of perfectly baked quick bread or a muffin should be 190°F. Anything over 205°F and the muffin or bread is going come out dry.

STRAWBERRY-BANANA MUFFINS WITH NUTELLA FILLING AND HAZELNUT-COCOA CRUMB TOPPING

makes 12 muffins

A friend of mine once asked me why the top of a muffin always tastes better than the rest of it. Sad muffin bottoms, they always get a bad rap. My friend was only half joking when he asked the question, but the answer is pretty easy. Muffin tops get a little punch of flavor and texture from their direct exposure to the heat of the oven. The exposed batter on top caramelizes, which creates all sorts of awesome flavor. Of course, the top also often has a nifty crumb or sugar topping, so there's that advantage. So the question remains, how can you jazz up your muffin bottoms? My solution is to give them a filling! I've added a dollop of Nutella inside these muffins, *and* given the top a sprinkling of crumb topping. Sure, it walks the line between breakfast and dessert, but every now and then it's a line worth walking.

NUTELLA FILLING

¼ to ⅓ cup (75 to 100 g) Nutella or other hazelnut-cocoa spread

CRUMB TOPPING

¼ cup (40 g) hazelnuts

½ cup (110 g) packed dark brown sugar

2 tablespoons natural cocoa powder (not Dutch-process)

1 tablespoon all-purpose flour

4 tablespoons (57 g or ½ stick) cold unsalted butter

MUFFIN BATTER

1 cup (140 g) all-purpose flour

¾ cup (115 g) whole-wheat flour

1½ teaspoons baking powder

1 teaspoon baking soda

½ teaspoon kosher salt

MAKE THE NUTELLA FILLING

Spoon 12 portions of about 1 teaspoon Nutella onto a plate and place in the freezer to chill while you make the muffins.

MAKE THE CRUMB TOPPING

Place the hazelnuts in a zip-top freezer bag and crush them with a rolling pin. You want them to be in fairly small pieces, but a few chunkier bits are okay. Empty the nuts into a medium bowl and add the brown sugar, cocoa powder, and flour. Cut the cold butter into ½-inch chunks and add them to the bowl. Using your fingers and hands, first toss the butter in the dry ingredients, then smash the butter into thin slivers, breaking them up as you go. Once the butter has been broken and flattened into small bits, place the topping in the refrigerator to chill as you make the muffin batter.

MAKE THE MUFFIN BATTER

Coat a standard 12-cup muffin tin with cooking spray. Preheat the oven to 425°F. Combine the flours, baking powder, baking soda, and salt in a bowl. Stir vigorously together with a whisk until the ingredients are evenly distributed. Place the bananas, both sugars, the vanilla, and ginger in the bowl of a stand mixer fitted with the paddle attachment. Mix on medium speed until the bananas are liquefied.

3 ripe bananas

½ cup (100 g) granulated sugar

¼ cup (55 g) packed dark brown sugar

1 teaspoon vanilla extract

1 teaspoon ground ginger

½ cup (115 g or 1 stick) unsalted butter

1 large egg

2 cups (320 g) sliced fresh strawberries

EASY ALTERNATIVE

You can replace the Nutella with peanut butter if you want a slightly less sweet filling.

Brown the butter in a medium skillet over medium-high heat. Stir constantly until the butter has melted and the milk fats start to brown and smell fragrantly nutty. Immediately remove from the heat and pour into the bowl with the bananas (there may be some sizzle), making sure to scrape all the browned bits into the bowl as well. Beat the puree until the butter is incorporated and the outside of the bowl is cool to the touch, 3 to 4 minutes. Add the egg and beat to incorporate. Remove the bowl from the mixer stand and fold in the strawberries by hand with a large spatula.

Fill each muffin cup about two-thirds with the muffin batter. Place the frozen Nutella in the middle of each muffin and cover with the remaining muffin batter. Sprinkle the crumb topping over each muffin. Immediately transfer the pan to the oven and bake for 5 minutes. Lower the oven temperature to 375°F and bake until a toothpick inserted in the center of a muffin comes out clean, 18 to 20 minutes more. Let cool in the pan for about 10 minutes, then slide a thin knife around the muffins' sides and carefully move them to a wire rack to cool completely.

·······>

More ways to improve the muffin bottoms

Muffin bottoms should be just as exciting as the tops. Be sure to bake your muffins in metal pans instead of silicone ones. The silicone ones are great for cupcakes, but the heat generated by metal pans is better for muffins. I also like to bake my muffins directly in the pan as opposed to using paper liners. The papers tend to insulate the muffins, leading to a bland muffin bottom. Baking directly in the pan will result in more evenly baked muffin bottoms. Just make sure to spray the pan well with cooking spray and remove the muffins while they are still warm. I like to leave them in the pan for 10 minutes, then slide a thin butter knife around the edge of the muffins and gently move them to a wire cooling rack.

The crunchy sugar often sprinkled on top of a muffin is one of the reasons everyone loves muffins so much. But you can add a sugary coating to the sides of the muffins: First, spray the muffin tin with cooking spray. Then cut out the bottoms of paper cupcake liners and use the round disks to line the bottom of each muffin cup. Sprinkle sugar all over the sides of the muffin cups. The cooking spray will help the sugar to stick to the sides. Fill the muffin tin and bake like you normally would. Once the muffins are done, immediately (don't let the muffins cool at all) insert a thin butter knife between the side of the muffin and the edge of the pan and move the muffins to a wire cooling rack. The paper on the bottom will keep the sugared muffins from sticking.

Finally, you can totally cheat by coating the baked muffins with cinnamon sugar. Melt 6 tablespoons butter. Stir together ½ cup granulated sugar and 1 teaspoon ground cinnamon. Brush or dip the muffin bottoms in the butter and then dip or sprinkle the sugar all over the bottoms. You'll have cinnamon-sugar flavor in addition to whatever muffin flavor you just baked! Mix things up further by using a different spice like ground nutmeg, ginger, or cardamom, or a blend of your choice.

BLUEBERRY-BANANA MUFFINS WITH ORANGE MARMALADE FILLING

Replace the strawberry slices with 1½ cups (190 g) fresh blueberries, the ginger with 1 teaspoon ground cinnamon, and the Nutella with 1 teaspoon Mandarin Orange Marmalade (page 63) or store-bought orange marmalade per muffin. No need to freeze the marmalade ahead of time. Skip the crumb topping and sprinkle sugar on top instead.

PEACH-BANANA MUFFINS WITH KIWI-LIME MARMALADE FILLING AND PECAN CRUMB TOPPING

Make the kiwi-lime marmalade a day ahead by peeling and chopping 4 kiwis into a large microwave-safe bowl. Add the zest and juice of 1 lime (about 2 tablespoons juice) and ¾ cup (150 g) granulated sugar. Stir to combine and then microwave for 5 minutes. Stir and then microwave for 6 minutes more. Stir and let sit on the counter until cool. Move to a smaller container once the marmalade reaches room temperature and refrigerate overnight.

In the muffin batter, replace the strawberries with 1½ cups (185 g) chopped peaches and replace the Nutella with the kiwi-lime marmalade. When making the crumb topping, replace the hazelnuts with chopped pecans and omit the cocoa powder, instead increasing the flour to 3 tablespoons.

THE CLASSIC MORNING BUN

makes 12 morning buns

I live a couple blocks away from the renowned Tartine Bakery & Café in San Francisco, a bakery with a line out the door—people waiting for their beautiful bread, their shatteringly crisp croissants, and most of all, their famous morning buns. They're a sophisticated, grown-up take on the cinnamon bun, made instead with croissant dough, and rolled and layered with cinnamon, brown sugar, orange zest, and specks of caramelized sugar bits. The idea of baking them at home might seem daunting at first. But I've simplified the process by making a rough puff pastry with yeast in the food processor, an idea inspired by a croissant dough that Nick Malgieri wrote about in his book *The Modern Baker*. The final product is an easy weekend project, worth the effort, without all the waiting in line!

DOUGH

1 cup whole milk, divided

4½ teaspoons (2 packages) active dry yeast

2¾ cups (440 g) bread flour

⅓ cup (50 g) whole-wheat flour

¼ cup (50 g) granulated sugar

3 tablespoons packed dark brown sugar

2½ teaspoons kosher salt

1¼ cups (285 g or 2½ sticks) cold unsalted butter, divided

FILLING

4 tablespoons (57 g or ½ stick) unsalted butter

6 tablespoons (75 g) granulated sugar, divided

¼ cup (55 g) packed dark brown sugar

2 tablespoons finely grated orange zest

2 tablespoons ground cinnamon

⅛ teaspoon kosher salt

MAKE THE DOUGH

Pour about ½ cup of the milk into a small pot and heat until it's lukewarm, 5 to 10 seconds over high heat. Stick your finger in the milk to check the temperature. You just want to take the chill off the milk, not make it hot. Pour the warm milk into a bowl or glass measuring cup and add the yeast. Stir to dissolve and let sit for 5 minutes, or until bubbles form on the surface of the milk.

While the yeast is proofing, place both flours, both sugars, and the salt in the bowl of a food processor. Process until the dry ingredients are blended and uniform in color. Cut up 4 tablespoons (57 g or ½ stick) of the butter into ½-inch cubes. Sprinkle the cubes of butter over the dry ingredients and pulse in 1-second bursts until the butter is chopped into small bits and mixed into the dry ingredients (it's okay if some of the butter is visible, but the pieces should be the size of small pebbles). Cut the remaining 1 cup (225 g or 2 sticks) butter into ½-inch chunks and add them to the food processor. Pulse just two times (there will be big fat chunks in the bowl; that's okay).

Add the remaining ½ cup milk to the warm yeast-milk mixture and mix together. Pour the milk mixture into the food processor and pulse three times only. There will still be big chunks of butter and a ball of dough will *not* form. That's normal. Empty the contents of the food processor onto a well-floured work surface and carefully (don't cut yourself) remove the blade. Gather the ingredients together

⋯⋯>

½ to ¾ cup (100 to 150 g) granulated sugar

with your hands and knead and fold the dough to incorporate all the dry ingredients until a ball forms. You should only need to fold and knead a few times. Push the ball on the floured surface and shape it into a rough rectangle. Toss some more flour under the dough and, with a rolling pin, roll the dough into a 12 x 15-inch rectangle with the long side facing you (it should be in landscape orientation). Try to make the rectangle edges and corners as even and square as possible. You'll notice that there are streaks of butter in the dough. That's totally cool. If the butter starts to get warm and sticky, just dust it with a little flour.

Brush as much of the flour off the dough with a pastry brush as you can. The more flour on the dough, the harder it is for the dough to laminate. Fold the top edge of the dough one-third of the way down toward the center, using a bench scraper to help lift it off the surface. Brush off any flour from the bottom of the dough that you just folded over. Then fold the bottom edge of the dough from the bottom up and over the first fold, as if folding a really long, skinny letter, again brushing off any flour. You should have three layers and a 4 x 15-inch rectangle.

Starting from one short end, roll up the dough, as if you were forming one huge cinnamon bun. Brush the dough as you roll it to remove as much flour as possible. You should end up with a tall, skinny roll with the spiral side facing you. Flatten the roll from the top down with the palm of your hand, flattening all the layers, to create a piece of dough 1½ to 2 inches thick. Put the flattened dough in a gallon-size zip-top plastic bag and let rise for 1 hour at room temperature. Once the hour is up, squish the dough down (it won't rise much but it will feel a little squishy) with your hand through the bag and then transfer the bag to the refrigerator. Let rest for at least 1 hour, or overnight.

MAKE THE FILLING

While the dough is chilling, melt the butter for the filling and brush half the butter (reserving the other half for later) inside and on top of a standard 12-cup muffin tin. Generously dust the inside of each muffin cup with granulated sugar, about a teaspoon per cup (2 tablespoons total—but you don't need to be exact about it). Place the pan on a rimmed baking sheet. In a small bowl, toss together the remaining granulated sugar (about 4 tablespoons), the brown sugar, orange zest, cinnamon, and salt. Set aside.

Once the dough has rested and chilled, take it out of the bag and place it on a floured surface. Roll the dough out into a 15 x 21-inch rectangle, with a long side facing you, trying to keep the edges and corners of the dough as square as possible. Fold the right edge of the dough one-third of the way toward the center.

Then fold the left edge over the first fold, forming a 7 x 15-inch rectangle with three layers of dough. Turn the dough 90 degrees and roll it out a bit until you have an 8 x 18-inch rectangle.

Brush the dough with the reserved melted butter and sprinkle the filling evenly over the dough. Tightly roll the dough from the bottom edge up, forming a long, skinny 18-inch roll. Slice the dough into 1½-inch pieces and place each bun in the prepared muffin tin, flat side down. Cover loosely with plastic wrap and let sit for 1 hour at room temperature to rise.

About 15 minutes before the buns are done rising, preheat the oven to 375°F. Once the buns have risen (they won't have doubled; they'll just look puffy and maybe have risen 1½ times), remove the plastic wrap and bake until the tops are golden brown and the sugar has melted, about 45 minutes. Immediately remove the buns from the pan with a fork or butter knife and place them on a wire rack. You don't want them cooling in the pan, or they'll harden and stick to it!

Let the buns cool on the rack for a minute, then move three of the pastries into a large bowl and sprinkle with 2 to 3 tablespoons of sugar, tossing and coating them with the sugar. Return them to the cooling rack and repeat with the remaining buns, coating three buns at a time. Serve immediately. These are best eaten the same day. If you serve them the next day, you can warm and crisp them up on a baking sheet in a 350°F oven for 5 minutes.

Blitz (rough) puff pastry

Blitz puff pastry, sometimes known as rough puff pastry, is a simplified version of the traditional laminated dough that consists of many alternating layers of dough and butter. This version also contains yeast.

Using the food processor makes this dough almost as easy to make as a pie crust. But if you want to try making true laminated dough, check out my recipe for Kouign Amann on page 279, which is a simplified croissant dough that uses a more traditional method for layering and folding laminated dough.

MUSCOVADO, GINGER, AND RED PEPPER MORNING BUNS

Make the dough as directed. Roll the dough into the 8 x 18-inch rectangle as instructed at the top of the previous page. To make the filling, substitute muscovado sugar, an unrefined brown sugar found at upscale grocery stores and natural food stores, for the dark brown sugar. Substitute 2 tablespoons finely chopped crystallized ginger for the orange zest and 2 tablespoons ground ginger in place of the cinnamon. Add 2 teaspoons red pepper flakes to the filling and increase the salt to ¼ teaspoon. Roll, slice, let rise, bake, and toss in granulated sugar as directed.

SAVORY MORNING BUNS WITH HAM, GRUYÈRE, AND GREEN ONIONS

Make the dough as directed. Grease the muffin tin with salted butter instead of unsalted, and dust the inside of the muffin cups with flour instead of sugar. Roll the dough into the 8 x 18-inch rectangle as instructed at the top of the previous page and brush with the butter as directed. Sprinkle the dough with 1½ cups (225 g) chopped thinly sliced ham, 1 cup (115 g) finely grated Gruyère cheese, ½ cup (115 g) chopped green onions, and 1 teaspoon kosher salt. Roll, slice, let rise, and bake as directed. Skip tossing the buns in granulated sugar. Serve warm.

KOUIGN AMANN

makes 12 kouign amann pastries

The first time I had a kouign amann was in New York, at Dominique Ansel Bakery, which would later became famous for deep-frying croissant dough and filling it with pastry cream. That particular pastry became a huge phenomenon, with lines around the block, but I'll always remember the shop for introducing me to the kouign amann, a different laminated dough pastry. Later I learned to bake them at the San Francisco Cooking School under the award-winning pastry chef Nicole Prue, who taught me not to be afraid of laminated dough. Layered with sugar that caramelizes as it bakes, the kouign amann isn't a difficult item to make at home, but it does take some time, because you have to let the dough rest in the refrigerator or freezer between folds (or "turns" as they are called by pastry chefs). These are best eaten the day they are baked. If you're up for a weekend project and have always wanted to learn how to make laminated dough, this is a great one to start with!

DOUGH

4½ teaspoons (2 packages) active dry yeast

1¼ cups warm water (110 to 115°F)

3¼ cups (490 g) bread flour

1 tablespoon granulated sugar

1 teaspoon kosher salt

BUTTER BLOCK

1½ cups plus 3 tablespoons (380 g) cold salted European-style butter

FINAL TURN

1½ cups (300 g) granulated sugar, divided

MAKE THE DOUGH

Sprinkle the yeast over the warm water in the bowl of a stand mixer fitted with the paddle attachment. Mix on low speed for about 5 seconds to dissolve the yeast, then turn off the mixer and let the yeast proof for 5 minutes, or until you see bubbles start to form on the surface of the liquid. Once the yeast has proofed, add the flour, sugar, and salt. Mix on low speed until the dry ingredients are incorporated. Switch to the dough hook attachment and mix for 3 to 5 minutes, until the dough is elastic. Remove the dough, coat the bowl with cooking spray, then return the dough to the oiled bowl. Cover loosely with plastic wrap and let rise for 1 to 1½ hours, until the dough has doubled in size.

Turn the bowl of dough upside down onto a clean surface dusted with flour. The dough should fall out (coax it out with your hands if you need to). Press down on the dough with the palm of your hand to make sure most of the air is out, then press the dough into a thick 10-inch square. Wrap tightly with plastic wrap, set on a thin cutting board or baking sheet, and place in the freezer for 15 minutes. Flip the dough over and return it to the freezer for another 15 minutes (for a total of 30 minutes).

·······>

* *You want the dough and the butter to be the same consistency and temperature. Neither should break but both should be cool and pliable. It helps to use a good-quality European-style butter like Plugrá or Kerrygold because it has less water and more butterfat, making it more pliable in general. If either the dough or butter is a different temperature or consistency, you run the risk of rolling out one of them faster than the other. Butter will ooze or the dough will tear. This laminated dough is a little more forgiving than croissant dough, so it's a good one to start with.*

* *Kouigns amann and all laminated dough projects benefit from a cool kitchen. Don't attempt this recipe in the middle of summer without air-conditioning. The butter will melt and ooze out of the dough, or worse, incorporate into it, making a dense, doughy product instead of separate layers of dough and butter. If at any point your butter starts to ooze and melt, place the dough in the freezer for 10 minutes or the refrigerator for 30 minutes to chill the butter.*

* *Working quickly also helps, as does working on a cool marble or granite countertop. But even if you don't have those available, just read the instructions thoroughly and work quickly and with purpose. It will make a difference in the end.*

MAKE THE BUTTER BLOCK

Meanwhile, pull the butter out of the refrigerator and place it between two pieces of parchment paper. Using a rolling pin, roll the butter out into a 10-inch square. You may need to whack the butter a few times with your rolling pin to make it pliable; don't be afraid to be rough with it. Once you get the butter to the right size, wrap it with parchment paper (or just sandwich it between the two pieces) and place it back in the refrigerator.

Unwrap the chilled dough and place it on a clean surface dusted with flour. Roll the dough out to 10 x 21 inches, with a long side facing you (landscape orientation). Remove the butter from the refrigerator, unwrap it, and place the butter in the center of the dough. Fold the left and right sides of the dough to the center of the butter, enclosing the butter with dough. Try to get the dough to just meet in the center, with no gap in the middle and no gap at the ends. This part of the process is called a lock-in or enclosure.

Turn the dough 90 degrees so the center seam is horizontal to you. Hold your rolling pin perpendicularly to the seam. Roll the dough sideways, first from the center of the dough to the left side, where the butter and dough are open, and then from the center to the right side. Roll the dough until it is 24 inches long by 10 inches deep, dusting the bottom and top lightly with flour if needed.

Brush off as much loose flour as you can from the top of the dough. Measure the dough into thirds from left to right by placing a ruler on the dough and lightly scoring with a butter knife at 8 and 16 inches. Fold the right side at the first scored mark to meet the second scored mark. Brush the flour off the dough, then fold the left side over so that you have an 8 x 10-inch rectangle, folded like a letter, with three layers of dough. This is called a letter-fold.

Turn the dough 90 degrees so the long (10-inch) side is facing you and the open sides of the dough are to the left and right. Roll the dough again to the left and to the right until it reaches 24 inches in length. Occasionally roll the dough from top to bottom as well so that it is 10 inches deep. Repeat the folding as in the last step, folding first the right one-third of the dough and then the left one-third to make a three-layer letter-fold.

Repeat the process one more time, turning the dough 90 degrees, rolling it out to 10 x 24 inches, then folding it into a letter-fold. You should have an 8 x 10-inch flat piece of dough. Wrap the dough tightly with plastic wrap and freeze for 15 minutes, then flip and freeze for 15 minutes more, then move the dough to the

.......>

refrigerator and let chill for about 1 hour, or until the dough is very firm. At this point, you can leave the dough in the fridge overnight if you like.

COMPLETE THE FINAL TURN

Coat a standard 12-cup muffin tin with cooking spray and place the pan on a rimmed baking sheet. Dust a clean surface with ¾ cup (150 g) of the sugar and place the chilled dough on the sugar with a long (10-inch) side facing you. Sprinkle another ½ cup (100 g) sugar on top of the dough. Roll it out as in the previous steps to a 10 x 24-inch rectangle and fold into a letter-fold, creating an 8 x 10-inch rectangle. Rotate the dough 90 degrees and roll the dough out into a 10 x 13-inch rectangle, then, using a sharp knife, trim all the edges of the dough by ½ inch in one even cut to make a perfect 9 x 12-inch rectangle. Do not saw back and forth; instead use a ruler as a guide and just slice cleanly once. Discard the edge pieces. Cut the dough into twelve 3-inch square pieces. Take each square of dough and fold the corners into the center of the dough, pinching down, then place into a prepared muffin cup, pressing down firmly so the dough is snugly fitted in the pan. Cover loosely with plastic wrap and let sit at room temperature for 30 minutes.

Meanwhile, preheat the oven to 400°F. After 30 minutes, remove the plastic wrap and sprinkle the kouigns amann with the remaining ¼ cup (50 g) sugar. Place the muffin tin in the oven and immediately reduce the heat to 350°F. Bake until the kouigns amann are deeply caramelized, about 45 minutes. Using a fork or butter knife, immediately remove the hot kouigns amann from the muffin tin and place them on a wire rack to cool. Don't wait for them to cool in the pan, as they will harden and stick to it. Let cool to room temperature before serving.

Suggestion ....

Split a room temperature kouign amann horizontally and sandwich a small scoop of your favorite ice cream inside for an insanely decadent ice cream sandwich. I've used vanilla, salted caramel, chocolate, roasted banana, and strawberry, but really any flavor that works well with caramelized sugar will lead to a ridiculously good treat.

DARK CHOCOLATE AND PISTACHIO KOUIGN AMANN

Make the dough as directed all the way through cutting the dough into 12 pieces after the final turn. In the center of each dough square, sprinkle 1 teaspoon chopped dark chocolate (bittersweet works best, as the kouigns amann are already pretty sweet) and ½ teaspoon chopped pistachios, then press the square corners over the filling and place in the muffin tin. Let rest, sprinkle with sugar, and bake as directed.

BLACK SESAME AND GINGER KOUIGN AMANN

Make the dough as directed. Before the final turn, place 3 tablespoons black sesame seeds in a food processor and process into a powder. Mix the black sesame powder and 1 tablespoon ground ginger into the 1½ cups (300 g) sugar for the final turn. Complete the final turn using the black sesame sugar. Before folding each dough square, place ½ teaspoon chopped crystallized ginger in the center, then press the square corners into the filling and place in the muffin tin. Let rest as directed, then sprinkle with the remaining black sesame sugar and bake as directed.

Laminated Dough

Laminated dough can scare even the most experienced baker. Croissant dough and puff pastry are examples of laminated dough, which is basically created by folding and layering butter with dough. The dough is folded multiple times, creating many thin layers of dough and butter. When the dough is baked, the butter melts and the steam lifts the dough layers, creating the signature flaky pastry of croissants, Danishes, and puff pastries. Making laminated dough is time-consuming, as you need to give the dough time to rest in the refrigerator between each turn (the pastry terminology for folding the dough), and you have to make sure the dough and butter are the same temperature and consistency.

If you want to try your hand at a simplified version of laminated dough, try my morning bun recipe on page 275, in which the dough is a yeasted blitz puff pastry (otherwise known as rough puff pastry). It skips the entire butter block step and instead mixes the butter and pastry in a food processor, much like you would do for a pie crust.

ALMOND-PEACH MONKEY BREAD

makes 8 servings or feeds 3 hungry monkeys

Even before I had tried monkey bread, I fell in love with the name. I had mental images of a group of monkeys crowding around the cobbled-together Bundt-shaped bread, picking away at the balls of baked dough and shoving them into their mouths with their tiny, adorable paws. Why monkey bread is called monkey bread isn't really known, but it's easy to make and even more fun to eat. Pulling off the pieces of sticky bread is a sure way to please a crowd, even if you all have to wash your hands afterward because of the sugary sweet residue. The use of almond slivers, almond extract, and almond milk really boosts the flavor and is a great complement to the peach and cinnamon. If you don't have almond milk, you can substitute 1 cup regular milk plus ⅓ cup water or use a different milk substitute of your choice (see page 286 for more information).

BREAD DOUGH

1⅓ cups unsweetened almond milk

¼ cup (50 g) granulated sugar

2 tablespoons unsalted butter, melted

2¼ teaspoons (1 package) active dry yeast

3½ cups (490 g) all-purpose flour

2 teaspoons kosher salt

COATING

½ cup (115 g or 1 stick) unsalted butter

¼ teaspoon almond extract

½ cup (50 g) slivered almonds, divided

1 cup (220 g) packed dark brown sugar

1½ teaspoons ground cinnamon

½ teaspoon ground nutmeg

½ teaspoon kosher salt

1 large peach, peeled and sliced into ½-inch chunks

MAKE THE BREAD DOUGH

Heat the almond milk until it's warm to the touch. Add the sugar, butter, and yeast and stir to dissolve the yeast. Let stand for 3 to 4 minutes, until the yeast starts to foam. Place the flour in the bowl of a stand mixer fitted with the dough hook. Add all the liquid to the flour and mix on low speed until a dough starts to form. Once the dough gathers, raise the mixer speed to medium and knead the dough for about 4 minutes. The dough should pull away from the sides of the bowl but still be sticky. You might need to hold on to the mixer during this time, as it might start "walking" across your countertop with the dough. Add the salt and knead for another minute on medium speed.

Oil a large bowl and place the dough in it, turning to coat the dough with the oil. Cover with plastic wrap and let the dough rise until doubled in size, 1 to 1½ hours.

MAKE THE COATING

While the dough is rising, melt the butter in a small saucepan on the stove or in the microwave. Brush some of the melted butter all over the inside of a 12-cup Bundt pan, making sure to cover every nook and cranny. Add the almond extract to the remaining melted butter and set aside. Sprinkle ¼ cup (25 g) of the almonds all over the inside of the Bundt pan; they should stick to the butter. Place the pan

.......>

in the refrigerator for the butter to harden until the dough has risen. Stir together the brown sugar, cinnamon, nutmeg, and salt in a small bowl and set aside.

Once the dough has risen, dump it onto a clean surface dusted lightly with flour. Divide the dough into 40 to 50 pieces and shape roughly into 1-inch balls. Roll each dough piece first in the reserved melted butter, then in the brown sugar mixture. This is messy business, so wear an apron and expect to get your hands dirty! Place each piece in the cold Bundt pan as you work until you've used about one-third of the dough. Sprinkle 2 tablespoons of the remaining almonds evenly over the dough, then half of the peach chunks. Repeat, adding another one-third of the dough pieces, then the remaining 2 tablespoons almonds and remaining peaches. Dip the remaining dough pieces in the butter and sugar and add them to the pan. The pan should be about two-thirds full. Cover with plastic wrap and let rise for 45 to 60 minutes, until the dough has risen slightly above the edge of the pan and is pushing against the plastic wrap.

About 15 minutes before the dough has risen completely, preheat the oven to 350°F. Set the Bundt pan on a rimmed baking sheet and bake until the top of the bread is golden brown and sounds hollow when you tap on it, 35 to 40 minutes. Let the bread cool for 5 minutes in the pan. Place a serving plate upside down on the pan, then invert the pan and serving plate together and remove the pan from the bread. Let cool for 15 minutes or so before serving slightly warm.

Alternative milks for flavor

Making yeasted bread often intimidates people, but yeast is pretty easy to work with, especially if you are using commercially available packets of yeast, which are designed for consistent results. As long as you proof the yeast by first dissolving it in a liquid and making sure it starts to foam (a sign that the yeast is active), the bread should rise as expected. Yeast sweet bread is extra forgivable as well, and if you are really nervous, you can add a little extra yeast to give the bread a boost, since the flavorings of the sweet filling and glaze will cover up any extra yeasty flavor.

One thing that bakers don't really think about, though, is the liquid they use to dissolve the yeast and hydrate the dough. Water, milk, and buttermilk are the usual suspects. Water is a neutral liquid that is great for artisan breads with a very crunchy crust. If you want something more tender, milk, with its higher fat content, and buttermilk, with a little bit of acidic tang, will give you a softer crumb. But nondairy milks can get overlooked when thinking about baking. These milks can add subtle flavor to baked goods. Consider using coconut milk to add richness and the mild flavors of tropical coconut and hints of vanilla. Or use a nut milk like almond milk for a slightly nutty flavor. Other nondairy milks like oat or soy milk will lend an earthiness to baked goods, while hemp milk will give you a hint of grassy flavor, which might work better for savory baked goods. Keep in mind that not all nondairy milks are made the same and that some brands are better than others. I recommend using a brand you like to drink, one with low sugar, in your baking.

TOASTED OAT, ORANGE, AND DRIED CHERRY MONKEY BREAD

Heat 1 tablespoon olive oil in a large pan until shimmering. Lower the heat and add ½ cup thick-cut rolled oats and 2 tablespoons packed dark brown sugar. Cook until the oats brown and become fragrant. Remove and let cool. Use in place of the slivered almonds.

Place 1½ cups (240 g) dried tart cherries in a pan and add ½ cup fresh-squeezed orange juice. Cook over medium heat until the cherries are plump and have absorbed the orange juice. Use in place of the peach chunks.

In the bread dough, use oat milk in place of almond milk. Add the zest of 1 orange to the brown sugar–spice mix. Assemble and bake as directed.

COCONUT-PINEAPPLE MONKEY BREAD

Substitute 1 cup coconut milk and ⅓ cup water for the almond milk and omit the almond extract. Place ¾ cup (65 g) unsweetened coconut flakes in a dry skillet and toast over medium-high heat, stirring constantly, until they start to brown. Pour into a bowl to cool, and use in place of the slivered almonds. Substitute 1½ cups (255 g) chopped fresh or well-drained canned pineapple for the peach chunks. Assemble and bake as directed.

CHOCOLATE-CINNAMON BABKA WITH CRUMB TOPPING

makes one 9-inch loaf

I don't do well with compliments. When someone praises me or my baked goods, I usually try to brush it off. This never works, of course, and I've slowly gotten better at just graciously saying "Thank you." But you can imagine my embarrassment when a mutual friend introduced me to Ruth Reichl, the famous food writer and former editor-in-chief of *Gourmet* magazine—and immediately my friend told her that not only was I writing a cookbook, but that I also made the best babka she had ever tasted! Ms. Reichl peered at me through her glasses as if she were sizing me up. Thankfully, she was very gracious and, sensing my discomfort, changed the subject, and we had a lovely conversation about New Zealand instead. But if I ever have a chance to meet her again, I'll bake her this babka.

DOUGH

¾ cup whole milk

¼ cup plus 1 teaspoon (54 g) granulated sugar, divided

2¼ teaspoons (1 package) active dry yeast

1 large egg

1 large egg yolk

1 teaspoon vanilla extract

3 cups (420 g) all-purpose flour

½ teaspoon kosher salt

4 tablespoons (57 g or ½ stick) unsalted butter, at room temperature

FILLING

½ cup (100 g) granulated sugar

2 tablespoons natural cocoa powder (not Dutch-process)

2 teaspoons ground cinnamon

MAKE THE DOUGH

Heat the milk and 1 teaspoon of the sugar in a medium saucepan until the milk is warm to the touch. Sprinkle the yeast over the milk and set aside to proof for about 5 minutes, or until bubbles form on the surface of the milk.

Pour the milk into the bowl of a stand mixer fitted with the paddle attachment. Add the egg, egg yolk, and vanilla. Mix on low speed for about 30 seconds to incorporate. Add the flour, the remaining ¼ cup (50 g) sugar, and the salt and mix on low speed until the flour is incorporated into the liquid and a sticky dough forms. Add the butter, 1 tablespoon at a time, waiting until it is incorporated before each addition.

Once all the butter is added, switch to the dough hook and knead the dough on medium-high speed until a smooth and slightly sticky dough forms, about 5 minutes. Gather the dough into a ball, stretching the dough so the top of the ball is smooth. Coat the mixer bowl with cooking spray, then place the dough back into the bowl, with the gathered rough part of the dough down and the smooth surface of the ball facing up. Cover with plastic wrap and let rise for about 1 hour, or until the dough has doubled in size.

·······>

½ teaspoon instant coffee powder

⅛ teaspoon kosher salt

2 tablespoons boiling water

6 tablespoons (85 g or ¾ stick) unsalted butter

6 ounces (170 g) dark chocolate (use what you like to eat)

STREUSEL

¼ cup (35 g) all-purpose flour

1 tablespoon granulated sugar

1 tablespoon packed dark brown sugar

½ teaspoon ground cinnamon

¼ teaspoon kosher salt

4 tablespoons (57 g or ½ stick) cold unsalted butter

TO ASSEMBLE

1 large egg yolk

1 tablespoon cold water

＊ *If you absolutely love chocolate, you can increase the chopped chocolate from 6 ounces to up to 12 ounces. It's a bit of a chocolate overload for the bread, but my partner, who adores all things chocolate, loves it this way. For most people, though, 6 to 8 ounces is enough.*

MAKE THE FILLING

Combine the sugar, cocoa powder, cinnamon, instant coffee powder, and salt in a small bowl. Pour the water over the dry ingredients and stir with a fork to form a paste. Add the butter and use the fork to mix together. Chop the dark chocolate into ¼-inch chunks.

MAKE THE STREUSEL

Combine the flour, both sugars, cinnamon, and salt in a bowl and toss together with a fork. Cut the butter into ½-inch chunks, then toss them in the streusel ingredients. Using your fingers, blend the butter into the dry ingredients until it is incorporated and the mixture forms clumps. Set aside.

Once the dough has doubled, coat a 5 x 9-inch loaf pan with cooking spray and line the bottom and sides with parchment paper, with an inch or two of the paper overhanging the edges of the pan. Dust a clean surface with flour and roll the dough out to a rectangle roughly 15 x 17 inches, with a long side facing you (landscape orientation). Spread the butter paste over the surface of the dough, then sprinkle the chocolate evenly over the paste.

Tightly roll the dough up from the bottom, making a 17-inch rope. Slice the dough in half lengthwise, making two 17-inch long pieces. The dough might start to fall apart because there's so much chocolate. Twist each long piece individually so the chocolate is trapped inside the dough, tucking in any chocolate that has fallen out. Then twist and wrap the two ropes of dough together. Squish the twisted dough together and transfer it to the prepared loaf pan, tucking in any stray pieces of chocolate and dough. This is messy business but worth it in the end!

In a small bowl, mix the egg yolk and water to make an egg wash. Brush the egg wash over the top of the dough in the pan. Sprinkle the streusel over the top of the dough and then cover with a piece of plastic wrap and let rest for 30 minutes.

While the babka loaf is resting, preheat the oven to 350°F. Once the dough has rested (it won't have risen much, just a tiny bit), place the pan on a rimmed baking sheet and bake for 50 minutes. Reduce the oven temperature to 325°F and continue to bake until the top of the dough is deep brown, 15 to 20 minutes more. Let cool in the pan for 15 minutes, then use the parchment paper to lift the babka out of the pan and transfer it to a wire cooling rack. Let cool to room temperature, or serve warm, in thick slices.

HAZELNUT-CHOCOLATE BABKA

Make the dough as directed.

Make the filling as directed, but omit the cinnamon. Sprinkle 4 ounces (115 g) chopped dark chocolate and ¾ cup (115 g) chopped hazelnuts over the filling. Assemble and bake as directed, using the same streusel topping.

APRICOT-BLUEBERRY BABKA

Make the dough as directed.

Make the filling by first chopping ¾ cup (150 g) dried apricots and placing them in a medium saucepan with ¼ cup water, 2 tablespoons fresh lemon juice, and 2 tablespoons granulated sugar. Bring to a boil, then reduce the heat and simmer for about 10 minutes. Scrape the apricot mixture into a medium bowl. Place ¾ cup (120 g) dried blueberries in the same saucepan (no need to clean it) and add ¼ cup water, 2 tablespoons fresh lemon juice, and 1 tablespoon sugar. Bring to a boil, reduce the heat, and simmer for about 10 minutes. Remove from the heat. To the bowl of a stand mixer fitted with the paddle attachment, add 8 ounces (225 g or 1 brick) room temperature cream cheese, 2 tablespoons sugar, 1 large egg yolk, 1 teaspoon vanilla extract, ½ teaspoon ground cinnamon, and ¼ teaspoon kosher salt, and then mix on medium speed until a smooth paste forms.

Roll the dough into the rectangle as instructed, then spread the cream cheese over the surface of the dough instead of the chocolate filling. Spread the chopped apricots over the bottom half of the cream cheese spread and the blueberries over the top half. Tightly roll the dough, then split and assemble the loaf as instructed.

Let rise and bake as directed, using the same streusel topping.

PLUM AND CARDAMOM SWIRL BUNS WITH LEMON–CREAM CHEESE FROSTING

makes 12 buns

In the summer of 2014, I went on a crazy canning and preserving kick. I had made jams in previous years, but usually in small batches, which I never bothered to can. Instead, I just stuck them in the fridge and used them up as quickly as possible. But that summer the plum tree in our backyard decided to produce buckets of plums, more than I (and my neighbors) could keep up with. This led to batch after batch of various plum jams (Vanilla Bean! Lavender! Cardamom! Cherry!). But since I wasn't writing a book about jams, I also came up with these fruit-filled swirl buns. One bite of these tender, sweet buns and I feel totally justified in my canning spree. They are basically cinnamon rolls filled with jam instead of cinnamon brown sugar. If you want a recipe shortcut, you can use store-bought jam instead of making your own, but remember that store-bought jam tends to be on the sweeter side, which of course will lead to a sweeter filling. I highly recommend making this plum jam because it's easy and fast (with only four ingredients!) and is as beautiful to the eye as it is on the tongue and in these rolls.

SWIRL BUN DOUGH

1 cup whole milk

⅓ cup water

2 tablespoons unsalted butter, melted

¼ cup (50 g) granulated sugar

2¼ teaspoons (1 package) active dry yeast

3½ cups (490 g) all-purpose flour

1 large egg

2 teaspoons kosher salt

Zest of ½ lemon

MAKE THE SWIRL BUN DOUGH

Combine the milk and water in a small pot and heat it over high heat until warm to the touch, about 15 seconds. Remove from the heat and stir in the melted butter and sugar. Sprinkle the yeast over the top of the mixture and stir to dissolve. Set aside for 3 to 4 minutes to proof, until the yeast starts to foam.

Once the yeast has proofed, place the flour in the bowl of a stand mixer fitted with the dough hook. Add the yeast-milk mixture and the egg. Mix on low speed until the ingredients start to form a dough. Once most of the dry ingredients are incorporated, raise the speed to medium-high and knead the dough for 4 minutes. Add the salt and lemon zest and knead for an additional 1 minute to incorporate. Transfer the dough to a well-oiled large bowl. Turn the dough around in the bowl to grease the top and sides, then cover with plastic wrap. Let rise for 2 hours, or until doubled in size. While the dough is rising, take the butter for assembling out to bring it to room temperature.

PLUM JAM FILLING

4 ripe but firm black plums
(about ¾ pound or 340 g)

½ cup (100 g) granulated sugar

1 tablespoon fresh lemon juice

¾ teaspoon ground cardamom

TO ASSEMBLE

4 tablespoons (57 g or ½ stick)
unsalted butter, at room temperature

¼ cup (55 g) packed dark brown sugar

LEMON–CREAM CHEESE FROSTING

4 ounces (115 g or ½ brick) cream cheese,
at room temperature

4 tablespoons (58 g or ½ stick)
unsalted butter, at room temperature

1 cup (115 g) powdered sugar, sifted

Zest of ½ lemon

2 tablespoons fresh lemon juice

MAKE THE PLUM JAM FILLING

Chop the plums (with skin on) into ½-inch chunks. You should have about 2½ cups. Place the plums, sugar, lemon juice, and cardamom in a medium pot. Bring the mixture to a boil over medium-high heat, then reduce the heat to low and simmer for about 10 minutes, uncovered, or until the fruit has disintegrated and the mixture has thickened to jam consistency. Remove from the heat and let cool completely before using.

ASSEMBLE THE BUNS

Coat a 9 x 12-inch baking pan with cooking spray and line the bottom with parchment paper. Once the dough has risen, dump it onto a lightly floured surface and roll it out to a 12 x 16-inch rectangle, with a long side facing you (landscape orientation). Spread the room temperature butter over the dough, leaving about ½ inch of plain dough at the top of the rectangle. Spread the cooled jam over the butter and then sprinkle the brown sugar over the jam. Tightly roll the dough from the bottom to the top, pinching the border of plain dough at the edge to the bottom of the roll to seal it. Cut the dough roll into 12 pieces. Place the pieces in the baking pan, forming a grid of 3 by 4 pieces. The buns won't be touching, so don't worry. Cover loosely with plastic wrap and set aside for 1 hour to rise, until the buns have doubled in size and look puffy.

Preheat the oven to 350°F about 15 minutes before the buns have completely risen. Bake until the tops of the buns are golden brown in the middle, 35 to 40 minutes. If the outer buns are browning too fast, you can cover them with aluminum foil to keep them from burning. Once baked, let rest for 5 minutes in the pan, then invert onto a baking sheet and remove the parchment paper from the bottom of the buns. Invert again so the buns are right side up on a wire cooling rack and let cool to room temperature.

MAKE THE LEMON–CREAM CHEESE FROSTING

Place the cream cheese and butter in a clean bowl of a stand mixer fitted with the paddle attachment. Beat on medium speed until the cream cheese and butter are fluffy and combined. Add the powdered sugar, lemon zest, and juice and beat on medium speed until combined. Frost the buns and serve immediately.

·······>

CINNAMON-PUMPKIN SWIRL BUNS WITH CARAMEL–CREAM CHEESE DRIZZLE

For the dough, first cook 15 ounces (425 g) canned pumpkin puree (not pie filling) in a large nonstick skillet over medium-high heat, stirring and scraping the bottom of the skillet with a wooden spoon, until the puree is reduced to 1 cup, 5 to 7 minutes. Remove from the heat and let cool. Make the dough as directed, adding 1 teaspoon ground cinnamon to the flour, reducing the milk to ¾ cup, and omitting the water. Add the pumpkin puree with the egg and omit the lemon zest.

Once the dough has risen and you've rolled it out, make the filling by combining 4 tablespoons (57 g or ½ stick) unsalted butter at room temperature with ¾ cup (165 g) packed dark brown sugar, 2 teaspoons ground cinnamon, ½ teaspoon ground nutmeg, ¼ teaspoon ground cloves, and ¼ teaspoon ground ginger. Mix with a spatula until the sugar and spices are incorporated into the butter, then spread it over the dough. Roll, slice, let rise, and bake as directed.

To make the caramel–cream cheese drizzle, put 1 cup (200 g) granulated sugar, 2 tablespoons light corn syrup, and 2 tablespoons water in a large microwave-safe glass bowl. Stir together and then microwave for 6 to 10 minutes. Start watching through the glass door after around 3 minutes and pay attention to the color of the liquid. Once it starts to brown, stop the microwave and remove the bowl. Watch the liquid continue to darken. Swirl it every now and then, but wait for it to darken to the color of dark rum or bourbon. Add 4 tablespoons (57 g or ½ stick) unsalted butter, 1 tablespoon at a time, then 4 ounces (115 g or ½ brick) cream cheese, about 1 ounce at a time, and stir with a fork until incorporated. Be careful, because the caramel will sputter and steam. Let the caramel cool until it has thickened to the consistency of honey, stirring occasionally. Drizzle the caramel over the top and sides of the cinnamon rolls. Serve warm.

DRIED BLUEBERRY AND STRAWBERRY LEMON THYME SCONES WITH MEYER LEMON GLAZE

makes 12 scones

Every time the subject of scones comes up (and you'd be surprised at how often this happens in my circle of acquaintances), people always emphatically say that they don't really care for them. Dry, crumbly, and not very flavorful, the typical scone you might find at a coffee shop isn't suitable for anything other than dipping into a cup of the overpriced coffee you just purchased. But then, those people haven't tasted *my* scones. Tender, buttery wedges of fresh-baked goodness, my homemade scones are the standard against which I judge all coffee-shop scones. And though I'm not really one to judge other people's baked goods (I leave that to my partner, who is actually a much harsher judge of food than I am), I just don't understand why other scones aren't better than they are, because it's not too difficult to make a good scone.

SCONE BATTER

2 cups (280 g) all-purpose flour

¼ cup (50 g) granulated sugar

2 teaspoons baking powder

1½ tablespoons fresh lemon thyme leaves (see note, page 296)

½ teaspoon kosher salt

6 tablespoons (85 g or ¾ stick) cold unsalted butter

2 large eggs

¾ cup buttermilk

⅔ cup (105 g) dried wild blueberries

2 tablespoons crushed freeze-dried strawberries

1 tablespoon water

MAKE THE SCONE BATTER

Preheat the oven to 350°F and line two baking sheets with parchment paper or Silpats. Place the flour, sugar, baking powder, thyme, and salt in a large bowl. Stir vigorously together with a balloon whisk until the ingredients are incorporated and uniform in color. Cut the butter into ½-inch cubes and sprinkle over the dry ingredients. Using your hands, first toss the butter in the flour, then smash the butter into thin slivers, breaking them up as you go.

Make a well in the center of the dry ingredients. Separate one egg and reserve the egg white in a small bowl. Place the egg yolk and the remaining whole egg in a glass measuring cup along with the buttermilk and beat with a fork until blended. Pour the buttermilk mixture into the middle of the well and gently stir and fold the ingredients together with a large spatula or wooden spoon. The dough will be wet. Scoop out about one-third of the dough and transfer it to another bowl. Add the dried blueberries to the larger portion of the dough and fold in gently. Add the crushed freeze-dried strawberries to the smaller amount of dough and fold in. Drop spoonfuls of the strawberry dough back into the blueberry dough and gently fold them together a couple of times, but not enough to fully incorporate. You want the doughs to stay separate.

········>

GLAZE

Zest of 1 Meyer lemon

¼ cup fresh Meyer lemon juice

1 cup (230 g) powdered sugar, sifted

1 tablespoon unsalted butter

Sprigs of lemon thyme, for garnish

Flour a clean surface and gather the dough on top of the surface. Divide the dough into two mounds and flatten and form each into a 6-inch circle about ½ inch thick. Cut each disk into 6 wedges and place the wedges on the prepared baking sheets. Add the water to the reserved egg white and beat with a fork until frothy. Brush each scone with the egg white wash. Bake until the scones start to just turn brown around the edges, 18 to 20 minutes.

Let the scones rest on the baking sheet for 5 minutes, then move them to a wire rack to cool completely.

MAKE THE GLAZE

Place the Meyer lemon zest, juice, powdered sugar, and butter in a small pot and heat over low heat, stirring constantly, until the butter is melted and all the sugar is dissolved. Let the glaze cool slightly to thicken, then drizzle over the cooled scones. Place a sprig or two of lemon thyme in the wet glaze to garnish and let set before serving.

✳ *Lemon thyme is an herb that tastes exactly like it sounds, with a slightly mellower green and grassy thyme flavor and a hint of lemony citrus. If you can't find lemon thyme (they occasionally stock it at upscale grocery stores, natural food stores, and farmers' markets), just substitute 1 teaspoon lemon zest and 2 teaspoons regular fresh thyme leaves.*

✳ *Freeze-dried strawberries are strawberries that have had all their moisture pulled out of them, making them brittle and dry. You can find them in well-stocked or upscale grocery stores like Whole Foods, natural food stores, or specialty stores like Trader Joe's. Look in the section near the dried fruit.*

DRIED CHERRY–ALMOND SCONES WITH EARL GREY GLAZE

Make the scone dough, omitting the lemon thyme leaves. Into one-third of the dough, mix ½ teaspoon almond extract, ¼ cup (30 g) almond meal, and 1 teaspoon crumbled Earl Grey tea. Into the larger portion of dough, add ⅔ cup (105 g) dried tart cherries instead of the blueberries. Proceed as directed.

Make the glaze by first making a strong cup of Earl Grey tea (2 tea bags or 2 teaspoons loose tea to 6 ounces nearly boiling water, steeped for 4 minutes). Sift 1 cup (115 g) powdered sugar into a bowl and stir in 2 tablespoons of the brewed tea. If the glaze isn't thin enough, add more tea, 1 teaspoon at a time, until the glaze is the right consistency. Glaze as directed.

PAPAYA-GINGER SCONES WITH COCONUT GLAZE

Make the scone dough, omitting the lemon thyme leaves. Into one-third of the dough, mix 1 teaspoon ground ginger, ½ teaspoon ground turmeric, and 2 tablespoons chopped crystallized ginger. Into the larger portion of dough, add ⅔ cup (100 g) chopped dried papaya instead of the blueberries. Proceed as directed.

Finish the scones by first toasting ½ cup (43 g) unsweetened shredded coconut in a dry skillet over medium heat until most of the coconut is golden brown. Pour the coconut into a bowl. Make the coconut glaze by sifting 1 cup (115 g) powdered sugar into a bowl and stirring in 2 tablespoons coconut milk. If the glaze isn't thin enough, add more coconut milk, 1 teaspoon at a time, until the glaze is the right consistency. Glaze as directed, then sprinkle with the toasted coconut before the glaze sets.

ITALIAN SPICE–TOMATO AND PARMESAN-GARLIC PRETZEL KNOTS

makes 12 pretzel knots

I have always loved the idea of soft pretzels. I used to see people on TV buying them on the streets of New York City and wished I lived there, just so I could eat them. Imagine my disappointment when I finally got to visit New York and found the street vendors serving up bland and dry pretzels, which apparently only tourists buy. Years later I discovered that making them at home is insanely easy, even if you are yeast averse. Packaged yeast is pretty fail-proof, and that means pretzels are only a single rise away from happening in your kitchen. I've given the classic soft pretzel a *twist* (see what I did there?) by splitting the dough in half and flavoring one half with Italian spices and tomato and the other with Parmesan and garlic. Twist them together, tie them in a knot, and it's like two New York classics combined: a slice of pizza and a garlic knot. Only better, because it's also a soft pretzel!

INITIAL PRETZEL DOUGH

1½ cups warm water (110 to 115°F)

1 tablespoon malt syrup, honey, or brown sugar

2¼ teaspoons (1 package) active dry yeast

3 cups (480 g) bread flour

1 tablespoon kosher salt

¼ cup extra-virgin olive oil

PARMESAN-GARLIC DOUGH MIX-IN

¾ cup (105 g) all-purpose flour

½ cup (60 g) grated Parmesan cheese

2 tablespoons granulated garlic

MAKE THE INITIAL PRETZEL DOUGH

Combine the warm water and malt syrup in a small bowl. Beat with a fork until the syrup is dissolved. Add the yeast and beat until the yeast is dissolved. Let sit for about 5 minutes, or until the yeast starts to bubble a little bit.

Pour the yeast mixture into the bowl of a stand mixer fitted with the paddle attachment. Add the bread flour, then sprinkle the salt over the flour and drizzle the oil over the flour and salt. Mix on low speed until the flour and liquid are incorporated. The dough will be very wet and sticky. Coat two medium bowls with olive oil cooking spray. Wet your hands and divide the dough in half (roughly 1 pound or 455 g each), and place one half in one of the greased bowls. Cover with plastic wrap. Leave the other half in the stand mixer bowl.

MAKE THE PARMESAN-GARLIC DOUGH

Change the mixer attachment to the dough hook. To the dough in the mixer bowl, add the flour, Parmesan, and granulated garlic. Mix on medium speed for about 1 minute, or until most of the dry ingredients are incorporated. Stop the mixer and, using your hands, knead the dough to incorporate the remaining dry ingredients. Turn the mixer back on and knead the dough for about 4 minutes,

·······>

TOMATO DOUGH MIX-IN

1½ cups (210 g) all-purpose flour

¾ cup (6 ounces or 170 g) tomato paste

1 teaspoon dried basil

1 teaspoon dried oregano

1 teaspoon paprika

1 tablespoon finely chopped
sun-dried tomatoes

TO PRETZEL-FY

10 cups water

⅔ cup (160 g) baking soda

1 large egg yolk plus 1 tablespoon water

1 tablespoon pretzel salt or coarse sea salt

1½ teaspoons granulated garlic

✱ *Barley malt syrup is my choice of sweetener for pretzels and bagels. Commercial bakers use it for its sticky, thick, distinctive malty sweet flavor. Of course, if you can't find it, or don't feel like ordering such a specialty ingredient, you can substitute honey, brown sugar, or even maple syrup in its place. If you're looking for something that is similar to barley malt syrup but is gluten-free or wheat-free, try brown rice syrup. Just make sure to read the label, as some brown rice syrup is treated with malt enzymes and may not be gluten-free.*

occasionally stopping and re-forming the dough into a ball if the kneading isn't uniform. The dough might still be a bit bumpy from the Parmesan, but that's okay.

Gather the Parmesan dough together and then stretch it so the top of the dough is a smooth ball, and place the dough in the second oiled bowl with the rough part of the dough face down. Cover with plastic wrap.

MAKE THE TOMATO DOUGH

Move the remaining initial pretzel dough to the mixer bowl and add the flour, tomato paste, basil, oregano, paprika, and sun-dried tomatoes. Mix on medium speed until incorporated (you shouldn't need to stop and incorporate anything by hand). Once the dry ingredients are incorporated, knead the dough on medium speed for about 4 minutes. Gather the tomato dough together and then stretch it so the top of the dough is a smooth ball, and place the dough into the oiled bowl with the rough part of the dough face down. Cover with plastic wrap. Let both doughs rise for 1 hour 15 minutes to 1 hour 30 minutes, until the tomato dough has doubled in size (the Parmesan dough won't rise as much).

MAKE THE PRETZELS

Once the dough has risen, preheat the oven to 450°F and line a baking sheet with a piece of parchment paper or a Silpat. Pour the water into a large stockpot and add the baking soda. Bring to a boil. While the water is heating up, divide each dough into 12 equal pieces. Roll one piece of the Parmesan-garlic dough into a rope about 10 inches long. Roll one piece of the tomato dough into a rope about the same length. Place next to each other and twist together. Tie each rope into a knot, then tuck the ends under the dough ball. Set aside and repeat with the remaining dough.

Once the water is boiling, reduce the heat to a simmer. Place 3 or 4 knots in the water, knot side down, and boil for about 45 seconds. Carefully flip the knots in the water and boil for an additional 20 seconds. Carefully remove the pretzel knots with a slotted spoon and place on the lined baking sheet, knot side up. Repeat with the remaining knots. Beat the egg yolk and water together, then brush each knot with the egg wash. Combine the pretzel salt and granulated garlic in a small bowl. Sprinkle each knot with a dusting of the garlic-salt mixture. Bake until the knots are a deep brown pretzel color, 15 to 17 minutes. If you have an instant-read thermometer, the inside of the pretzels should be about 190°F. Let cool on the baking sheet for 5 minutes and then move to a wire rack to cool completely.

BLOODY MARY PRETZEL KNOTS

Make a Blood Mary version of this recipe by omitting the oregano, basil, and sundried tomatoes from the tomato dough. Instead, add 1 teaspoon freshly cracked black pepper, ½ teaspoon cayenne pepper, and 1 tablespoon each Worcestershire sauce and Tabasco sauce. Omit the Parmesan and garlic in the other half of the dough and instead add an additional ½ cup (70 g) all-purpose flour, 1 tablespoon prepared horseradish, and 2 teaspoons each celery salt and onion flakes. Mix, knead, shape, and boil as directed, then brush with egg wash and sprinkle the tops with celery seeds instead of the garlic salt before baking.

APPLE, RYE, AND CINNAMON-RAISIN SOFT PRETZELS

First, chop up (or break up) 1 cup (40 g) baked apple chips into ½-inch chunks. Cover with boiling water and let soak for 10 minutes as you make the initial pretzel dough. Repeat with ½ cup (75 g) golden raisins. Make the dough as directed, omitting the malt syrup and using 1 tablespoon boiled cider (a super-concentrated apple cider available by mail order and from specialty shops) in its place. Divide the dough in half as directed. Drain the apple chips and add them to one half of the dough along with 1¼ cups (135 g) rye flour. Knead the flour and chips into the dough and set aside to rise as directed. To the other half, add 1 cup (140 g) all-purpose flour, 1 teaspoon ground cinnamon, and the drained golden raisins. Knead the ingredients into the dough and set aside to rise as directed. Assemble, boil, and brush with egg wash as directed. Skip the coarse sea salt or pretzel salt, and use 1½ tablespoons coarse sparkling sugar. Sprinkle over the pretzels and bake as directed.

LEMON MATCHA YEASTED WAFFLES WITH ROSEMARY MAPLE SYRUP

makes 5 or 6 Belgian-style waffles or 8 to 10 regular waffles

When presented with the question of waffles or pancakes, I almost always choose waffles. The crunchy crevices of crispy batter that create tiny little cups for the maple syrup make waffles the clear winner in my book. But I'm always looking for new ways and flavors to enhance my waffle experience. Marbling waffle batters together is an impressive (and unexpectedly easy) way to serve a standard brunch item. This batter is convenient because you make it the night before, letting it rise overnight on the counter. The yeasted batter cultures a bit from the overnight rest at room temperature, leading to a nice, ever-so-slightly tangy waffle. The addition of cornmeal gives a shattering crispness to the waffles and, because of the overnight rise, has enough time to soak, resulting in a flavorful waffle that isn't gritty at all. Add a little bit of infused rosemary maple syrup over the freshly made waffles and you've taken everything to the next level.

WAFFLE BATTER

2¼ cups plus 1 tablespoon whole milk, divided

2¼ teaspoons (1 package) active dry yeast

½ cup (115 g or 1 stick) unsalted butter, melted and cooled

2 cups (280 g) all-purpose flour

⅓ cup (50 g) cornmeal

1 tablespoon granulated sugar

1 teaspoon kosher salt

2 large eggs

¼ teaspoon baking soda

Zest of 2 lemons

2 tablespoons fresh lemon juice

2 tablespoons matcha green tea powder

MAKE THE WAFFLE BATTER

Warm up 2¼ cups of the milk in a small saucepan on the stove. It doesn't have to be hot, just warm to the touch, or at the very least room temperature. Stir in the yeast and let sit to proof, about 5 minutes or until you see bubbles forming at the top of the milk.

Pour the yeasty milk into a large bowl. Add the butter, flour, cornmeal, sugar, and salt and stir thoroughly until a uniform batter forms. Cover with plastic wrap and let sit overnight on the countertop.

The next morning, stir in the eggs, baking soda, lemon zest, and lemon juice. Beat thoroughly to make sure the eggs are incorporated. Pour out about 1 cup of the batter into a large glass measuring cup. Stir in the remaining 1 tablespoon milk and the matcha green tea powder.

Heat your waffle iron according to the instructions, and once it's ready, drizzle a little bit of the matcha batter (2 to 3 tablespoons if it's Belgian-style or 1 to 2 tablespoons if it's a regular waffle maker) over the iron, then fill the remaining space in the iron with the lemon batter on top. Cook as directed, until golden and crisp.

ROSEMARY MAPLE SYRUP

2 (3-inch) sprigs fresh rosemary
(do not use dried)

1 cup maple syrup (do not use artificially
flavored pancake syrup)

Repeat with the remaining batter.

MAKE THE ROSEMARY MAPLE SYRUP

Place the rosemary and maple syrup in a small saucepan and bring the syrup to a boil. Reduce the heat to a bare simmer and cook for about 5 minutes. Taste the maple syrup (carefully, as it will be hot), and if the rosemary flavor isn't strong enough for you, cook for an additional 2 to 3 minutes, or to your own taste.

alternative

VANILLA AND CHOCOLATE WAFFLES

Make the batter as directed for the overnight rise. The next morning, omit the lemon zest and lemon juice and add 1 tablespoon vanilla extract to the batter with the eggs. Scoop out 1 cup of batter and, instead of adding the matcha powder, add 2 tablespoons natural cocoa powder (not Dutch-process). Cook as directed. Serve with regular maple syrup, or dust with powdered sugar and serve with fresh berries and whipped cream.

A LITTLE BIT MORE

I'M A BIG FAN OF THE "LITTLE BIT MORE" SORT of twist ending. The late Steve Jobs was the master of this, always saving the big announcement of whatever spectacular Apple product he was introducing for the very end of his talk. Great and unexpected desserts are the dinner version of a twist ending. For me, an excellent dinner isn't complete without a sweet bite at the end to punctuate it. It doesn't have to be big—it can be a small nibble to finish the meal. Show-stopping desserts have their place too, but sometimes a simple bite of ice cream is all it takes.

From cheesecakes to parfaits, from ice cream to éclairs, here are a few extra recipes that are unexpected in their flavors or execution. Think of this as my own twist ending, but a little sweeter and a lot less expensive than anything Apple would announce.

"L'ORANGE" CURD CHEESECAKE WITH PISTACHIO CRUST

makes one 9-inch cheesecake; 12 to 14 servings

My partner, A.J., has a crush on Meyer lemons, which are a hybrid of regular lemons and common oranges. A.J. is usually more of a chocolate guy, but the fragrant scent of Meyer lemons when they come into season always gets him excited. A.J. has nicknamed Meyer lemons "l'oranges" (pronounced with an outrageous French accent), and he looks forward to finding them in the grocery store every year. Meyer lemons had a surge in popularity when Alice Waters started using them at Chez Panisse in the late 1990s, and then all of sudden they were everywhere. They are becoming more and more common across the country at upscale grocery stores and farmers' markets. This bright and cheery cheesecake has a swirl of Meyer lemon curd in a lemon cheesecake base. It's the best sort of hybrid dessert.

MEYER LEMON CURD

½ cup (100 g) granulated sugar

2 teaspoons Meyer lemon zest

Pinch of kosher salt

½ cup fresh Meyer lemon juice
(from 2 or 3 lemons)

3 large eggs

4 tablespoons (57 g or ½ stick)
unsalted butter

CRUST

1 cup (2½ ounces or 70 g)
plain animal crackers (not iced)

⅔ cup (3½ ounces or 100 g) shelled
unsalted pistachios (see note, opposite)

⅓ cup (67 g) granulated sugar

¼ teaspoon kosher salt

5 tablespoons (70 g) unsalted
butter, melted

MAKE THE MEYER LEMON CURD

Place the sugar, lemon zest, and salt in a food processor and pulse in 1-second bursts until the sugar is uniformly yellow. Pour the lemon sugar into a medium pot and add the lemon juice and eggs. Whisk together and place on the stove over medium-low heat. Add the butter and cook, whisking constantly, until the butter melts. Reduce the heat to low and cook until the curd coats the back of a spoon and holds a line when you drag a finger through the curd, anywhere from 4 to 8 minutes. Pour the curd through a fine-mesh sieve into a heatproof bowl. Let cool to room temperature as you continue with the recipe.

Preheat the oven to 350°F. Arrange the bottom of a 9-inch springform pan upside down (lip side down) to make removing the cheesecake easier. Smear a little softened butter in the bottom of the pan and line it with a 9-inch parchment paper round. Place two large sheets of aluminum foil on a table, crisscrossing each other. Place the springform pan in the middle of the foil and then wrap the foil tightly up and around the sides of the pan.

MAKE THE CRUST

Place the animal crackers, pistachios, sugar, and salt in the food processor (no need to clean it) and pulse in 1-second bursts until the nuts are finely ground and the mixture is uniform in color. With the processor on, drizzle in the melted butter. Once all the butter has been added, turn the processor off and dump the

CHEESECAKE FILLING

24 ounces (680 g or 3 bricks) cream cheese, at room temperature

1 cup (200 g) granulated sugar

3 large eggs

¾ cup (180 g) sour cream

2 teaspoons vanilla extract

1 teaspoon lemon zest (regular or Meyer)

✱ *Shelled unsalted pistachios can be hard to find. If your grocery store only has salted nuts, use those and omit the salt in the crust. If they only have nuts in the shells, start with 1⅓ cups (7 ounces or 200 g) and shell them by hand. You should have ⅔ cup pistachios once shelled.*

wet crumbs into the prepared pan. Using the back of a spoon, press the crumbs evenly into the bottom and halfway up the sides of the pan. Bake until the edges of the crust start to brown a bit and the crust smells fragrant, 8 to 10 minutes. Remove from the oven and reduce the oven temperature to 300°F.

MAKE THE CHEESECAKE FILLING

Place the cream cheese and sugar in the bowl of a stand mixer fitted with the paddle attachment. Beat on medium speed until fluffy, 1 to 2 minutes. Add the eggs, one at a time, waiting for each to incorporate before adding the next. Add the sour cream, vanilla, and lemon zest and beat to incorporate. Scrape down the sides of the bowl.

Place the foil-wrapped springform pan in a large roasting pan. Carefully spoon two-thirds of the filling into the crust and spread evenly. Spoon two-thirds of the curd over the filling and swirl with a butter knife. Cover the curd with the remaining cheesecake filling and drizzle the remaining curd over the top of the filling. Swirl with a butter knife. Pour boiling hot water into the roasting pan until it goes halfway up the sides of the springform pan. Bake until the edges of the cheesecake start to puff up and look solid, 50 to 60 minutes. The center of the cheesecake will still be wobbly, but don't worry; it will firm up as it cools. Once the cheesecake is done, remove it from the oven and immediately run a thin butter knife around the edge of the cheesecake to loosen it from the pan. Let the cheesecake cool until the water is at room temperature, 30 to 45 minutes. Remove from the water and discard the foil. Let cool on a wire rack for about 2 hours more, or until the bottom of the pan doesn't feel warm to the touch anymore. Cover the pan with aluminum foil (don't let it touch the top of the cheesecake!) and refrigerate overnight or for at least 8 hours.

Serve straight from the fridge, or let it sit at room temperature for about an hour before serving for a slightly less firm texture.

BALSAMIC, STRAWBERRY, AND LIME CHEESECAKE WITH PINE NUT CRUST

Replace the Meyer lemon curd with balsamic-strawberry curd: First, puree 2 cups (225 g) chopped strawberries in a food processor. Transfer the pureed strawberries to a saucepan and add ½ cup (100 g) granulated sugar, the zest of 1 lemon, 1 tablespoon fresh lemon juice, a pinch of salt, 3 large eggs, 4 tablespoons (57 g or ½ stick) unsalted butter, and 1 teaspoon balsamic vinegar. Cook over medium-high heat, stirring constantly, until the curd coats the back of a spoon and holds a line when you drag a finger through the curd, 5 to 6 minutes. Pour the curd through a fine-mesh sieve into a heatproof bowl.

Make the cheesecake as directed, substituting ⅔ cup (95 g) pine nuts for the pistachios in the crust and 1 teaspoon lime zest for the lemon zest in the cheesecake filling. Stir 1 tablespoon fresh lime juice into the sour cream before adding. Assemble and bake as directed.

BLUEBERRY-MAPLE CHEESECAKE WITH PECAN CRUST

Replace the Meyer lemon curd with blueberry curd: Cook 1 cup (130 g) fresh blueberries with ½ cup (100 g) granulated sugar, the zest of 1 lemon, 1 tablespoon fresh lemon juice, and a pinch of salt over medium heat until the blueberries have popped and softened, 7 to 10 minutes. Remove from the heat and stir in 4 tablespoons (57 g or ½ stick) cold unsalted butter, letting the residual heat melt the butter and cool the cooked blueberries. Let cool for 10 minutes, then add 3 eggs and stir with a whisk. Return to medium heat and cook, stirring constantly, until the curd coats the back of a spoon and holds a line when you drag a finger through the curd, about 5 minutes. Pour the curd through a fine-mesh sieve into a heatproof bowl.

Make the cheesecake as directed, replacing the pistachios in the crust with ⅔ cup (67 g) pecans. In the filling, reduce the granulated sugar to ¾ cup (150 g) and add ¼ cup maple syrup, and omit the lemon zest. Assemble and bake as directed.

RASPBERRY-ROSE SWIRLED HONEY CHEESECAKE

makes one 9-inch cheesecake; 12 servings

Though it's fairly common in Indian and Middle Eastern desserts, using rose in desserts seems strange to a lot of people. However, rose is one of those flavors that goes really well with raspberry, as long as you don't use too much of it. One bite of this heavenly combination in this honey-flavored cheesecake and you'll be singing the praises of rose and raspberry. It actually might become your new favorite!

CRUST

⅔ cup (90 g) all-purpose flour

2 tablespoons granulated sugar

¼ teaspoon kosher salt

6 tablespoons (85 g or ¾ stick) unsalted butter, melted and cooled

1 teaspoon raspberry extract

ROSE-RASPBERRY CURD

4 tablespoons (57 g or ½ stick) unsalted butter

3 cups (12 ounces or 340 g) fresh or frozen raspberries

½ cup (100 g) granulated sugar

¼ teaspoon kosher salt

5 large egg yolks

2 teaspoons rose water

CHEESECAKE FILLING

24 ounces (680 g or 3 bricks) cream cheese, at room temperature

¾ cup (150 g) granulated sugar

¼ cup (85 g) honey

3 large eggs

MAKE THE CRUST

Arrange the bottom of a 9-inch springform pan upside down (lip side down) to make removing the cheesecake easier. Place two large sheets of aluminum foil on a table, crisscrossing each other. Place the springform pan in the middle of the foil and then wrap the foil tightly up and around the sides of the pan. Combine the flour, sugar, and salt in a bowl. Form a well in the middle and add the butter and raspberry extract. Using a fork, work the ingredients together into a soft, sticky dough. Press the dough into the bottom of the springform pan. Refrigerate for 20 minutes. While the crust chills, preheat the oven to 400°F. Bake the crust until golden brown, about 15 minutes. Let cool to room temperature.

MAKE THE ROSE-RASPBERRY CURD

Melt the butter in a medium saucepan. Reduce the heat to low and add the raspberries, sugar, salt, and egg yolks. Cook over medium heat, whisking constantly, until it coats the back of a spoon and holds a line when you drag a finger through the curd, anywhere from 4 to 8 minutes. Stir in the rose water and pour the curd through a fine-mesh sieve into a heatproof bowl. Let cool to room temperature while you make the filling. Lower the oven temperature to 300°F.

MAKE THE CHEESECAKE FILLING

Combine the cream cheese, sugar, and honey in the bowl of a stand mixer fitted with the paddle attachment. Beat on medium speed until fluffy, 1 to 2 minutes. Add the eggs, one at a time, waiting for each to incorporate before adding the next. Add the sour cream, rose water, and vanilla and beat to incorporate.

·······>

¾ cup (125 g) sour cream

1 tablespoon rose water

1 teaspoon vanilla extract

Place the foil-wrapped springform pan in a large roasting pan. Carefully spoon half of the filling into the crust and spread it evenly. Spoon most of the curd over the filling (reserving about 2 tablespoons) and swirl with a butter knife. Cover the curd with the remaining cheesecake filling and then drizzle the reserved curd over the filling. Swirl with a butter knife or chopstick. Pour boiling hot water into the roasting pan until it goes halfway up the sides of the springform pan. Bake until the edges of the cheesecake start to puff up and turn slightly brown, 45 to 50 minutes. The center of the cheesecake will still be wobbly, but don't worry; it will firm up as it cools. Once the cheesecake is done, remove it from the oven and immediately run a thin butter knife around the edge of the cheesecake to loosen it from the pan. Let the cheesecake cool in the roasting pan until the water is at room temperature, 30 to 45 minutes. Remove from the water and discard the foil. Let cool on a wire rack for about 2 hours more, or until the bottom of the pan doesn't feel warm to the touch anymore. Cover the pan with aluminum foil (don't let it touch the top of the cheesecake!) and refrigerate overnight or for at least 8 hours.

Serve straight from the fridge, or let it sit at room temperature for about an hour before serving for a slightly less firm texture.

alternative

LAVENDER, BLUEBERRY, AND ORANGE GOAT CHEESECAKE

Make the crust as directed, omitting the raspberry extract.

Instead of making the rose-raspberry curd, replace the raspberries with ¾ pound (340 g) fresh or frozen blueberries. Add 3 tablespoons culinary lavender to the curd while you are cooking it. Omit the rose water. Strain through a fine-mesh sieve once the curd has thickened to remove the blueberry pulp and lavender.

To make the filling, reduce the cream cheese to 16 ounces (455 g or 2 bricks) and add 8 ounces (225 g) soft goat cheese. Omit the rose water and add 3 tablespoons Cointreau or Grand Marnier to the filling. Swirl and bake as directed.

NO-BAKE GINGER AND CINNAMON CHEESECAKE WITH BLUEBERRY SAUCE

makes one 9-inch cheesecake; 8 to 12 servings

My mom had two desserts in her repertoire: a marble Bundt cake and a cheesecake bar with blueberry pie filling poured over it. She rarely made either, saving them for special occasions or company. But when she did, my sweets-deprived family clamored for them. I was particularly taken with the bars, with their sticky, deep violet blueberry sauce oozing over the creamy cheesecake and buttery crumb crust. I've reinterpreted her dessert in this no-bake cheesecake. If you've never made a no-bake cheesecake, you'll love the ease with which it comes together. No hot oven (making it ideal for summertime) and no worrying about the cheesecake over- or under-baking. Just make sure to bring the cream cheese to room temperature before you make this. The resulting cheesecake filling will be lumpy if you don't!

CRUST

8 ounces (225 g) store-bought gingersnaps

6 tablespoons (85 g or ¾ stick) unsalted butter, melted

CHEESECAKE FILLING

1 tablespoon (1½ packages) powdered gelatin

¼ cup cold water

16 ounces (455 g or 2 bricks) cream cheese, at room temperature

1 cup (115 g) powdered sugar, sifted

2 cups cold heavy cream

1½ teaspoons ground ginger

½ teaspoon ground turmeric

1½ teaspoons ground cinnamon

1½ teaspoons natural cocoa powder (not Dutch-process)

MAKE THE CRUST

Lightly coat a 9-inch round springform pan with cooking spray. Place the ginger-snaps in a food processor and process into crumbs, then drizzle in the melted butter and process until the crumbs start to clump together. Dump the buttery crumbs into the pan and press into a thick crust over the bottom of the pan.

MAKE THE CHEESECAKE FILLING

Sprinkle the gelatin over the cold water in a microwave-safe bowl or glass measuring cup and stir to moisten. Set aside for 5 minutes to soften. Once softened, microwave the gelatin for 20 to 30 seconds, until the gelatin is dissolved. Set aside to cool.

Place the cream cheese and powdered sugar in the bowl of a stand mixer fitted with the paddle attachment. Mix on low speed and then raise the mixer speed to medium and mix until the sugar is incorporated and the cream cheese looks fluffy.

Switch the mixer attachment to the whisk and add the cream. Mix on low speed until the cream is incorporated, then raise the speed to medium. Stop the mixer and scrape down the sides of the bowl, then continue to mix, slowly increasing the speed to high, until soft peaks form. Reduce the speed to medium and slowly

·······>

BLUEBERRY SAUCE

Zest of 1 orange

½ cup fresh-squeezed orange juice

1 tablespoon cornstarch

1 tablespoon granulated sugar

2 cups (9 ounces or 255 g) fresh blueberries

drizzle the warm gelatin into the bowl. Return the mixer speed to high and beat until the mixture forms firm peaks.

Scoop half the filling into a bowl and fold in the ginger and turmeric by hand with a large spatula. To the remaining filling, add the cinnamon and cocoa powder and fold in by hand with a different large spatula. Spoon the fillings into the pan, alternating small spoonfuls of each filling, then smooth the top. Refrigerate for at least 1 hour or overnight to firm up.

MAKE THE BLUEBERRY SAUCE

Combine the orange zest, juice, cornstarch, and sugar in a small saucepan. Stir to dissolve the cornstarch and sugar. Add the blueberries and cook over medium heat until the sauce thickens and some of the blueberries have popped, about 5 minutes. Let cool to room temperature, then spoon over the chilled cheesecake and return to the refrigerator to chill for an additional hour or overnight.

alternative

NO-BAKE PEANUT BUTTER AND JELLY CHEESECAKE WITH GRAHAM CRACKER CRUST

Make the crust using ½ pound (225 g) graham crackers instead of the gingersnaps. Make the filling as directed. Omit the ginger, turmeric, cinnamon, and cocoa powder. Into half the filling, fold ½ cup (130 g) peanut butter by hand (this might take a bit of elbow grease, but it will eventually fold in). Stir ¼ cup (85 g) grape jelly in a small bowl until it has loosened, then fold it into the other half of the filling. Assemble and chill as directed.

Warm 1 cup (340 g) grape jelly in a small saucepan over low heat until it just starts to melt. Spread over the chilled cheesecake in place of the blueberry sauce.

Fruit sauces

The blueberry sauce for this cheesecake really brings everything together, and I highly recommend that you don't skip it. In fact, fruit sauces in general are a great way to easily tie together desserts or make desserts look fancy-pants. My mom used a shortcut by just opening up a can of pie filling, but making them from scratch is easy. I generally use tapioca starch or cornstarch to thicken the fruit and add a little bit of sugar to help bring out the fruit's natural sweetness. The nice thing about fruit sauces is that you can adjust them on the stovetop to make them a little bit sweeter or a little thicker or thinner depending on what sort of consistency you want. I've even been known to microwave the ingredients for a super-fast fruit sauce. It's not ideal, but it's a good shortcut if you want to glam up a dessert without a lot of effort.

When making sauce, remember to always add the cornstarch or tapioca starch to cold or room temperature fruit before cooking it, or to dissolve it in cold or room temperature liquid first before adding it. If you add any sort of starch to hot liquid, it will get lumpy. If you have it, tapioca starch is a great choice for making fruit sauces and pie fillings. It sets up faster than cornstarch at lower temperatures and is more stable when frozen or when working with really acidic fruit. You can find tapioca starch at upscale grocery stores and natural food stores. Also, remember that the sauce will thicken when it cools to room temperature, and more if it is chilled.

I try to add minimal amounts of sugar as well, tasting the sauce as I go to see if I need to add more. Some fruit is sweet enough on its own.

MAKE-AHEAD RASPBERRY CRANACHAN

makes 6 servings

Parfaits are simple and easy to make. Unless you're me, that is. I keep on futzing with the recipes for them, often making them more complicated than they need to be. But every now and then I figure out a recipe that is worth the extra bit of effort. Take, for instance, the cranachan, which is a traditional Scottish version of a parfait. Basically, it's a layering of toasted oats (rolled or steel-cut), whipped cream with a little honey and whiskey (it is Scottish, after all), and raspberries. As much as I love the simple version, I wanted something that was a little more stable, that I could make ahead of time for a dinner party and not have to assemble on the fly. So here, I cook mixed grains with some oil and maple syrup, giving them a nice, slightly sweet coating (almost like granola), as well as stabilize the whipped cream so it can sit in the fridge for up to 8 hours before serving. This leaves me plenty of time to make the cranachan ahead of time for a dinner party. Plus, I've thrown in a few cacao nibs for added crunch and earthy chocolate notes. All those extras make for a more complex layering of flavors and textures. Of course, if all of this seems too fussy for you, just skip to the alternative recipes on page 318, where I've included instructions on how to make a standard simplified cranachan.

TOASTED GRAINS

1 cup (100 g) mixed rolled grains or thick-cut rolled oats

1 tablespoon extra-virgin olive oil

1 tablespoon maple syrup

½ teaspoon vanilla extract

1 tablespoon cacao nibs (optional)

1 large pinch kosher salt

RASPBERRIES AND RASPBERRY SAUCE

3 cups (12 ounces or 340 g) fresh raspberries, divided

2 teaspoons granulated sugar

MAKE THE TOASTED GRAINS

Toast the grains in a dry skillet over medium-high heat, stirring constantly, until they start to smell slightly nutty and fragrant, 5 to 7 minutes. The grains won't color much, so just give them a sniff now and then. Once the grains are starting to smell nicely toasty and nutty, drizzle the oil, maple syrup, and vanilla over the grains and stir to evenly coat. Cook for an additional 2 to 3 minutes, stirring constantly, until the grains start to darken slightly and take on a sheen. Pour the grains onto a baking pan and sprinkle with the cacao nibs, if using, and salt. Set aside to cool.

MAKE THE RASPBERRY SAUCE

Place 1 cup (4 ounces or 115 g) of the raspberries in a fine-mesh strainer and press them through the strainer into a bowl with the back of the spoon. Discard the pulp and seeds and stir the sugar into the juice. Set aside.

STABILIZED WHIPPED CREAM

1 teaspoon powdered gelatin

2 tablespoons cold water

2 tablespoons honey

2 tablespoons whiskey or bourbon

1½ cups cold heavy cream

2 tablespoons cold plain
Greek-style yogurt

2 tablespoons granulated sugar

Combine the gelatin and water in a small microwave-safe bowl. Let sit for 5 minutes for the gelatin to soften, then microwave for 10 to 15 seconds, until the gelatin is liquid. Let cool. Place the honey and whiskey in a small glass measuring cup and stir to dissolve the honey into the whiskey. Place the cream, yogurt, and sugar in the bowl of a stand mixer fitted with the whisk attachment and whip on high speed until soft peaks form. Reduce the speed to medium and drizzle the liquid gelatin into the bowl with the mixer running, then add the whiskey mixture. Raise the speed to high and whip until firm peaks form (be sure not to over-whip it; you don't want butter).

Assemble the cranachan by spooning a layer of whipped cream into each serving glass, then adding some raspberries on top of the whipped cream. Drizzle a little raspberry sauce over the raspberries and sprinkle with some of the toasted grains and cacao nibs. Repeat, layering in the same order, then finish with a dollop of whipped cream, a raspberry or two for garnish, and a light sprinkling of the toasted grains and nibs. Refrigerate until ready to serve. The cranachan can be made up to 8 hours in advance, though the grains will soften the longer it sits in the fridge.

·······>

TRADITIONAL (SIMPLIFIED) RASPBERRY CRANACHAN

Use steel-cut oats for the grains, toasting them in a dry skillet over medium-high heat until they smell slightly nutty and fragrant, 5 to 7 minutes. (Do not add the oil, maple syrup, vanilla, cacao nibs, and salt.) Pour onto a baking sheet to cool. Crush 1 cup (4 ounces or 115 g) of the raspberries through a fine-mesh strainer into a bowl, then add 2 tablespoons granulated sugar to the raspberry juice.

To make the whipped cream without the gelatin mixture, whip 1½ cups heavy cream and 2 tablespoons granulated sugar until soft peaks form. Stir together the 2 tablespoons whiskey and 2 tablespoons honey and add to the whipped cream. Whisk by hand until firm peaks form. Fold in most of the toasted oats (reserving 2 tablespoons for garnish). In each serving glass, alternate layers of whipped cream, some fresh raspberries, and a drizzle of raspberry sauce. Sprinkle the reserved toasted oats on top.

Serve immediately.

MUSCOVADO, BLACKBERRY, AND PISTACHIO CRANACHAN

Toast the mixed rolled grains as directed, omitting the cacao nibs. Toast 2 tablespoons pistachios in a dry skillet over medium heat until fragrant and nutty, 7 to 10 minutes. Let cool, then chop and add to the grains.

In place of the raspberries, use 12 ounces (340 g) fresh blackberries, pressing 4 ounces (1 cup or 115 g) of the blackberries through a fine-mesh strainer and adding the sugar to the blackberry juice.

Make the whipped cream, skipping the gelatin mixture. Reduce the cream to 1 cup and replace the yogurt with ⅓ cup (80 g) cold sour cream. Use ¼ cup (55 g) packed muscovado sugar in place of the granulated sugar. Whip on high speed until soft peaks form. Add 2 tablespoons whiskey or bourbon (omit the honey) and continue to whip until firm peaks form.

Assemble the cranachan as directed.

BLUEBERRY CRISP BUTTERMILK ICE CREAM

makes about 1 quart

In St. Louis, where I grew up, there's a stand called Ted Drewes Frozen Custard where everyone (and I mean everyone) goes for their concretes, a blend of frozen custard and mix-ins like Oreos, cherries, or M&M's. The signature Ted Drewes concrete is so thick you can turn it upside down and it won't fall out of the cup. If that sounds familiar, yes, it's what inspired Dairy Queen's Blizzards and Shake Shack's concretes. When I go back to St. Louis, my favorite mix-in is the apple pie. It's an honest-to-goodness slice of apple pie, blended into the vanilla frozen custard, and it's as good as it sounds. I've taken inspiration from that treat to make this ice cream. Because it's left in the freezer to harden overnight, it's more of a scoop-and-serve ice cream than a blended soft-serve–consistency frozen treat like the concrete. So no turning this one upside down!

BUTTERMILK ICE CREAM BASE

6 large egg yolks

¾ cup (150 g) granulated sugar, divided

1½ cups heavy cream

½ cup whole milk

Pinch of kosher salt

1 cup buttermilk

1 teaspoon vanilla extract

BLUEBERRY SAUCE

1½ cups (6¾ ounces or 190 g) fresh or frozen blueberries

¼ cup (50 g) granulated sugar

2 teaspoons cornstarch

2 teaspoons balsamic vinegar

3 tablespoons crème de cassis, Chambord, kirsch, or Cointreau (see note, page 322)

MAKE THE BUTTERMILK ICE CREAM BASE

Combine the egg yolks and ¼ cup (50 g) of the sugar in a medium bowl. Whisk together into a paste. In a medium saucepan, combine the remaining ½ cup (100 g) sugar, the cream, milk, and salt. Cook over medium-high heat, stirring constantly with a heatproof spatula, until small bubbles start to form on the sides of the pan.

Turn the heat off and scoop out ½ cup of the hot milk with a heatproof measuring cup. Drizzle it into the egg yolk paste, whisking constantly to make sure the eggs don't cook but just warm up. Repeat with another ½ cup of the hot milk. Scrape and pour the entire hot egg mixture back into the saucepan and turn the heat to medium-low. Continue to cook until the custard thickens and coats the back of a spoon and holds a line when you draw a finger across the custard, 4 to 6 minutes.

Open a 1-gallon zip-top plastic bag and place it in a large bowl. Place a fine-mesh strainer inside the bag and pour the ice cream base into the bag through the strainer. Fill the bowl with ice from two ice cube trays and water. Submerge the bag in the ice water and let sit for about 30 minutes, or more, until the ice cream base is cold. Move the bag to a smaller bowl and refrigerate overnight. (You will add the buttermilk and vanilla later.)

·······>

CRISP MIX-IN

1 tablespoon honey

1 tablespoon hot water (from the tap is fine)

½ teaspoon ground cinnamon

¼ teaspoon ground nutmeg

¼ teaspoon ground allspice

¼ teaspoon kosher salt

¾ cup (25 g) cornflakes

¼ cup (25 g) thick-cut rolled oats

2 teaspoons olive oil

MAKE THE BLUEBERRY SAUCE

Add the blueberries, sugar, and cornstarch to a small saucepan and cook over medium-low heat, stirring constantly, until the sauce has thickened and about half the berries have popped, about 5 minutes. Remove from the heat and let cool to room temperature, then stir in the vinegar and crème de cassis. Transfer to a zip-top plastic bag or airtight container and freeze overnight.

MAKE THE CRISP MIX-IN

Line a rimmed baking sheet with parchment paper. Stir the honey and hot water together in small bowl or glass measuring cup until the honey dissolves. Stir in the cinnamon, nutmeg, allspice, and salt. It won't all dissolve, but that's fine. Gently crush the cornflakes until they are roughly the same size as the oats. Toast the cornflakes and oats in a large nonstick skillet over medium-high heat, stirring constantly with a heatproof spatula, until they start to smell a bit fragrant (they won't darken much), 2 to 3 minutes.

Drizzle the oil over the cornflakes and oats and continue to cook until the oil is absorbed and the ingredients start to darken a bit, 1 to 2 minutes. Drizzle the spiced honey water over the cornflakes and oats, using a spatula to scrape out any spices that are left behind in the bowl. Continue to cook, stirring constantly, until the moisture from the honey water is absorbed into the cornflakes and oats and they have both darkened slightly and look toasty, 2 to 3 minutes. Dump the cornflake-oat mixture onto the baking sheet. Spread it out slightly but not completely (you want some clumps). It will feel lightly moist, but don't worry; it will crisp up as it dries. Once cool, break up any of the really big chunks and store in an airtight container or zip-top plastic bag until ready to use.

Once the custard has chilled, open the bag and add the buttermilk and vanilla. Seal the bag and massage and shake the custard to incorporate the buttermilk and vanilla. Snip the corner of the bag and squeeze the custard into the bowl of your ice cream maker. Freeze according to the manufacturer's instructions. While the custard is freezing, take the blueberry sauce out of the freezer to thaw.

Once the ice cream is frozen, spread a bit of blueberry sauce in the bottom of an airtight container, then scoop some ice cream out on top of it. Add a little more blueberry sauce and sprinkle some crisp mix-in over the sauce. Repeat layering the ice cream, blueberry sauce, and crisp mix-in until it is all used. Place a piece of parchment paper over the ice cream to keep the air out and then seal the container. Freeze overnight to harden.

APPLE PIE ICE CREAM

Make and churn the ice cream base as directed.

Skip the blueberry filling and make an apple filling instead by peeling, coring, and chopping 2 cooking apples (Braeburn, Gala, Golden Delicious, or Jonagold) into ½-inch chunks. Melt 4 tablespoons (57 g or ½ stick) unsalted butter in a large nonstick skillet. Add the apples and sauté over medium heat, stirring frequently, until the apples are soft, about 10 minutes. Stir 2 teaspoons cornstarch into ¼ cup apple juice until dissolved. Add to the skillet, along with 2 tablespoons packed dark brown sugar, ½ teaspoon ground cinnamon, and ¼ teaspoon ground nutmeg. Cook until the sauce thickens, about 2 minutes, then let cool. Once cool, stir in 1 tablespoon dark rum or bourbon.

Skip the crisp mix-in and make a pie crust instead by combining 1 cup (140 g) all-purpose flour and ¼ teaspoon kosher salt in a bowl. Cut 6 tablespoons (85 g or ¾ stick) cold unsalted butter into ½-inch chunks and sprinkle over the dry ingredients. Using your fingers and hands, first toss the butter in the flour and then smash the butter into thin slivers, breaking them up as you go. Once the pieces have been broken and flattened into small bits the size of peas, sprinkle 3 tablespoons water over the butter and flour. Toss with a fork until the dough starts to come together. If the dough still isn't forming, add another 1 tablespoon water. Massage the mass with your hands until it forms a cohesive dough. Flatten into a disk about 1 inch thick and wrap tightly with plastic wrap. Refrigerate for at least 1 hour. Once chilled, preheat the oven to 450°F. Line a baking sheet with parchment paper or a Silpat. Roll out the dough into a 10-inch diameter circle and transfer to the baking sheet. Mix 1 tablespoon ground cinnamon with 2 tablespoons granulated sugar. Melt 1 tablespoon unsalted butter. Brush the butter over the crust, then sprinkle with the cinnamon-sugar mixture. Bake until golden brown and crisp, 8 to 10 minutes. Let cool on the baking sheet, then transfer to a large cutting board and cut into 1-inch squares.

Once the ice cream is churned, layer the ice cream with the apples and pie crust pieces as directed in the recipe.

·······>

easy alternative

HUCKLEBERRY CRISP GOAT'S MILK ICE CREAM

Swap out the blueberries for huckleberries for a little bit more intensity of flavor. To balance the strong, sweet huckleberry flavor, try using fresh goat's milk in place of the buttermilk.

Alcohol in the sauce

Adding a touch of alcohol like the crème de cassis in this sauce keeps the sauce from freezing completely, as alcohol has a lower freezing point than water. I like to add liqueur in a complementary flavor, but if you don't have any of those suggested, you can use vodka, which is neutral in flavor. If you don't have any alcohol on hand or you don't drink alcohol, increase the sugar by 2 extra tablespoons to keep the sauce from freezing completely. Of course, the resulting sauce will be sweeter.

EARL GREY PAVLOVAS WITH ORANGE-SCENTED WHIPPED CREAM AND SUMMER BERRIES

makes 2 pavlovas; 8 servings

Pavlovas are one of those infinitely adaptable desserts that you can make with just a few ingredients and whatever fruit you happen to have on hand. I always have frozen egg whites because I use a lot more egg yolks in my baking. This results in some creative recipe uses, including pavlovas. A layered dessert with a meringue shell, whipped cream, and fruit on top, the pavlova is incredibly popular in Australia and New Zealand, where it originated, but not as common in the United States. Which is sad, because the crisp and marshmallowy dessert is easy to make and customize. Here I've infused the meringue with Earl Grey tea, added a touch of orange to the whipped cream, and topped it all off with a blend of summer berries. One thing to note: I infuse the egg whites with the tea overnight, so plan accordingly.

MERINGUE

7 large egg whites, divided

4 bags Earl Grey tea

½ teaspoon cream of tartar

Pinch of kosher salt

1½ cups (200 g) superfine sugar (see note, page 325)

¾ teaspoon vanilla extract

4 teaspoons cornstarch

FRUIT

6 cups (1 pound 11 ounces or 765 g) mixed fresh berries, divided

3 to 4 tablespoons granulated sugar

2 tablespoons saba (or balsamic vinegar; see note, page 325)

MAKE THE MERINGUE

Place 6 of the egg whites and the tea in a zip-top plastic bag. Seal it, place it in a bowl (in case of leakages), and refrigerate for 8 hours or up to overnight. Don't be alarmed if the egg whites turn an unappealing greenish gray color. That's natural and won't be as noticeable once whipped and baked.

Once the egg whites have steeped, fill the bowl with warm water from the tap to warm up the egg whites in the bag. Warmer egg whites whip up faster and higher. While the egg whites are warming up, preheat the oven to 200°F. Lightly coat two rimmed baking sheets with cooking spray. Draw three 6-inch diameter circles with a pencil on each of two pieces of parchment paper (six circles total), then flip the paper over so the pencil marks are on the underside and place on the baking sheets. The cooking spray will keep the paper from moving around.

Once the egg whites are at or close to room temperature, snip the corner of the bag with scissors and squeeze the egg whites into the bowl of a stand mixer fitted with the whisk attachment. Gently squeeze the tea bags to extract as much egg white and flavor as possible. Add the remaining 1 egg white, along with the cream of tartar and salt.

·······>

WHIPPED CREAM

3 cups heavy cream

3 tablespoons granulated sugar

1½ tablespoons Grand Marnier
or Cointreau

1½ teaspoons vanilla extract

Zest of 1 orange

✱ *You can buy superfine sugar at the grocery store, where it is sometimes labeled baker's sugar. If you can't get ahold of superfine sugar, just process a cup of regular granulated sugar in a food processor or blender until a fine powder forms.*

✱ *You can find saba, a syrup boiled down from grape must (a liquid made up of crushed grapes, skin, seeds and stems), at upscale grocery stores, specialty stores, and online. But if you can't find it, use the same amount of balsamic vinegar and then taste the resulting fruit and their juices. If they need more sweetness, add a little more sugar.*

Whip the egg whites on medium-high speed until soft peaks form. Reduce the speed to medium and slowly sprinkle the sugar over the whites. Once all the sugar has been absorbed, raise the speed to medium-high and continue to whip until firm peaks form and the egg whites are glossy and white. Add the vanilla and whip for another 10 seconds to incorporate.

Remove the bowl from the mixer, sift the cornstarch over the egg whites, and fold it in gently with a large spatula. Evenly divide the meringue onto the baking sheets, scooping it into the middle of each 6-inch circle (to make 6 disks). Use the back of a spoon to smooth and shape each meringue so that the edge is slightly higher than the center.

Bake for about 1 hour. Turn the oven off and let the meringues sit in the oven for about 1 hour more.

PREP THE FRUIT

After the meringues have sat in the oven for about 30 minutes, place the berries in medium nonreactive bowl (glass or ceramic). Sprinkle with 3 tablespoons of the sugar and the saba, and then taste and add more sugar if necessary (keeping in mind the meringue and whipped cream will be sweet as well). Let the fruit sit for 30 minutes, or until the meringues are cool and you are ready to assemble the pavlovas.

MAKE THE WHIPPED CREAM

Place the whipped cream and sugar in a clean bowl of the stand mixer fitted with the whisk attachment. Whip on high speed until soft peaks form. Add the Grand Marnier and vanilla and whip until firm peaks form. Remove the bowl from the mixer and fold in the orange zest with a large spatula.

Place one meringue disk on a serving plate and spread some whipped cream over the top. Add some of the fruit and then a dollop more whipped cream. Layer on a second and third meringue disk, adding more whipped cream and fruit on top of each disk. Drizzle with some of the fruit juice from the bottom of the bowl. Repeat with the remaining meringue disks, whipped cream, and fruit on a second serving plate.

ORANGE PEKOE PAVLOVA WITH ORANGE-SCENTED WHIPPED CREAM AND SUMMER STONE FRUIT

Swap in Orange Pekoe tea for the Earl Grey tea. Infuse and bake the meringue as directed. Swap out the berries for 4 cups (1 pound or 455 g) cherries and 2 each pitted and sliced apricots and plums. Pit 3 cups of the cherries to layer inside the pavlovas, and use the remaining 1 cup unpitted cherries with stems to garnish the tops.

The deep steep: cold brewing

Most people are familiar with iced tea and iced coffee. Both are typically made with hot brewed liquid and then cooled in the refrigerator or with ice cubes, although it is becoming more common to find cold-brewed iced coffee, with the ground coffee beans steeping in cold or room temperature water for up to 24 hours, slowly extracting flavor. You can use ground coffee to infuse flavor into your baked goods in the same way, steeping it in the baking liquid for 24 hours.

You can actually cold-brew tea using much the same method, with the tea steeping in a cold or room temperature liquid for a long period of time. A cold-brewed coffee or tea will have a different flavor profile, smoother and with less caffeine and bitterness. For making beverages, all you need to do is leave the tea in the water at room temperature for a period of time depending on the tea.

White teas take 4 to 6 hours, green teas and oolongs 6 to 8 hours, and black teas 10 to 12 hours.

You can also use this technique in baking to infuse baked goods with flavor without adding ground tea leaves or heating the liquid. If you are using a liquid like milk, buttermilk, or cream, just measure it into a bowl or glass measuring cup and immerse the tea (in a bag or loose), cover with plastic wrap, and refrigerate overnight. This will infuse the dairy with the tea flavor. This is a good method if your recipe calls for buttermilk especially, as buttermilk separates when heated. Be sure to gently squeeze the tea bag to extract as much liquid and flavor as possible, or press down on the loose tea when you are straining it. Also keep in mind that each bag (no matter how much you squeeze) will absorb anywhere from ½ to 2 teaspoons of the liquid and that the amount of

time needed will vary depending on how much fat is in the dairy (cream takes longer to steep, while a thinner liquid like milk will take less time). Measure the liquid afterward to make sure you have enough, then adjust accordingly with a little bit more of the plain base liquid.

You can even steep tea in egg whites (like I do in this recipe), as egg whites are 80 percent water! Egg yolks are only 50 percent water and have more fat and protein in them (which explains why they are so viscous and thick), so I don't recommend steeping tea in them. The best way to steep tea in egg whites is to place the egg whites and tea bags in a zip-top plastic bag and refrigerate. Once the steeping is over, snip a corner of the bag with scissors to create a small hole and squeeze the egg whites into a bowl. You can squeeze all the liquid from the tea bags as well, and the tea bags stay in the zip-top bag. No mess!

CHOCOLATE PAVLOVAS WITH WINTER FRUIT

Omit the Earl Grey tea and use 6 plain egg whites for the meringue. Reduce the vanilla to ½ teaspoon and add ½ teaspoon balsamic vinegar. Replace the cornstarch with 3 tablespoons Dutch-process cocoa powder, sifting it over the meringue and folding as directed. Bake as directed.

Supreme 3 blood oranges and 1 grapefruit (remove the fruit segments) by slicing off the top and bottom of the citrus. Stand the fruit on one of the flat sides, then cut down around the sides of the fruit, making sure to cut off all the white pith. Follow the rounded contours of the fruit as you do this. You should have a citrus fruit devoid of peel. Holding the fruit in the palm of your hand over a bowl to catch any juice, cut between the membrane of each segment, removing each segment and dropping it into the bowl. Once you've supremed all the fruit, add ½ cup (90 g) pomegranate seeds. Decrease the sugar to start with 2 tablespoons, tasting the fruit and adding more sugar if necessary.

When making the whipped cream, omit the Grand Marnier and orange zest. Instead, add ½ cup (50 g) Dutch-process cocoa powder to the cream and sugar and stir with a fork until dissolved. Make sure all the cocoa is dissolved before whipping the cream.

Assemble the pavlova as directed, sprinkling 2 teaspoons roasted cacao nibs over the fruit in each layer (optional, but it adds a really nice crunchy and earthy chocolate note to each bite).

ETON MESS

Eton mess is basically a layered pavlova made with smaller bits of meringue in a parfait glass or bowl. It's the perfect dessert to make if your meringues crack or break. Follow the recipe as directed (or make a simplified meringue, using 6 egg whites and no tea or overnight steeping), but don't bother to carefully measure the meringue into 6-inch circles. Just spoon it into 2- to 3-tablespoon heaps on the baking sheet, and bake as directed.

Traditionally berries are used in Eton mess, but you can use whatever fruit you want. If you go the traditional route, use about 1½ pounds (675 g) fresh strawberries, hulled and sliced. Use a potato masher to mash about half of the strawberries with 3 tablespoons sugar and 1½ teaspoons balsamic vinegar. Assemble the Eton mess in parfait glasses or a bowl, layering broken or small pieces of meringue, whipped cream, sliced berries, and mashed balsamic berries, and then repeating the layers until you have filled up the glasses or bowl.

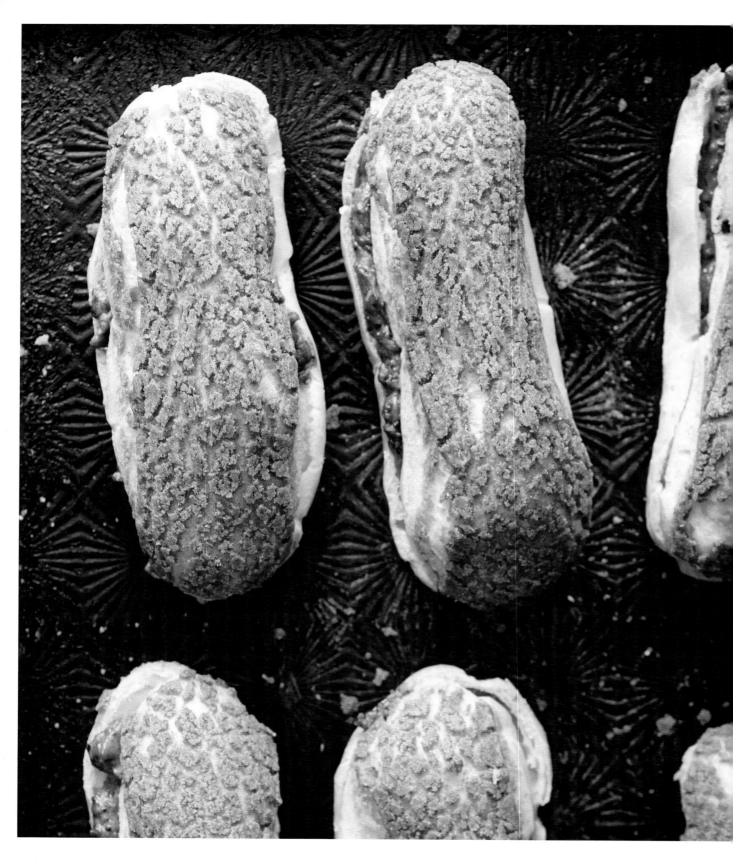

GINGER ÉCLAIRS WITH BLACK SESAME PASTRY CREAM AND FIVE-SPICE CRAQUELIN

makes 6 or 7 éclairs

Despite being Taiwanese-American, it took me a while to embrace my Asian heritage when it came to desserts. I grew up in the Midwest, where desserts are sugary cakes, gooey brownies, and warm slices of pie, all of which I ate with gusto at friends' houses. At home, we rarely ate desserts. Occasionally my parents' friends (also Taiwanese) would serve us red bean paste–filled pastries and little rectangular pineapple cakes. I was not impressed. It's only as an adult that I've come to fully appreciate these Asian flavors. This classic French éclair marries ginger, black sesame, and five-spice powder into a treat I bet even my younger self would appreciate.

CRAQUELIN

¼ cup (55 g) packed dark brown sugar

6 tablespoons (55 g) all-purpose flour

3 tablespoons unsalted butter, at room temperature

2 teaspoons five-spice blend

PÂTE À CHOUX DOUGH

2 ounces (60 g or about a 3-inch piece) fresh ginger

½ cup whole milk

¼ cup water

6 tablespoons (85 g or ¾ stick) unsalted butter

1 tablespoon granulated sugar

⅛ teaspoon kosher salt

1 cup (160 g) bread flour

1 teaspoon ground ginger

4 large eggs, at room temperature

MAKE THE CRAQUELIN

Combine the brown sugar, flour, butter, and five-spice in the bowl of a stand mixer fitted with the paddle attachment and mix on medium speed until well blended, smooth, and uniform in color. Scrape the mixture onto a piece of parchment paper and lay another piece of parchment on top. Using a rolling pin, roll the craquelin out to about a ¼-inch thickness. Place the craquelin, still sandwiched in the parchment, on a baking sheet and transfer to the freezer.

MAKE THE PÂTE À CHOUX DOUGH

Rinse off the ginger, then slice it thinly (about ⅛ inch thick), leaving the peel on. Place the ginger in a medium saucepan and cover with water by about 1 inch. Bring to a boil and cook for about 2 minutes. Drain and rinse the ginger. Boiling the ginger removes an enzyme in the root that makes dairy curdle and also removes bitterness. Rinse out the saucepan and put the ginger back in the pan. Add the milk and the ¼ cup water and heat over medium-high heat until bubbles start to form on the sides of the pan. Turn the heat off, cover, and let the ginger steep for about 1 hour. Strain ½ cup of the ginger-infused milk into a measuring cup and discard the rest.

Preheat the oven to 425°F and line a baking sheet with a piece of parchment paper or a Silpat. Add the ginger-infused milk, the butter, sugar, and salt to a medium

·······>

BLACK SESAME PASTRY CREAM

¼ cup (35 g) black sesame seeds

3 large egg yolks

¼ cup (50 g) granulated sugar

1 tablespoon all-purpose flour

2 tablespoons plus 2 teaspoons cornstarch

1 teaspoon vanilla extract

⅛ teaspoon kosher salt

¾ cup whole milk

1¼ cups heavy cream, divided

saucepan. Cook over medium heat, stirring frequently, until the milk is boiling and the butter has melted. Remove the pan from the heat. Sift the flour and ground ginger over the liquid, stirring, until the flour is incorporated and a dough has formed. Return to the heat and cook for an additional 2 minutes. You should see a little starch coating on the bottom of the pan (don't mix it into the dough, just stir gently without scraping), but if it doesn't form and you have an instant-read thermometer, check the temperature of the dough. It should be 170°F.

Transfer the dough to a clean bowl of the stand mixer fitted with the paddle attachment. Mix on medium speed for 90 seconds to cool the dough slightly (to about 115°F), then add one egg to the dough and continue to mix on medium speed until the dough has absorbed the egg. Scrape down the sides of the bowl with a spatula and repeat with the remaining 3 eggs, beating until each egg is fully absorbed before adding the next. The dough will be really sticky and shiny.

Scoop the dough into a pastry bag fitted with a ¼-inch plain round tip. Pipe the dough into 1½ x 4-inch strips, leaving about 2 inches of space between each strip. Wet your finger and press down on any points to smooth out the dough. You should have 6 or 7 strips of dough. Take the craquelin out of the freezer. Peel off the top paper and, using a sharp knife or pizza cutter, cut six or seven 1½ x 4-inch rectangles. Place a rectangle on top of each éclair.

Bake for 10 minutes, then reduce the oven temperature to 350°F and continue to bake until the tops of the éclairs are golden brown and sound hollow when you tap them, 25 to 30 minutes.

MAKE THE BLACK SESAME PASTRY CREAM

Process the sesame seeds to a powder in a food processor or blender. Transfer to a bowl and add the egg yolks, sugar, flour, cornstarch, vanilla, and salt. Beat together until a paste forms. Place the whole milk and ½ cup of the cream in a medium saucepan and cook over high heat until bubbles start to form on the sides of the saucepan. Drizzle about half of the hot cream mixture into the egg yolk paste, whisking constantly until the paste has loosened up and thinned. Pour the paste back into the saucepan with the remaining cream mixture and cook over medium heat until the pastry cream thickens, 1 to 2 minutes. Remove from the heat and pour into a bowl. Press plastic wrap directly on the surface of the pastry cream to keep a skin from forming and transfer to the refrigerator for a minimum of 1 hour, or until the pastry cream is cool to the touch.

·······>

Pierce the side of each baked éclair with a sharp paring knife to let the steam escape. Let cool completely. Once the éclairs and pastry cream have cooled and you are ready to assemble, place the remaining ¾ cup cream in a clean bowl of the stand mixer fitted with the whisk attachment. Whip the cream until firm peaks form. Scoop the pastry cream into the whipped cream and fold together until incorporated. Cut each éclair in half lengthwise with a sharp serrated knife, fill the bottom half with pastry cream, and replace the top. Refrigerate for 1 hour to set, then serve the same day.

Pâte à choux

The classic French pâte à choux (often referred to as choux pastry) is the foundation for a number of pastries like éclairs, profiteroles, croquembouches, cream puffs, and gougères, as well as beignets and French cruller-style doughnuts. The hallmark of pâte à choux is that it is first cooked on the stovetop, then piped and baked. The steam in the paste puffs up, creating a hollow pastry to be filled with pastry cream, ice cream, whipped cream, or whatever else you want. A few tips:

Make sure to really bring your liquid to a rolling boil initially. This allows the fat to evenly distribute throughout the liquid. A lot of recipes use just water, but I find a combination of water and milk helps the browning when you bake. That said, you can certainly use just water or something like carrot juice, which I use in the alternative recipe for pumpkin spice éclairs. If you use a very sweet juice, you should adjust the sugar in the recipe accordingly.

Make sure to remove the pan from the heat before adding the flour and stirring it in. If you stir in the flour on the heat, you're liable to get clumps of flour, which you don't want. You want all the flour absorbed into the liquid without any lumps, which is also why sifting is recommended.

Returning the batter to the stove and cooking it just a little more helps to ensure excess moisture is driven off the paste and also activates and denatures the gluten protein in the flour. You want a balance of the gluten protein, active enough to stretch when you bake it but not so strong that it snaps back and collapses.

Make sure your eggs are at room temperature when you add them to the paste. If they are cold, they'll drop the temperature of the paste too fast. But in addition, make sure to beat the paste for the full 90 seconds to cool it before adding the eggs; if the paste is too warm, it will cook the eggs.

Finally, I bake at a higher tempera-ture first to get a burst of steam, which makes the éclairs rise. Once the dough has risen and the outside has started to set, lowering the temperature allows the remaining dough on the inside to bake and dry out.

PUMPKIN SPICE ÉCLAIRS WITH CHOCOLATE-BEER PASTRY CREAM AND CHOCOLATE-BEER GANACHE

Skip the craquelin.

Make the pâte à choux dough as directed, skipping the ginger-milk infusion. Replace the water and milk with ¾ cup carrot juice and proceed, adding 1¾ teaspoons pumpkin spice (or 1 teaspoon ground cinnamon, ½ teaspoon ground ginger, and ¼ teaspoon ground nutmeg). Bake as directed.

For the pastry cream, chop 2 ounces (57 g) semisweet chocolate into ¼-inch chunks. Place the egg yolks, granulated sugar, flour, cornstarch, vanilla, and salt in a bowl and add 1½ teaspoons natural cocoa powder (not Dutch-process). Beat together until a paste forms. In a medium saucepan, replace the milk with ¾ cup beer. Add ½ cup of the heavy cream, reserving the remaining cream for later, and the chopped chocolate and cook on high heat until bubbles start to form on the sides of the saucepan. Lower the heat and stir until the chocolate has melted. Combine the cream mixture and the egg yolk mixture as directed and cook as directed until the pastry cream thickens, 1 to 2 minutes. Transfer to a bowl, press plastic wrap on the surface of the pastry cream to keep a skin from forming, and refrigerate.

To make the beer-chocolate ganache, chop 4 ounces (115 g) semisweet chocolate into ¼-inch chunks and place in a microwave-safe shallow bowl. Microwave in three 30-second intervals, stirring between each interval, until the chocolate is smooth and melted. Stir in ¼ cup beer until incorporated and smooth.

To complete the éclairs, whip the remaining cream and fold in the pastry cream as directed. Cut the éclairs in half lengthwise and spoon the pastry cream into the bottom half of each éclair. Dip the top of each éclair in the ganache and then set it on top of the filled bottom half.

MANGO AND FRESH MINT ICE CREAM

makes about 1 quart

There's definitely a difference between fresh mint ice cream and the stuff made from mint extract or oil. As much as I love the easier mint extract ice cream, especially when getting a scoop at an ice cream shop (extra-green, please!), I always gravitate toward the fresh mint if I have the option. The bright, herbaceous, tingly mint flavor actually tastes green (like herbs) without the neon artificial coloring. The classic mix-in for mint ice cream is chocolate chips, and I've gone ahead and given an alternative for making that version, but the addition of honey-sweet mango pulls the ice cream in a decidedly different tropical and lush direction.

MINT ICE CREAM BASE

5 teaspoons tapioca starch
(see note, opposite)

2 cups whole milk, divided

1¼ cups heavy cream

½ cup (100 g) granulated sugar

3 tablespoons mild-flavored honey

⅛ teaspoon kosher salt

2 cups (80 g) fresh mint leaves, divided

3 tablespoons cream cheese,
at room temperature

MANGO MIX-IN

1 medium (12 ounces or 340 g) mango

2 tablespoons dark rum

½ teaspoon fresh lime juice

¼ teaspoon kosher salt

6 tablespoons (75 g) superfine sugar
(see note, opposite)

MAKE THE MINT ICE CREAM BASE

Mix the tapioca starch and 2 tablespoons of the milk in a small bowl or glass measuring cup. Place the remaining milk, the cream, sugar, honey, and salt in a large pot. Tear apart 1 cup (40 g) of the mint leaves and toss them into the pot as well. Bring the mixture to a boil, then lower the heat to a bare simmer. Simmer for about 4 minutes, occasionally checking the heat and stirring the pot. Slowly drizzle the tapioca mixture into the pan, stirring with a whisk. Cook until it has thickened slightly, about 1 minute more. Remove from the heat and add the cream cheese. Whisk to incorporate. Let sit in the pot for 20 minutes to steep.

Open a 1-gallon zip-top plastic bag and set it in a large bowl. Place a mesh strainer inside the bag and pour the ice cream base through the strainer into the bag, pressing down on the leaves to extract as much liquid as possible. Discard the mint and seal the bag. Fill the bowl with ice from two ice cube trays and water. Submerge the bag in the ice water and let sit for about 30 minutes, or more, until the ice cream base is cold. Once cold, tear up the remaining 1 cup (40 g) mint leaves and add them to the mix. Transfer the bag to a smaller bowl and refrigerate for 8 hours, or overnight.

MAKE THE MANGO MIX-IN

Peel the mango and dice it into ½-inch chunks. Place the mango, rum, lime juice, and salt in a food processor or blender and process until very smooth. Pour the mango puree through a fine-mesh strainer, pushing all the liquid through with a spoon. Discard the solids. Stir the sugar into the mango puree until dissolved.

Transfer the mango puree to a zip-top plastic bag or airtight container and freeze overnight.

Strain the ice cream base into your ice cream machine to remove the mint leaves and then churn according to the manufacturer's instructions. Remove the mango puree from the freezer and let thaw on the counter while you churn the ice cream.

Once the ice cream is done churning, layer the ice cream in the bottom of an airtight container, alternating layers of mango puree and mint ice cream. Place a piece of parchment paper over the ice cream, seal the container, and freeze overnight to harden.

✱ *You can find tapioca starch at upscale grocery stores, natural food stores, and online. If you can't locate it, you can replace the tapioca starch with the same amount of cornstarch.*

✱ *You can buy superfine sugar at the grocery store, sometimes labeled baker's sugar. If you can't get ahold of superfine sugar, just process a cup of granulated sugar to a powder in a food processor or blender.*

alternative

FRESH MINT CHOCOLATE CHIP ICE CREAM

Make the mint ice cream base as directed.

Skip the mango puree. Instead, line a small rimmed baking sheet with parchment paper. Chop 4 ounces (115 g) semisweet chocolate into ¼-inch chunks and place in a microwave-safe bowl. Microwave for 30 seconds, then stir. Microwave for 1 minute more, stopping and stirring after 30 seconds, until the chocolate is completely smooth and melted. If there are still a few stubborn solid pieces, microwave for 15 seconds more. Stir 2 teaspoons olive oil into the chocolate. This creates a lower melting point for the chocolate so that it will melt in your mouth when you eat the ice cream. Pour the melted chocolate onto the parchment paper and freeze for at least 15 minutes or up to overnight. Once the chocolate is solid, chop into small chips. Add the chips to the ice cream in the last 2 minutes of churning.

RESOURCES

GENERAL

Amazon
www.amazon.com

Whole Foods
(check their Web site
for store locator)
www.wholefoodsmarket.com

VANILLA BEANS, EXTRACTS, PASTES

Beanilla
www.beanilla.com

Nielsen-Massey
www.nielsenmassey.com

Rodelle
www.rodellekitchen.com

WHEAT FLOURS AND OTHER BAKING SUPPLIES

Arrowhead Mills
www.arrowheadmills.com

Bob's Red Mill
www.bobsredmill.com

Central Milling
www.centralmilling.com

King Arthur Flour
www.kingarthurflour.com

GLUTEN-FREE FLOURS

Arrowhead Mills
www.arrowheadmills.com

Authentic Foods
www.authenticfoods.com

Bob's Red Mill
www.bobsredmill.com

Cup4Cup
www.cup4cup.com

King Arthur Flour
www.kingarthurflour.com

SUGAR AND OTHER SWEETENERS

Wholesome Sweeteners
www.wholesomesweet.com

India Tree
www.indiatree.com

Big Tree Farms
www.bigtreefarms.com

EXTRACTS

Beanilla
www.beanilla.com

LorAnn Oils
www.lorannoils.com

Star Kay White
www.starkaywhite.com

SPICES

Frontier Co-Op
www.frontiercoop.com

Penzeys Spices
www.penzeys.com

FREEZE-DRIED FRUITS

Crispy Green
www.crispygreen.com

Karen's Naturals
www.shopkarensnaturals.com

**Trader Joe's (check their Web
site for store locator)**
www.traderjoes.com

CHOCOLATE

Callebaut
www.callebaut.com/usen

Ghirardelli
www.ghirardelli.com

Guittard
www.guittard.com

Scharffen Berger
www.scharffenberger.com

Theo
www.theochocolate.com

Valrhona
www.valrhona-chocolate.com

ACKNOWLEDGMENTS

This book would not exist if it weren't for the numerous people who helped me. First and foremost, thank you, A.J., for being the absolute best partner in the world. You believed in me when I didn't and you carried me through some rough times. You did my dishes, you ran last-minute grocery runs, you troubleshot computer issues, and you held me together when I felt like I would fall apart. I'm so happy we've made a life together.

Thank you, Justin Schwartz; you took a chance on me with this book, and I can only hope I didn't let you down. Thank you, Stephanie Fletcher, for the time you took to work on this book and for gently helping me along the way. Thank you to the rest of the Houghton Mifflin Harcourt team, from the art department to marketing and sales to administration. You went above and beyond.

Thank you, Linda Xiao, for your beautiful photography. Thank you, Suzanne Lenzer; your styling made my food look stellar. Thank you, Kara Plikaitis, for designing a gorgeous book.

Thank you to the best agent in the world: Stacey Glick. You held my hand when I didn't know what I was doing and were always there when I needed it.

Thank you, Mom, Dad, Rob, and Natatia. I love you guys.

Thank you, Alice and Gary Bates and the entire Bates clan. You're my second family.

Thank you Tori Avey, Elise Bauer, Ree Drummond, Lori Lange, David Lebovitz, David Leite, Dan Lepard, Alice Medrich, and Amanda Rettke. Your support means everything.

Thank you to Shauna James Ahern for opening doors. Thank you to Gail Dosik, Kate McDermott, Stella Parks, Jennie Schacht, and Shauna Sever for answering my weirdo pastry questions. Thank you to food pals Dianne Jacob, Garrett McCord, Sabrina Modelle, Gabi Moskowitz, Stephanie Stiavetti, Sean Timberlake, and Annelies Zijderveld.

Thank you, Pat Fusco, for telling me to start a blog. Thank you, Rita Huang, Damon Nagami, Peter Nguyen, and Grant Kalinoswki, for being my biggest cheerleaders!

Thank you, Tina LeCount Myers and S. B. Hadley Wilson. First Writer's Club forever! Thank you to all the amazing recipe testers who gave me invaluable feedback: Eugenie Berg, Jennifer Botkin, Mia Broad, Meg Brown, Chris Callahan, Candace Chen, Debra Darlington, Kay Davis, Scott Davis, Allison Day, Susie Decker, Lindsey DiLoreto, Michael Flanagin, Alexis Green, Jeff Hanson, Ariel Hernandez, Suzanne Hickman, Aislinn Hyde, Stacey Indeck, Nancy Kellerman, Nate Klass, Jennifer Martinez, Joanna Meyer, Jamie Nesbitt, Jen Nurse, Tracy O'Banion, Kevin O'Leary, Amy Peterson, Steven Reigns, Jessica Schunke, Lauren Sims, Kelly Schoenberg, Lilah Sutphen, Kim Tabor, Michele Taylor, Darlene Veenhuizen, Felisa Yang, Gin Yang, Stella Yang, and Tiffany Zhou.

And finally, a huge thank-you to my readers at *Eat the Love*. This wouldn't have happened without you. I love you all.

INDEX

"Love this book. It's packed with all the style and brilliance that made Irvin Lin such a must-read food writer online. This book is all about incorporating big flavors into your baking with style: swirling, studding, and supercharging recipes to a magical effect. Cakes are cut to reveal extraordinary fillings or sliced to show beautiful marbling. Cookies and bars offer striking geometric effects. Recipes are easy enough to encourage, but with enough intricacy to keep you interested and, yes, impress friends and family. Five-star baking at its best."

—DAN LEPARD, food writer and baker

"This book is captivating. The recipes are unique, but more so, they are carefully crafted. The ingredients were chosen to complement each other to create the most magical experience. I found myself smiling as I read this book. The combination of amazing recipes and entertaining words makes it one of my favorites!"

—AMANDA RETTKE, best-selling author

"I couldn't be more excited for *Marbled, Swirled, and Layered*. Irvin's recipes are so unique and his flavor combinations inspire me to be more creative in my own kitchen. This book belongs on the bookshelf of every baker, no matter their level of expertise."

—TORI AVEY, PBS food columnist and creator of *ToriAvey.com*